Praise for THE KNOWING

"*The Knowing* is a masterwork by one of our most essential storytellers. Tanya Talaga once again bears witness to the truth and shares it with searing clarity and a deep compassion. She exposes history denied and compels a new understanding of the Canadian story. *The Knowing* is deeply researched and urgent storytelling at its finest. At a time when journalism is in crisis, Tanya Talaga shows us the power of rigorous and thorough reportage and in doing so honours the survivors and their descendants with the gift of truth. This may be my favourite book ever."

—JESSE WENTE, author of *Unreconciled*

"The story of one woman gone missing becomes the story of all the children who never came home. Tanya Talaga fearlessly takes on Canadian history and presents it through the lens of indigenous experience—an absolute prerequisite to understanding how we got here from there and how we must move forward. In a time when denialists are finding their whitewashed story on the bestseller lists, Talaga provides an antidote to their poisonous resistance to the truth. *The Knowing*, a meticulously researched and startling rearticulation of the inherent violence in colonial disregard for Indigenous peoples, in particular the children, takes a deep dive into the story Indigenous people know all too well but remains stubbornly supressed by the colonial mindset of Canadian institutions. *The Knowing*, written in beautiful, often heartbreaking prose, is a handbook for reaching beneath the myths of Canadian history and finding the truth of a Canadian genocide as horrific as any other."

—MICHELLE GOOD, bestselling author of *Five Little Indians*

"Any attempts to eliminate or literally bury any evidence of the Indigenous concentration camps' malicious architecture are no match for the mighty Tanya Talaga. In *The Knowing*, we witness one of the most significant Truth Sayers of our time embark on an epic, generations-long quest to find the unmarked grave of her ancestor. Talaga employs both her keen investigative eye and her tender author's heart to transform the political into the personal; cryptic paperwork into the details of precious lives lost; this country's shame into a call to action."

—CATHERINE HERNANDEZ,
author and screenwriter of *Scarborough* the book and film

"*The Knowing* is a deeply personal account of Talaga's search for her missing and disappeared family members. By sharing her family's story, she is helping to address what the Truth and Reconciliation Commission identified as an urgent need—to create historically literate citizens. We find and feel Annie's spirit with every turn of the page, despite the government's efforts to disappear her. This book teaches us all that knowing our ancestors, is knowing ourselves."

—KIMBERLY R. MURRAY, Independent Special Interlocutor for Missing Children and Unmarked Graves

"This is about a Canada that you do not know, but one we all must confront. *The Knowing* is harrowing, illuminating and necessary reading."

—CAROL OFF, author of *At a Loss for Words*

"*The Knowing* is everything we've come to expect from a Tanya Talaga book— meticulous research, impassioned advocacy, searing prose. But this is her most personal story yet, an epic retelling of one family's story that illuminates both the repugnant history of Indian residential schools in Canada and the inspiring reclamation of Indigenous identities."

—DUNCAN MCCUE, author of *Decolonizing Journalism: A Guide to Reporting in Indigenous Communities*

"Through the lens of our nation's most prescient truthteller, an unspeakable hurt is painstakingly excavated. This is the story of Tanya Talaga's lineage, an eighty-year search to unravel the mysteries that shroud her great-great-grandmother's fate. This is, also, the story of how Canada came to be. These pages give voice to generations of abducted and discarded souls, a land stolen, a way of life eradicated. Tanya's profound empathy and unwavering determination to discover their truth honours their resilience and spirit. This book is a path forward."

—MARK SAKAMOTO, author of *Forgiveness*

THE KNOWING

THE KNOWING
ᑭᓇᖃᓂᑕᒍᐅᓐ

TANYA TALAGA

HarperCollins*Publishers*Ltd

Published by HarperCollins Publishers Ltd

First edition

HarperCollins Publishers Ltd
Bay Adelaide Centre, East Tower
22 Adelaide Street West, 41st Floor
Toronto, Ontario, Canada
M5H 4E3

www.harpercollins.ca

Map on pp. x to xi by Bora Tekogul

Library and Archives Canada Cataloguing in Publication
Title: The knowing / Tanya Talaga. Names: Talaga, Tanya, author.
Description: Includes bibliographical references and index.
Identifiers: Canadiana (print) 20240368711 | Canadiana (ebook) 20240368800 |
ISBN 9781443467506 (hardcover) | ISBN 9781443467513 (ebook)
Subjects: LCSH: Indigenous peoples—Canada—History. | LCSH: Canada—
Ethnic relations—History. | LCSH: Generational trauma. | LCSH: Talaga,
Tanya—Family. | CSH: Indigenous peoples—Canada—Residential
schools. Classification: LCC E78.C2 T35 2024 | DDC 971.004/97—dc23

Printed and bound in the United States of America
24 25 26 27 28 LBC 5 4 3 2 1

For my uncle Hank Bowen

They just made this damn thing up, the entire thing.
A fiction that is absolutely made up and it shapes the world.
—Montreal Lake Cree Nation author Harold Johnson,
in conversation with Tanya Talaga, Vancouver Writers Fest,
October 2021

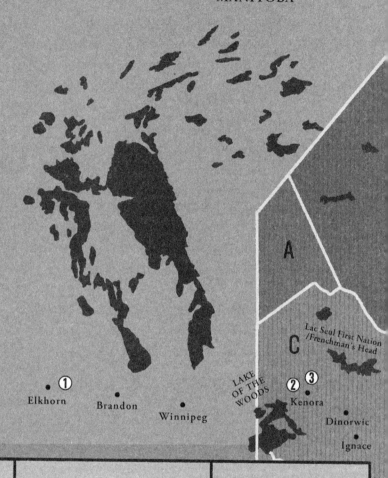

N

MANITOBA

A

Lac Seul First Nation
/Frenchman's Head

C

LAKE
OF THE
WOODS

② ③

Elkhorn   Kenora

Brandon   Dinorwic

Winnipeg   Ignace

TREATY ZONES	1905 TREATY SIGNING LOCATIONS	INDIAN RESIDENTIAL SCHOOLS
A Zone 1	❶ *Osnaburgh Post* Mishkeegogamang First Nation	① Elkhorn IRS
B Zone 2	❷ *Fort Hope Post* Eabemetoong First Nation	② Cecilia Jeffrey IRS
C Zone 3	❸ *Marten Falls Post* Ogoki First Nation	③ St. Mary's IRS
D Zone 4	❹ *Fort Albany Post* Kashechewan First Nation	④ Pelican IRS
E Zone 5	❺ *Moose Factory Post* Moose Cree First Nation	⑤ St. Joseph's IRS
F Zone 6	❻ *New Post* Taykwa Tagamou First Nation	⑥ Shingwauk IRS
		⑦ St. Anne's IRS
		⑧ Bishop Horden Hall IRS

KITCHI WEENEEBAYKO
HUDSON BAY

B

ATTAWAPISKAT RIVER

Peetabeck

⑦

④

⑧

WEENEEBAYKO
JAMES BAY

Mishkeekogamang

②

③

KISTACHOWAN SIPI
RIVER

⑤

LAKE
ST.JOSEPH

④

①

ONTARIO

ENGLISH RIVER

MOOSE RIVER

Moose Factory

⑥

Sioux
Lookout

Lake
NIPIGON

D

QUEBEC

Graham

⑤

E

Animiki Wajiw
/Fort William
First Nation

Raith

Thunder Bay

ANISHINAABEWI-
GICHIGAMI
LAKE SUPERIOR

⑥

Sault Ste. Marie

F

USA

ININWEWI-GICHIGAMI
LAKE MICHIGAN

CONTENTS

CHA-KA-PESH
AND THE DIRTY SEA

CHA-KA-PESH WAS A TEENY, TINY PERSON. A MYSTICAL, SPIRITUAL, CHILDLIKE man who held special powers and liked to do what he wished. He was small but mighty. He had extraordinary gifts. In the blink of an eye, he could transport himself to other places. He loved to explore the great unknown, to go where he shouldn't and to see things that he was told not to see. He challenged everything and anything, his actions ruled by zest and wonder.

Cha-ka-pesh's story has been told and retold by the Omushkego.[1] It comes from a time before memories are remembered, so long ago that no one can say when the events occurred. Winisk First Nation Elder Louis Bird tells us this story, one that was passed down through the generations. This story comes with a warning.

Cha-ka-pesh lived with his older sister. She was said to be the wisest person who ever lived. She knew all the knowledge there was to know. So, the little man would go on his adventures and return home to his sister, to ask her what it all meant. She would always tell him the truth, and that truth always came with pieces of advice. One thing she always said was, "Do not do anything that puts your life in danger or harms your health."

But like any child, Cha-ka-pesh would head out secretly on adventures, constantly doing the opposite of what he was told. Because he was a shaman, he could travel far and wide using his mind powers. He could transport himself, instantly be where he wanted to, to places where, sometimes, he shouldn't go.

Cha-ka-pesh lived inland, away from the giant body of water that looked like a sea. It is called Ki-sti-ka-min: big water. Ki-sti-ka-min is stinky. It tastes salty and it is water that you cannot drink. If you did, it would make you sick. The people called it the "dirty water" and they avoided it.

The dirty water got its name because of Mi-she-shek-kak, the feared and deadly Giant Skunk. Mi-she-shek-kak killed anyone who ever tried to cross its path. Everyone knew that. It was just not allowed. But one day, a tired weasel, desperate to get home, dug a hole in the snow under Mi-she-shek-kak's trail. Sneakily, he went underneath. Mi-she-shek-kak knew as soon as the weasel did this. He went after the weasel and an epic battle ensued, one that pitted all the animals that lived—the caribou, the mice, the eagles, the bears, wolverines and the bobcats—against Mi-she-shek-kak. It was in the middle of this clash that the Giant Skunk sprayed the wolverine, and the wolverine ran. He ran and he ran until he reached the largest body of water he'd ever seen. Then he washed himself, and the stink stayed in the water forever.

Cha-ka-pesh liked to go to the edge of the dirty water. He liked to look out on its vastness, watching and listening to all of the white shorebirds who came to soar above the water, dipping and diving and flying through the air. But since he lived so far away, he had to use his mind to transport himself there. So, one day, he used his power and he willed himself there. As soon as he did, he found himself standing on the shore.

There were thousands of shorebirds. He thought it was okay to take a few, for he and his sister were hungry. So he used his bow and arrow. The sun was setting and the water was so very calm.

Suddenly he heard a noise. An echo. It seemed to be coming from overtop of the dirty sea.

"Hoo hee, hoo hee, hoo hee," came the strange sounds. Cha-ka-pesh listened some more. It was a human voice! He stood there and wondered, "Who could be out there? Is there a land I cannot see?"

The sun was setting fast. Cha-ka-pesh had to go. So he thought in his mind of home and whoosh, there he went.

As soon as he arrived home, Cha-ka-pesh gave his sister his bag of birds. Right away she questioned him. "When did you go to the shore?"

He told her he'd just gone, not long before the evening.

"So you fooled around, eh?" She was angry.

Then he told her everything. He said he'd wanted to go so badly, that he just had to do it. But when he was there, he heard voices. He told her what they sounded like.

She listened and said, "Well, do you remember I told you that you had to watch yourself, what you do? Sometimes when you travel with this power, sometimes you can land somewhere and you don't know what or where it is."

She said he could have gone back into the past or far into the future. "And this is one of the most dangerous things to do."

Cha-ka-pesh told his sister that she scared him. He promised never to do it again, and he went to bed.

But Cha-ka-pesh was not telling the truth. He could not let go of what he'd heard. He wanted to know more.

The next day, when he was hunting out on the land, he waited until it was dusk. Until it was the same time that he heard the strange sounds. Then he did what he'd promised his sister he would not do. He closed his eyes and returned to the shores of the dirty water.

This time, he heard nothing. He waited, but there was silence. Only the sounds of the shorebirds. So he decided to travel over the dirty water to look for the strange sounds. He picked up a rock and threw it at one of the shorebirds, knocking it to the ground. The bird was stunned. Cha-ka-pesh entered the bird and they became one. Then he took flight. He flew over the dirty sea until he could hear the sounds again.

There they were! The voices! Coming from a strange wooden island.

This island had a few tall trees and on top there were clouds. He perched up high and then he saw the men with pale skin. Together, they shouted, "Heave-ho, heave-ho, heave-ho!"

After a while watching, he decided to get closer.

One of the men was chewing on something, eating it. He threw a piece to the floor. Being a shorebird, Cha-ka-pesh swooped in and picked it up. One of the other men grabbed a stick and prepared to throw it at him. So he flew high into the sky and away, back to the shore. Once there, he jumped out of the bird's body and became himself again. He still had what it was the men were eating. He stuck it in his bag, closed his eyes and went home. Since he'd defied his sister, he decided not to tell her what he did.

Feeling bad, he went hunting, so he wouldn't go home with empty hands. He snagged a few rabbits and stuck them in his bag. When he got home, without a second thought he gave the bag to his sister. He'd forgotten about the piece of food the sailor threw on the floor.

She pulled it from the bag and asked him what it was.

He stammered, could give no good answer, then blurted, "A mushroom!"

She did not believe him. She knew he had not listened to her. She bit it and knew it was no mushroom. She told him never to go there again—because he would be lost, and she would never be able to find him.

He tried to say he was sorry and to apologize, but his sister was very angry. For this story pointed to a greater threat, the coming of white people on small wooden islands.

She asked him what would have happened if the strange man had hit him with the stick. "You would die, and that's what I've been trying to tell you. You would lose your life. I would never find you."

The coming of the We-mis-ti-go-si-wak. White men, the men with wooden boats.

Men holding sticks, threatening and waving them in our faces. Men who could take our lives if they wished, and men who did.

BOOK ONE

Yellow

I throw my arms out wide and begin to spin in a circle. With each turn, my fingertips touch the inner circumference of all of Creation. As I spin, I am the centre. The four stages of life, the four directions of the Medicine Wheel, bound together by sacred laws and ceremonies. The Anishinaabe believe all life is connected: to the tree people, the stones, the earth, air, water and animals. All have spirits; we are all part of the circle of Creation.

The four directions of the Medicine Wheel whirl with me as I spin, from the east to the south and from the south to the west, and then from the west to the north. We enter our human life through the yellow east door—the same colour as the rising sun—and we gain knowledge as we strengthen into youth and adulthood, and the sun glows so strong on our journey through the red south door. As it sets, darkness falls, but it leaves enough light to shine on our Elder path as we reach the black west door. We share and grow, and then we die with the coming of winter, in the white north door. The cycle begins again as we continue to whirl. The circle is the beat of the human heart. The sound of the drum.

This is the movement of life and of time itself.

The end is the beginning.

CHAPTER ONE

THE KNOWING

ANNIE CARPENTER LIES IN AN UNMARKED GRAVE JUST SOUTH OF A GIANT BLUE-
and-yellow IKEA, directly off one of the busiest thoroughfares in North
America, the Gardiner Expressway, part of the Queen Elizabeth Way,
which cuts west and east across the city of Toronto. It feels like an area
you drive through to get somewhere else, not a destination.

I have lived in Toronto my entire life, born and raised in this city
of immigrants, a city built on the land snatched from the Mississaugas
of the Credit by the Toronto Purchase agreement of 1805. The British,
looking to secure trade routes and the safety of the growing city of York,
as Toronto was then known, entered into a now disputed treaty with
the Mississaugas, an Anishinaabe group of families who had made their
home here for centuries. The Anishinaabe say they were duped by the
British and that the agreement they signed was blank. They said it did
not, in fact, cede to the Crown any land, much less the area on which
the cities of Toronto and Vaughan are built—their concrete office towers
and condos pocking the land with thick, crusty pavement.[1] Our peoples
have walked on this land, now trapped beneath the cities' hard shell
of concrete, asphalt and steel, for tens of thousands of years. The soil
remembers our footsteps.

I have travelled along this highway too many times to say. Heading
in and out of the city. Ferrying my children to Hamilton and back, to see

their father's relations. How many times have I taken this route to get to the airport, or to go to Sherway Gardens, a giant shopping mall smack in industrial west-end Toronto?

All this time, until five weeks before writing this, I did not know that I was driving past my great-great-grandmother's grave.

How cruel reality is. She was right there. All this time. Since 1937.

Gone from us. From her language. From her Ininiw (Omushkego Cree) family, and so very far away from the water that knew her, the giant Albany River and James Bay basin. Gone from her clothes, her beads and her rocking chair, gone from the sweet smell of burning sage, the softness of a floor of furs and the guttural sounds of a flock of geese making their way south in the brilliant blue sky.

Gone from her children, from the beautiful embrace of a gaggle of grandchildren, my grandmother Margaret among them, who used to listen to her as she sang the sweet sounds of ten thousand generations of our families. We carry our knowledge through our songs. Never written down, our knowledge was lifted and passed from one to the other through our singing, through the beat of a drum. The circular sound of a drumbeat, the sound of a human heart beating.

She used to sing as she rocked.

This is my grandmother's only memory of her. She said Annie spent hours singing softly and rocking. She did not stop.

Oh, Annie. What happened to you? What did you see? How did you feel when you were sent 2,500 kilometres from your home, away from everything familiar, away from your way of life, and shoved into—of all horrific places—a "lunatic asylum"? Did you even know what kind of place it was? It must have been disorienting, frightening, as if your world had ended. Were you trapped in a dingy cell? Did you comprehend any of what the whites said to you as they poked and prodded your body, strapped you on a gurney and locked you away? They spoke a language that did not come from you, in sounds that did not come naturally from your lips and that were not understood by your ears. Did they torture you? Hurt you? Did it not matter anymore because this physical pain was nothing compared to what it felt like to be ripped away from your children, your home and family, everything you knew?

We looked for you. Since the 1930s, the decade you were taken away, never to return.

Your grandson, Hank Bowen, my grandmother Margaret's brother, led the charge, constantly searching for traces of who we were. Do you remember him? He was a loner, a hunter, a lover of the sounds of the bush and the sting of the drink. He nearly died in a Thunder Bay tuberculosis sanatorium, kept hidden away for years as his lungs suffered and heaved from the bacterial infection that ate at his insides. He never settled, never stopped trying to figure out exactly where you were, and who you were. His brown collapsible file folder stuffed with papers, maps, letters and notes was never far from his grasp. Inside were places carefully circled on photocopied maps of all the First Nations, communities nestled deep in the boreal forests and freshwater lakes of northern Ontario stretching from the Manitoba border to Hudson Bay and James Bay. Eabametoong. Lansdowne House. Whitefish Bay. Long Lake 58.

Could she be from here? From these places? Where did her blood come from? His quest was relentless. It consumed him.

The Ontario Hospital, on the shores of Lake Ontario, was the provincial lunatic asylum. Annie Gauthier (née Carpenter) became a patient here in 1930 until her death. (Courtesy of Lakeshore Grounds interpretive Centre)

EVERY SINGLE FIRST Nations, Métis and Inuit family has a story like ours, has lived through a similar trauma. Every single family. Not one was left unscathed by the demonizing policies of the Canadian government and those of the provinces, the British Crown and the Christian churches. Laws were written with the sole intent of crushing First Nations into submission so that the colonizers could easily take the land and everything on it or underneath it.

This is a hard but true reality for Canadians to realize, but it is one that Indigenous Peoples have always known.

The Knowing contains stories of lives lived through these genocidal beginnings to the present day. Annie is one Cree (Ininiw) woman born in Rupert's Land—the vast plantation that was the Hudson's Bay Company—around the time of the birth of what we now call Canada, as one empire was dying and another beginning.

This is the story of my hunt for Annie, her children, their children and theirs. It is by no means complete. It is told with the fragmented, semi-accurate government and church records and letters that we have been able to locate in dioceses, down website wormholes, in dusty archives and through memory.

Annie was five years old when the race-based, genocidal policies of the Indian Act became law in 1876. She was the first of five generations of Anishinaabe and Ininiw women in my family to live under its yoke.

The Indian Act, a paternalistic piece of legislation that remains in effect to this day, was and is a framework for subjugation and control. The government explained the purpose of the act by saying that it rested on the principle "that the aborigines are to be kept in condition of tutelage and treated as wards or children of the State. . . . The true interests of the aborigines and of the State alike require that every effort should be made to aid the Red man in lifting himself out of his condition of tutelage and dependence, and that is clearly our wisdom and our duty, through education and every other means, to prepare him for a higher civilization."[2]

The government did not refer to "Indian women," as they were not considered or thought of as persons with rights when the patriarchal act was drawn up. Who was "Indian" was determined only through the male lineage until changes were made, most significantly in 1985, when enfranchisement clauses were removed. The word *Indian*, which describes people who are First Nations in Canada, will be used in this book, where warranted. *Status Indian* is the Canadian term used to describe those still governed under the Indian Act of 1876. The act contains a race-based registry, a list of names of those Canada officially recognizes with treaty rights and restrictions.

The newcomers who designed the act assumed they were superior to the Indians because that is what they believed as part of the tenets of Christianity: from the divinity of man flowed power structures and kingdoms. Christianity provided the spiritual foundation of the papal bull known as the Doctrine of Discovery. These newcomers set the table for how British and European arrivals would view the Indigenous Peoples already living on Turtle Island, the continent of North America.

To the settlers, Indians looked different, dressed differently, ate different food and did not live by recognizable European laws or customs. And they did not follow the Christian faith. They might have been living here for tens of thousands of years, but since they did not hold land titles or property deeds familiar to and acceptable to Europeans, the conquerors pushed Indigenous Peoples out of the way. They did not understand we moved around the land, taking care of it before moving again when the land told us it was tired. Indigenous languages come from the land; our way of life, our very being is tied to it. The aki, the earth, is alive. And as such, we never owned it. We held no property deeds or titles. How could you claim ownership over a living entity?

Annie, like all other Indigenous people on Turtle Island, was cast aside by the British ruling class and churches. This was a common practice in British rule, as seen with the Irish tenant farmers, as well as in Great Britain's dominant involvement in the slave trade. By the late eighteenth century, nearly seventy-eight thousand slaves were being brought to North America every year—primarily on British ships. Merchants were making a killing buying, selling and oppressing people.

Great Britain's political rules and systems of parliamentary government "othered" populations all over the world to exploit the land and profit all they could for the mother country. The ideals and practices of class and racial superiority that allowed the slave trade to exist—and the British and European "higher" classes to profit from it—came crashing across the Atlantic along with their ships.

The foundations of Canada's and America's class and race-based policies of domination—which gave permission to kill both Indian and buffalo, to steal children away from their parents, their language, families and everything they knew—constructed a society that was built to keep us consistently as second-class citizens, governed by a different set of rules and served by a different set of schools and services. The burgeoning caste system in Canada was clearly illustrated by how Annie was treated throughout her life as an Ininiw woman, scraping to survive in a growing country that considered hers a life without value.

The great tool of subjection in Canada was the Indian residential school system, while in the United States, boarding schools played a similar role. The mantra of the schools was: "Kill the Indian, save the child." This hints at the underlying belief that Indigenous children could be "saved" once they were force-transferred to institutions and turned into something "useful" to the emerging Canada.

The effect was devastating. Destroying and separating generations, the newcomers' policies and actions left tens of thousands of children, youth, women and men in unmarked graves, buried out of sight and out of conscience. Buried in school grounds with graveyards dug by the students themselves. Buried in hospital grounds, sometimes in mass graves. Buried unceremoniously, anonymously, on forgotten plots of land in fields or city centres, or in church graveyards—not good enough for headstones and, sometimes, buried on the other side of the cemetery fence because, apparently, Jesus Christ did not want to save these particular souls.

None of the residential schools provided Indigenous children with an education sufficient to propel them to university or law school or that would allow them to become doctors. The Indian Act made that illegal anyway: if you went to university, you were no longer counted as an "Indian."

The proof of the plan was in the pudding: residential schools had children work in fields, in laundry rooms, picking apples, building churches, baking bread and digging graves. The children were to grow up and benefit the lives of their masters, to work in kitchens, become domestics, to toil away in the mines and to farm the fields.

Indian women were at the bottom of the social hierarchy. It was not until 1985 that the Indian Act was amended to include women, giving them the same rights as Indian men.

The original purpose of the act and its list of names was not to protect Indians and their rights, but to get rid of them—to reduce their numbers until they were fully assimilated into Canada. Various amendments have been made in an effort to change the law, but it still is a law aimed at annihilation.

If you want to destroy a nation, you destroy the women. That is what the lawmakers, governments, churches and institutions have been complicit in doing through harmful legislation, through policies that made Indian women property and that aided and abetted Indian residential schools. These foundations set the stage for the murder and disappearances of thousands of our children and women. This was the beginning of the murdered and missing Indigenous women and girls crisis we live with today.

This is the background you need to understand in our hunt for Annie.

I FIRST HEARD the term "the Knowing" in Tk'emlúps te Secwépemc, along the Thompson River's banks in the Interior of B.C. where the Kamloops Indian Residential School was located. Kamloops was once the largest residential school in the area. The surviving children from Kamloops tell stories of being woken up in the middle of the night to dig graves in the apple orchard.[3] They remember their friends that disappeared. For years they told the stories, but few listened, and certainly no lawmakers or governments. They called this knowledge "the Knowing."

The Knowing provides a different way of seeing.

Every Indigenous family is missing loved ones. Everyone knows of a brother or sister, an aunt or uncle, a friend, grandparent or great-grand-parent who has vanished at the schools, at the Indian hospitals or sana-toriums, in lunatic asylums or from the streets. There are entire branches of family trees that are unknown or erased.

My family is made up of pieces of what is left behind. The stories of who we were, where we came from, passed down from generation to generation. We always knew there were others out there—missing. Stories whispered, late at night, among my grandma, my aunties.

Perception is everything.

I am a descendant of both those who have lived on this land for tens of thousands of years and of those who settled it from eastern Europe, of those fleeing oppressive regimes and persecution based on class and racial hierarchy. I write this book informed by the perspective of two separate family trees that have been shaken by two different genocides, the one here on Turtle Island and the other in a part of the world that is still shaking in hatred, a blood feud that has continued for a thousand years.

My father's family comes from Galicia, a part of southeastern Poland where the borders have shifted countless times and where bombs and bullets still fly. His family fled to New York in 1911 with Austrian pass-ports, on ships ferrying thousands across the ocean. The Talagas were a large mixed family of many branches that I know next to nothing about. But I do know that those with the last name "Talaga" were sent to Nazi concentration camps as labourers, as prisoners. What I do not know is how many of these Talagas I am related to. The Talagas left behind faced unbelievable suffering, some surviving and others dying, in places that are burned into the world's memory: Dachau. Flossenbürg. Sachsenhausen.

No one in my father's family spoke of the past. We did not keep in touch with anyone who stayed. Were we part of the Polish resistance or persecuted Catholics? A mixture of both or none of the above? I still cannot answer these questions.

From this world view—from the legacies of these dual branches of genocide, one on Turtle Island and one far off in eastern Europe—comes my knowing.

UNCLE HANK'S BROWN file folder came to me after he died, in the summer of 2011. (I always knew him as Uncle Hank and refer to him that way in this text, but actually, as my grandmother's brother, Hank was my *great*-uncle.) My mother brought it over. It had come to her from Hank's sister, my aunt Connie. She gave it to me with great care. It was as if she were handing me highly confidential state secrets wrapped in a plastic shopping bag. "He'd want you to have this," she said quietly.

The brown folder was heavy, full of letters, inquiries, death certificates and baptism records. They were all the clues we had left of who Hank's grandmother, Annie, and his mother, Elizabeth, were. Annie was stolen away from us and Liz was silent. Her silence deafened. It told everyone to back off, to not ask questions. What was she hiding, other than who she was?

Time and time again, both the federal Department of Indian Affairs and Ontario's vital statistics branch had told Hank they had no records for his mother.* They told him that so many records had been destroyed and hers were probably gone with them.

How many times have Indigenous people heard this sentence: "The records have been destroyed"?

A 1933 federal government policy led to the destruction of fifteen tons of paper between 1936 and 1944; two hundred thousand Indian Affairs files were destroyed.[4] It is possible these records could have helped in my family's research. It wasn't until 1973 that the Department of Indian Affairs agreed to place a moratorium on the destruction of records. But that begs the question: Was the moratorium followed? And what about all the other government ministries and departments that may have held residential school records? What happened to them?

---

* The department has had various names, and has been under the domain of various departments, since 1867, but for simplicity's sake I will mostly call it the Department of Indian Affairs throughout.

The bottom line, for us: the Government of Canada and the Province of Ontario declared Liz Gauthier wasn't an "Indian" because they could find no official piece of paper that said she was.

My uncle Hank would not accept this. He tried to document her. He went in search of those who had known her and her mother Annie. He tracked down, cold-called and visited former neighbours and friends. He interviewed them, asked them to testify that his mother and grandmother were of red skin just like himself. He wrote down their memories. Each swore up and down that Liz was an Indian through and through. In some cases, he even asked them to write letters to the government, sign their names, swear to this truth—affidavits, if you will.

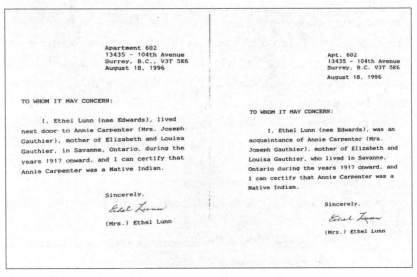

Uncle Hank asked Ethel Lunn, Annie Gauthier's neighbour, to write a letter to Indian Affairs confirming that Annie was indeed an "Indian."

Why was he so hell-bent on finding her? In part because while Canada told him he was an Indian under the terms of the Indian Act, something he already knew, Canada also had the audacity to tell him he was not Indian enough by excluding his mother. That he, and all his descendants, and the children of his brothers and sisters, could not pass their Indian status down to their children because Liz, their mother, was not an

Indian. A bureaucratic decision, baked into the Indian Act's sexism, along with enfranchisement, combined with incorrect and missing records—the absence of which helped obliterate an entire family's heritage and sense of belonging. Of knowing who their mothers were, where they came from.

Uncle Hank spent his life looking for Annie. But more importantly, he was looking for himself and for the spirit of his mother Lizzie, a complicated, strong woman. She never spoke of who she was or where she was from, never mind what school she had attended or what she endured while she was there. She took those secrets to her grave. It is as if she hated being an Indian. What happened to Liz that she would want to erase every single trace of herself and, in doing so, refuse to share herself with her own children, leaving them with no knowledge of themselves, cursing generations to blindly walk ahead in the dark?

With Uncle Hank gone, it was up to me, the journalist, to pick up where he left off.

For years I avoided looking through Uncle Hank's file. It was just too daunting and upsetting. Both Annie's and Liz's spirits were completely eviscerated and blown dead away by colonization and the Indian residential school system in Canada. I would pick up that heavy folder, only to put it back down again, overwhelmed by the sadness in the pages, as well as by what seemed to me the nearly insurmountable challenge of trying to figure out why these women—and so many others—were erased.

Canada, as a state, has an obligation under its United Nations Declaration on the Rights of Indigenous Peoples Act, passed in 2021, to facilitate the finding of the truth, not to impede it. Yet after the Truth and Reconciliation Commission heard from thousands of Survivors and other witnesses who told about the missing and dead children, when the three commissioners, Murray Sinclair, Wilton Littlechild and Marie Wilson, petitioned the federal government for enough funds to start looking for them, Canada refused. Canada refused even though the TRC had identified 3,200 deaths and compiled registers of confirmed deaths of named and unnamed students. The TRC did this independently, with what little resources and records it had; Canada wouldn't hand over most government records to the commission, citing privacy reasons.[5]

That official list was used to produce a long, flowing red banner containing about 2,800 (known) names of children who died while at school, a banner that is unfurled at events such as the 2022 papal apology at Maskwacis, Alberta, to remind Canada what has happened here. Among the names on that banner are those of five members of my own extended family: Gabriel Carpenter, Charles Carpenter, Thomas Skelliter, Samuel Skelliter and Doris Carpenter.

But those 3,200 children represent only a small fraction of the Indigenous children who disappeared, who died. Finding each child, bringing them home spiritually or physically, is why we hunt. To give them the dignity and respect they were never offered in their brief time on this earth.

We are still searching for their names. On that official list of 3,200 children, the names of just under one-third were not recorded by the government or the schools. For another one-quarter, we don't know whether they were boys or girls. And for just under one-half of the deaths, no cause of death was recorded.[6] Almost all of the children who died were never sent back home.

What exhausted me about Uncle Hank's file was that this wasn't only in my family: we were one family among thousands who had lived the genocide. Inside that folder was information not just about us but about the colonial history of erasure that every other First Nations family faces. The brown folder was heavy with the forces at play that resulted in Annie's disappearance and those of several of her own children, and the resulting damage it did to the next generation and the next.

Uncle Hank's brown folder represents what the state did to all of us.

Genocide is impossible to retell. The connections between generations are fractured. It leaves us as intimate strangers, looking for the names and faces of those we've lost. And if we find them, we then begin the process of reclamation. There is another choice: the alternative is to just shrug your shoulders and move on. But that is precisely what the architects of genocide want. And I could not do that. The ancestors restless in the back of my mind would not let me.

The day I first felt the meaning of the term "the Knowing" sink in, standing on the grounds of the Kamloops residential school in 2021, after the announcement that nearly two hundred possible gravesites of children had been found, I could not have foretold what the song of those children's spirits would awaken in me and across all Indigenous Peoples on Turtle Island. That the ancestors within me would respond with such force. On that first day in Kamloops, I listened to the bang of the drums, and with each beat, my ancestors' voices got louder: *Find Annie.*

I knew I had to locate her, bring her home. And in that process, I would find myself.

WHEN I THINK of Annie, I am full of a near-indescribable shame and a hollow sadness that spans generations, both so deep they're underwritten with a howling, seething anger at the smugness of this postcolonial world, a world of supposed acceptance and understanding, of plastic attempts at reconciling the past made by those hosting human rights dinners in glitzy hotel ballrooms.

They do not have a damn clue. How could they?

But Indigenous Peoples see. We know—a deep understanding that comes from the marrow of our bones, one that is passed down through the whispers of our kin, lips on our ears breathing words of truths heaving within ourselves. We know what was done to our children, to our parents, to their parents and to all our relations.

Our bodies were, and are still, tossed away like used plastic bags to be buried in a landfill site and never seen again.

It has taken us eight decades to find Annie, in an unmarked grave off the side of a major highway in present-day Toronto.

Annie died alone.

With no complete set of records to tell the story and no family around to remember, we did not know where she was, where she had disappeared to. One day she was just gone. Was she sent away by doctors? By the Indian agent? By her husband? Did he no longer want her?

Chapan. Oh, how I mourn you.

My blood is your blood. I am born from you, from an egg formed in my mother's ovaries when she was developing inside my grandmother Margaret's womb. And she, Margaret—who was born and raised on the trapline, near Graham, Ontario, at the bottom of Treaty 9, where the waters on Turtle Island split, flowing either north to the Arctic Circle or south to the great cities that line the QEW thoroughfare—was born of an egg that first felt the electricity of life inside of Annie Carpenter.

We now know—and the story that unfolds in the coming chapters will reveal how, through years of thwarted efforts, painful disappointments and exhausting persistence, we finally came to learn—that Annie Carpenter lived with her family in Keewatin. The north, or, as the mapmakers of the day put it, the Northwest Territories.

The Lakeshore Cemetery is where Annie Gauthier (née Carpenter) lies in an unmarked grave. The cemetery was created by the Ontario Hospital, and patients dug the graves. It is just off the Gardiner Expressway in Toronto. (Photo by Tanya Talaga)

The Albany is a thick, wide river that, for 982 kilometres, cuts and curls its way through the top one-third of Ontario. It begins in Cat Lake, deep in the heart of the rich, dense boreal forest in the northern centre of the province and it flows northeast into James Bay. The water has always been our great carrier, bearing us along from community to community, providing us with life-giving sustenance, nourishing food.

The Albany was named after the Duke of Albany, who became King James II, the last Catholic monarch of England, Ireland and Scotland. But we never called the river that. For tens of thousands of years we did not know this living, flowing life-giver of a river as the Albany.

No, it was called Kistachowan Sipi.

Annie lies so far, far away from the movements of that big, wide, fast-moving river. She is here in Toronto, in the Lakeshore Psychiatric Hospital Cemetery. In a dark, cold, dirty, earthy pit, underneath dead, yellow grass. Unknown and unseen since 1937. In a final resting place that is three feet wide by eight feet deep, and three feet away from that of her neighbour, Pte. Walter Mills Landrie, of the 240th Battalion, Canadian Expeditionary Force, which formed in Renfrew, Ontario, in 1916. He was born in 1894 and died in 1933. I mention him because there are twenty-four Great War veterans buried here, at Evans and Horner Avenues, just off the Gardiner, mixed in among 1,511 souls. The soldiers are the only ones who have, in recent years, been given grave markers. The majority of these forgotten are just impressions in the ground, which awkwardly, ever so slightly, rolls all the way to the cemetery's highway edges here in Canada's largest city.

This is where the remains of those who died at the Ontario Hospital and Mimico Asylum between 1890 and 1979 were dumped. There is no other word to describe it. For decades this graveyard was completely overgrown; it was a field full of brush, bush and garbage.

But we do not forget. We remember.

We live to tell the truth of what happened and what continues to occur.

Kistachowan is our guide, a constant flow, anchoring us to the past and moving us towards the future.

Chapter Two

THE END IS THE BEGINNING

I HAD MISSED THE EMAIL FROM RACELLE KOOY, WHO WAS THE ACTING MEDIA relations coordinator for Tk'emlúps te Secwépemc, a First Nation in the southern British Columbia Interior that is also home to the Kamloops Indian Residential School, the largest school of its kind in Canada. She had sent it two days earlier. "Crap," I thought. "Here she was offering me an exclusive and I, typically, neglected to read my email." Exclusives, in the news business, are a rarity, and every journalist strives to get them, to be first with the news before everyone else.

I did not know Kooy, but I knew of her. In 2019, she ran in the federal election for the Green Party in Victoria. Kooy is well known in the Indigenous media world as a sharpshooter, one who often works as a moderator for Assembly of First Nations events—which means trying to keep more than six hundred Chiefs in line and keep meetings running like clockwork. Kooy is someone who doesn't suffer fools. If she sends an email offering an exclusive, you respond.

Her message began: "Weytk Tanya, I am honoured to be working with Tk'emlúps te Secwépemc to bring forward some tragic news that was a 'knowing' before but is now confirmed."

Kooy said they were sending out an embargoed press release to select journalists who they felt could bring the devastating news to light with sensitivity.

The release categorized the unthinkable. It began to say that with a "heavy heart" Tk'emlúps te Secwépemc Kúkpi7 (Chief) Rosanne Casimir confirmed what Survivors of the Kamloops Indian Residential School knew: that there were children buried on the former school ground. It further said that ground-penetrating radar used over the past weekend had indicated the "confirmation of the remains of 215 children" who were students of Kamloops.

I could not believe what I was reading. The magnitude of Kooy's words was hard to comprehend and process. The release went on to say that the Tk'emlúps leadership acknowledged their responsibility to care for these lost children.

Sick to my stomach, I dialed Racelle's cell. She picked up instantly. She sounded like she was in the middle of chaos. I wasn't sure if she could hear me. I got to the point. I apologized for not reading her email two days earlier. I told her I wanted to write the story and that I was flying to Kamloops. The words came out of my mouth before I even understood them myself.

She yelled into the phone, "How soon can you get here?"

This was one of those moments. I booked my flight and then sent a note to David Walmsley, the *Globe and Mail*'s editor, and Natasha Hassan, the Opinion editor and my direct boss, to let them know I was heading to Kamloops and why. By then, the story was breaking across social media. As I got on a plane to Kelowna, they put me in touch with investigations editor Renata D'Aliesio.

THE DRIVE FROM the Kelowna airport to the city of Kamloops isn't long—two hours—but it is breathtaking. A long stretch of Highway 97, white-dusted mountains and endless skies. Near the end of the route, the highway turns west, becoming Highway 1, which follows the South Thompson River, a wide, glacial, deep, blue fast-moving river that is the largest tributary of the Fraser River. There are two Thompson Rivers, one north and one south, and where they meet, the confluence, is a spirit centre for the Secwépemc (Shuswap) people.

Ceremonies have been held where these rivers meet for thousands of years.

As you follow the river into Kamloops, on the north side of the Thompson sits a large, imposing red-brick building. You can't help but notice it. It comes out of nowhere. *Imposing* isn't the right word. It is menacing. An obelisk-shaped spire shoots up out the top of the three-storey centre block of the building. The building itself is boxy, equally proportioned. On either side of the centre block it rises to four stories. It looks like an institution. Concrete steps lead up to the green double doors that look like a mouth. Its eyes are the windows, equal distances apart, repeating across each floor. If you stand before it, Kamloops Indian Residential School feels exactly how Survivor Dennis Saddleman—who was six when he was first dragged in through the front doors of the so-called school—describes it in his poem "Monster." For all intents and purposes, this school *was* a monster.[1]

Kamloops Indian Residential School was the largest school in Canada, opening in 1890 and operating until 1969. It was run by the Catholic Church. One Survivor, poet Dennis Saddleman, described it as "the Monster." (Photo by Tanya Talaga)

Across from the steps, down a short slope, is a large green soccer field, and beyond that the land slopes away towards the river. As you drive west down the highway, slightly past the physical school, the land widens and here is a large powwow arbour, the largest in southern B.C., made of rich red cedar. Between the school, the soccer field and the arbour is a large wooded area. An old, sprawling apple orchard. The knotty branches of the apple trees reach out in all directions.

Kamloops is a sleepy town. Train tracks run through its core. The main street is small, with a library, a Wednesday farmers' market, an old movie theatre that hosts the Kamloops Film Festival and a tiny CBC radio station.

I checked into my hotel and quickly changed into my ribbon skirt, linen with orange felt flowers, made for me by the Indigenous students at Seneca College. Anishinaabe women wear long skirts with brightly coloured ribbons hemming the bottom to be respectful during times of ceremony. We wear them in the Sweat Lodges, and we often wear them to any important gathering with our people. The ribbons are often symbolic, and they show the sacred colours that were given to us in ceremony.

Then I called Racelle. "Come down to the school," she told me. "I'm in meetings but I'll text you when I'm free."

THE TK'EMLÚPS TE Secwépemc First Nation is firmly interwoven into the city of Kamloops. That is as it should be, as the Secwépemc and Nlaka'pamux peoples have lived here for thousands of years, although the recent history of the Nation, meaning the last two hundred years or so, reads like an old western film.

That's because non-Indigenous settlers arrived in the early years of the nineteenth century, around 1811, when the fur trade was established. The trade in pelts lasted for a generation, buoying and employing many, who later transitioned to looking for gold or to making their fortunes as drovers, driving cattle in the mountainous region, an enterprise that eventually gave way to modern-day ranching.

Tk'emlúps straddles the South Thompson River as it makes its way to the confluence. The Canadian Pacific Railway line also runs along the river. There is an old rickety bridge over the Thompson from the Tk'emlúps-owned industrial park. The Secwépemc People have always been traders, keen on commerce and defending their way of life and land from their enemies. Cross the bridge from the park and you are in Kamloops—the English word for Tk'emlúps, or "where the rivers meet"—a small city established in 1893.

Chief Louis is credited with creating the Tk'emlúps Nation as it is today. He was Chief for more than six decades, from 1850 until 1916, the year he passed away. He lived through the smallpox epidemics that tore through the area in 1862 and 1863. He was thought to have been born in 1832 or 1833, which means he experienced many of the changes that took place with the coming of the white man, including the 1840s Oregon gold rush that spread north, followed by the arrival of the overlanders, or drovers—the cowboys—and the development of ranches, which led to the exploitation of land and, ultimately, to the stealing of most of modern-day British Columbia.

Amidst all this upheaval, Chief Louis knew life was drastically changing and that something must be done to stop it. But then came perhaps the biggest change of all: the railroad.

It was the vision of Sir John A. Macdonald, Canada's long-serving nineteenth-century prime minister and one of the early builders of Indian residential schools, to construct a transcontinental railway that would join the entire country economically and bring the western province of British Columbia into Confederation. Construction of the CPR began in 1881 at Callander Station (now Bonfield), in eastern Ontario. The railway cut right through lands that had been occupied by First Nations. But Macdonald knew how to get around them: from 1871 to 1877 Canada signed the Numbered Treaties 1 to 7, thus enveloping the prairies, displacing hundreds of thousands of Indigenous Peoples to guarantee the railway's westward expansion.[2]

Before the Canadian Pacific Railway, the majority of the people in B.C. were First Nations. Their communities had their own complex social structures, laws and agreements. They dictated their own forms of governance and policies, and they even collected taxes off miners, drovers and the timber trade. As Manny Jules, a long-serving former Chief at Kamloops and a Survivor of the Kamloops Indian Residential School, says, "We were the masters of our traditional territory. With the influx of the miners, only after the railway did that fundamentally change."[3]

Author interviews Kamloops Indian Residential School Survivor Manny Jules in his office inside the former school. The building has been repurposed by Tk'emlúps te Secwépemc. (Photo by Melissa Tait/*Globe and Mail*)

The railway dispersed and removed the people by laying down tracks wherever its engineers deemed best. The railway belt required ten miles on each side of the line cleared for the use of the CPR. The railway did not care whose land it was busting through.

By the 1880s, Chief Louis knew his people needed a school—that the community needed to keep up and stay ahead of the wave of settlers by educating Shuswap doctors, lawyers and teachers. He believed education would help them keep control over their land and safeguard their ways of life. He worked with Father Jean-Marie-Raphaël Le Jeune, a Catholic priest and linguist who spoke many of the B.C. Interior languages. The first priests had started to come into the Kamloops territory three decades earlier, in the 1850s, and had been baptizing whomever they could. Chief Louis himself became a convert, and by 1856 the community had built its first Catholic church.

Chief Louis's wish of a school would finally be granted, but it would not unfold as he planned. The Kamloops Indian Residential School would be run by the French Catholic order the Missionary Oblates of Mary Immaculate, the order that would operate some of the most notorious and abusive Indian residential schools in Canada. The Oblates oversaw fifty-seven residential schools in Canada, ten of them in British Columbia, including Kuper Island, St. Mary's, St. Joseph's and the Lower Post school.[4]

However, Kamloops would become one of the largest institutions of its kind in the West. The actions of those who ran the schools, their violent disruptions and continued abuse of children who were placed under their care for nearly eighty years, would echo throughout history and send shockwaves around the world when the truth of what happened inside the Monster came out.

The discovery of the 215.[5] The Missing. Le Estcwicwéy.

I HOPPED INTO my rental car. I had to cross the Thompson River, then head on to Tk'emlúps. I hung a right at the first lights over the bridge, on Shuswap Road, passed the gas bar, and two roads in I turned right again on Chief Eli Larue Way, which then becomes Chief Alex Thomas Way, which leads behind the school. I drove by an older wooden building with a white sign that said "Moccasin Square Gardens Community Centre." Beside it, I saw a tipi and a sacred fire. These fires are lit to call in the spirits, to honour those that are around us and to acknowledge them. The sacred fire is just that—sacred. Once lit, the fire is tended and cared for by Firekeepers. This is ceremony: there are rules around the fire.

A dozen people were loosely standing around. Some had on orange T-shirts commemorating "Every Child Matters" and ribbon skirts. Most looked like how I felt, a bit dishevelled, emotional, uncertain of what to do. They sat on white plastic lawn chairs.

Would I be welcome as an outsider? I sat in my car until I saw another car slowly pull up into the spot beside me. The driver, an older man, smiled at me and rolled down his window. He asked if I was new in town. I told him I was. He smiled and said, "Get out of the car and join us."

He carried his hand drum in one hand, a drumstick in the other. He walked into the circle, me behind him, and all who were there smiled and greeted him. He told everyone that he drove hours to the school after he'd heard the news, which was spreading to Survivors and community members throughout the B.C. Interior. He was a Survivor of this place. He knew he had to come. He introduced me as a Nish friend from Toronto.

He placed his drum on a plastic chair that someone vacated for him. Then we walked over to a table where the sage was burning strongly in a smudge bowl. An Elder wearing a ribbon skirt and bright-coloured T-shirt beckoned us in, one at a time. I stood there as she lifted the smudge bowl, fanning the comforting smell of the smoke over my head, her eagle feathers moving it over my shoulders, down my arms, all the way to my feet. Then I turned around and she did it again.

My unease dissipated. We were in ceremony. I joined my brothers and sisters around the sacred fire and we let the spirits come.

FOR THE NEXT few days, as the world reeled with the headlines coming out of Canada at the end of May 2021—that there were potentially 215 children's graves located here at the Kamloops Indian Residential School—ceremonies were held in the Powwow Arbour, which is located right off of Shuswap Road, past the gas station and the Tim Hortons on Powwow Trail. The Tk'emlúps arbour is a large open-air gathering space on the West Coast. When you walk inside it, you can't help but be struck by its warm beauty. It feels like you are being welcomed and embraced by giant red cedars. Sunlight streams down onto gleaming green grass. Each of the four directions is marked with a statue: a wolf, a steer, a bear and an eagle.

These were heady days, chaotic, like a bomb had gone off. International news crews were dropping onto the scene. The leadership of the Tk'emlúps council was drowning in media requests. All levels of government and First Nations leadership from coast to coast to coast were trying to get in touch. Tk'emlúps valiantly tried to push them all aside in order to make sure they got hold of community members first— the Survivors of Kamloops. They did not want the news to reach them via the TV set or internet. The community wanted to be the first to let them know.

But that was virtually impossible as the world found out about the 215.

Racelle was the one and only person tasked with handling communications, and she was besieged with inquiries from all over the globe. I would meet and speak with her sporadically, whenever she came up for air. She couldn't keep up with the requests and she was telling everyone to stay *away*. Barricades were set up at each of the driveways into the school and into the powwow grounds. Secwépemc youth and men wearing bright orange vests stood at the entrances, stopping each car and turning them away if they were not part of the community, if they had not been invited here to pay respect and to mourn.

There would be no media at this time, except those select few who, like me, were invited. How could there be?

As a *Globe* columnist, I was also fielding questions, but they were coming from the *Globe's* Parliament Hill bureau. On one of my first nights there, my editor called me. It was late, and I was in my hotel room, exhausted. She apologized for what she was about to ask me and then she said, "The Prime Minister's Office, the RCMP, is questioning the numbers—the 215." There was more. "There is talk that there is internal strife in the community."

As an Anishinaabe journalist my back went up. As a political reporter, I had seen this before. Calls from the centre of power, the PMO, those who run the highest office in the land in Canada, to reporters in a polit-ical bureau, questioning where the truth lies, poking what they're hearing, looking for off-the-record information in exchange for sharing a bit of their own.

When Canadian political leadership behaves this way, it shows its true colours and perpetuates the unfortunate biases that have plagued Indigenous–Canadian relations and reporting since the time of Sir John A. Macdonald: a lack of trust, a downplaying of what Indigenous Peoples have experienced or discovered. Then, to top it off, the old "There is division in the community," an age-old divide-and-conquer tactic seen at the negotiation table and in the practices of the press. It is the same old trope.

I told my editor that what she heard was categorically not true. The number was correct. And furthermore, that I had not seen any division. In fact, I'd seen the exact opposite: unity. She said she'd tell everyone what I'd said, and she apologized for having to be the messenger. We hung up.

My head was spinning, but I had one clear thought: we needed Murray Sinclair. Tk'emlúps needed Murray, former senator and the for-mer chair of the Truth and Reconciliation Commission of Canada, or TRC. He was my next call.

When I reached him, I told him what was occurring, what I was seeing. He said, "You are in the eye of the storm now. Be careful."

FIRST NATIONS COMMUNITIES across the B.C. Interior and all over Turtle Island were in mourning. It was as if someone had woken up the dead. Someone had—215 spirits—and their call was reverberating around the earth. Why the blow felt so hard was because we *knew*. Every single Indigenous person in the country has been touched in some way by the schools. Now after generations of our kin crying and trying to get someone's attention over finding their loved ones, of looking for them and bringing them home, the spirits of the 215 had come screaming from the ground.

At its peak, five hundred students lived at the Kamloops school. Its imposing design mirrored Indian residential schools across Canada: the entranceway was in the middle, to the right was the girls' dorms and to the left, the boys'. A chapel was attached to the school, and a working farm—including, here in Kamloops, a notorious apple orchard—occupied much of the students' time.

For more than eighty years, the Canadian government and the Christian churches had moved mountains to take children away from their families and bring them to this place and others like it. No expense was spared in what they described as the saving of souls. RCMP officers were dispatched to bring the children in. Trucks used to patrol the communities surrounding Kamloops, the agents who drove them snatching First Nations children. Cars, trains and buses were hired to transport them.

The deputy superintendent general—the equivalent of deputy minister—of Canada's Department of Indian Affairs, Duncan Campbell Scott, the top-ranking civil servant in charge of Indigenous people, willingly signed off on the cost of bringing Indian kids to the school, but he wouldn't pay a damn cent to send them home. Nor would he invest in their well-being. In 1918, Scott is purported to have made this comment: "It is readily acknowledged that Indian children lose their natural resistance to illness by habituating so closely in residential schools and that they die at a much higher rate than in their villages. But this does not justify a change in the policy of this department which is geared toward a final solution of our Indian problem."

Scott held the children in his grip, refusing to let them go home even though he knew they died at unprecedented rates inside the school walls. Because that was the point. The abuse going on in the schools—the maltreatment, the neglect, the meanness and the torture—the Department of Indian Affairs did not care. Government bureaucrats had other things to worry about. Children of Indians were not the same as the children of everyone else. They were of a lesser class. As Tk'emlúps former Chief Manny Jules says, this is what led to the missing.

This whole notion of missing is important. It corresponds to what has happened in Argentina and in other countries. They called them "the disappeared." For us, it is "the missing." As Jules said to me: "It is encapsulated in the single word, *missing*. When we talk of truth and reconciliation that is what we have to look at—this truth. Why did the government develop policies that would allow this to happen?"

All religious denominations that participated need to be held responsible, he added. Blame can't be cast on the Catholic Church alone. "We should have the ultimate jurisdiction to deal with it. We should have access to the resources needed for [the work] to be done."

"We continue to have a mistaken belief the federal government will do this for us and they will not. Part of the reason is when they look at our issues, they immediately see liability. And when they see it they think a trillion dollars. When you think of a trillion dollars of liability, you are thinking of how can I save a few to deal with it?"

In 2015, the Truth and Reconciliation Commission published an entire volume called *Missing Children and Unmarked Burials* that is 286 pages long. The report states, "The most basic of questions about missing children—Who died? Why did they die? Where are they buried?—have never been addressed or comprehensively documented by the Canadian government."[6]

The TRC recorded 3,200 deaths, but that is just a small fraction of the true number. Murray Sinclair has told me it is more likely 15,000 are lost, as there were 1,300 different types of schools across Canada that Indigenous children were sent to or attended. Canada only sanctioned the 140 federally supported schools to be part of the commission's purview.

Yes, that is another dirty secret: 1,300 schools that received no federal support—meaning they were solely financed by a religious denomination, privately run or provincial schools. Survivors have tried in vain to petition the government to add more schools to the acknowledged federal compensation list.

I have been lucky to have had Sinclair as a sounding board, a needed ear when I grapple with the intent and meaning of reconciliation in Canada. While I was writing my second book, *All Our Relations*, on why Indigenous children have been dying by suicide in record numbers in colonized nations, Sinclair told me that the commissioners wrote the TRC report to "arm the reasonable," to fight the deniers in this country who say the schools weren't that bad or that this was not a genocide. He told me he wanted to "ensure that those who are learning about reconciliation have at their disposal, have in their hands, information they can use to challenge people who challenge them. This is to arm the willing."

Sinclair called me in early May 2023, when I was in the final throes of writing this book. His call was like a giant hug, a boost to keep writing, not to be afraid to say what needed to be said, what Canada needs to hear. He told me there are three audiences: "Those who believe in what we are doing, who want to be the allies and be at the forefront of process. Secondly, there are those that will deny it and scream bloody murder, who will call the Survivors liars—they will always be there. But the group we need to be concerned with is the large group in the middle. As they become aware—there is something not quite right in what I have been taught in school, something not quite right—we need to give them knowledge to know more."[7]

ONE EVENING I walked down to the powwow grounds and sat on one of the benches. Survivor Evelyn Camille was there. She smiled at me, her lips tight together, her eyes taking it all in—what was unfolding before her. Many of the surrounding Nations had come. They were pouring in, carloads of community members from all over: they just got in their vehicles and showed up. From Pavilion, Penticton, Adams Lake, Bonaparte, Fountain, Douglas Lake, Okanagan, Quilchena, Shulus, Little Shuswap Lake, Coldwater and Seabird Island. They brought their drums, their coolers full of cold water and snacks. They brought their tissues and their tears. They stood in a circle, they held hands and they cried.

Oh, how we all cried.

There was a moment when a young boy, not more than ten, suddenly sang out in a clear, mournful tone as he banged on his hand drum along the edge of the giant circle on the powwow grounds. His voice rose above all the rest, so everyone quieted and let him sing. His voice carried and swirled over us, dancing around the arbour and floating up, out of the open roof, then caressing the grounds around us, where the 215 were lying in the ground.

As his voice waned, he was answered by nearly one hundred hand drummers who had come and formed a circle. They boomed in imposing unity, then they would fall silent and wait for him to sing again. He did, his voice rising and falling over all of us. Then the larger group would answer with fierce power. Then the boy sang again. They went on and on like this in rotation.

This is the sound of all Indigenous Peoples on Turtle Island as we mourn what we knew—what Canada knew all along. That the children are buried here. Underneath our feet. Where they have been for decades.

Little pairs of shoes, boots and sandals started to appear everywhere across Canada shortly after the announcement of more than two hundred potential graves at Kamloops as a reminder of the children lost. This is what appeared on the front soccer field at Kamloops Indian Residential School, each with a solar light. (Photo by Tanya Talaga)

THE SUN TORE through the sky in a steady beam of heat. It was nearly thirty-five degrees Celsius in the shade on the lawn of the Kamloops school. It was less than a week after I'd arrived in Tk'emlúps. I took my phone out and saw a text from a friend that said Mike Metatawabin's 104-year-old father, Abraham, had died.

Abraham was a beloved Elder, an Ininiw language and Knowledge Keeper, who lived in Fort Albany. He was a direct link to the land, to the old ways. He had lived his life on the shores of Kistachowan; he knew how to watch the stars and the skies for patterns about the coming weather, something taught to him by his ancestors. He knew the shore-lines of the Albany, where the bends and the rocks were, how the water flowed from northwest to northeast. Abraham had been troubled by the changes he was seeing in the climate around him, especially in what he'd observed about the river. Sometimes, he had told Mike, it looked as though the mighty Kistachowan was changing direction. There were birds along the shores, birds the Elders had never seen before, birds they had no names for, no words to describe.

Abraham had seven sons. I have known three of them, Mike, Leo and Edmund, for more than a dozen years. Mike had relayed his father's concerns to me in the summer of 2019 when I was writing a feature story on climate change for the *Toronto Star*. By then I had been a journalist at Canada's biggest city newspaper for nearly twenty years, finally working my way up to being a columnist, covering Indigenous issues. As part of a series on climate change, I'd pitched a story about what the warming of the earth meant for First Nations communities along the James Bay coast.[8] The winters were getting shorter in the north, which meant the hunting seasons were altering, the spring goose hunt was earlier. Colossal ice jams occurred each spring in the mouth of Kistachowan, which caused extensive flooding every year in two First Nation communities, Kashechewan and Fort Albany. The ice jams and the floods seemed to be coming on faster, with less warning, and turning more ferocious.

I'd first contacted Mike in 2011, eight years before his father's contribution to the climate change series. That time, I was reaching out from the *Star*'s Queen's Park bureau, about a story I was pursuing on Ralph Rowe, an Anglican priest and Boy Scout leader who flew himself into nearly twenty First Nations communities in northern Ontario during the 1970s and 1980s. After taking the time to learn to speak Oji-Cree and gaining the trust of First Nations parents and community Elders, no one batted an eye when Rowe offered to take adolescent boys on "camping" trips.

In 1994, Rowe pleaded guilty to thirty-nine counts of indecent assault against fifteen boys, and a plea deal he made with the Ontario Crown meant he did not serve more than four and a half years in prison for his crimes.[9] More convictions followed in 2005 and 2009, and after pleading guilty in 2012, he was sentenced to two years' house arrest. In 2017, a class-action lawsuit was filed against Rowe, the Anglican Church's Diocese of Keewatin and Scouts Canada. A $13.25-million settlement was approved by the Ontario Superior Court in Thunder Bay in October 2023.[10] Ralph Rowe is still alive. His last known address was Lake Cowichan on Vancouver Island.

These light sentences were beyond damaging, considering it is believed Rowe had upwards of five hundred victims and the time he served did not reflect the fallout from his crimes. It is believed in both the Indigenous community and by those familiar with this case that his prolonged sexual abuse resulted in dozens of men taking their lives in the Nishnawbe Aski Nation territory—an area encompassing two-thirds of the province of Ontario. The abuse some of the men suffered tore through families and communities, causing a cascading effect of abuse and suicide in their children.

When Mike was deputy Grand Chief of Nishnawbe Aski Nation, he worked with the men supporting Survivors—there were just so many of them—in healing groups, trying to help them rebuild their suffering families. He also tried to assist twenty-four other men who had come forward to the Ontario Provincial Police to say they had been abused by Rowe as children.[11] (Rowe had briefly served as an officer with the OPP on Manitoulin Island before leaving to become an Anglican priest.)

While I was researching that article and learning about Mike's efforts to help his community heal, I was a political reporter, covering the Ontario legislature. I worked alongside three veteran male political journalists who lived and breathed politics. While they were more than happy to handle the ebb and flow of political news, I went in another direction, using the opportunity of being away from the supervision of the downtown Toronto newsroom to write stories about First Nations communities in northern Ontario. In the early 2010s, writing about First Nations was nowhere near as popular—or tolerated—as it is today. It wasn't until after the Truth and Reconciliation Commission released a summary of their final report, with its ninety-four Calls to Action, in June 2015 that things began to change in Canadian newsrooms. The TRC was a turning point in Canadian–Indigenous relations and in the media. No longer could Canada look away from the reality and national fallout of at least 150,000 First Nations, Métis and Inuit children being ripped away from their homes, languages and everything they knew to attend the Christian Church–run, federally funded institutions from the mid-1800s until 1996, when the last "school" closed. Until 2015, it is fair to say Canada's mainstream media had completely ignored the genocide going on right underneath its nose.

On June 2, 2015, the *Globe and Mail*'s front page screamed "Residential Schools Amounted to 'Cultural Genocide.'"[12] That was one of the first times the word *genocide* had been used and heard by non-Indigenous media. Notably, a week before the summary report's release, Beverley McLachlin, the chief justice of the Supreme Court of Canada, had given a speech in which she'd accused Canada of "cultural genocide" against Indigenous Peoples.[13]

The public discourse around use of the word *genocide* marked a sea change for Canada. The six-volume final TRC report, authored by lead commissioner Murray Sinclair along with commissioners Chief Wilton Littlechild and journalist Marie Wilson, would drop on Canada's conscience with intensity.

STRAINING TO SEE my phone screen in the sun's glaring brightness, I texted Mike: "Good morning. I am so very sad to hear about the passing of your father. I know this must be a difficult time for you and your family—and what a family he has!! So much strength among you. I hope you are able to find peace and comfort at this time. Please send my condolences to your family and take care."

He replied, "Hi, yes and thank you, the comfort is knowing he is finally at peace. He has long yearned to be reunited with his long-lost family. For myself, I am happy I was able to be here in the community. They are going through a lot here, more in regards to the spike in positive COVID cases being discovered. It makes it hard to have the proper and usual protocols for laying loved ones to rest."

I said, "I am thinking of you all. I am here in Kamloops writing about the school."

Within a blink, he wrote back: "It has opened the scars of all survivors. I was just listening to an Elder who came and sat with us for a bit this morning and that's what he shared. He said he shed tears once he heard the news of the 215. He said he could relate to the pain and suffering they must have went through. The 215 is the talk of the nation today and rightfully so. The truth has finally caught up to Canada, and hopefully caught the attention of the world."

Mike and his brother Edmund were both Survivors of St. Anne's Indian Residential School, the school run by the Missionary Oblates of Mary Immaculate and the Grey Nuns on the shores of the Albany River. The Oblates had also run the Kamloops school, among forty-seven other residential schools across Canada. Both Mike and Ed have publicly shared details of their time at St. Anne's, which was open from 1906 until 1975. Their experience at St. Anne's almost broke the brothers. Among the litany of abuses that happened there, children were whipped until they bled, they were forced to eat their own vomit, and the institution had a homemade electric chair that they used on students, whom they called "inmates." Survivors report being strapped to the chair and electrocuted until they were semi-conscious.[14]

For over three decades, Ed has been leading a group of St. Anne's Survivors in their quest for justice, in an OPP investigation into child abuse, criminal charges and trials, and civil litigation for compensation. The OPP force undertook a widespread investigation into the school in the mid-1990s in response to Survivors' claims that they had been subjected to violent sexual and physical abuse.

Ed and other Survivors proved in 2014 that the government and church lawyers had withheld all that evidence (generated through the Ontario justice system from about one thousand former students) and that false reports had been filed in the confidential child abuse hearings under the settlement agreement. Despite winning that year, Ed and other Survivors have brought court action upon court action against the Canadian government, trying to enforce the 2014 court order for individual victims of child abuse, and trying to obtain the fair and just hearing process owed under the settlement agreement. Hundreds of St. Anne's Survivors had their child abuse claims rebutted by false government reports that claimed there was no sexual abuse at St. Anne's. Those reports failed to include forty-seven thousand pages of factual evidence of the abuse and about the abusers—all of which was withheld by government lawyers. The legal dispute went all the way to the Supreme Court of Canada, which declined to hear an appeal. The Indian Residential Schools Settlement Agreement, or IRSSA, received final court approval in 2007. The IRSSA is a class-action legal settlement. It is not federal legislation and it is not a private contract that Indigenous People are responsible for enforcing.

Before the IRSSA was negotiated, there were about eighteen thousand civil actions against the federal government and churches in which Indigenous people gave testimonies about the abuse they had suffered in these schools.[15] The legal settlement came in principle, in 2005, after the Supreme Court of Canada confirmed that the federal government and churches were liable for child abuse in these schools. The IRSSA is meant to help aid in Canada's reconciliation effort towards Survivors of the schools by ensuring a monetary compensation to individual Survivors based on their verified attendance in a recognized institution. It has five main components. It gives Survivors a set Common Experience Payment, while an Independent Assessment Process, or IAP, resolves claims for sexual and serious physical and psychological abuse. The IRSSA also set up the Aboriginal Healing Foundation (Ottawa discontinued its funding in 2014) and established the Truth and Reconciliation Commission. The fifth part of the settlement is the continued support of commemorative events.[16]

St. Anne's Survivors say they never received their proper payment because the Government of Canada and the Catholic Church failed to file all the child abuse evidence in their possession with the claims adjudicators, the victims or lawyers for the victims. As their lawyer, Fay Brunning, explained to me, "We established in 2014, it was the law that government officials were supposed to file all documents with 'allegations of child abuse' for the Truth and Reconciliation Commission and for each child abuse hearing under the IAP. We were able to prove in 2014 that the Department of Justice lawyers had breached the IRSSA because the lawyers had withheld criminal trial transcripts, Ontario Superior Court pleadings and all the OPP investigation documents that the government and church obtained in 2003 through the courts."[17]

But since 2014, the Government of Canada has failed to comply with that court order to file the truthful reports and documents for each Indigenous victim of abuse at St. Anne's. Individual victims were not given the new evidence for their claims, and the chief adjudicator did not give notice that there was new evidence to people whose claims had already been breached prior to 2014. Furthermore, the Ontario court and its agents did not enforce the 2014 order.

Ed and other Survivors have bravely stood up for the rights of those victims, who are too scared to go to court or who do not know their claims were breached. The Ontario court had the claims reviewed in 2021 and 2022, without any involvement of the Indigenous victims and without any procedural rights owed under the IRSSA.

Regardless, in October 2022 the Supreme Court dismissed the application for leave to appeal.[18]

The denied claims of Survivors from schools like St. Anne's, of those who suffered abuses like those described by Mike and Ed, form part of the Knowing.

＝

WEEKS BEFORE KAMLOOPS, I had picked up Uncle Hank's brown file folder and started to sift through its contents. I felt guilty that I had ignored it for a long while. Sometimes what was inside both perplexed and depressed me to the point of stagnation. It represented the elusive identity hunt my family was constantly on and our aching lack of knowledge. All the bureaucratic dismissals my uncle Hank had received seemed like so many doors slamming shut in his face. It was so disrespectful to Uncle Hank, a veteran, no less, who'd been willing to put his life on the line for whatever this country represented.

I had just started researching this book. I knew I was going to write about the missing children who'd disappeared at residential schools, but I did not know how I would tell the story.

The idea of this book had been living with me for a long while, at least since the TRC report came out in 2015. As a journalist, I wanted to know what had happened to the children, to the 3,200 deaths on the TRC's registers of confirmed deaths of both named and unnamed residential school students, referenced in the fourth volume of the report.[19] Before I wrote my first book, *Seven Fallen Feathers*, I had actually pitched two books to Janie Yoon, the nonfiction editor at House of Anansi Press. Over lunch in spring 2016, at my first-ever meeting with a book editor, I nervously told her about both ideas that were occupying my mind. I told her about residential schools and the thousands of children gone, and how the country did not seem to care. And I told her about the deaths of seven First Nations students in Thunder Bay, who had no high school to go to in their home communities so they had to leave home, leave their families and everything they knew behind, and move by themselves at age thirteen or fourteen to be boarded with people in a faraway city who were paid to take care of them. I told her a high school education was the fundamental right of any child in Canada, but not if you were a First Nations student.

She listened thoughtfully and then, at the end of the lunch, she said I should write the book on the seven first. Set the table, and then, when Canada is ready, write the next book.

So here I was, five years later, sitting at the tiny white desk that used to be my daughter's, in my east end Toronto home, with Uncle Hank's brown file folder in my hands. The contents were spread out over my messy desk. I didn't know how a book on the disappeared and dead children at residential schools fit with the story of Annie, but I knew they were related. We had stories in my family—of children that were missing, gone—but they were just whispers, no names, nothing. My mother had three brothers, Maurice, Bill and Alvie, who were taken in the Sixties Scoop, the term used to describe what happened when the residential schools started to close across Canada and child welfare authorities swooped in. Convinced Indigenous people could not be good and proper parents under the colonial lens, provincial authorities started to take the children, en masse, and stick them into the foster system. My older sister Donna was adopted out and raised by a white family in Manitoba. I knew that this entire story of the long destruction of First Nations families was also related to Annie. That she was the beginning for what had happened to our family.

I looked through what Uncle Hank had collected: all the birth and death certificates, the maps, the family trees that seemed to go nowhere. As a reporter, I knew the most logical place to start was with Annie's death certificate. But it left me with questions more than anything else.

Dated 1937, it stated that "Ann Gauthier" was "French-Indian," and that her place of residence was Graham, Ontario. Graham was where my grandma Margaret and all her brothers and sisters were raised, along with my mother, deep in the bush at the southern end of Treaty 9 territory. She must have been staying with her daughter Elizabeth Gauthier—Hank's mother—and Liz's husband, my great-grandfather Russell Alphonse "Rusty" Bowen. He was from Fort William First Nation, but he had a trapline near Graham and the family lived in what they called "the big house" because it was a log cabin with more than two rooms. Rusty also worked the railway as a labourer.

Why was Annie listed as "French-Indian?" Was it because her husband was Joseph Gauthier, a French Canadian from Quebec? Did being married to a French Canadian man cancel out her very identity? We used to joke among the women in our family, who couldn't understand the "French-Indian" label, that she was a "fancy Indian."

And what was the Ontario Hospital? We had heard she was in a "lunatic asylum." Is that what the Ontario Hospital was? If so, why was she in there for nearly eight years? Had she been committed? Why?

Annie's place of burial was given as the "Institution Cemetery, New Toronto," and the only other clue to where that was, was the word "Mimico."

Why did her death certificate list her parents as "Unknown," and the same for her birthdate and place of birth? During her seven long years as a patient, did no one ever ask her who she was or where she was from? Wasn't that basic information?

For a medical record, the death certificate's lack of information stunned me. Was the incomplete, cold document an indication of the level of care she received?

But the most troubling aspect of the document was that it reveals Annie died of broncho-pneumonia. Further, a "morbid condition" that contributed to her death was acute peritonitis and gangrene of the intestines. Reading this, I had visions of her lying in a nondescript, dirty cell-like room, suffering, rotting from the inside out. This vision sat with me for a long time. It still does.

The third and last "morbid condition," but not one that was causally linked to her death, was "chronic mania," an incredibly loose term that could mean many things.

I knew I needed assistance, a records hunter who could navigate through piles of government documents and bureaucracy. Fortuitously, several months beforehand, I had been introduced to Ryan Shackleton, the owner of Know History, a firm of professional historical archive hunters based in Ottawa. Ryan offered Know History's services to me, knowing that I might need help delving into Canada's vast treasure trove of hidden records stashed in church and government archives and in other places. Now, as a stuck journalist, I knew this offer was something

I could not pass up. I called him up and told him about my search for Annie, how I needed help in going deeper, looking for any information I could about her, and that I honestly didn't know where to start. All I had was her death certificate and her maiden name: Carpenter.

Ryan mentioned the importance of census records. I told him I knew that there were Carpenters in two distinct places in Ontario: northwestern Ontario and along the James Bay coast, particularly in Attawapiskat. I knew there were Carpenters in Attawapiskat because I'd met journalist Lenny Carpenter, who was from there, at a journalism conference a few summers before. And I had read about the death of Elder James Carpenter, a Canadian Ranger also from Attawapiskat, earlier that year. Attawapiskat was just up the James Bay coast from Fort Albany.

Albany. My mind was rumbling. That was when I reached out to Mike Metatawabin on Facebook: "I think I have asked you this before, but, are there any Carpenters in Fort Albany?"

As always, he replied quickly: "You mean the last name right? We do. But the last one is now hospitalized. I don't know about the younger family members. The other Carpenter family are in Moosonee. And Attawapiskat."

I asked if they were all part of the same family. That is when he told me the last remaining Carpenter in Albany was François and that his father was Elder James Carpenter. Then Mike wrote, "I have a Treaty and land entitlement report document which might provide some information."

THE REPORT MIKE sent to me is titled "Fort Albany Treaty Land Entitlement Claim: Historical Report." Right on the first page it lists the families who had lived along the western James Bay coast in 1905, at the signing of Treaty 9.[20]

The Province of Ontario was intent on expanding its borders so it could explore the economic potential of the north. They needed to know who lived where—and how many Indigenous communities they needed to enter into a treaty with. Before 1905, the northern border of Ontario was the Albany River. Treaty 9 in 1905 encompassed 331,500 square kilometres, or two-thirds of present-day Ontario.[21]

The report notes that Fort Albany was established in 1705 as a Hudson's Bay Company trading post. By 1800, the population was two hundred, consisting of twenty-five to thirty families of Homeguard Cree—those who lived close to the post and provided the staff with fowl, fish and other foods.[22]

It mentions the 1881 Canadian census, the first census taken in the area, which listed those residing at Albany Factory, including the "native and non-natives." The census documented "137 heads of family, 10 of which are not 'Indian' totalling 679 'Indian' people (not counting native wives and children of whites)."

The report lists the names of 203 hunters who had an account at the HBC and notes that the sheer number of hunters meant an "aboriginal population of at least 1000." According to the report, many of the hunters had come down to Albany from Attawapiskat: "The distant northern Indians are the mainstay of the post."

But the growing Ontario, the report explains, was getting antsy. It wanted to expand its borders—all while "extinguishing aboriginal title." As such, a provincial government head counter from Port Arthur (now Thunder Bay) claimed that only 150 Indians were at Albany. Fewer Indians meant fewer people to deal with and pay treaty annuities to.

I scanned the document, looking for the last name Carpenter. There were references to George Carpenter, Joseph Carpenter and Charles Carpenter in 1921. They were listed as "Albany Indians" hunting in Attawapiskat. Then came more Carpenters, those who were counted as "visitors to Attawapiskat" in the ten years before 1929: George Carpenter, James Carpenter, Jacob Carpenter, Joe Carpenter, Joseph Carpenter, Pat Carpenter.

The Carpenters had a strong family presence along the James Bay coast. My mind raced.

This is the 1881 Census of Canada, taken in what was then "The Territories, Albany Factory," which shows Annie Carpenter as a ten-year-old "Indian" girl along with her parents Jean-Baptiste Carpenter and Jane Bunting, also listed as "Indians," along with Annie's six siblings. (Library and Archives Canada / RG 31 / Reel C-13286)

There she was: Annie Carpenter. Born in 1871. The census showed she was attending school along with her brother James. But it didn't say where.

Mike had pushed me in the direction of where to look for Annie and my family. Our long friendship had helped guide the way.

FROM WHAT I now understand from the documents Mike gave me, the Carpenter family is from Keewatin, the northernmost point of the four directions. Omushkego is the anglicized name of the people who live here, in the swampy lands full of waterways that lead to the dirty sea, which was only called Hudson Bay after the English came and failed to show any respect for what once was.

To the Omushkego, Kitchi Weeneebayko is the great Hudson Bay and wayshaybayow describes the shoreline of the coast. It is a place where the great white bears have roamed, king of all they survey, while seals and beluga whales frolic in the cold, salty water that is constantly dotted with floating chunks of glacial ice and snow—so white in spots that the snow looks like it bleeds aqua blue. The people also call themselves the Ininiw, or Innino, and if you are from the traditional Môsonîw Ililiw or what the English called Moose Factory, the dialect and name changes to Ililiw. All essentially mean "the original people."[23]

So, where did the name Omushkego come from? John S. Long, whose book *Treaty No. 9: Making the Agreement to Share the Land in Far Northern Ontario in 1905* is one of the few well-known and beloved books on the history of the area, describes the origin of the term like this: A group of Elders once deliberated on the name by which the people refer to themselves and they made this statement: "Mushkegowuk can mean two things. One refers to the muskeg. Long ago, the Ojibway Indians from the west came to see us, and they saw that we were living along the coast. So they named us Mushkego Indians. The Indians who lived here were very strong and powerful, and that is the second reason we were given the name Mushkegowuk. Our grandfathers unloaded the Hudson's Bay Company ships when they came in. The word Mushkegowuk also reminds us of our traditional religion, when we use powerful spirits to protect ourselves."[24]

The French, when they first encountered those on the shore, called them the Kiristinon. This was shortened to Cri. Then the English said they were Cree.[25]

On the dirty sea's southern shore, there are no trees and the ground is flat, seemingly endless. The rich, brown sand is full of swooping ripples running up and down the wide, wide shores, water resting only momentarily before it is swept out again. Smooth round rocks in dark purples, shades of grey, yellows and coppers, white and marbly black, litter the coast—along with spent oyster shells, their pearly insides gleaming. Large dark rocks, their tops smooth like tabletops, expose themselves in clusters, the long tide of the sea washing in and out over them.

On the shores of Kitchi Weeneebayko, there are no trees, just bits of dead seaweed and old weathered driftwood from other southerly places. The view is unobstructed for as far as the eye can see. This land is the subarctic.

Turn away from the endless beach of rock and sand and your feet begin to plunge deep into vast plush, spongy ground. Te-ni-sha-wow. The lowlands. The land that sinks. For miles the land slopes, gradually leaning towards the dirty sea. With every step, it is like walking on clouds of various shades of mossy green, from the darkest colours of the forest to light pea green to browns and dark yellows, accented every once in a while with patches of small white daisies, yellow or purple flowers. Bright beauty lives amongst the starkness.

The muskeg runs in zigs and zags, like stripes on a tiger's back, for thousands of kilometres up from the treeline to the water. The quiet is uncanny. Your feet sink into the muskeg, your heels sucking in and out with each step. Your legs ache for higher ground. Your ears are full of your efforts and the sound of the wind whooshing past, obstructed only by your presence, as there are no structures, no buildings. Nothing but rock and moss, sand and water.

The wind comes and it howls with all the screaming might of the four directions off the back of the turtle's shell. This is where the air of this continent we now call North America comes to dance, twirl and bend before it decides to swoosh off as fast as it came.

The only thing that can survive and break this land, this harshness carved out of the dirty sea, are the commanding mighty serpentine rivers. In some places they can be as wide as lakes or dribble down to spaces as skinny as creeks. They begin here in the rolling, mineral-rich area of the Canadian Shield and they flow away from the southern cities.

The rivers are living, breathing entities, flowing and moving depending on their moods and on the skies above. The Ininiw named each of these living, flowing entities to describe what it does, what its spirit means, and that is how you know where you are. This is the map you use to figure out time and space and where you need to go.

Kistachowan Sipi. Fast, strong moving river. Albany River.

At-a-wa-pis-kat-sipi. Gorge stone river. Attawapiskat River.

Moososiibii. Moose river.

Wa-shs-hoe-wi-sipi. The bay within the bay river. Severn River.

Wi-nas-sko-sipi. Ground hog river. Winisk River.

Pa-wa-ni-na-kaw-sipi. River of white water. Nelson River.

I had been to this place before I understood the women in my mother's family were from here, before my great-grandmother arrived as a residential school Survivor, on the shores of Gichigami, Lake Superior. For some inexplicable reason I have, countless times, been drawn back to Keewatin, so familiar to me yet also so foreign. Like the members of my own family, ripped from the wombs of our mothers, stolen and sent away to the arms and abuses of others. When they return they are intimate strangers. We know them but we do not. That is what this place has always felt like to me. I know it but I do not.

I have travelled from Toronto, thousands of kilometres south, to get to the First Nations communities in the lowlands and on the coast so I could write about them, understand them. Weenusk. Webequie. Marten Falls. Neskantaga. Moose Factory. The only way in to most of these communities is by small, rickety charter plane or, depending on the season, by ice roads. There are no paved roads here. No highways, toll booths, gas stations, variety stores or Tim Hortons. You carry what you need on your back or in your boat. You bring your food with you or you fish or kill it.

There is only one train in this space running from the small northern mining town of Cochrane to Moosonee, or Moose Factory. That train is the Polar Bear Express, the real one, not something out of a child's fantasy book. But true to its name, it's a magical locomotive from another time that chugs its way to the James Bay coast, every once in a while stopping to let out passengers—seemingly nowhere—at prearranged stops along the line.

I have written about Keewatin endlessly in newspapers and in books. For years I came up with story ideas and excuses, doing my damnedest to convince newspaper editors with only vague interest that I needed to be in this place in order to tell its stories. That these stories mattered to them and to their children and to their children's children. Eventually, they reluctantly sent me, for no other reason, I'm convinced, than to shut me up.

Kistachowan. You knew me before I knew you. You welcomed me like my beautiful kokum—or like an angry relative wondering where the hell I've been. I have sailed you, been held in your sway. You showed me my people, introduced me to the youth, to your bountiful gifts that fed us well every night after we gathered the fish in our nets. I slept under the open skies, embraced by your soft, mossy ground. You sustained me as you had sustained my mother's people for thousands of years.

You welcomed me home with your tears after I landed on your waters in the summer of 2014, joining Edmund and his brother Mike on a raft Ed had made of cedar logs. Two Survivors of the ruinous so-called schools that the men waving the sticks built. We laughed and called it the river cruise of Crees. When I arrived, there was an onslaught of torrential rain for three solid days. I could not help but feel you, breathe you in. There was no part of me that was not touched by you, seeping through every garment, every stitch I owned. Nothing was spared from your rage. I was the river.

Kistachowan, you were so angry. Mad that it took so long for me to recognize you, to pay you the respect you were so due. Mostly, you cried for what had been taken, for all that Cha-ka-pesh's sister foresaw, for the warning she gave to her baby brother and to us all.

===

HOW DID WE get here? How did the women in my family get so far from Kistachowan to the point where we didn't know who the hell we were?

To understand, I needed to go back and find where the rupture was.

I needed to start with Hudson Bay. James Bay. Why did we know these by their English names only? What came before?

It was on Henry Hudson's fourth attempt to find a northern passage to the Pacific Ocean that the wealthy English merchant met his fate. Hudson was born of privilege in 1570, to a family that was part of London's prestigious Company of Merchant Adventurers, a prosperous group of traders of foreign goods with tentacles all over Britain. He was schooled in mathematics, in the stars and the skies, in celestial movements and in the stories of faraway lands—lands that were the talk of all society during the sixteenth century, a time when the Europeans crossed the oceans, armed with their papal bulls, with their missions from Christian churches and governments to conquer any and all lands that they could find. He was a child unaware of the diseases of poverty that plagued the lower classes in his country, which was also heaving with religious insurrection. From all available accounts, Henry Hudson was a boy whose head was full of wonder. As soon as he was adult and able, he filled a massive seafaring boat with men and supplies and took off for the great unknown.

He was first hired in 1607, by the Muscovy Company of London, to find a quick passage to Asia along the top of the world. But twice he was forced back to England after his boat, *Hopewell*, encountered thick, unmovable ice. While he was on his second voyage, Hudson recorded in his journal that the ship's men had spotted a pair of mermaids, their long, black hair hanging down their backs, their tails the size of a dolphin's and speckled like a mackerel.

After these two failed attempts, the Muscovy Company declined to back any more of Hudson's voyages, so he turned to the Dutch East India Company for support.

By his third try, he had learned his lesson. He sailed the East India's ship *Half Moon* southward, hitting the shore of Turtle Island and then following it south to the opening of a giant, gaping river that had first been "discovered" by a Florentine explorer named Giovanni da Verrazzano. There, he made his way inland. This river would later be known as the Hudson, bearing the name of the first known Englishman to sail down it. For Hudson himself, this trip proved fruitless. But for the Dutch, it was another story: it would begin their migration to North America, particularly to the island the Lenape Peoples called Manhatta, an island the East India Company allegedly purchased from them in 1626, founding what they called New Amsterdam. This $24 "purchase" of fifteen thousand acres would eventually become the city of New York. The Lenape (their Anglicized name is the Delaware) were driven out of the area, and the Dutch built a giant wall to keep them out. Where this wall once stood is now known as Wall Street. Their trading route, Brede weg, is now known as Broadway Avenue.

On Hudson's fourth attempt, both the Dutch East India Company and the Muscovy Company footed the bill, jointly paying to outfit the fifty-five-ton ship *Discovery*. Hudson left England in April 1610, and this time he turned north, or so he thought, finding his way to what he must have thought was the long sought-after "northwest passage." Instead, he had sailed south of what is now known as Baffin Island and above the northern shores of Quebec. Hudson fatefully turned south and inland, thinking he was on his way to the Pacific and all of the riches of Asia. After all, the body of water that spread before him looked like open sea. It was salt water, full of white whales bursting up towards the sun, seals slithering beside the ship. The horizon must have looked like it went on forever.

Hudson and his men—who by this time were starving—continued to sail south, but the temperatures didn't change. They unknowingly had made their way from one bay to another. The cold stayed with them. They only discovered more ice and snow. Clearly it was not the Pacific.

Desperate, and crazed from hunger, the crew mutinied, seizing control of *Discovery* and casting Hudson, his seventeen-year-old son John and a crew of seven men, all suffering from malnutrition, adrift in a small wooden dinghy, with nothing to aid their survival. *Discovery* turned around and headed back into the open ocean, the remaining crew—eight of the original twenty-three—starved and half-mad, floating in a boat of scurvy and death. The men were eventually rescued by the Irish and taken back to English shores. But the fate of Hudson, his son and the other sailors is unknown. They were never seen or heard from again, all believed drowned in the bay that now bears Hudson's name on the maps of the conquerors. Hudson Bay is second only in size to the Bay of Bengal in the northeastern Indian Ocean, a place Hudson had so hoped to find.

It took another two decades, but another Englishman came to the dirty sea. In 1631, Thomas James sailed this way, also in search of a passage to Asia. His intent was to visit the Emperor of Japan, with letters from His Majesty. He never made it. James was the only Englishman to land on the Omushkego southern coast from Severn east along to the bay that would, once he'd published an account of his incredible voyage, take his name on all the maps: "James his Baye." He sailed his ship along the southern shore and found the entrance to a cape, which he named Henrietta Maria after the king's bride, and then another bay. He then landed on a large treed island that he called Charles Town, after the king. When James returned to England, he wrote *The Strange and Dangerous Voyage of Captaine Thomas James, in his intended Discovery of the Northwest Passage into the South Sea. Wherein the Miseries indured both Going, Wintering, Returning; & the Rarities observed, both Philosophicall and Mathematicall, are related in this Journall of it.* In this book he told of landing at Cape Henrietta, of erecting a giant wooden cross, of seeing strong healthy deer but not being able to hunt them and neither could his dogs, which they left behind. He was astounded by the winter ice and by the ferocity of the mosquitoes.

Neither Hudson nor James were towering figures in British history. They were practically unknown, barely remembered in their homelands. But the mark they left on the geography and trajectory of the continent of North America and its existing people—on my own family—would be immense.

What would begin, following Hudson's and James's arrival, was the fur trade. It would lead to the formation of a large economic monopoly to govern over Canada, the creation of something called Rupert's Land, a monstrous plantation for the British and for what was to become the fur-trading giant, the Hudson's Bay Company, a vast area encompassing nearly eight million square kilometres. Europe's greed for furs would feast off of a sinister combination of colonial hunger and slave-based economics. It would feed off of racism, classism, cultural superiority and Christianity's belief in its right to dominate and convert. Ultimately, it would lead to residential schools and to the tragic consequences of that supposed system of "education" that remain so potent today.

Those two voyages would have a profound effect on Annie's life, ending a long line of Ininiw women and families who'd been braided together for thousands of years, to the land and to each other. It was the beginning of my mother's family's violent rip from the aki, the land, of being torn up and tossed into a system of supposed Western modernity that would nearly crush us, along with hundreds of thousands of our fellow Indigenous families on Turtle Island.

As I stood on the front steps of Kamloops Indian Residential School, I thought about the children lying here somewhere on the school grounds, and I thought of Annie—just like the 215, she was missing. Did she have more than the two children my family knew about? If she did, where were they? The question was so simple, and so enormous. Its answers—whatever they were—contained everything I did and didn't want to know about the last two hundred years for my people, and for my family.

Chapter Three

TK'EMLÚPS AND THE STICK WAVERS

MOTIONLESS RED DRESSES WERE HANGING FROM A LARGE, THICK OAK TREE ON the front lawn of the Kamloops Indian Residential School. The dresses are symbolic of murdered and missing Indigenous women and girls. There were three made from cardboard, adorned with flowers, tiny silver jingles hanging on them. The tree is across the driveway from the Monster's front door. It stands beside a grey rectangular granite monument that reads: "To honor all survivors from the Secwepemc Bands who attended the Kamloops Residential School; who all suffered the genocide period in the history of the Kamloops Indian Residential School; and to honor all survivors who are not with us today, but are with us in spirit."

The base of the monument was surrounded with store-bought flowers, sweetgrass, little running shoes placed carefully side by side, along with tiny winter boots and teddy bears. On the school's soccer field, someone from the Tk'emlúps council had placed 215 solar lights in two long rows. At each light, a pair or children's boots, shoes or sandals, plus the odd stuffed toy, was carefully placed. Almost every single pair looked like they had been recently worn by a child.

Across Canada, this phenomenon was repeated in public places. Regular Canadians set pairs of children's shoes, boots and sandals on church steps and out in front of significant buildings or landmarks such as the Ontario legislature, Parliament Hill and the Vancouver Art Gallery. They were everywhere: a grassroots pull-together of deep mourning.

I was lying on the grass, taking everything in, when I saw two pickup trucks pull in at the far end of the field. One of the trucks carried an extremely long, thin cedar canoe. The doors opened and a pile of people got out. Cars drove up and parked behind the trucks. Nearly three dozen people had suddenly gathered on the field, out of nowhere. Almost all wore orange T-shirts and cedar hats, and most held hand drums. Some wore traditional Stó:lō regalia, the men in all black, with headdresses of eagle feathers.

Some of the men lifted the long, white-and-teal-painted canoe off the truck and carried it to the centre of the soccer field. Those who'd gathered around the trucks followed them, drumming and singing a mournful song. The procession moved slowly, rhythmically, to the centre of the field, where they lowered the big canoe—named Xwe Xwos (thunder and lightning)—down on the grass. Then they arranged themselves in a long line in front of it.

Everyone who had gathered to lounge on the front steps, or to remember the 215 with gifts of teddy bears and shoes, stopped what they were doing. We were transfixed. Once again, we were thrust into ceremony.

Red dresses, a reminder of murdered and missing Indigenous women and girls, were made out of cardboard and cloth and stuck to the tree outside the entranceway of the Kamloops Indian Residential School shortly after the discovery of more than two hundred potential graves. (Photo by Tanya Talaga)

One man stepped forward. He spoke in his language and introduced himself as Russell Williams. He said they had driven 250 kilometres from Chilliwack. He said the family knew first-hand the horrors that had unfolded in that red-brick building behind us. That they had relatives who'd come to this place and never returned. He said, in a booming voice, that they would hold ceremony on the grounds, the empty canoe serving as a vessel to bring the spirits of the missing, Le Estcwicwéy̓, home.

We rose to our feet and, in utter silence, watched.

Russell and his cousin Justin Williams began to speak in clear, powerful voices. They called for the spirits of their family's children, and any other children who wished to leave this horrible place, to come with them, to climb into the canoe and come to the Skwah First Nation in the Fraser Valley. Then Justin spoke to the children's captors: He told them to let the children go. He told them they could no longer have the children.

He said to the children, "There is room for you all." He told them they didn't need to be afraid. They could move past what was keeping them there and climb into the canoe.

They could leave this horrific place, return to the Stó:lō forests in the valleys at the bottom of the great mountains, to the warm embrace of the family once lost and never found.

The Williams family had come to bring home Le Estcwicwéy̓.

TWO DAYS AFTER I saw the Williams family come to Kamloops Indian Residential School to take the children's spirits home, I drove with *Globe and Mail* photographer Melissa Tait to Skwah First Nation to visit the family—specifically, Justin Williams's father Gary, the oldest surviving family member, and Gary's brothers and sisters.

Their community is nestled deep along the Fraser River valley outside Chilliwack, the small B.C. city with the Stó:lō name borrowed by the 1970s Canadian pop band. As we drove, we couldn't help but take in the harsh reality around us: The deep Interior of B.C. had been devastated by forest fires. There were acres of black, charred trees, the remnants of what was burned alive when the last fire blew through. The fire spares nothing. It burns through whatever it touches. Outside of Kamloops is the turnoff for Lytton, a small town of 250 that, just one month later, would be completely destroyed by a fire. Lytton First Nation, where the temperature hit 49.6 Celsius that summer, the hottest ever recorded in Canada, would be flattened—homes, the hotel, the emergency services buildings, everything gone.

Still, the landscape tells many stories. Amid the evidence of wild-fires, we passed by the Interior's lush green valleys that echo another time. Here, you can feel the glaciers' presence. The flat earth once lay at the bottom of great bodies of water. Now it is some of the best farmland in the country, growing all kinds of fruits and vegetables. You pass places like Hope, deep in the Fraser Valley. The Stó:lō Nation has been living along this fast-moving river for at least ten thousand years. The Stó:lō are river people.

When Melissa and I pulled into the community, the family were all waiting for us. They sat under a small white tent on the banks of the Hope Slough. The tent was perfect in the time of Covid-19, when, even during the pandemic's summer lull, we had to worry about meeting indoors and spreading the virus. Gary, eighty-four, was already seated under the canopy with his daughter Collette Williams, his constant companion. He is thin; his shoulders don't quite fill out his shirt. His hair is salt-and-pepper, and his gaze is intense with meaning.

Gary comes from a large Stó:lō family that knows the Fraser Valley's water systems like the backs of their hands. The river is the constant, always there. His fifteen brothers and sisters were Russell, Vernon, Frenchie, Beverly, Victor, Leslie, Marcia, Patricia, Anthony, Stephan, Rosalita, Susan, Anastasia, Andy and Dean. From those original fifteen, there are now 61 first cousins and 350 cousins living in the community of nearly seven hundred people.

Gary's younger sister Bev remembers who went where and when. She says forty family members were sent to some of the worst Catholic schools in Canada, three of those run by the Missionary Oblates of Mary

Immaculate: Kamloops, St. Mary's Mission and Residential School, and Kuper Island Residential School, in the southern Gulf Islands. Students at each of the three schools had complained about abuse, particularly sexual abuse, since their inception.

Of the Williams family siblings, seven—Russell, Vernon, Frenchie, Beverly, Leslie, Patricia and Gary—went to Kamloops. The younger ones, all but Victor, went to St. Mary's Mission. (Tragically, Victor had drowned in the slough in a canoe race when he was six years old.)

Gary started at Kamloops in 1949 and was there until 1953. But before Kamloops, when he was just seven, he was sent to Coqualeetza Indian Hospital, in Sardis in the Fraser Valley. It was one of the largest Indigenous tuberculosis facilities in the province. He spent two years there: alone, sick and unable to go home.

Unspeakably, it was typical for hospitalized First Nations children to be neglected, receiving little care or attention. The sanatoriums received more government funding the more patients they had. For decades, the Indian Act made it a crime for First Nations people to refuse any medical treatment or to try to leave a hospital of their own accord. The RCMP arrested and returned patients to the hospital or took them to jail. Indian hospitals and sanatoriums were like prisons. And if you died at the hospital, the government did not return your body home.[1] Gary remembers taking twenty-nine pills a day. He was threatened with jail if he did not take his treatment. "It was no picnic. You didn't know if you'd ever get out. And there was no cure."

Coqualeetza was both a hospital and a residential school. By the time Gary left, Indian hospitals were starting to appear across Canada. They were awful places, created essentially because regular hospitals didn't want Indians in them. Indigenous patients who *were* admitted to regular Canadian hospitals were often placed in basements or in spaces with poor ventilation. But the Indian hospitals were consistently poorly funded and poorly staffed, supplying neglectful or second-class care. Some were the site of medical, surgical and nutritional experiments. By the 1960s in Canada there were twenty-two fully functioning Indian hospitals.[2]

When he was well enough to leave Coqualeetza, Gary was sent to St. Mary's Mission School to "recover." After two years there, he was sent to the Kamloops school. Eventually, Gary would make it home from Kamloops, but other children in his large family did not.

Roderick Charlie, a cousin six years older than Gary, disappeared after he went to Kamloops. He remained an unknown face in old family photographs. As a child, Gary clearly remembers his aunt Verna waiting by her front door, hoping Roderick would come home from school.

A second child, George Williams, also died but little else is known. The Stó:lō Nation knows his name, birth and death dates and has a note that he is buried in the Skwah First Nation Cemetery.

Of the siblings who went to Kamloops, Gary and his brother Leslie are the only ones who are still alive. Justin, seated under the tent near his father, Gary, tells us after they heard the news of the 215, they knew they had to act. They took one of the community's most elegant cedar canoes, got in their vehicles and went to the school. It was time to take the lost children's spirits home.

Standing on the Kamloops soccer field, it was Justin who told the children not to be afraid of the nuns, that their spirits could leave. "We can feel all that sorrow, grief and pain."

GARY WILLIAMS LIVES across the street from the fast-moving Hope Slough, in a two-storey split-level with a well-used blue trampoline in the front yard. A big, fierce, barking dog is chained up at the side of the driveway.

His walls are covered in old photographs, spanning more than seven decades. The pictures all depict different times and faces. Some are on bristol board, some are stuck with tape to the wall, others are wedged into the hutch that holds the dishes. The wide-screen TV is prominently displayed in the main room, along with Gary's easy chair and a couch covered with various blankets. Children, grandchildren and great-grandchildren race in and out, charge up and down the stairs, rummage through the kitchen for snacks.

When he heard the news of the discovery of Le Estcwicwéy̓ in Kamloops, he was numb, unsure of what to do or feel. *Helpless.* Yes, that's how he felt: helpless.

"I knew some of our people were there," he says quietly.

The property the school sits on covers eighty hectares. There is a lot of ground to cover. Just like other students, Gary wasn't shocked when he heard on the news that anthropologist Sarah Beaulieu and a team from the University of the Fraser Valley had found indications of shallow little graves in the orchard.

During his own time at Kamloops, Gary had always wondered about the apple orchard. He'd never liked it there. He remembers constantly being hungry at Kamloops, and naturally kids were drawn to the apples. But a man named Brother Joseph was in charge there. He was mean, with menacing black dogs. He threatened any kid who tried to take an apple.

Gary doesn't remember much else about the school, but he does recall one thing very clearly: watching from the dorm window for someone to come and take him home. He had seen other children climb into taxis or cars during holiday time or on the weekends. "We weren't lucky enough to have people in taxis for us," he says.

The news of the missing found at Kamloops has thrown him, taken him back to a lifetime lived with those schools, Kamloops and Mission, lording over him and his family. "They separated us, wouldn't allow us to talk," he recalls. "Everything seemed like a sin. They called us savages, but the savages are the ones who did that to the people."

Bad as it was, the pain of what he saw and experienced at Kamloops was nothing compared to the deaths of his sons. Two of them. Gary Jr. and Rick. Gary says St. Mary's Mission School took them.

His sons did not physically die at that school up the hill in the middle of the trees, a place that looked like any other public elementary school of its day: low-rise, brownish, flat. But St. Mary's did steal their lives. Both Gary Jr. and Rick had been taken into the foster system, where they were sexually abused. They were also sent to the St. Mary's

Mission in the early 1970s, where their family feared the abuse continued, amplified.

There is a photo of Gary Jr., his beautiful wavy black hair and easy, slow smile, his plaid shirt opened to show off his smooth, muscular chest. He is frozen in time. The picture of him hangs taped to Gary's wall.

Gary Phillips Jr., who attended St. Joseph's Mission school and was also in the child welfare system, is the son of Kamloops Indian Residential School Survivor Gary Phillips. Gary Jr. died by suicide. (Photo courtesy of Phillips family)

Gary Jr. lived with unspoken demons. He tried to take his life twice. The second time, he succeeded. He was thirty-two years old, full of life and torment, when he stood in front of a speeding train on October 27, 1994. The Canadian Pacific train runs alongside the river, right through some of the Stó:lō Nations. This is how many young men in the area take their lives.[3]

The year that Gary Jr. died was the year that the Royal Canadian Mounted Police, at the urging of First Nations leadership, established the Native Indian Residential School Task Force. It began work in 1995 and, over the next 8 years, would investigate 15 schools and 974 allegations, 515 of which were allegations of sexual offences involving 374 victims.[4] Another 435 allegations of physical assault involved 223 victims, many of whom overlap with the victims of sexual abuse. Sadly, by the end of the investigation in 2003, one-third of the 180 alleged abusers were deceased. The RCMP reported that 14 individuals were charged; the number includes charges laid prior to the creation of the task force.[5]

Rick held on, raging, until he was fifty-seven. But eventually his body gave up to the abuse. He died in April 2021, of health complications due to his addictions.

The trauma is cyclical; it spins around like a circle. "They did not die naturally," Gary says. "Who do you blame? No one wants to take the blame."

Gary does not know exactly what happened to his sons at the mission school. It was the first residential school to open in B.C., in 1863, and it was the last to close, in 1984. More than 120 years of pain and suffering unfolded on the grounds of that school bearing St. Mary's name.

TO UNDERSTAND THE Indian residential school system, which enslaved and tried to assimilate First Nations, Métis and Inuit children, violently breaking apart families and ways of life all across Turtle Island, you must understand where the ideals behind its creation came from. Where the attitudes germinated and took root. How the righteousness of Crown, king, merchants and missionaries was based on steadfast Christian beliefs of racial and class superiority. The dominance of one race over the other.

You must return to the dirty sea and the land of Keewatin, to the men on floating wooden islands that Cha-ka-pesh encountered.

The English came back, soon after Hudson and James, in 1668, on the ship the *Nonsuch*, commanded by Capt. Zachariah Gillam. Their aim: to trade for furs in Hudson Bay.[6] The trip was so successful that two years later, in 1670, investors received an exclusive royal charter from the British Crown to start the "Governor & Company of Adventurers of England Tradeing into Hudsons Bay."[7] The Hudson's Bay Company was born.

The charter was massive, like no other business transaction ever executed—and it was an outright land grab, carried out with zero regard for those who already lived on the land. It gave the merchants of the HBC control over all of Hudson Bay's waterways: everything that flowed into that giant sea. The drainage area was huge. It encompassed an area five times larger than the country of France: 3.9 million square kilometres, stretching from the Atlantic Ocean to the Rocky Mountains. The charter also gave the British governors and directors the right to colonize.[8] This was, in effect, the inception of a giant plantation, with slave owners presiding—collecting the wealth, while breaking bodies, minds and spirits with no qualms.

Unsure of what lay inland, away from the great sea, the newcomers set up their trading posts on the shores of the bay, at the mouths of the wide rivers that led to river junctions and geographic points, or rest areas, well used by Indigenous peoples. They did this in order to be close to traders, hunters and trappers.[9] The earliest, Rupert House (originally Charles Fort), was built on the Rupert River. Fort Albany was built in and around the mouth of the Kistachowan; Moose Fort (later Moose Factory) on the southern shore of James Bay; York Factory near Pa-wa-ni-na-kaw-sipi, or the Nelson River; and Fort Severn on Wa-shs-hoe-wi-sipi, or the Severn River.

In the beginning, a wealthy English merchant acted as governor and oversaw the entire operation from London. Chief traders were stationed at each fort, and word quickly spread that the magical objects the foreigners brought with them in the ships could be traded for at the forts. All the Europeans wanted were the skins of the animals—primarily beaver. During this beginning period, the coastal Omushkego, along with the Anishinaabe—those living inland, up Kistachowan and throughout the interior—were the important middlemen, acting for the communities, bringing in the pelts, doing the trades. They were the early day brokers.

The Europeans wanted beaver. It took five to eight beaver pelts to make one coat. The process of refining the fur could take years. Beaver fur has an outer layer of greasy, stiff hairs known as guard hairs. The furs had to be worn, facing inward, before the guard hairs dropped off and the soft under-fur could be exposed. Then, the softer products that had been worn in by the brokers and their families were shipped off to England for sale.[10]

The fur trade changed our relationship with each other and with the land. For the first time ever, our families began to take more than what we needed. We began to compete with other families in order to gain more and more. That had never happened before. Since time began, the land had been taken care of by Indigenous Peoples. We had shared for survival; we were never greedy.

But Europeans viewed the world through a completely different lens. The colonial history of this country we now call Canada was profoundly shaped by warring European fiefdoms, notions of cultural superiority and class biases.

The English upper classes had long practised feudalism, reigning over lands, first in England and then in Scotland and Ireland, making serfs or servants of anyone who did not have the means or the social standing to own their own land. Among the people the wealthy few governed over, anger and desperation reigned.

The very definition of imperialism is living and feeding off exploited colonies. Imperialism dominates for the good of the Crown, whoever wears it. Colonialism is the tool of the imperial state. Colonies are built, set up and exist with the intention of keeping the Crown well fed and whole, by claiming what resources are available and sending the riches back home.

And so, from 1670 onward, the HBC ruled, largely unchecked and unfettered, over a vast territory named after King Charles II's cousin Prince Rupert. Two enterprising Frenchmen, Médard Chouart des Groseilliers and Pierre-Esprit Radisson, were among the first to trade with the Ininiw in the upper Great Lakes area. Refused a trading licence from the French, who even jailed Groseilliers for trade New France didn't sanction, they wound up working with the English. The two realized the abundance of fur, how rich the area was in beaver and mink.

In 1680, a little over a decade after the fur trade's establishment, England went to war with France and captured control of its coastal trading posts. For decades, the coast was alight with warring factions. Supply ships could not reach the posts, and many posts were left without food staples or anything to trade. Meanwhile, the Omushkego and Anishinaabe were coming in, looking to unload their pelts and get paid. But instead, they were met with infectious diseases: the middlemen were exposed to smallpox, which they carried back home to others.[11]

Amid all this upheaval, the settlers could not survive without the Omushkego or the Anishinaabe or the Haudenosaunee—or whichever Indigenous Peoples best knew the land they'd taken it upon themselves to settle. They could not explore or build structures of wood in the right spot or even hunt and eat without support and help from those who lived on the land. Indigenous Peoples were their guides, their eyes and ears, their teachers.

In short order, the fur trade had become the economic engine of the area, and in the beginning, Indigenous Peoples somewhat benefited and welcomed these newcomers and their trade goods—from handheld mirrors to steel axes to large metal pots that could sit in the fire. Without Indigenous labour propping up the fur trade, being the ones to go inland and to seek out the furs to bring back for trade—without them being the middleman—the entire structure of the fur trade would have collapsed. But eventually—it was inevitable—the balance of power would shift. The colonial ways would become dominant. Hierarchies constructed around land ownership and material possessions would rule.

To the British, the French, the Spanish—whichever imperial force led the day—Indigenous Peoples became nothing more than blockers on the land, a hindrance that needed to be moved out of the way. By 1840, Herman Merivale, who would become the British permanent under-secretary at the Colonial Office, had declared that there were four basic approaches an imperial power could take in its relations with Indigenous Peoples: it could exterminate them, enslave them, separate them from colonial society, or assimilate them.[12]

The victor writes the story. But with little recorded history outside of treaty papers and the ledgers of a four-hundred-year-old department store, what truly happened in Rupert's Land during the fur trade can only ever be partly known, especially with regards to what happened to Indigenous Peoples and, particularly, to Indigenous women.

We do know this: the chief beneficiary of empire was, is and always will be the colonial state and the head of the empire, plus their children and then their children. That holds true to today.

We also know that the British felt that their laws, their customs, the cities and towns they built, the clothes they wore, the food they ate, the culture they fostered—and, of course, the religion they followed—were superior. And if those in faraway lands, way off in the colonies that fed the Crown, weren't following the same script, then they did not know or understand what was good for them: what it was like to be "civilized."

Given this, it was inevitable that the upholders of the European Crowns would bring more than economic trade and sickness. They also brought the wemaystigoosh or the men who wave wooden sticks. That was the name our people gave to the white Christian missionaries who literally waved pieces of wood—the cross—in front of the Indigenous faces they first encountered. These missionaries would prove near catastrophic to Indigenous Peoples, an absolute irony considering that they wanted to "save" us.

From the start, the missionaries dismissed the Omushkego and Anishinaabe spirituality, languages and ways of life. Colonizers had convinced themselves they were bringing salvation and progress to the people they were encountering in the so-called New World. They believed the only religion that counted was Christianity—everything else was heresy.

Belief in dreams, visions and third-eye seeing, Sweat Lodges, fasts, Sundances and Potlaches were, in their eyes, pagan rituals and the work of the devil. The patterns of life as we knew them—from naming ceremonies, to coming-of-age rituals, to how we formed family units and explained the spiritual existence of human beings in relation to the earth, air, water and all the four-leggeds—were discouraged, called into question, declared to be the rantings of pagans. And unless Indigenous Peoples' souls were saved by God, we would be lost in an unchristian purgatory.

The newcomers brought with them their own beliefs, new stories, to replace ours. They told us that what they were teaching us represented the ultimate truth, that the stories they carried held more weight than any other—that they came right out of the mouth of a mighty God who lived in the sky and watched all, knew all. They brought the Bible, which contained this omnipotent force's teachings within its stories. They told us that if we wanted to trade, we must follow these teachings and listen to these stories. This began to alter our beliefs and our understanding of the spirit world. It changed our relationship with the Creator. What we'd always believed and passed down through the generations became confused, diluted and weak.[13]

What gave these men, who travelled by strange wooden islands with cloud puffs on top, the authority to do what they were doing? Why were they fuelled by righteous superiority?

They believed they were empowered by Christianity; they were followers of Jesus Christ, the son of God, who they said created the world. Christianity may not be a religion that comes from a book, but nevertheless it is a book—and chiefly the interpretation of what is written in that book—that has shaped it. The missionaries who first encountered Indigenous Peoples on Turtle Island believed the Bible contained all the necessary instructions about life, and that the words found in this book came directly from the one God who lives in heaven—the all-knowing and all-powerful God who they believed created man, then used his rib to create Eve. A good story, that one. It has all the elements: an evil snake, a handsome alpha man, food, prime real estate and even a gorgeous naked woman.

The story of Christianity is one fantastical combination of many smaller stories, some historical and factual, some imaginative and hyperbolic. All stories have bits of truths, facts and historical knowledge. Christians built theirs up, improved on them, made endless variations to explain the unexplainable, and gathered them in a big book dressed up in glittering metaphors. These are the stories Christians told themselves, over generations. These are the stories that have been used by some to prop up entire states and empires, and as catalysts for devastating wars that have killed untold millions. Hundreds of millions have lived and died by this story. The Ten Commandments: revealed to a man named Moses on Mount Sinai. Written in stone by the finger of God and then kept in the Ark of the Covenant. Another good story.

In part because their stories deemed their God the one "true" God, Christians believed that they were given the right to spread the word of God wherever they found nonbelievers. But there was more than spirituality at play: there was land, and the wealth it could bring. Christian nations acted based on a belief in their right to "discover" and claim any land, as long as they converted—read "saved"—those living on it.[14]

Since first contact, the papacy sanctioned colonization and legitimized imperial expansion through papal bulls, religious charters or decrees issued by the pope that at the time were held to be law. They handed these out, conveniently fat with detailed instructions for how to adhere to their principles, to whichever country was earning their favour (not to mention keeping the church's coffers stuffed with riches to keep the machine running). The papal bulls relevant to colonization were the foundation of the concept of the Doctrine of Discovery. They were at heart the orders that seemingly allowed Portugal and Spain to conquer Africa and beyond and to engage in the slave trade.

Romanus Pontifex, issued by Pope Nicholas V in 1455, granted Portugal's king the right "to invade, search out, capture, vanquish, and subdue all Saracens and pagans whatsoever, and other enemies of Christ wheresoever placed, and the kingdoms, dukedoms, principalities, dominions, possessions, and all movable and immovable goods whatsoever held and possessed by them and to reduce their persons to perpetual slavery, and to apply and appropriate to himself and his successors the kingdoms, dukedoms, counties, principalities, dominions, possessions, and goods, and to convert them to his and their use and profit."[15] In case that wasn't clear enough, Pope Alexander VI chimed in with *Inter caetera* in 1493, which authorized Spain and Portugal to colonize, convert and enslave the Americas and its Native people.

To make a long story short: North and South America was "given" to Spain, while Portugal got Brazil and the South Atlantic.

The newfound Church of England also believed in converting the "savages" and in the concept of *terra nullius*, that land inhabited only by non-Christians—i.e., Indigenous Peoples—belonged to no one. The British used the principle of *terra nullius* to take over the entire continent of Australia, where it remained the basis of law until 1992. The British argued they could take the land because Indigenous People did not claim ownership of it: the British believed they did not use it to grow food or farm it. And if Indigenous Peoples weren't using it to farm, the settlers coming from crowded England, Ireland and Scotland must have thought it was going to waste.

Indigenous Peoples were also thought to be genetically inferior—unworthy—because they did not look the same. Their skin colour was different, due to climate, geography and their ways of life. In turn, those ways of life meant that, to the colonizers, not only were they of a different race, but they were also of a different class.

Because Indigenous Peoples did not live in societies that the colonizers understood, we were considered not civilized enough to govern ourselves. "It is on the British race, whether in Great Britain, or in the United States, or in the Colonies, or wherever it may be, that rest the highest hopes of those who try to penetrate the dark future, or who seek to raise and better the patient masses of mankind," Britain's Lord Rosebery told an Australian audience in 1883.[16]

Most importantly, it wasn't believed we could educate ourselves in the way that Western "civilization" required. And so residential schools were set up under the conviction that Christianity would save us from ourselves. Some settlers actually thought they were helping.

After five hundred years, the Catholic Church has, officially, walked back the foundations it laid in support of colonization. On March 30, 2023, the church formally repudiated the Doctrine of Discovery that gave explorers, missionaries and mercenaries the "right" to conquer and take away all land held by Indigenous Peoples in the Americas.[17] (It's worth highlighting that the doctrine was repudiated by the first Latin American pontiff, Pope Francis.)

This is a welcome, if long overdue, step forward. But so much damage has been done in the name of that doctrine, a seemingly unquantifiable amount, that the Catholic Church's newfound enlightenment won't come close to changing the lives of Indigenous people any time soon. This will take generations.

AT THE TIME of my trip to Tk'emlúps and my visit with the Williamses in Stó:lō, I had no idea how many of my family members had been taken by the schools, never to come home. Never would I have thought that the number of deceased in my family, that our common experience under colonization, would be similar to what the Williams family had experienced.

This sad truth is one I would soon discover.

But the Williamses, too, still had sorrows waiting to come to light. In 2022, one year after our first meeting, a journalist called and told them that one of Gary's missing cousins, Roderick Charlie, had been found. He was buried in Victoria.

Uncertain what it all meant and where to turn, the family called to tell me. After we spoke, with the help of the *Globe and Mail*'s librarian I began to look for records of Roderick. She found a document titled Return of Death of an Indian. The title, in black bold letters, made my stomach turn. This was what was sent to the federal government and filed away after an Indian died.

BRITISH COLUMBIA
Certified True Copy of a Registration Document
on file with the Vital Statistics Agency, Victoria, British Columbia, Canada.

71127036
Certificate number

Date issued: **MAY 1 2 2022**

VICTORIA

Division Number Three,

VITAL STATISTICS ACT.
(Being Chapter 208, R.S.B.C. 1924.)

RETURN OF DEATH OF AN INDIAN.

To the Indian Agent,

New Westminster _____ Agency,

New Westminster _____ , B.C.

1. Full name of deceased.	RODERICK CHARLIE	
2. Where died.	Jubilee Hospital, Victoria, B. C.	
3. Reserve and band or tribe.	Skwah Band	
4. When died.	May 28, 1941	
5. Sex.	Male	
6. Single, married, widowed, or divorced.	Single	
7. Age.	11 years. months. days.	
8. Where born.	Skwah Indian Reserve.	
9. Religious denomination.	Roman Catholic	
10. *Occupation of deceased.	None	
11. Name of father.	Not-known *Shaw Charley*	
12. Birthplace of father.	Not-known *Skwah Indian Reserve, Chilliwack BC*	
13. Maiden name of mother.	Not-known *Rosie Phillips,*	
14. Birthplace of mother.	Not-known *Skwah Indian Reserve, Devenle, BC*	
15. In case no physician attended, reported cause of death to be herein entered, together with duration of illness.	---- *13 B*	
16. Place of burial.	Songhees Reserve, Esquimalt, B.C.	
17. Name and address of informant.	B.C.Funeral Co.(Hayward's) Ltd., 734 Broughton Street, Victoria, B. C.	

This is a correct return of the death of .... RODERICK CHARLIE

as reported to me this .. 31st .. day of .. May .. 19 41

_____ for Indian Agent.

* If under 16 years of age, the occupation of father.

Jack Shewchuk
Registrar General
Vital Statistics Agency

FOR RESTRICTED USE ONLY pursuant to
Section 36, 37 or 38 of the Vital Statistics Act.

BRITISH COLUMBIA
VSA 439 (14/08)

"Return of Death of an Indian" is the name of the death registration certificate for Roderick Charlie, a student at Kamloops Indian Residential School. He was from the Skwah First Nation in the B.C. Interior but he died in a Victoria, B.C., hospital and was buried on the Songhees Reserve, in Esquimalt, B.C. (B.C. Vital Statistics Agency, Victoria, B.C.)

Under the title, the document reads, "To the Indian Agent, New Westminster Agency, New Westminster, B.C." A list of seventeen numbered items runs down the left side of the page. The first states his full name, Roderick Charlie. Number 2 says, "Where died: Jubilee Hospital, Victoria, B.C."

I scanned the rest of the list and wondered why the Indian agents couldn't have created another form to use for children. This one was so cold. Number 6 on the list was "Single, married, widowed or divorced." It reads "Single." He was a child. Number 10 was "Occupation of deceased." That box was filled out to read "None." Number 16 was "Place of burial." It reads "Songhees Reserve, Esquimalt, B.C."

Roderick was buried in Victoria, rather than where his family lived. This, apparently, was something hospitals did when they had a dead First Nations child and they didn't know what to do with them: they sent them to the nearest First Nation to bury. Songhees wasn't far from the hospital.

The *Globe* librarian and I found something else: Roderick's death certificate from B.C. Vital Statistics. It states that Roderick was eleven when he died, on May 28, 1941, at the Jubilee Hospital. The certificate says he was a Roman Catholic and a member of the Skwah Indian Reserve. Gary told me the family had no idea that Roderick had been in hospital, yet he had apparently been at the Jubilee for nearly a year. The "Physician's Certificate of Cause of Death" states he'd been in hospital from July 5, 1940, until he died, just under eleven months later, of complex tuberculosis. The record notes contributing causes of death were acute toxemia and spinal paraplegia.

Studying Roderick's death certificate, I could not help but think about Annie's. Both were so matter-of-fact, so grey. Both offered more questions than answers. How did Roderick get to Victoria without his family knowing? How did Annie get to Toronto? Did anybody know she was there, or for how long? The similarities between the treatment and death of eleven-year-old Roderick and sixty-six-year-old Annie were clear. They had both been transferred, without their family's knowledge, to an institution and kept there. They had both been quietly disposed of.

CHAPTER FOUR

PROFIT HUNTERS
AND THE FALSE PROPHET

JEAN-BAPTISTE CARPENTER, MY GREAT-GREAT-GREAT-GRANDFATHER, WAS BORN
near present-day Fort Albany in 1841, at a time of cataclysmic cultural
change and intense starvation among the Omushkego along the James
Bay and Hudson Bay coast.

Jean-Baptiste's father, Metikonabe, was from somewhere in the
Keewatin area north of the Albany River. There are no records of
Metikonabe other than that he was married to Madeline, who was
born in 1802, and that she gave birth to five of his children: Jane, Jean-
Baptiste, Charles, Lindsay and Joseph. Metikonabe's name was Cree.
Just Metikonabe, The One Who Knows How to Work with Wood,
hence the last name given to his children: Carpenter.

It is remarkable that we have been able to find any trace of him.
Documentation of most First Nations peoples from this time only
comes from archived Christian church registers for events such as
baptisms and marriages. Records were also kept by the Hudson's Bay
Company if it entered into a contract with a person as a labourer or
servant—and "servant" was a loaded term that signified unfreedom, an
inability to chart one's own destiny. In HBC records, payments were
noted, and sometimes additional, scant information regarding how

many children an employee had, or if he'd been fired and why.

I was lucky that Lawrence Martin, a respected Omushkego Elder, knowing the research I was doing into my family's history, suggested I reach out to his son Jason Martin, an amateur genealogist in Moose Factory. It was Jason who found Jean-Baptiste's father, Metikonabe.

When Jean-Baptiste was born, merchants had been trading in and around the area for nearly 180 years. Who dominated would flip between the two warring empires of France and England, and between the North West Company and its rival, the HBC. During his infancy and early childhood, winters up and down the coast were brutal. The land was in a deep freeze. The geese were slow to return in the spring, and when they did come, there weren't very many. There was overhunting in the south, because of the fur trade, and meat was scarce: there was no beaver, no moose. The caribou were gone. One bad year rolled into another, with no relief in sight.

The English and French—right down to the merchants in what the HBC claimed as Rupert's Land—were equally well versed in cultures of conquest, born into the European history of fiefdoms and the belief that Christianity trumped all other religions. Hundreds of years earlier, from the eleventh to the thirteenth centuries, Europeans had engaged in the Crusades, conquering the Middle East and North Africa in the name of the cross. The Crusaders were violent, rampaging soldiers sanctioned by popes to steal, loot and take non-Christian land. Towards the end of the thirteenth century, the list of who could be conquered had expanded: it now extended to pagans and commoners, including the European peasantry. Entire nations were colonized: Scotland, Wales, Ireland, Bohemia, the Basque Country and Catalonia. Peasants were evicted from lands, while languages and songs were banned and cultures destroyed. The English even paid bounties for the heads of the Irish (a practice that was later adopted in the United States, where bounties were given for scalps).[1]

By my great-great-great-grandfather's time, the European royal houses and states were thriving due to the expropriation of land and exploitation of human labour. Meanwhile, just as Cha-ka-pesh's sister had forewarned, more and more white men, bringing Christianity and market forces, were crashing through the thick black spruce, beyond the treeline, up the rivers and down from the coast of the dirty sea. The English and French Christian missionaries were arriving now in full force, heading deeper and deeper into Rupert's Land, hauling with them their multitudes of denominations and competing faiths. What came altered everyone's lives forever—in the darkest ways possible.

By the 1840s, the war had heightened for the souls of the Omushkego. The coast was wild with religious conversions, up and down the settlements that appeared around the trading posts from north of the Red River Settlement to Norway House and York Factory in present-day northern Manitoba, to all around the Hudson and James Bay coastline. The Anglicans, the Methodists, the Presbyterians and the Jesuits were racing to convert as many Indians as they could, saving their souls and bodies from the supposed evils of being pagans, or from the Ininiw spiritual teachings that had sustained them since time immemorial. Those teachings were dismissed as heresy by the wemaystigoosh—the white men who wave wooden sticks.

Remember, these were especially hard times. At Albany, the HBC's George Barnston wrote, "I have never seen any post so distressed by poor, indigent, starving, and sometimes, unfortunately, lazy natives." He noted conditions were the same up and down the coast. "It seems to be a dead heat for who shall decline fastest. The Albany District from one end of it to the other scarcely exhibited half a trade and I am sorry to say there is no evidence as yet of a turn in the times."[2] Away from the big bodies of water and inward along the Kistachowan, among the black spruce at Marten Falls, other HBC agents recorded the same destitution and starvation. HBC letters from the spring of 1843 include report after report like this one: "Indians were hungry all along the Bayside."[3]

While people starved, Methodist missionaries were penetrating the area from Norway House, Kinosao Sipi, in central Manitoba, up the coast and all the way along to Moose Factory. Among them was the Reverend James Evans, a Methodist preacher who'd spent years travelling throughout what is now southern Ontario—Rice Lake, St. Catharines, Guelph—indoctrinating many Indigenous Peoples. He had even invented a written language of syllabics for translating scripture into Ojibwe. Now he brought that experience to central Manitoba.

When Evans arrived at Norway House, he discovered it was near impossible to convert the Cree because they were hunters and always on the move. So he developed the phonetic syllabic characters that became the syllabics still used by the Cree. He did so for one reason: to try to teach them the word of the Christian Lord.[4] He made the language accessible so the people could take this form of scripture and share it among themselves, thus spreading Christianity. The Cree would copy the symbols onto birchbark, the paper of the time. The missionaries said this caused "intense excitement" among the people. One Methodist missionary wrote: "That birch bark could 'talk,' and above all that it could talk about the Great Spirit and say His words, was indeed a thing of mystery and astonishment."[5] Evans began to use an old Hudson's Bay fur press to produce syllabic books with pages sewn into deerskin covers. His first paper was fine birchbark. Some of the books contained hymns, which the Cree took to instantly.

Among the men who came to learn the Methodist teachings were Abishabis (Small Eyes) and his friend Wasiteck. They took the teachings of the Great Spirit and the Bible a step further, spreading the "word" themselves, with more authority than the HBC's white overlords appreciated.

Shortly after Jean-Baptiste's birth, in the spring of 1843, the Omushkego descended on Albany for their spring gathering. The HBC officer in charge at the time, George Barnston, thought he should warn the hunters about Abishabis, who had begun to call himself Jesus Christ, and Wasiteck, who was calling himself "the Light." Barnston told the Omushkego that the two believed they'd "been in heaven, and returned to bring blessings and Knowledge to their Brethren."[6] He called them "Imposters" and emphasized that the Indians had learned about Jesus Christ, the Son of the God that all the white people believed in, from the missionaries. Barnston said the imposters were telling people they had a "'Track to Heaven,' with lines drawn on paper or wood," and that this was not only false, it was the "wiles of the Devil."[7]

There are no written Cree accounts of Abishabis and the coming of Christianity. Anything we know comes from whatever the missionaries or the HBC's British employees wrote down. The HBC's James Hargrave reported in a letter that Abishabis was acting like some sort of prophet, "taking upon himself the character of a preacher, giving out the most blasphemous stories of his intercourse with the supreme Being, and stating that all our white missionaries know nothing in comparison with him."[8] Academics have surmised that Abishabis had delusions of grandeur. He used to tell other Omushkego that they must give him things—food, clothes, other goods—so that he could carry on and spread the word. Apparently, he became so greedy and drunk with power that he started to demand fathers give him their daughters, insisting he needed five or six wives.

This must have been a spiritually confusing and distressing time for the Omushkego. What were they to believe? Imagine them at that time, living as they always had, with their own ancient spiritual practices, their own stories and ceremonies. Then, suddenly, white people appear with weapons made of steel that change their hunting ways. They have rum drinks that make them lose their heads. And they have books that speak.

Symbols—pictographs—have been used among the Ojibwe people (whose name means "people of the pictograph") for at least a millennium, and so the talking books made an impact among them. Missionaries and other spreaders of God's word such as Abishabis constantly told the Omushkego that they must believe, they must pray and do the bidding of the Lord, and that if they did, they would be rewarded.

At Albany, in 1844, the missionaries found that the starving Indians seemed to be staring at, even worshipping, pictures of animals, in the hopes they would magically appear. George Barnley wrote:

The outline of a female figure was carved and round her several squares contain several crooked marks, and having appropriated to each a song about berries deer &c &c. A second board had the outline

of a male figure a good deal larger and surrounded by various ani-
mals as a Cow, a goat, a buffalo, a sheep &c. They were taught that
if they worshipped the latter figure the animals they needed would
be supplied without further trouble, and reposing confidence in this
gratifying doctrine they lay down in their tents gazing on the figure
and of course almost starving . . . expecting to find deer &c so accom-
modating as to bring their throats to the knife. . . . These boards were
worn next to the heart.[9]

Was Abishabis an opportunist, or was he an overzealous believer in what he was learning from the talking books and the white men? Was he running to community after community and telling families to warn them—or to convert them? Was he out of his mind with fear, was he suffering from mental illness, or was he confused after the white missionaries said the pieces of paper and wood that his Cree followers inscribed with syllabics were worthless and should all be burned and damned? But didn't those papers contain the biblical path to heaven?

Without hearing from the Cree, it is impossible to know.

Eventually, tragically, things came to a head with Abishabis. With the HBC continually questioning and discrediting him, he became alienated from everyone and withdrew. He was also starting to be questioned by the people themselves because of his insistent demands for goods (and wives). Support for him gradually disappeared. In July 1843, by then an outcast, Abishabis murdered an Omushkego family in the York Factory area, stealing their goods so he could head home to Severn House. Once there, he was captured and imprisoned. But the people found out and sought their own justice: they beat him to death, then burned his body. They were trying to destroy the Windigo inside him—an evil cannibalistic spirit.[10]

THE GOVERNOR OF the Hudson's Bay Company during Jean-Baptiste Carpenter's youth was Sir George Simpson, who lorded, from 1820 to 1860, over 250 trading posts throughout Rupert's Land. In 1820, Simpson landed in North America, knowing nothing about the fur trade but bringing with him many years of experience in the West Indian sugar industry. Despite his lack of fur trade experience, he quickly rose to the governorship of the entire HBC.[11]

Simpson had been sent to help oversee the 1821 merger of the HBC with its long-time rival, the North West Company, a prosperous fur trade company started in the 1770s and based in London and Montreal. For nearly two hundred years, the North West Company, the short-lived New North West Company (also known as the XY Company and formed by disgruntled NWC workers) and the HBC had engaged in violent competition, each jockeying for control of the continent's fur trade business. Each had repeatedly leapfrogged over the other, rushing to exploring areas inland to claim as their own. However, in 1800 the New North West Company merged with the North West Company, which then, in 1821, merged with the HBC, giving that company an absolute monopoly over much of the land considered to be part of Canada.[12]

Simpson was a Scot and a ruthless businessman who started his fur-trading career consolidating and closing trading posts, laying off staff and banning the sale of alcohol (he didn't like any distractions from business).[13] Vain and egotistical, he reportedly travelled with his own piper.[14] He was also a misogynist and abuser of women, profoundly racist and by all accounts a bastard.[15]

He was a man of his time. His uncle Geddes Mackenzie Simpson was a partner in the sugar brokerage Graham and Simpson, which had merged with the brokerage Wedderburn and Company in 1812. The Wedderburn family owned plantations and slaves in the Caribbean. Since 1810, senior Wedderburn partner Andrew Wedderburn Colvile had been on the board of directors of the HBC, and had taken note of the hard-working Simpson. By the 1820s, the slave trade was disintegrating, and the Wedderburn family looked to invest its money in the fur trade. It was Colvile who was largely behind sending Simpson to Rupert's Land.

Given this, perhaps it's no surprise that human slavery of those seen as less-thans would come to form part of the story of the Hudson's Bay Company.

This is a part of Canada's history that is not widely known. It deserves a greater place in the national narrative. It is corrective history, and vital that Canadians understand that slavery existed in the fur trade in Canada. The HBC, the North West Company and the XY all had strong roots in the violent slave-owning empires of England and France. There was a complex web of relationships involving class, family dynasties and business interests of the fur trade, which intersected with the African slave trade and other interests of empire. They brought their laws, their morals and their values with them, and they were the foundations of Canada.

In fact, Prince Rupert, the HBC's first governor, was also a director of the Royal African Company, which in 1660 received a royal charter to run trade in West Africa. Fronted by James, Duke of York, who later became King James II, and Prince Rupert, King Charles II's cousin, the RAC quickly became the monopoly licence controlling the transatlantic slave trade, a position guaranteed by a change in its charter in 1663.[16] Thus, two British companies were instrumental to imperialism and to propping up the British economy during the height of the fur trade: the Royal African Company and the Hudson's Bay Company.

Many of the HBC's first governors had served as directors of the RAC. Not only did they profit immensely from slavery, but they were themselves slave owners and plantation owners in both the Caribbean and in British North America. They also worked for a third British firm: the East India Company.

Meanwhile, for a full eighty-one years between 1670 and 1799 the HBC had clear, direct, strong ties between several of its governors and the RAC.[17] HBC governors who also served as directors of the RAC included Sir Stephen Evance, the fourth and sixth governor, serving from 1692 until 1696 and from 1700 to 1712; Sir Bibye Lake, who served as seventh governor from 1712 until 1743; and Sir Atwell Lake, the tenth governor, and son of Sir Bibye, who served from 1750 until 1760.[18]

The connections to slavery don't end there. William Baker, alderman of the City of London before he went to work for the HBC, served as deputy governor from 1750 to 1760 and then governor until 1770. He was also at one time the chair of the East India Company and he personally owned slaves in the Bahamas, Barbados and Dominica.[19]

Edward Ellice, an HBC director, owned at least 308 slaves on his plantations in St. Lucia, Granada and Jamaica.[20] A major artery in Winnipeg is named after him.

Jean Selkirk is said to have been a full partner with her husband, Thomas Selkirk, in running the HBC. From her home in Montreal, while Lord Selkirk was actively involved in armed rebellions in Manitoba, Lady Selkirk made decisions on how to handle the conflict between the HBC and the North West Company and in running the HBC's daily affairs.[21]

Jean Selkirk was born in Edinburgh in 1768 to a prosperous Scottish family who were slave owners in the Caribbean. She married Thomas Selkirk and moved to Montreal. While he handled the armed rebellions in Manitoba, she was key in negotiating the conflict between the Hudson's Bay Company and the North West Company. (Manitoba Historical Society)

Lady Selkirk came from a prosperous slave-owning family, the Wedderburns—the family that had joined forces with Simpson's relatives in their slave-based sugar enterprises. She was the daughter of James Wedderburn Colvile and her uncle was John Wedderburn; both had gone to Jamaica and declared themselves surgeons, though they apparently had no such qualifications. They ultimately became wealthy plantation and slave owners with at least four estates.[22] Aside from Lady Selkirk, many other members of the Wedderburn family also worked for the HBC—Andrew Colvile among them—and are listed in the Legacies of British Slavery database.

IT IS CLEAR that the foundational support for the fur trade in Canada came from slave-owning English and Scottish businessmen, who thought nothing of building an empire on the labour of Indigenous slaves. Few scholars study this neglected part of Canada's history, but the University of Winnipeg's Dr. Anne Lindsay is one historian who does. Her research reveals that many untold examples of chattel slavery existed in the imperial world in the late eighteenth and early nineteenth centuries, extending from Montreal, over the Canadian Shield and into the Prairies. "Chattel slavery, alongside other forms of unfreedom, traced out along these webs, might be encountered any place that fur traders travelled, reflecting the racialized constructions of freedom and unfreedom they were familiar with," she writes.[23]

From the seventeenth century all the way through to the nineteenth century, on the basis of class, or caste, the colonizers built a segregated society in Canada.

Slavery—unfreedom—had strong and long roots in the James and Hudson Bay coasts and extending all the way into Manitoba's Red River. One of the earliest surviving records of HBC activity around Hudson Bay, *The York Factory General Account Book* for 1688–89, notes a transaction of "one short English Gun given for a slave man, One Long: Eng: Gun given for a woman."[24]

Lindsay notes that the history of unfreedom—of slavery in Canada, of the buying and selling of Indigenous people and of their forced labour—is rarely discussed. It is a history framed by erasure, by a lack of record-keeping in a colonial narrative.

Indigenous slaves were mostly women or young boys. They were stolen by war parties, then bought and sold like possessions. Our people were kept as HBC guides, translators, general labourers, domestic workers, passed around from one post to another. Slavery made many of our people economically dependent on the fur trade. Our women were stolen, they were trafficked, they were "married" off to the workers, the labourers and the traders of empire and given the most ridiculous, romantic name of "country wives."

George Simpson openly referred to Indigenous women and those who were called "half-breeds" at the time as "brown bits," "commodities" and "brown jugs."[25] He had at least thirteen children whose mothers were Indigenous. After the women gave birth to his offspring, he threw them—and the kids—away. He tried to marry women off to subordinate employees, begged his friends to help cover up his behaviour, or he just walked out. "If you can dispose of the Lady it will be satisfactory as she is an unnecessary and expensive appendage," he wrote to a friend. "I see no fun in keeping a Woman, without enjoying her charms . . . but if she is unmarketable I have no wish that she should be a general accommodation shop to all the young bucks at the Factory and in addition to her own chastity a padlock may be useful."[26]

Simpson believed the nature and moral character of Indigenous Peoples meant they needed to be "ruled with an iron fist" and kept in a "proper state of subordination."[27] In fact, he thought educating Indigenous Peoples was a complete waste of time, that schooling, like religion, was just another distraction from the fur trade. Educating them, he once wrote, "will be attended with little other good, than filling the pockets and bellies of some hungry Missionaries and schoolmasters and rearing the Indians in habits of indolence."[28]

It is essential that Simpson and his attitude be remembered as an important part of the Hudson's Bay Company story: in him and in his conduct we are shown the principles of the men who ran it and how they viewed Indigenous People, particularly women.

By the time Simpson had taken over, French and English fur traders had taken Indigenous women as wives for more than a century. Men needed partners on the land. If you weren't from here, if you weren't Indigenous, life was hard. It was even worse if you didn't have the support of community. You did not know how to survive, where and when to travel, what to pick to eat, where to hunt, how to make clothes, canoes, proper shelters. The list is endless.

The women who became those wives were essential to the success of the fur trade, but, excepting the valuable research done by Jennifer Brown and Sylvia Van Kirk in particular, they have been mostly forgotten by most historians—those who wrote Canada's story as found in many school textbooks. This is in part because there was scarcely no record of their existence. Such was their level of disdain, the men and ruling classes at the time did not see the women as worth recording. That the lives of Indigenous women and children were poorly documented meant that, if they were separated from their families, they were subject to exploitation and easily enslaved. The sons of French and British workers and Indigenous women had no social standing. This left them, when they grew up to become young men and labourers, at the mercy of their employers.[29]

Unfreedom thus defined the fur trade. It was a form of slavery unique to Canada that spread throughout all the lands the settlers touched. And it shaped the future of Canadian policy for centuries.

There are some records of buying and selling Indigenous people during fur trading. At Fort Albany in 1694, records show the HBC paid out a gun and a blanket plus a few other items for "an As'scomore slave boy for the use of ye factory." The HBC director James McKnight was no stranger to enslavement or warfare. He managed to hold down the HBC's only fort left, at Albany, during turbulent years with the French. He even "owned" a slave girl that the HBC shipped to him when he returned to London. It was recorded, "An Indian Girle being come with Capt Grimington from Hudsons Bay Ordered that Capt Knight may dispose of her if he think fitt according to his Instructions from Governor Fullerton."[30] She was left in London.

Another unknown child, an Inuit boy this time, was sent from Moose Factory to be with his "owner" in London in 1738. Richard Staunton, who presided over the region, noted, "Upon the request of Captain Middleton I have sent your slave home, the Escomay boy, he saying how serviceable he will be in informing them relating to the trade in the Straits relating to the whalebone."[31] (When war occurred between Cree, Dene and Inuit, sometimes youth were taken from the opposing group and used as labourers. Those youth had little support and could claim no rights: they could be easily bought and sold.) Six decades later, during the 1780s, the HBC's Samuel Hearne wrote in his journal, "I desired some Indians that were going to war to bring me a young slave, which I intended to have brought up as a domestic."[32]

The references go on, unmistakable, through HBC and government officials' correspondence, journals and other historical documents, through the years. NWC partner Archibald McLeod, a Scot, writing in his journal of a journey through the Ottawa area, recorded, "I left Alexandria accompanied, by Collin & my slave boy Jack all three on horseback," as well as "Took the Slave Woman, whom next Fall I shall sell for a good price to one of the men. She was wife to the Deceased old man."[33] In 1798, after moving to Brandon from Fort Albany, postmaster Jack McKay wrote in his journal, "At 10 PM 10 Canadians arrived from the Mandles with two Natives of that place and two slave women."[34]

Only occasionally, if women crossed paths with HBC or North West Company workers and ended up becoming one of their "country wives"—or, as the French called these arrangements, mariage à la façon du pays—do we ever hear of their existence. That phrase may conjure up some Hollywood-style images of "pioneer" times, men and women proudly working together to eke out a livelihood. But life then was brutal, not a storybook romance, and these women had little to zero choice in their lives. Daughters were treated as commodities, traded for ammunition or land, sold to ensure a family's survival. Without the voices of the women to tell us what really happened, those phrases and descriptions are naive at best. They are ridiculous and insulting.

What is written in the history books shows there was little respect or regard for Indigenous women: they were rarely seen as equals. How many of our women—and I include those the history books have called "half-breeds"—were abused, lost and murdered during this time? Thrown away, treated as less than dogs? What happened back then speaks to how Indigenous women are still treated in this country. Those centuries normalized seeing Indigenous women as tools, easily expendable, the most vulnerable and forgotten.

In contrast, the strength of Indigenous women cannot be overstated. We learned fast and quick how to survive, how to protect and fend for our children, and of the importance of the bonds of family, of kinship. Those survival skills and instincts have not let up, and all of us who are here now know that we come from a long line of Indigenous women who fought for our survival, who gave everything of themselves to ensure that we would be here to step forward and speak up, right now in the twenty-first century, to challenge the stories told by this country.

Those stories, written by historians and generally believed by Canadians for over 150 years, are not our stories. They have not been told by us but were taught in classrooms alongside the tales of the adventuring English and French who reached our shores and boldly explored the country—so-called "explorers" who came here, planted flags and declared the land theirs. They made us sick with their diseases, wiping out entire communities. They made Indigenous Peoples dependent on them, they enslaved us, and if we did not comply with their rules, they imprisoned us. Or they just killed us.

And for centuries, they stole our women.

Sure, there was love in some of the unions. But even the unions revered now as symbolizing, for example, "the greatest fur trade love story ever told," have got to be questioned. Much has been written about Englishman David Thompson and his storied fifty-seven years with Charlotte Small, daughter of a Cree mother and a French fur trader from the Red River. But Small was fourteen when she was "given" to

Thompson.[35] What Indigenous girl of fourteen wants to marry a foreign white man she's never met before? Not to mention, Small's mother had also been abandoned by her European husband.

Such abandonments were rampant—indeed, they were expected of white traders and workers. During his four-decade tenure in the mid-nineteenth century, Simpson set the tone. While he privately slept with and criminally abused Indigenous women—one, named Mary Keith, was thought to be ten years old—he made it clear that considering a "country wife" as a serious relationship was a nonstarter. He did not think such unions real, as the women held no class or social standing as those were understood in British culture. Simpson was also a hypocrite. He had his own "country wife," named Marguerite Taylor, at Red River. He even had two sons with her: George Stewart in 1827 and John Mckenzie in 1829. After John was born, though, Simpson split. He took off to London to marry his eighteen-year-old cousin Frances. He left nothing behind for his two sons.

Simpson's plan was to marry his cousin and bring her back to Rupert's Land. An accomplished musician, Frances was in every respect a Victorian lady, right down to her delicate constitution. Simpson, who had grown up in poverty without knowing who his mother was, was obsessed with class and how people viewed him. His new wife, he believed, would show the traders the sort of woman they should marry: someone from back home, with class standing. True enough, English and French employees began to abandon their "country wives," abandoning them and their children to the climate and to fate.

While the couple was at the Red River Settlement, Frances met one of her husband's children by chance. Andrew Dominique Pambrun, who was an HBC trader himself at the time, wrote that Simpson's wife had not been there long when she went for a walk and "met a little boy in tatters, with bare legs and cracked feet and asked him his name. 'George Simpson' was his reply. Who is your father, was the next query and prompt answer was '*The Governor.*' Convinced she had found a stepson, she took him to the store and dressed him up, then took him to her husband, remarking, 'This is a nice smart little boy, and you must send him to school without delay.' Subsequently she found others of the same noble name, a boy and two girls but claiming different mothers."[36]

Though he was away for much of the time, leaving Frances either in Lachine, Quebec, or sending her home to London, Simpson kept her impregnated for the course of their marriage. She bore five children. She never recovered from the last birth, and she died at age forty-three.

Throughout Canadian history, "country wives" have been romantically portrayed, as seen in this 1859 painting by Alfred Jacob Miller, "The Trapper's Bride." First Nations and Métis girls and teens were treated as commodities, taken against their will by European and British trappers and labourers for wives, unlike in the romantic narrative. (Commissioned by William T. Walters, 1858–1860 / The Walters Art Museum online collection / Creative Commons Zero)

IN 1818, a little over two decades before the birth of Jean-Baptiste Carpenter and two years before the start of Simpson's long and brutal reign as HBC governor, British legislators announced they would no longer provide any money for the colonies to purchase Indian land. Upper Canada's lieutenant governor, Sir Peregrine Maitland, knowing he had a huge problem on his hands—what to do with Indigenous Peoples who continued to populate lands the colony wanted for its own growing population—devised a scheme that would see no more large one-time payments for tracts of land. Instead, Indigenous Peoples would be given small annual payments called annuities.

In essence, this was a deferred payment system: a few dollars a year to everyone who was entitled, meticulously recorded and counted by government officials. Payments also included blankets, provisional goods, sometimes clothing and ammunition. This new system would become one in a long line of ruinous financial deals and policies aimed at undercutting Indigenous Peoples' position and role in the greater economy.

In 1820, Governor Maitland proposed a "civilization policy" for the people of the Grand and Credit Rivers, in what is now southern Ontario. This policy was said to be economically, educationally and spiritually based. Boarding schools would open for the area's children, allowing training to "civilize" Indigenous Peoples so they could participate in— that is, serve—the growing settler-led economy. The schools would also Christianize the young pupils from an early age, changing their way of life and who they were, integrating them by assimilation. A sick bonus was that this program would pay for itself, by charging what was essentially tuition: the small treaty-based annuities the people were receiving from the Crown. The result, in theory: a mass conversion to the British Canadian way of life. Such a shift would also free up tracts of land for settlement as the Indians were assimilated into the wider community.[37]

By this point, the early 1820s, treaties signed with Indigenous Peoples in Upper Canada included provisions for the establishment of reserves, lands set aside for Indigenous Peoples to "protect" us from the encroachment of settlers. We were supposed to be *sharing* the land and all the bounty that came from it, as was the stated intent in every single signed treaty. Indigenous Peoples, even though they were negotiating with a foreign conquering power, and in a different language with its own set of legal rules, never *gave* land away. But this separation, which was the basis for the land reserve system, the boxing in of Indigenous Peoples onto small squares of land, became the foundation of Indigenous relations and policy in Canada as well as in the U.S. The intent, at the same time as our children were being ushered away into settler-run schools, removed from their families, their language and their culture, was to isolate us even further from the growing economic and "civil" society around us.[38]

At the boarding schools, beyond religious conversion to Christianity, the students would learn the basics: reading, writing and arithmetic. The curriculum would also include half days during which the boys would be taught to farm and work a trade while the girls would be taught to cook, sew, garden and keep house. Part of Christianizing the Indians involved making sure they settled in small nuclear families, rather than living in large roaming hunting parties. Households pinned them down on patches of land that would be worked to feed the economic engine.

Although Maitland devised this plan in 1820, it did not come to pass until later that decade, around 1828. At that time, Lord Goderich, Britain's colonial secretary, recommended that the Indian Department, run out of London, be closed. The thought was to turn it into a domestic department or bureaucracy, closer to the people it was trying to control.

In 1828, Anglican missionary Robert Lugger established a day school at a Six Nations settlement known as the Mohawk Village.[39] Lugger worked for the New England Company, a Puritan outfit that had long roots on the eastern shore of Turtle Island. It had earlier tried to open a school in New Brunswick but had failed to convince the Mi'kmaq parents to send their children to the school, which provided free room and board.[40] The school at Six Nations, though, called the Mohawk Institute, would keep operating until 1970, making it one of the longest-running schools in Canada.

The British Colonial Office agreed to support this policy of civilization. And so, in 1830, the Department of Indian Affairs was born, creating a domestic branch of the government tasked with "gradually reclaiming the Indians from a state of barbarism, and introducing amongst them the industrious and peaceful habits of civilized life."⁴¹ Branches were established in Canada West (now Ontario) and Canada East (now Quebec). The establishment of the department was pivotal. It was now *policy* to assimilate and civilize Indigenous People to Christianity and the British way of life. An official system was in place to achieve the goal of getting land away from Indigenous People. This system would grow and grow until it ate up the entire continent.

THIS WASN'T THE only seismic shift under way. In 1833, just three years after the Department of Indian Affairs was born, Great Britain passed the Slavery Abolition Act, which outlawed slavery throughout the colonies.

This move freed nearly one million enslaved peoples in the Caribbean, South Africa and Canada. It also kick-started a movement that hinged on a philosophical belief—enhanced by spiritual convictions—that it was important for morally conscious people to become friends and guides to the recently freed slaves, as well as to Indigenous Peoples. What better gift, they believed, than the moral teachings of the Christian church?⁴²

At the back of the Mohawk Institute Residential School, begun by the New England Company in 1831 and then taken over by the Anglican Church, children have carved their initials and messages into the bricks. The institute closed in 1970. (Photo by Tanya Talaga)

The new movement put pressure on Simpson. Remember how he thought teaching Indigenous people anything, including religion, was a waste of time? He'd also discouraged missionary work on his plantation because he thought it would distract people from working. Now he quickly found himself on the wrong side of public opinion. In 1836, he was criticized by the powerful Aborigines' Protection Society, a humanitarian organization that considered itself a check on the British moral conscience for not doing enough to bring Christianity to Rupert's Land. The society had friends in the British Parliament, so its displeasure meant that Simpson's inaction on the spiritual front imperilled the HBC's charter. So, in 1837, he changed his tune and allowed Methodist ministers to infiltrate the coasts and Norway House, an important post in central Manitoba.[43]

Now we come full circle, back to the conversion frenzy along the James Bay and Hudson Bay coasts at the time of my great-great-great-grandfather's birth in 1841.

When George Barnley arrived in Moose Factory in 1840, a full century after the French Jesuits had come north, he was twenty-three years old and infused with the preconceived notion that he would encounter Indians who were "good with the bow and arrow" and "ferocious."[44] He was also confident he'd find people ready to embrace the teachings of the Wesleyan Methodist Missionary Society of London.

But his scripture and teachings seemed lost on the Omushkego, who seemed to get excited about religion only if Abishabis was teaching it. The Omushkego he encountered weren't the Indians of his imagination. Instead, he described them as people who only wished "to satisfy the wants of the body, to eat, and drink and sleep." This did not fit his Eurocentric desire to turn them into assimilated British subjects. Barnley believed that their brains were shrinking from lack of knowledge about Christianity, literally starving from a lack of its "mental food," and that once injected with Christian "truth" they would be saved, especially against the false dogma of Catholicism.[45] And he worried that everyone was a drunk, as rum was regularly traded and handed out to hunters and those returning from long canoe journeys.[46] He came up with a plan of reform targeted chiefly at, in the words of historian John S. Long, "Native motivation, mental capacity, ingratitude, lack of cleanliness, domestic life, liquor and what he called superstitions."[47]

The plan was to save the souls of the Omushkego by holding mass baptismal sessions up and down the James Bay coast. He started his rapid-fire baptisms at Moose Factory, where he performed 148 of them in four days. Barnley was on a roll. He went on to do 235 baptisms in one day at Rupert House and the same at Fort George, with a two-day stint in Fort Albany, where he tallied 89 baptisms.

Everyone baptized was given a Christian name chosen by Barnley. Some Omushkego were named after the biblical Adam and Eve. Others were given the names of Jesus's disciples: Matthew, James, John. As Long notes, Tekokumaw (Caribou Boss) was renamed Adam Goodwin. Wapunewoetum (Morning Cry) and Shkwashest (Small Woman) were baptized and renamed John and Susannah Wesley.[48]

Tahkoonahkun (Cradle Board) and his wife—my four times great-grandparents—were included in those frenzied speed baptisms. My relations were renamed Jabez Bunting and Dorcas Bunting. Both were twenty-one years old at the time. A man named Jabez Bunting already existed: he was a popular white revivalist preacher with the Wesleyan Methodist Church. Jabez and Dorcas would give birth to Jean (or Jane) Bunting—depending which record you use—in 1846. Decades later, in July 1899, Dorcas Bunting died of influenza. She had been sick for one week. Records show she was eighty years old, a widow, born in Fort Albany, and she passed away in Frenchman's Head, Lac Seul. Her friend Mrs. Goodwin reported the death.

Her daughter Jane married Jean-Baptiste Carpenter.

All of their birth and marriage records say that the families were from Albany. The HBC records used the Christian names Barnley gave to the Omushkego families. The names he had chosen were obviously anglicized, easier for the whites to spell and pronounce.

One can't help but think that, at the time, the Ininiw were being accommodating, that they didn't really care: "Sure, if that is what you want and it will make trade easier, let's do it" might have been the attitude. For, as soon as they got away from the traders and back out onto the land, they would revert to their traditional ways—and names—and none would be the wiser.[49] Not to mention each convert was given free sugar and free tea.

An 1886 photograph of Fort Albany, where the HBC had been trading for more than two hundred years. This is what the community would have looked like when Annie was fifteen years old and presumably still living along the James Bay coast.

As for Barnley, the young preacher became dejected and demoralized by his lack of spiritual power over the Ininiw. He abandoned his post after seven years.[50]

Tragically for the Ininiw, he'd accomplished far more than he realized. How could they possibly know what conversion had in store for them? What Christianity really meant, and, diabolically, what was to come?

IN 1869, five years after Jane Bunting and Jean-Baptiste Carpenter married, the fledgling Government of Canada's prime minister, Sir John A. Macdonald, paid the HBC $1.5 million for Rupert's Land. The company had gone into serious decline after the slave trade wound down and furs were no longer in fashion. The English merchants who had profited from and backed these enslaving and monopolizing ventures were turning their eyes elsewhere. Macdonald had dreams of expanding the British colony and keeping it out of the hands of the Americans, who were actively courting the land after their purchase of Alaska.[51]

Rupert's Land was seen as a natural extension of Canada, which already encompassed what are now Quebec, Ontario, New Brunswick and Prince Edward Island. The British government knew it was advantageous to enlarge the colony and keep it in the fold, and it had urged the HBC merchants to sell the land to Canada. George Brown, editor of the *Globe*, believed taking over this new land was Canada's right, calling it a "vast and fertile territory which is our birthright—and which no power on earth can prevent us occupying."[52]

No thought was given to the Indigenous Peoples who made their living off the fur trade or to the women and families left behind by Scottish and British HBC workers. Everyone was discarded and forgotten, thought of as nonentities. This was yet another historical moment that would imprint upon colonial Canadian culture the underlying notion that Indigenous Peoples, women especially, were disposable.

Macdonald knew all this. He knew that Canada was taking over land that was already populated with millions of Indigenous Peoples and that the HBC had its own "treaties" with Indigenous People and communities in order to be on the land. "No explanation it appears has been made of the arrangement by which the country is to be handed over. All these poor people know is that Canada has bought the country from the Hudson's Bay Company and that they are handed over like a flock of sheep to us," Macdonald wrote at the time of the turnover.[53]

The Indians were a problem that Macdonald and his government had to deal with. Much of Ontario had been settled with treaties made by the Crown and Canada, from those made in Niagara in the eighteenth century, to the top of Lake Superior, with the Robinson-Superior Treaty of 1850. Now it was time to go west. Truthfully, Macdonald had no interest in making treaties with Indigenous Peoples, whom he saw as a nuisance, standing in his way along the path to the country he wanted to build.

In 1870, one year after the HBC was turned over to Canada, Macdonald wrote, "Sir, We are looking anxiously for your report as to Indian titles both within Manitoba and without; and as to the best means of extinguishing [terminating] the Indian titles in the valley of the Saskatchewan. Would you kindly give us your views on that point, officially and unofficially? We should take immediate steps to extinguish the Indian titles somewhere in the Fertile Belt in the valley of the Saskatchewan, and open it for settlement. There will otherwise be an influx of squatters who will seize upon the most eligible positions and greatly disturb the symmetry [organization] of future surveys."[54]

This bloody, violent, racist mess that defined the beginnings of Canada is what my great-great-grandmother Annie Carpenter was born into.

BOOK TWO

Red

The southern direction of the Medicine Wheel is a time of nurturing all of Creation, where everything is awake and dancing. It should be a time of growth and discovery, a coming of age. But for our youth, this has been nearly impossible as we live through the effects of Canada's genocidal past.

CHAPTER FIVE

THIS IS ANNIE

EVERYONE WITH ME ON THE RAFT WAS FROM FORT ALBANY FIRST NATION,
Peetabeck—Mike Metatawabin, his brother Edmund, and a dozen
youth and Elders. It was early summer 2011, cold and wet. I'd travelled there as a journalist and had landed on Kistachowan in an old
de Havilland float plane with members of the Wildlands League, who
worked with the Omushkego in efforts to safeguard the unique ecosystems of Kitchi Weeneebayko, or Hudson Bay, and the lowlands of
Weeneebayko, or James Bay. I'll never forget landing on the river, hop-
ping out of the plane to the shore and then getting onto the homemade raft crafted by Edmund from long cedar logs. There were so
many people on what seemed like such a small boat—we were crowded
together, hiding under the only shelter the boat offered. They stared at
me and Anna Baggio, the conservationist from the Wildlands League
who had convinced me I needed to come north and see the lowlands,
which, at the time, were under threat by one of the world's largest
diamond mines. One of the women on the boat looked at me and said:
"I've seen you before. I had a dream about you. You were wearing a
red coat."

I didn't know at the time how close I was to Annie—to where her
blood was from. Looking back now, I can't help but wonder: Was anyone
on that boat with me related to my family? To me? Did our ancestors

mingle? Were they friends? Did they live together on the land, hunting in large groups, listening to the stories of Cha-ka-pesh?

How could I have been so close and yet so far from a part of myself? Did the woman who had the dream know?

Fort Albany First Nation's Edmund Metatawabin pulls his canoe to shore along the Albany River in summer 2011 during his river trip with Fort Albany youth. Author Tanya Talaga was also on the trip. This photo hangs in the author's home. (Photo by Tanya Talaga/*Toronto Star*)

It was the researchers from Know History that pointed me in the direction of the 1881 census, something Uncle Hank had not been able to do back in the day. The census for the Territories district No. 192, Albany Factory, listed a Jean-Baptiste Carpenter, forty, the head of the family, a labourer. His race was listed as "Indian"—not French Canadian. Recorded along with him were his wife Jane, thirty-five, and their children, including ten-year-old Annie. There she was! There they all were!

But it was the sight of Annie's name that stopped me cold. After all this time. "Annie." Not a formal "Anne" with an *e*. She was "Annie."

Here she was, part of a big family—so many sisters and brothers.

Her oldest brother Joseph was nineteen, also a labourer. She had a sister Jane, who was seventeen; a twelve-year-old brother, James; another sister, Sarah, who was seven; a brother Charles, age four; and one more younger sister, Clara, who was two. At ten, Annie fell exactly in the middle, between three older and three younger siblings. They must have loved her so much. "Annie," not stuffy "Anne." I imagined her as a laughing girl, with long black hair, black sparkling eyes and a mischievous smile.

I reread the census multiple times, poring over every aspect of it for hours, and reading about the other families who were there: the Louttits, the Faries. There it was, what we had been looking for, where Annie was from, and it was right there in the federal government's ultimate counting tool. After all this time. Canada had counted her all along.

An oral people, we did not keep diaries, books or journals of who we were, what lands we'd conquered, or what we thought the rules of life should be. We had to rely on the others for that. The census, written out in cursive, unambiguous, said so much—yet so little.

Notably, Annie and her brother James were the only two children in the Carpenter family who had a tick mark in the column "Going to School." Where they went to school was not recorded.

RUPERT'S LAND HAD been in Sir John A. Macdonald's hands for only two years at the time of Annie's birth. She was born into a strange, unsettled period of intense conflict for our people, when Indigenous culture and spirituality were under direct attack from various fronts. Then, in 1876, when she was just five years old, the Indian Act became law.

The Indian Act was used to control, tame and diminish the Indian population in the country of Canada. With the acquisition of Rupert's Land—which Canada took upon itself to scoop up from the British, as if they owned the place—came, suddenly, hundreds of thousands of Indians living on the land.

The Indian Act was never meant to give First Nations peoples rights, or to protect such rights. Instead, it was created to deal with the "problem" of those Indians who were living on what Canada now saw as its own property. The act upheld the premise that Indians are incapable of taking care of themselves, that they are unequal to European or British men who follow the teachings of Christian churches. It mandated a federally kept registry containing the names of all Indigenous people Canada deemed to be Indians in the eyes of the law. Those Indians were—and, I would argue, still are—a different class of citizen, complete with their own sets of laws and services that have served to keep them under the thumb of federal authorities.

The act historically gave full fiscal control of Indian Affairs to the government. The department controlled band governance, including the designation of band councils and Chiefs, with elections to be held every two years. In 2015, a legislative amendment changed this requirement to every four years, just like Canadian federal elections. Imagine that until 2015, the Indian Act imposed such insanely tight time frames, forcing band councils to form a new government every two years. It would have been nearly impossible to get anything done.

The act also made it illegal for us to practise our cultural ceremonies, banning Potlaches and traditional dances. Finally, it required parents to hand over their children to the state in order to attend Indian residential schools. The act itself framed an apartheid—it kept us apart from settler Canadians.

As I related earlier in this book, in 1876 the Department of the Interior, which then included Indian Affairs, justified their legislation by saying "it is clearly our wisdom and our duty, through education and every other means, to prepare him"—him being "the Red man"—"for a higher civilization by encouraging him to assume the privileges and responsibilities of full citizenship."[1]

This "prepare him for a higher civilization" method of control was just reaching full power when Annie was a toddler. The act became the scaffolding upon which Canada would build its regressive colonial policies, including identifying the broadly known Indian people (one misused word to describe hundreds of different Nations) as belonging to, and registering with, one geographical community as opposed to another.

While the Indian Act prohibited Indigenous spiritual practices, the

European missionaries of different denominations all competed to fill what they saw as a spiritual void with their own particular versions of God and religion. Evidence of our communities' struggles with persistent efforts to turn them into Christians, combined with Ottawa's policies created to control us, can be seen in how Annie's own family was wedged apart.

During the signing of Treaty 9, these First Nations women were seated with their animals and holding a tikinagan, a traditional baby carrier. (Library and Archives Canada / Treaty No. 9 fonds / 3366788)

Is Annie in this photo? These are women lined up against the wooden fence during the signing of Treaty 9 at Osnaburgh HBC post. The community would become Mishkeegogamang First Nation. (Library and Archives Canada / Treaty No. 9 fonds / 3367544)

The people in the Treaty 9 photographs are mostly unidentified so I don't know if any are my kin. (Canada. Dept. of Indian Affairs and Northern Development / Library and Archives Canada / PA-059533)

I got some inkling of this by digging into the online Hudson's Bay Company Archives, an extensive collection of records that is part of the Archives of Manitoba. The archives site reads "HBCA acquires and preserves archival records of HBC and other records related to HBC history, such as private records of individuals and subsidiary companies (including the North West Company), and encourages the use and understanding of these records."

The collection is impressive in what it says and details, and in what it does not.

Though other evidence suggests that Annie's father Jean-Baptiste could both read and write, in the HBC records he signed his contracts for his position as an HBC servant with an "X." Since he was an "Indian servant" he was not written about or made note of in any company documents—unlike white HBC staff. At best, he would have been a voyageur, a tradesperson or a labourer. He was barely recorded or noticed by anyone but the accountant.

The records also reveal that at the time of Annie's birth, her father's family was split along religious lines. The archives show that Jean-Baptiste was an Anglican, a servant both of the Church Missionary Society of the Church of England and of the HBC fort at Albany.

Where did Jean-Baptiste come from? And what did it mean to be a "servant" of the HBC? That suggested an element of unfree or forced labour. As a journalist, I had covered the Omushkego communities sporadically over the past decade. I began to reach out to some of my sources and speak to friends who could lead me towards more information, and perhaps other relatives. My friend Stephanie Moses led me to Elder Lawrence Martin. Lawrence was a former Grand Chief of the Mushkegowuk Council. He was also a Juno Award–winning musician and, at one time, the mayor of Cochrane, a small town north of Timmins. I tracked him down on Facebook—all Indians are on Facebook; it is the moccasin telegraph of the times—and he gave me his phone number.

Lawrence's kindness came through on the phone. Our conversation meant a great deal to me: he was one of the first people from the community along the coast I was approaching with Annie's story—or at least what I'd found of it so far. And Lawrence is a well-known and respected Elder who works hard to safeguard his community. He is heading up the Omushkego effort to use both Traditional Knowledge and Western science to protect the coasts of Weeneebayko and Kitchi Weeneebayko.

I told him what I knew about Annie, who her parents were, her brothers and sisters. I asked him if he had any clue about the Carpenters. Without wasting a moment, he told me he knew who I needed to talk to: his son Jason, the family historian.

I reached out to Jason Martin on—of course—Facebook. I told him that I was an author writing a book on residential schools and that the book starts with my great-great-grandmother Annie Carpenter, from Fort Albany.

"Interesting," Jason replied. "Wow, who were her siblings?"

Jason, I learned, spends a lot of time going through church records from Fort Albany and Moose Factory. He also gets a lot of help from his cousin Paula Rickard, who lives in Moose Factory. He told me that he had a Jane Carpenter from Fort Albany in his family tree, born in the 1840s. That was around the same time as Jean-Baptiste, Annie's father.

Jason said I needed to get on Ancestry.ca, that he had a large family tree and I could see it. Through my own sleuthing on Ancestry, I already knew Jean-Baptiste had a younger brother named Charles Johnny Carpenter, who was born in Attawapiskat, north of Fort Albany on the coast. He had married Henriette Edwards (Etget). They were Catholics who had eight children: James, Mary, Jack, Sarah, Jean-Baptiste, Maggie, Jasper, and an as yet unnamed baby boy.

So Jean-Baptiste was Anglican and his brother Charles, Catholic. It looked as though the family was split in half along religious lines. Did the Barnley mass baptisms have anything to do with this? Or was it the arrival of the Catholics at Albany? Attawapiskat was north of Albany. They had no school at Attawapiskat. They sent their children to St. Anne's Indian Residential School at Fort Albany.

My head was exploding. Something had caused the Carpenter family to grow branches in different directions. My bet was that "something" was a combination of competing religious missionaries and schools and government policy. No doubt divides like the one playing out in the Carpenter family were occurring in every other Ininiw family along the coast. Separation by religion, by a treaty system and an Indian Act that assigned families to communities based on where they happened to be when the treaty officers managed to encounter them.

What I hadn't known, and what Jason pointed me towards, was that Jean-Baptiste and Charles had a sister named Jane. She was Jason's great-great-great-grandmother. His father Lawrence Martin's great-great-grandmother. Jane Carpenter and my great-great-great-grandfather were brother and sister.

I messaged Lawrence Martin to let him know. He wrote back: "Hahahaha told you we could be cousins."

Martin's family was entrenched in Moose Factory and around the Moose River. If he was my relation, what other distant family did I have there?

At every turn, in the midst of coming face to face with these divides that colonialism had led to, I also found new relations, like Jane

Carpenter. Like the Martins. Could I, person by person, insufficient record by insufficient record, piece my family back together?

There are things I will never know about the Carpenter family: what drove them, how they wound up in the Nations and communities that they did. We see only in hindsight the restrictions placed on them, their lack of freedom, the policies that controlled their movements.

Three Carpenter children died at St. Anne's: Gabriel, Onesime and Michel Carpenter. I found Michel's death record quite by accident late one night while searching on Ancestry. It says he was buried at Fort Albany, according to the Catholic priest who was there at the time, and that he died of "unresolved pneumonia." What does that mean?

I assumed these Carpenter children, being Catholic, were from Charlie's branch of the family. Regardless of religion and the divisions that ensued because of it, they were still family. How did they die?

ANNIE WAS BAPTIZED by an Anglican missionary named Thomas Vincent at Fort Albany on September 26, 1871. Born at the Osnaburgh trading post in Ontario, Vincent was a unicorn of his time, a rarity held up as an example by the Anglican missionaries. He was of "mixed race," being the grandson of a fur trader and a Native grandmother named Jane Renton. Educated in Winnipeg, he became a labourer, teacher and translator to the Reverend John Horden, whose name would be applied years later, in 1905, to a new residential school in Moose Factory: Bishop Horden Hall. Horden Hall, I was soon to learn, would prove to be a disastrous, looming presence in the lives and deaths of the Carpenter family. But that comes later.

In 1851, John Horden arrived in Moose Factory, about 160 kilometres south of Fort Albany, with his new bride, Elizabeth Oke, a teacher and missionary enthusiast. Upon arriving, they were surprised to discover that the Omushkego knew of the Ten Commandments and the Bible. That was thanks to James Evans and the Cree syllabics he'd invented.

Horden had been hired by the HBC to set up a school at Moose Factory. The school was built on an island: a wooden house two storeys high made of dark wood clapboard, with a tin roof. A picket fence enclosed a small yard at the front.[2]

Given the distance from their home, Fort Albany students were boarded with Moose Factory families, and the children were sent across by boat from their "boarding homes" on the mainland. The school had a different practice than what most residential schools would adopt: children were first taught to read and write in their own language, and then they were taught English. Horden himself was a linguist who spoke Cree, Inuktitut, Ojibwe and Norwegian.[3]

In Thomas Vincent, Horden believed he had found someone who could act as a missionary to his "countrymen."[4] However, no matter how well educated and subservient Vincent was, Horden never thought he'd get anywhere, owing to his genetics. Horden said a man of mixed race was inferior because of the "declension of the European intellect in the second or third generation." He felt Vincent's father, instead of marrying a Métis (Charlotte Thomas from Moose Factory), should have married a European woman so children of "fair intellect" would result. Vincent himself married a Native woman (Eliza Gladman, who is described as mixed race from Rupert House), and to Horden, this was even worse, making all his children "stupid."[5]

Even though Vincent was upheld as an example of what a Christian Indian could be, Horden and the church refused to promote him or give him any real control over the Anglican Church in the area. Horden felt someone of "European origin" should be in charge.[6]

Despite his own Indigeneity, Vincent did not believe in Omushkego or Anishinaabe ceremony, and he outlawed the use of the drum, a sacred item that has been used for ceremonial purposes by our peoples since the dawn of time. Much change came to the area after Barnley left and Horden and Vincent joined forces in Moose Factory. The Omushkego began to wear European clothes and they changed their burial customs to reflect the Christian way. By the time of Horden's first vacation to England, he had baptized more than eighteen hundred souls, from York Factory in Manitoba all the way to Moose Factory.[7]

Horden wanted to assimilate Indigenous Peoples to Christian and

European ways, but he failed to adjust himself to his new environment. He could not get over the harshness of the winter and the starvation that occurred along the coast. One winter, he travelled onto the land and, at one settlement of 120 people, he found that one-sixth had starved to death. One man, he reported, had saved his own life by killing and eating six of his children.[8]

Winter on the coast eventually gives way to spring, but during the in-between time, before the thaw comes, the ice of the rivers comes crashing into James Bay. The collision is intense, leaving those who live through it in awe of nature's power—just like Thomas James noted in his travels; it can destroy homes and communities on the water's edge. Horden couldn't believe it when he saw it first-hand:

On the night of May 21st the noise, as of distant thunders, told of the conflict going on between the rushing waters and the still compact ice, great masses of which were being occasionally thrown up in heaps. Soon the alarm bell rang, which told us of our danger, and some gentlemen from the Factory instantly came to conduct us thither, as our house is in a very exposed position. The river was now twenty feet above its usual level, and large hills of ice, twenty feet high, were thrown up in several places. The water continued to rise, until it was five feet higher, by which time every house on the island, except the Factory, was flooded; the water, as we afterwards ascertained, having been five feet nine inches deep in my own kitchen.[9]

The English school at Moose Factory was of utmost importance to the Anglican mission. They had a day school at Albany, but little information is available about it. Did Annie and her brother James attend? The 1881 census said they were in school, but not which school. The Anglican Church of Canada's main archives are in Toronto, and more records are held at Laurentian University. I contacted both, but neither had records of Annie or James.

Where else could they have gone? Horden's day school at Moose Factory, 160 kilometres away? It's difficult to say. Given Jean-Baptiste's position at the HBC he would have been in the sight lines of the missionary Anglicans. And there are hints in the records that they took control of the educations of Jean-Baptiste's children.

Someone taught Annie how to read and write in English and to use Cree syllabics. It is possible her parents taught her. After all, her mother and father could both read and write, according to the 1901 census. (This is despite the HBC's records showing Jean-Baptiste's signature as an "X.") Her mother Jane's parents, Jabez and Dorcas Bunting, were some of the original Omushkego baptized by the now absent Rev. George Barnley, and so the family was clearly on the church's radar.

We do know that Vincent taught Joseph Carpenter, Annie's eldest brother, at the Moose Factory school. We know this only because Lawrence and Jason Martin's cousin Paula Rickard found it in a magazine, a piece of Anglican missionary propaganda published monthly in London, England, to help raise funds for Coral Fund schools around the world, including the James Bay school. Imagine. Nowadays, parents must sign a media release for an image of their child to appear in the school newsletter, but back then, an Indigenous parent might not even know where their child was, within a range of several hundred kilometres. They might have been moved, or died, without anyone in the family being notified.

In the November 1, 1874, edition of the *Coral Missionary Magazine*, one dozen children are "advertised," including Joseph Carpenter. Reverend Vincent describes Joseph as a "strong, stout, healthy boy, about twelve years of age. He attends school regularly and is doing very well. He finds it very difficult to learn to read English, but latterly he has been doing much better. In his writing and arithmetic he does very well indeed, especially in the former, in which he seems to take great pleasure. I have always found him very obedient, and in school his conduct is good."[10]

The next year, Joseph again appears in the magazine, where this time Bishop Horden writes that he "still continues a strong, healthy boy, and is beginning to be of some use to us. He finds it difficult to learn to read in English, he is now, however, doing pretty well, and is able to read in the Testament; I trust that hereafter his progress will be more rapid."[11]

In 1877, however, the magazine takes a different tone about Joseph. It reports that he has left the school and gone inland with his friends. Vincent notes that he's found a "sharp, intelligent," replacement for Joseph.[12]

PAULA RICKARD'S NAME kept coming up—Jason Martin's cousin. In late 2022, I turned to Facebook to find anything to do with James Bay and the Carpenters. I found the James Bay FYI page, which seemed a good place to start. Remarkably, the administrator was Paula Rickard. I sent her a message: "Hi Paula, my name is Tanya Talaga. I'm an author who lives in Toronto. I tried to join your group . . . I saw a 1915 Treaty paylist that has my relations on it. The Carpenters. My great-great Grandma is Annie Carpenter. Her brother Charlie Carpenter was Charlotte Carpenter's wife. John and Henry Carpenter, also on the same paylist, are all part of the same family. Anyhow, would love to connect."

She wrote back forty-five minutes later: "Hello Tanya! That's amazing! The other night I stayed up until 3 am trying to sort out the Carpenters! My family tree is forever a work in progress. My research on the Carpenters taught me that Metikonabe is Carpenter in Cree. How do you descend from Annie?"

I told her that my great-grandmother Liz Gauthier was Annie's daughter and that Liz raised my mom Sheila in the bush, in Raith and Graham, Ontario. I told her that Annie's dad was Jean-Baptiste Carpenter, that her mom was Jane Carpenter (Bunting) and that they were from Fort Albany.

A couple of days later, Paula sent me a message that changed everything: "Good morning! Annie Carpenter-Chapish (Wemaystikosh)—Annie's first husband is Samson my great-great uncle."

My heart stopped. For decades, our family had had no idea who this "Samson" was or what Annie's or our relationship was to him. There is only one reference to a Samson in Uncle Hank's documents and that was scrawled on Annie's second marriage registration, when she wed Joseph Gauthier in late 1908. This told us she had been married before. But this one name was a big clue to who Annie was. The marriage registration had always raised more questions about her than answers. Annie's parents were listed as Carpenters, but she was Annie Samson, listed as a widow aged thirty-five. (That was off by a few years, but what woman hasn't lied about her age?) No one in my family had a clue who this Samson was. But Paula did.

She told me Samson was Annie's first husband, my great-great-grandfather. On October 29, 1888, when Annie was eighteen, she wed Samson Chapish Wemaystikosh (also spelled Wemistekos), a twenty-one-year-old Omushkego hunter, at Moose Factory.

Paula had found a copy of their marriage registration. She sent me a photograph of it. The two were married at St. Thomas' Anglican Church, a small red-roofed wooden church that was built by the HBC and still stands in the community. Both Annie and Samson signed their names in Cree syllabics. The certificate lists her father Jean-Baptiste as a "servant" of the HBC. Remarkably, they were married by Rev. Thomas Vincent, who at the time was taking care of the Moose Factory diocese while Bishop Horden was in England.

So many questions ran through my mind. Thomas Vincent had been in Annie's brother's life as his teacher, and he was the person who officiated at her marriage to Samson. He had known her practically since birth: he'd baptized her. Was she also his student? And did she meet Samson at school in Moose Factory, which was down the coast from Albany?

Seeing their signatures in syllabics, seeing a piece of paper Annie had physically held in her hands, something they had both touched and written their names on, made me break into a smile. I was elated for her. There she was, about to embark on a new life, as women just like her had done for thousands of years. She was marrying an Omushkego hunter, a provider, and they were going to live on the land.

Theirs was a Christian service, a break from the past, a change from what the tradition had been for generations of Ininiw women. Were there any Ininiw rites of passage or ceremonies around the marriage? I have no idea. Nothing is recorded.

The tragedies that I knew lay ahead for Annie—of being violently ripped away from everything—had not yet come. This registration of her marriage with Samson represented, to me, joy and promise. I hoped she was deliriously in love.

It was incredible to see this—the October 29, 1888, marriage certificate Paula found that records Annie and Samson's marriage at the St. Thomas Anglican Church in Moose Factory. The certificate says Annie, eighteen, was a spinster from Albany and Samson, twenty-one, a hunter from Moose. (Photo by Paula Rickard)

SAMSON WEMAYSTIKOSH WAS born in 1867, the year celebrated for Canada becoming a country. According to Ancestry.ca, his mother and father, Hannah Oskidgee (Ooskeche) and James Wemaystikosh, had ten children altogether between 1859 and 1877. All were born in Moose Factory: Margaret, Elizabeth, Isabella, George, Charles, James, Rachel, Job, Samson and William. The name Wemaystikosh means a few different things. It is "wooden shoe" or "hard-soled shoe" in Ininímowin (Cree language), but a variation of this name is also the nickname for a white man. Somewhere around this time, the name was changed, by either the French or the English, who perhaps thought the Ininímowin was too confusing. Depending on where one lived, Wemaystikosh was—

inexplicably—changed to Chapish or Chapais. Sadly, in 1877, James died. His death left Hannah a forty-year-old widow with ten children. Her oldest son, James, would have been eighteen at the time. He would have inherited the responsibility to help feed and care for the family.

The 1881 Canadian census gives us a glimpse into her life a few years later. James had moved out and married, but lived beside his mother and siblings. She was heading up her own household in Moose, and two older women were living with her: her seventy-year-old mother Emma Starblanket and eighty-year-old Sarah Royal. I do not know the relationship to Sarah. Hannah's sons William and Samson were seventeen and fourteen. Their occupations were listed as hunters. They lived off the land to provide for their family.

Paula's next bit of news left me stunned. She had found records of Samson and Annie's three children in the Anglican Church archives in Moose Factory.

Annie had more children! I had suspected from the record of her second marriage, which stated she was a thirty-five-year-old widow, that she probably had children from before. Now that I knew they were real, who were they? And where were they? These were my great-great-uncles and great-great-aunts. What happened to them? I could not help but wonder: Did they go to residential school? And did they ever make it home?

As I read through what Paula had found, I learned the answers to some of these questions—but nowhere near all. The documents showed that Annie's three children had all lived in Moose Factory. George Wemaystikosh (Chapish) was the young couple's firstborn son. Anglican church records show he was baptized on July 16, 1890. George's burial record from St. Thomas' Church showed he died of whooping cough on July 2, 1895, at the age of seven.

Paula had also discovered the baptismal record for a girl named Sarah, the "daughter of Sampson Wamistikosh (Chapish) and Annie, his wife, both Indians, of Moose Factory, from the third day of November, A.D. 1895," who "was baptized on the fifteenth of June following, by me, Jervois A. [Newnham, Bishop of] Moosonee."

And she found a third child, James, born in the summer of 1894. His baptismal record reads: "James, son of Samson Wamistikosh and Annie his wife of Moose Factory Indians born during the previous August was baptized this 23rd day of September A.D. 1895 by me, Isaac John Taylor."

So now I knew: Annie and Samson had children and spent the 1890s and the first few years of the 1900s living traditionally on the land in and around Moose Factory. But Annie and Samson's union would be a short one. I can only hope there was much love in it because I suspect this was the only matrimonial love Annie would know in her lifetime. Life was about to go dark.

Samson died sometime in 1905. There is no record of what happened to him.

Samson's death must have led to a cataclysmic shift in the life of Annie Carpenter. Beyond the gut-wrenching horror of losing a partner, family units, community, meant survival. Our families always moved in hunting parties, close together. Traces of this practice, which held our communities together since our spirits have embodied physical form, can be seen in census records.

The census began in this area in 1881, after the "sale" of Rupert's Land to Canada. That was when the Government of Canada started collecting information about the Omushkego, those living in Eastern Rupert's Land, a vast area including Qu'Appelle, Oxford House, Norway House, Fort Albany and Moose Factory. The census was taken every ten years. Through it, you follow the movements of families. Each family house was given a number, the head—or, if the census official was French, the "chef"—of the house was named, and then every family member living there was listed in order of age. Louttits, Faries, Archibalds, Goodwins, Wesleys, Sutherlands—these were the families that were constantly in the Carpenters' orbit.

Sarah and James, Annie's children, would have been about ten and eight at the time of Samson's death. A thorough scrub of records and archives reveals nothing about their lives: they seem to have vanished without a trace. At the time of this writing, the National Centre for Truth and Reconciliation could not locate Annie's children, a task made difficult by the many different spellings that were used when recording their last name.

The only documented evidence of the children being alive are census records and their baptismal records at the Moose Factory Anglican church. But what happened afterwards? Beyond George, there is no record of any deaths or burials. Were they sent away to school never to return?

The school that it makes sense for Annie's children to attend is Bishop Horden Hall, named after Thomas Vincent's mentor, which opened in 1905.* Sarah and James would have been of age to attend.

The Hall was the converted bishop's residence, constructed on the southwest end of Moose Factory Island, near the Hudson's Bay Company post. Funds were provided for the school from the Church of England. It was a rectangular building about thirty-eight feet long and twenty-eight feet wide, with a flat roof in the central portion that sloped on each side.[13] There was a dining room and classrooms on the first floor. Upstairs were the sleeping quarters, in a space measuring nineteen by fourteen feet, with a wall dividing it into dorms. Each dormitory housed sixteen students.[14] A smaller hospital building is where the staff slept. By 1916, the school was in dire shape and it was rebuilt, with a basement and a couple of new outbuildings.[15]

In the early years the Hall drew its students from the coastal communities of Attawapiskat, Fort Albany and Moose Factory, as well as from the interior, including Marten Falls, Chapleau, Fort Hope and even Fort George in Quebec. As the school grew over the decades, the student body grew, taking in more children from Quebec and children listed as "Eskimo" or Inuit. Children came from such far-away places as Fort Mackenzie, Great Whale River, Eastmain, La Sarre, Mistissini, Nemaska, Pointe-Bleue, Rupert House, Senneterre, Waswanipi and Oskélanéo in Quebec; Coral Rapids, Island Falls and Peterbell in Ontario; and Creswell Bay and Boothia Peninsula in what is now Nunavut.[16]

---

* At the time it was known as Moose Fort Boarding School. It went by a number of names over the years, but for simplicity's sake I'll call it Bishop Horden Hall throughout.

Like almost every other residential school in Canada, the Hall had structural and administrative problems from the start.

THE GOVERNMENT OF Canada and the Anglican Church each had their own ideas on how to bring "civilization" to the students and instill in them the qualities of good workers. But these ideas clashed against thousands of years of Ininiw spirituality and ways of life. For the British, land (much like a people and its culture) was something to be tamed, not respected or listened to.

Part of the overarching residential school plan was to turn young Indigenous men into farmers: first while at school, and then back home in their communities.

That is a bit of a riot considering the land and waters surrounding Moose Factory. The community is in the Hudson Bay Lowlands, a vast expanse of ancient rock covered by muskeg. The area rises in a shallow elevation from Hudson and James Bays. It is a giant flat, swampy plain with nearly four metres of organic sediment—just one metre in the Moose area—with poor drainage. Everything holds water—as it should, since this is a coastal community, a marine area where ocean currents, open water and countless waterways all move and flow together This land and the creatures on it, in it and above it—from migratory birds such as the millions of snow geese that move in during the spring and fall to beluga whales, polar bears and even walruses—are essential not only to spiritual well-being but to ways of life. Along the coast of Weeneebayko, winters are long and cold, the summers are short, and the ice jam-ups are legendary. Farming techniques from the Prairies or England would have been properly out of place in aski-gitchi bayou, the traditional lands of the Omushkego.

Moosonee is about thirteen kilometres upriver from the mouth of the Moose River, which empties into Weeneebayko. Kistachowan and the Moose Rivers account for two-thirds of Ontario's Arctic water discharge, and the Hudson and James Bay tides affect Kistachowan and the Moose for up to twenty kilometres inland. In spring, during ice breakup, the flow of water is intense and powerful; water levels are known to rise fifteen metres. Flooding is always a concern. In short, the movement of water rules the land and the people who live here.

Bringing farming to the area—making the students attempt to find, let alone work, arable land—was ridiculous. Yet the Anglican leaders of the school were convinced it must be done. Winters were hard and the students were always hungry. Anglican officials in Moosonee begged the federal Indian Department's top-ranking civil servant, Duncan Campbell Scott, for more provisions and equipment. In an April 16, 1912, letter, Bishop John G. Anderson requested tools for the school's potato garden, plus a gasoline engine and a saw from the T. Eaton Company to cut wood up the river. (Wood to heat the school had to be brought in from at least a mile away.) School officials also desired livestock, writing that food continued to be scarce and that, the previous winter, the "Indian children" had existed entirely on canned meats that might have been bad. "If we had four or five cows we would soon be able to kill an animal and live every winter."[17]

It will come as no surprise that the bureaucrats in Indian Affairs were micromanagers from the start. At the time, an angry letter from Scott, who was then the acting deputy superintendent general, was sent to Revillon Frères, a general store in Moose that had started out as a French furrier outpost, questioning who had authorized eighty dollars' worth of freight to bring bedsteads from Montreal by steamship for the school.[18]

Everything was vastly more expensive to construct and to get in places like Moose Factory, where the nearest rail stop was a couple of hundred kilometres away and the only way in was by the rivers. Mail was infrequent, and steamships had to be rented to come through the bay from Montreal with goods.

This reality continues, in the twenty-first century, to mystify some bureaucrats and government departments who do not understand it costs more to live and work in the north. First Nations communities have long argued for more money to be budgeted for construction and transportation of goods, as bringing in needed supplies can be prohibitively expensive in isolated areas. These days, First Nations communities call it "the northern quotient."

Before the First World War, the management of Bishop Horden Hall was in flux. Principal R. J. Renison, a young Irish-born Anglican archdeacon, managed the school for barely a year around 1911 before leaving. Letters and records in the archives indicate there was a strong female presence at the school, and non-Indigenous matrons were not afraid to challenge the leadership.

One of those women was matron Miss Quartermaine, who adopted one of the "orphaned" Carpenter children from Fort Hope, a six-year-old boy named John. There were four Carpenter children at the school, and they were not orphans: they were Annie's nieces and nephews, her brother James's children, something I was able to piece together with census records from Eabametoong, or Fort Hope, which is upriver about 440 kilometres from Fort Albany. Along with John, Annie Carpenter's seventeen-year-old niece Mary, born in 1894, was then a student at Bishop Horden and, although I haven't been able to find any record of them, it is possible that Annie's children James and Sarah could have been students there in the early 1900s.

After Renison's fight with Miss Quartermaine, he left and never returned, leaving the matrons to run the school. The Reverend William Haythornthwaite was the missionary in charge and then principal from 1912 until 1921. From the letters I've found in the archives, he was a cruel, abusive and delusional man. He used to beat and whip the girls in the small upstairs dormitory. One of the matrons, Miss Mary A. Johnson, wrote to the secretary of the Department of Indian Affairs to complain about his treatment of the students: "On the evening of 2ND February the Rev. W. Haythornthwaite, Missionary in charge, came into the school, went to the girls' bedroom after I had sent them to bed, brought them down, took them over to his study and had two of them cruelly whipped, so much so that their hands were swollen and discolored for two days afterwards, for the simple reason that they were playing outside our own door not <u>his</u> and with my permission. One was Clara Sutherland, a Moose girl and an orphan, the other Mary Snipe of Marten's Falls, motherless. He had also at different times previously chased the girls around their bedrooms."[19] Miss Johnson added she had been appointed by Bishop Anderson "in charge" of the school since October 1911.

Haythornthwaite fought back. Bishop Anderson reported that, according to the principal, the allegations were untrue and that "the punishing of these girls was the climax of a long process of provocation." According to Anderson's letter to the department, the situation between Johnson and Haythornthwaite had become very unpleasant, that she told the HBC inspector (who did nothing) and that she was encouraged by another matron, Miss Bennett, whom he accused of being a "suffragette."[20]

Anderson, whose job it was to oversee all that was going on along the James Bay coast, was aware of Reverend Haythornthwaite's abuses. His letter took Haythornthwaite's side against the matrons, yet, at the same time, questioned his behaviour. Anderson wrote that he had been "summoned to see a third child die" at the school. That child was named Malcolm Cowboy. No reason was given for how he had died. The names of the two other students who had died are unknown, and so is what happened to them. It is as if they never existed. "I was kept in ignorance of this boy's state until five minutes before his death," Anderson wrote to Indian Affairs.

Months later, in October, Principal Haythornthwaite said a public meeting had been held to discuss the accusations against him and that he had been acquitted of all charges. (Anderson wrote about this meeting, saying the women ganged up on the principal.) The assistant deputy minister and secretary for the Department of Indian Affairs praised all for their handling of the situation, noting that the resignations of two matrons and the exoneration of Haythornthwaite was most welcome.

After the incident of the principal running around the girls' dorm, chasing and whipping them, some parents pulled their children out of the school. But some girls, who were from other coastal or inland communities, had no choice but to stay. Lizzie Nipineskum, her brother Peter and their other siblings, the twins Henry and Ellen, were from Albany and were grieving the loss of both their parents. They'd been shipped nearly two hundred kilometres south and had no ability to get themselves back home.

Haythornthwaite, meanwhile, installed his wife as the head matron in place of the matrons who'd complained about him.

The mismanagement under Haythornthwaite was criminal, and he got away with it. Complaints about his behaviour and the situation at the school under his watch were constantly ignored by or explained away by diocese officials. It would appear they just did not care. Yet the "unpleasantness" that Ottawa and church officials permitted and turned a blind eye to would only escalate after Haythornthwaite had full control of the school. In the coming years, their inaction at the severe neglect and brutish behaviour of Reverend Haythornthwaite would cost multiple lives.

In the spring of 1914, a fire destroyed the school. It started when two boys hung the laundry in the kitchen too close to the stove. Bishop Anderson, who lived in Cochrane, two hundred kilometres west, described the scene to Duncan Campbell Scott in Ottawa, writing that the boys, "becoming alarmed, ran out." The fire destroyed the school, the storehouse and the barn, along with all the farm equipment. Everything was gone. "It is a most dreadful loss for us," he wrote, "and there was no insurance."[21] The school's boys were now living at the hospital and the girls at the old mission residence. "What can you do for us?" pleaded a despondent Anderson. He said they were living on donations from the HBC.

Scott replied by telegram: "Will give every consideration to needs of Moose Fort school but in absence of any special appropriation cannot state definite extent at present."[22]

Haythornthwaite, a man who lorded over the school with his anger and temper, was on his own, with his bishop two hundred kilometres away. It would take years to rebuild the school, and the battle for funds was never-ending, especially during the First World War.

But for Haythornthwaite, things were soon to get even worse. Fast-forward five years, to July 29, 1919.

══

THE FAST-MOVING MOOSOSIIBII surges for nearly a hundred kilometres from its beginnings at the Missinaibi and Mattagami Rivers, emptying out into the salty Weeneebayko, or James Bay, at the southern end of the Arctic Ocean. This area experiences the southernmost breakup of sea ice in the winter. Seals and beluga whales play in the waters. Near the mouth of the river is Moose Factory Island, where Bishop Horden school was located. There are several smaller islands in the bay, and the children were often sent there to pick berries. To reach these islands, they had to cross the river by boat. When the tide is high, it often isn't safe to cross. Worse, they were using a rickety old canoe.

For months, staff and parents had warned that the students needed a new boat so they could safely make the journey. Regardless, the students were expected to make this crossing on their own, in a canoe that reportedly had open gashes in the lining. The canoe was held together with nails and cedar; the gum used to gel everything together was missing in places.

On that July day in 1919, twelve boys from the school had canoed out to do some berry picking. On the return journey, the tide was high, the water moving. The boat took water, overturned and sank.

John Carpenter, the fourteen-year-old son of Annie's older brother James—the "orphan" adopted by Miss Quartermaine—was there. In the chaos of the boat sinking, John managed to grab onto an eight-year-old boy and hold him above the water until help came. Three others managed to get to safety.

But seven boys drowned. Their names were Alfred Louttit, Thomas Louttit, Arthur Sutherland, James Sutherland, Harry Wesley, John Sailors and Sinclair Nepaneshkum.[23] They must have been terrified. And the boys who survived would have had to live with the horror of seeing their classmates drown.

Indian Affairs and the Anglican diocese seemed to downplay the tragedy. They called what happened "very sad," and they urged Reverend Haythornthwaite to not blame himself. "Their death is regretted and the Department sympathizes with the parents and the school in their loss," wrote the assistant deputy and secretary in September. The letter continued, "No blame can be attached to yourself or the other members of the staff, but it is considered that to allow such a large number of boys in a canoe should not have been permitted. It is hoped that this accident will not result detrimentally to the future recruiting of pupils for the school."[24]

The Moose community, devastated by the boys' deaths, was outraged. The families were in shock. The principal had systematically terrified their children, and now this mass drowning had occurred under his watch. In October, four Moose Factory members wrote a letter in Cree syllabics to the deputy superintendent general of Indian Affairs, Duncan Campbell Scott, demanding justice for the death of the seven children.

A report from Moose Factory, Ontario.

I, Chief Woomastoogish, and George Hardisty, Andrew Butterfly, and John Dick.*

> *We want to give the Government a true report of the drowning of the children.*

> *There were twelve children in the canoe and the children were alone, and the canoe which they were using was very bad. A canoe which was not fit for anyone to use. The canvas of the canoe was half ripped.*

> *How these children were allowed to go crossing the river every day in it and very often twice one evening. The canoe was that far gone that the thwarts were just nailed on top of the gunwale.*

> *There was not one boy big enough to have any sense.*

> *I don't know if this report was sent in yet or not, but this which I say is exactly what happened, and this is the weight which I am carrying.*

> *Now you know just the same as I do, about that which I am speaking of.*[25]

---

* Paula Rickard tells me that Chief Woomastoogish was Samson Wemaystikosh's relation—it is yet another spelling of the name.

Their translated letter was sent on by William Rackham, the commissioner in charge of taking affidavits in Timiskaming. He wrote his own letter about what happened to the boys, to accompany the Chief's letter. That he felt he had to write another description seemingly undermines the Moose community members. He wrote:

"I regret to have to report a very serious drowning accident in this District. It occurred on July 29TH at Moose Factory. It appears that twelve of the school children from the Church of England Mission of which The Rev. Haythornthwaite is in charge, were allowed to crowd into an old canoe, for the purpose of crossing to an Island to pick berries. It was high tide with quite a big sea running. When about in mid channel the canoe capsized and seven out of the twelve children were drowned. The remaining five were saved by an Indian named Archie Sailor who in a small canoe managed to pick them up. Mr. Gaudet sent out his entire staff of Servants with all canoes available, to search for the bodies, and by 1 a.m. on the 30th the seven bodies were recovered. Two of the boys drowned were sons of one of our Servants, Samuel Louttit who is employed at Fort George."[26]

It is clear that the principal made a lapse in judgment in sending the children berry picking in such conditions. But where is the outrage by the officials? The Chief's concerns and those of the Moose community were ignored. There was no police investigation, inquest or inquiry into the death of seven children. Principal Haythornthwaite did not lose his job. There is no record of his being reprimanded, fined or sanctioned. The evidence suggests this tragic event was quickly forgotten by Canadian officials and they all moved on.

Sadly, the same could be said, by and large, for all complaints from Indian families about residential schools. It was as if the children were all expendable, nuisances.

In a bittersweet twist, in 1921 John Carpenter received a medal of bravery from the Royal Canadian Humane Association in Ottawa, whose patron was the governor general of Canada. It must have been an awkward occasion for a boy who'd lost seven of his classmates in a horrific drowning incident that was completely avoidable.

An Indian Affairs commissioner sent a report to the Humane Association proudly describing the ceremony in detail: "The presentation was made to him in the presence of Chief Wamistagoosh, his Councillors and about three hundred members of the Moose Factory Band. The Indians seemed to be greatly pleased to see the gallantry of one of their race acknowledged by your Society, and I am sure your generosity will not be forgotten, but will produce among these Indians a higher incentive to do good to others."[27]

But our peoples do not forget. The last written account of Haythornthwaite's life speaks for itself. Everything is circular and, just like the Christian biblical saying goes, you reap what you sow.

A FRONT-PAGE HEADLINE in the *New York Times* on January 3, 1921, read "Lost Balloon Safe Near Hudson Bay; All the Men Alive." The subhead read "Naval Aircraft A-5598 Landed on Dec. 14 at a Far Northern Trading Post."[28] All the news that's fit to print had arrived in Moose Factory after three naval airmen, all veterans of the Great War, crash-landed about thirty kilometres northeast of the community.

It must have been a sight: a giant air balloon on the coast. A storm on December 14 had caused the crew of three to go wildly off course and fall into the bush. They'd left Long Island the day before, the *Times* reported, to make "an experimental flight with some point in Canada as its indefinite objective."

The crew spent four days in the frozen forest with provisions for only three days, before finding their way to the HBC trading post in Moose. It wasn't an easy journey, and the men were weak. Farrell was reportedly distressed and "suggested that the others should just cut his throat and use him for food or just leave him behind."[29]

The U.S. Army had sent two planes up to Fort Albany to conduct daily searches for the crew, but they could find nothing. After the three lieutenants walked into the trading post, an "Indian runner" was sent to Mattice to give word on the telegraph line. It took the unnamed runner two weeks to get there.

Principal Haythornthwaite reportedly took an "active part" in helping the lost balloonists.

That is almost the last we know of Haythornthwaite's activities. In
1921, one year after the balloon crash and two years after the seven boys
drowned, he shot himself dead.

Haythornthwaite's demise was reported in the *Morning Citizen*
newspaper, in a news brief dated August 31, 1921. The headline reads
"Pathetic End of Anglican Rector." The blunt piece reads, "Rev. W.
Haythornwaite [*sic*], who was injured recently, ended his suffering with
a bullet, according to word just received here from Rev. J. G. Anderson,
bishop of the Anglican diocese of Moosonee."

According to Anderson, Haythornthwaite had broken his shoulder
while helping to move a piano, after which he suffered for weeks "without
medical attendance, the nearest doctor being at Cochrane 180 miles distant." He was delirious with the pain when he "escaped from his Indian
attendants and shot himself."[30]

There is no written account to suggest anything malicious happened
to the hated principal, but the use of that phrase "escaped from his Indian
attendants" is striking. Truth is stranger than fiction. And truth always
comes for you, hunts you down and engulfs you. Haythornthwaite was
forced to rely on the very people he'd tortured and abused. He was helpless, and, like generations of Englishmen before him, reliant on the
Omushkego to survive.

The article says only this about his life.: "Mr. Haythornwaite [*sic*]
was principal of the Indian school at Moose Factory. He was well known
here where he was stationed as rector for 12 months, ten years ago. He
took an active part in helping the lost American balloonists when they
descended in the vicinity of Moose Factory last winter."

It is fascinating that the only positive thing that could be said
about the late reverend was in relation to three stranded American
balloonists. Nothing about his kindness or stellar career in education
in the community.

In a report to the Department of Indian Affairs the following month,
Commissioner Awrey wrote that for some time the principal had been

suffering from dementia precox, a phrase used at the time to describe psychosis or madness.

Awrey also noted that a tuberculosis epidemic had swept through the small school of not more than twenty-five pupils, and that a "weeding out" was necessary to stop the spread. The report mentioned one orphaned Nipineskum child named Lizzie who had died of the disease the previous winter.[31] Three other children who had TB were sent to live with their grandmother. They weren't allowed to return to school until they had money in hand to pay their fees.

The Canadian government had a diabolical way of charging Indigenous children to attend residential schools. Each pupil who was counted as a Status Indian received treaty payments yearly. The money was held in trust while they were at school, and funds were taken out of their accounts to pay for their room and board. How cruel, that children were made to pay their tormentors to torment them and, in some cases, to cause them to die or to suffer such trauma that they, and generations after them, would not recover.

Awrey's report is troubling to read. He wrote that another boy was permanently paralyzed from the waist down due to a TB infection. He was being sent out to the Wesley family to be cared for.

And, in an act of ultimate neglect, Awrey reported that yet another boy, Charlie Carpenter, was on death's doorstep with TB. Awrey had authorized the purchase of a tent—paid for by Charlie's own treaty money—where the boy would remain, alone. "I authorized Bishop Anderson to purchase a tent in which to place Chas. Carpenter another orphan boy who has been several years in the school as this boy has funds to his credit in savings. I told Bishop Anderson to submit vouchers for any expenditures made. Dr. Day states this boy cannot possibly live very long."

Monsters.

I was enraged reading this. Once again the Carpenter children were dismissed as orphans. They were not. They were brothers, Annie's nephews, and they had a large extended family. Given the chance, I am certain the family would have taken the children back. It is not uncommon for grandparents, aunties and uncles, sisters and brothers and other kin to help raise our children.

My uncle Hank knew their names. He had tried to search for records of them, hoping to figure out where they fit in relation to Annie. He knew they were related, but he wasn't sure how. He had both boys' baptism records. And I uncovered further records on Charles, after seeking the help of the National Centre for Truth and Reconciliation, where, in early 2023, I had filed a request for any information on Charles Carpenter, Elizabeth Gauthier, James Chapish Wemaystikosh and Sarah Chapish Wemaystikosh.

In December, I received a letter from Hunter Clemons, the NCTR's access and privacy coordinator, with a package containing only Charles's available records. There was nothing for Elizabeth, James or Sarah. I am not surprised by this, given the name changes, wrong spellings and the lack of records during that time.

Clemons wrote, "Please note that Student Memorial Register Reports are generated from records that are located in the NCTR collections, that indicate certain children passed away or went missing while attending residential school. However, this does not mean that any of your family members passing away or disappearing can be excluded. The NCTR does not currently hold all records related to the residential school system." From what the NCTR did have in their collection, they were "able to generate a Student Memorial Register Report for Charles."

According to their records, Charles was a boy when he was sent to the Mohawk Institute Residential School, or what Survivors later called the Mush Hole after the sludgy, mushy food constantly served there. This school was about two thousand kilometres away from Eabametoong, or Fort Hope, where he was last captured on the census with his father James Carpenter, Annie's brother.

Why was he sent so far away?

At the time of Charles's attendance at the Mohawk Institute, it was being run by the New England Company. An Anglican missionary working for the company had established a day school at the Six Nations community, near what is now the city of Brantford, in 1828.

The New England Company were Puritan missionaries who had established the New England colonies in the 1630s. They drove the colonization of modern-day America, while preaching the virtue of work. They thought that if Indigenous Peoples didn't have an education and didn't work hard, they'd fall into the grip of Satan.[32]

The Anglican Church took over the school in 1920 and ran it until 1970, making it one of the longest-running Indian residential schools in Canada. The Mohawk Institute lists Charles as a "troublesome" student on what is labelled an "Explanatory" document that details the students' performance in 1914. The good students received "badges," and the others were put on the "Black List" for such misdemeanours as talking back, trying to run away or stealing apples.

According to the "Explanatory" document, only the children who misbehaved (in the eyes of the school official who kept the report) and did not get badges were mentioned. Here are but a few of them:

A fourteen-year-old girl who "belongs to low caste, her face is often repulsive in appearance." Her mother had lived with a man who is said to have murdered her in a drunken brawl. "We have lately admitted by special request."

Another girl whom the Mohawk Institute planned to transfer to the Shingwauk Home, "as she needs discipline and to be away from the influence of her mother."

A thirteen-year-old girl, whose mother had died, was described as a "low type, her face is defiant, any amount of gentle persuasion is lost on her . . . We are not hopeful of improving this girl's conduct, a reformatory is the place for her—it's too bad to have her here contaminating the many nice girls in the school and we will be glad if you can remove her."

Charles Carpenter had three minor reports in two years and "none at all in 1 1/3 years."

In 1916, Charles was ping-ponged more than two thousand kilometres up to northwestern Ontario, to Cecilia Jeffrey Indian Residential School. I have no idea why he was sent to Cecilia Jeffrey but a letter sent by Ottawa on August 21, 1916, confirmed his health was good enough for him to be admitted there.

The NCTR found no further mention of Charles at Cecilia Jeffrey, and he must not have been there for very long. He was transferred one more time, up to Bishop Horden Hall on Moose Factory Island. When he was there, the Hall had ten rooms and an attic. Besides the school building, the site consisted of the principal's house, a carpentry building, an engine house and a cowshed. Charles attended Bishop Horden when tuberculosis stalked residential schools across Canada.

A lack of proper health care, nutrition and basic kindness added to the children's suffering. This, according to a Dr. A. S. McCraig in 1919, regarding a young girl who had a tuberculosis infection in her right elbow at the Wawanosh school for girls in Sault Ste. Marie: "The trouble is about two years of duration. About a month ago, the joint became acutely inflamed, due to additional infection, and ten days ago the abscess opened and is now discharging freely from several openings. It will improve slowly but the Shingwauk Home is not a suitable place for a case of this kind."[33]

By 1907, Dr. Peter Bryce, the chief medical officer for the Department of Indian Affairs, had written a report on the number of children dying of infections in residential schools. He visited schools and collected data on 1,537 deceased students: 35 per cent of the students had died of TB and, in one school alone, that number was 69 per cent. "It is apparent," the report read, "that general ill health from continuous respiration of the air of increasing foulness is inevitable, but when sometimes consumptive pupils, and very frequently others with discharging scrofulous glands, are present to add an infective quality to the atmosphere, we have created a situation so dangerous to health that I am often surprised that results were not more serious than they have been shown statistically to be."[34]

His report makes it clear that children being sent to residential schools were being sent to die.

By 1905, two years before Bryce's scathing report, Duncan Campbell Scott was already aware of what was happening in the schools. He knew because he was a micromanaging bureaucrat who received letters consistently and constantly from Indian agents and school principals telling him about the states of the schools and how many children were dying.

It was in every single school annual report: the number of children who were "discharged" due to death.

He knew, and chose to do nothing.

Charles Carpenter is one of the 2,800 names on the National Centre for Truth and Reconciliation's memorial red banner, containing the known names of children who died while at residential school by the time of the commission's reports in 2015.

Charlie died by himself on October 13, 1921.[35] He lived alone for one month in the tent he was forced to buy with his treaty money.

All my relations.

AFTER HAYTHORNTHWAITE'S SUICIDE, life carried on at Bishop Horden Hall. The school was reportedly overcrowded, and arrangements were being made to bring in another principal.

H. N. Awrey, the department's man in James Bay whose reports and correspondence we had some glimpse of above—when the Horden schoolchildren drowned, and after Principal Haythornthwaite died—kept watch at the school, regularly travelling to Moose and performing inspections. On one occasion in 1927, he found an unauthorized woman sleeping in the dormitory with the girls.

"I discovered that an idiotic creature was sleeping in the same apartment as the girls," he wrote when he handed in his annual report to the government. "I strongly protested against this, and I believe steps are now being taken to have her removed."[36]

In Ottawa, this news sent officials scrambling and firing letters off to the Anglican diocese. "The Department considers that insane Indians should not be allowed to reside in Indian residential schools owing to the danger to the young children," wrote the acting assistant deputy and secretary later that month. He called for the woman's removal "at once."[37]

There is no mention, anywhere, of the woman's name or who she was, other than an "insane Indian." What if this woman was not "insane"? What if she was just a mother who refused to leave her daughter's side?

After Haythornthwaite's death, the Hall was desperate for a new principal. An unusual one arrived in 1926 from Shingwauk Indian Residential School, where he'd graduated after being a student there: John Albert Maggrah, who was Anishinaabe and would go on to be ordained as an Anglican priest.[38] But his posting was only temporary until someone else could be found. They couldn't leave an Indian in charge.

Meanwhile at Indian Affairs, Awrey would continue to climb the career ladder. He would go on to become one of two commissioners in charge of negotiating the adhesions to Treaty 9 in 1929.

BY THIS TIME, Annie had long since left Moose Factory. Her children James and Sarah were gone, unaccounted for. Also gone from her was her son John.

Yes, John. After I had written this chapter, Paula contacted me to say that she had found that Annie and Samson had another son, John Charles Chapish, born on June 12, 1892.

What had happened to their three children? Did they disappear at Bishop Horden Hall? At another school up the James Bay coast? Were they the nameless, faceless children who received no medical care and died of tuberculosis or other respiratory ailments?

Annie left Moose in the early 1900s. She fled back to her family. Her brothers and sisters were on the move, so she joined them as they went up the Albany River. At the time of Samson's death, she would have been pregnant or had just given birth to my great-grandmother Elizabeth, who was born in 1904 (according to her death record).

She joined her eldest brother Joseph, his wife Mary, and their five children at Osnaburgh, an old HBC trading post at the head of the Albany River. We know this because Annie's name was put on the Treaty 9 paylist in July 1905, after the very first community signed on to a treaty that effectively granted to the federal government two-thirds of the present-day province of Ontario land mass—from the Manitoba border to Hudson Bay and then over to James Bay in the east.

According to that first paylist, Annie had another daughter with her, and her name was Christina. I had no idea who she was. Christina would have been born in the early 1900s. She would have been a toddler at the time of Samson's death.

Lost are the official records of either Christina's or Elizabeth's births.

I remember Elizabeth, holding me in her warm, huge embrace. More than anything, I remember her faint smell of clean soap, her horn-rimmed glasses and a feeling of being safe in her thick, strong arms.

According to the Province of Ontario, Elizabeth is not a person. Twice, Uncle Hank asked the Ontario government to conduct a search for her birth record. Twice, searches of vital statistics records yielded no results.

I now know why. Elizabeth was registered as a Gauthier at her 1911 Roman Catholic baptism in Kenora after Annie married Joseph Gauthier. But she wasn't a Gauthier or even an Elizabeth. She was a Wemaystikosh, a Chapish—or, as she is listed in the Anglican baptism record of February 3, 1907, she was Lizzie Samson. Lizzie's mother was Annie "Sampson" and the witness to the service was Mrs. John Jeffreys— her older sister Jane Carpenter.

For her entire life, my great-grandma Elizabeth or Lizzie, a Survivor of Indian residential school, a traditional midwife and mother of nine children, was not counted as a person, much less an Indian, by the Province of Ontario. She grew up with the wrong name, nation-less, and unrecognized by Canada, Ontario or her communities.

CHAPTER SIX

SEPARATION AND
THE HUNT FOR RECORDS

PAULA RICKARD IS MOOSE FACTORY'S RESIDENT FAMILY HISTORIAN. SHE IS ALSO a descendant of the Wemaystikoshes and, as such, my cousin. Paula has become a constant confidante, a late-night Facebook message buddy and a partner on reclamation.

While the rest of the world finds other platforms for communication, Facebook remains the main vehicle for Indigenous people on Turtle Island. It is how we keep each other posted on the goings-on, with lots of photographs and with comments ranging from political commentary to the traditional foods or Kraft Dinner and hot dogs consumed last night. Everyone is connected.

In an email after one of our late-night chats, Paula wrote about the legacy of how, when recording the names of First Nations people, the church and the government wrote down what they wanted or whatever they decided they'd heard. Different names, different spellings. "Often, our Indigenous family history can only go back so far because of the lack of documentation of our grandmothers," her message read. "They were often not listed, and if they were listed, only their first name was noted, or they were noted as 'Indian woman.' This made it near impossible to connect a grandmother to any family."

Before the settlers came, there was no need for paperwork for families to keep track of each other, to not lose one another. Records were not needed to find people. What the settlers gave us were inadequate accounts of who was who, not to mention hidden, inaccurate, sloppy and inexcusably casual accounts of who went where. They showed a callousness towards the value of the lives being "recorded."

In the face of this, through years of determined hunting, Paula has been building an epic digitized family tree of the James and Hudson Bay Omushkego Cree. Her tree has branches entwining nearly *twelve thousand* names. It spans like a giant blanket over the coastlines and inward into the interior of what we now call Ontario, Quebec and Manitoba. She is the one who led me to Samson, after our family's fruitless search for him for over five decades—and, through him, to his and Annie's children.

Samson Wemaystikosh, Annie's first husband and my great-great-grandfather, is a prime example of church and census officials having no idea what to do with an Indigenous family's last name. There are at least seven different spellings and iterations of Wemaystikosh. Church records, census and vital statistics give different spellings in different areas. The spelling of Wemaystikosh is wildly different throughout the documents. Almost always, the recorder was either a member of the church or with the HBC or, later on, an Indian agent. Wemaystikosh in Moose Factory is also Wemistagoose, Wemastikos and, oddly, Chapish. Move south to Longlac, Timmins, Mattagami and North Bay, and Chapish is seen again. Up and along the James Bay coast to Fort George it becomes Chapais and Chapaisse.

The screw-up on the spelling has been a big contributor to at least three generations of loss. The "found" part happened by looking for a needle in a haystack.

Paula was the one, up so late every night for months, scanning through census records from 1881 to 1921 until her tired eyes couldn't see straight. But her persistence paid off. She is determined to find all of our lost and forgotten loved ones. She believes each deserves to have their story told.

Her devotion to finding out the truth puts the mom and health-care worker in high demand. Everyone knows who she is and how talented she is when it comes to finding the impossible. The Toronto Police Service has sought her out to help them find the identities of Jane Does who are sitting in the morgue, waiting to be called home. She also assisted police in the investigation of Moosonee's Joseph George Sutherland, who pleaded guilty to first-degree murder in late 2023, almost forty years after Susan Tice, forty-five, and Erin Gilmour, twenty-two, two Toronto women who did not know each other, were sexually assaulted and violently stabbed in 1983.[1] Sutherland's arrest surprised the coastal James Bay town of Moosonee, population 1,500. He was a quiet man whom Paula remembers worked in IT for Payukotayno, James and Hudson Bay Family Services.

Toronto Police used the new field of investigative genetic genealogy to find Sutherland, who was never a suspect in the killings previously. Paula's Indigenous knowledge about James Bay family history was crucial to creating a family tree based on DNA matches. DNA found at the crime scenes was uploaded to the website GEDmatch, which identified matches that were used to build a family tree of the suspect's relations.

But even those decades-old crimes and those caught up in their investigation count as recent, with relatively accessible records, compared with the generations-back Omushkego Cree family tree Paula is constructing. She needed all her well-honed skills to find Annie and Samson's children, considering the English missionaries recorded the names of Samson and Annie and their descendants so many different ways.

In Annie's case, her last name changed to Samson after her husband's death in the early 1900s. This was something my uncle Hank, Elizabeth's son, did not know. All he knew was that his mother's last name was Gauthier, because that is what he was raised knowing. And his mother never spoke about who she was. Did Annie's last name change to Samson because of a language barrier? Did she tell the Indian agent and authorities that she was Samson's wife after he died? Paula knows of evidence in church records of children carrying their father's first name as their surname.

For decades our family had no idea about Annie's children from her first marriage. For lifetimes, my grandmother and aunties and uncles did not know about their uncles George or John or James or about Auntie Sarah and Auntie Christina. More importantly, we did not know that Elizabeth Gauthier was not, as we'd thought, Annie's daughter with her second husband Joseph Gauthier. Elizabeth was Samson and Annie's last child. The 1907 baptism record for Lizzie Sampson gives proof to this.

This is hard to comprehend in 2023, but a hundred years ago, I wonder if the assimilative lessons drilled into her head may have convinced her that it was better to be the child of a French Canadian man than an Indian. (Gauthier's marriage and death certificates list him as French Canadian, born in Quebec.) Sometimes I can't even imagine she thought this, that she willingly abandoned her own father. Was that possible? Did she not know who he was?

We live in a vast, uncharted country of memories. So little was written down; so much is unknown about who was forced into the Indian industrial, residential and day schools. So many have disappeared along with the memories of those who are no longer with us. We do not know their names, or their whereabouts, and we'll never know the extent of the loss and annihilation achieved by the policies of conformist destruction.

MY UNCLE HANK could not find any government records that proved Elizabeth Gauthier was an Indian. At every turn he met roadblocks, some of them put in place by his own mother. Bowen was my great-grandmother Liz's married name. Before that, as far as anyone knew, she was a Gauthier. My mother clearly remembers her grandmother being teased by her husband Rusty as being "from the Factory." (Did he mean her home of Moose Factory, or the "factory" of residential schools?) But she herself would say nothing about where she was from, and she refused to talk about residential school other than to say that the nuns had taught her how to bake bread. She also insisted that the family eat fish on

Fridays. Those clues didn't really narrow down the possibilities, other than suggesting that it must have been a Catholic institution. Did she go to a school in northern Ontario? Manitoba? Quebec?

Where do you start looking when you have no clue which First Nations community to search in? There are 133 in Ontario alone.

Uncle Hank turned to the province. Twice he wrote to Ontario's vital statistics branch to try to obtain Elizabeth's birth record. In response to his first inquiry, in 1993, he received this one-sentence reply on March 6, 1993, from Ontario's Consumer and Commercial Relations department, where birth records and vital statistics were kept: "THIS IS TO CERTIFY THAT WE HAVE SEARCHED THE PROVINCE OF ONTARIO INDEX FOR THE PERIOD OF 1902–1906 AND THERE IS NO RECORD OF A REGISTRATION FOR THE NAME(S) INDICATED IN THE PERIOD COVERED."

Uncle Hank wrote another letter, three years later, again asking for the birth information of Elizabeth Gauthier, born between 1905 and 1909. He received this reply on May 15, 1996: "IN RESPONSE TO YOUR REQUEST FOR A CERTIFICATE/SEARCH, WE HAVE SEARCHED THE PROVINCE OF ONTARIO RECORDS FOR THE PERIOD AND NAME INDICATED ABOVE, AND FOUND NO REGISTRATION THAT EXACTLY MATCHES THE INFORMATION YOU HAVE PROVIDED."

In Ontario, Elizabeth Gauthier simply did not exist. Not in Quebec either. Nor in Manitoba, or in any other province or territory in Canada.

We now know why. It is because Elizabeth Gauthier was not her original name. It was Elizabeth Wemaystikosh. And even *that* name, when she was very young, was changed to Samson.

It was Paula who found, in 2023, during one of her crawls through the endless records, the 1911 Rainy River census, in the "unorganized territory" of northern Ontario, which lists a Joseph Gocha—yet another wrong spelling of a name written down in an "official" record. Joseph Gocha was a trapper with a wife named Annie and a "step-daughter," Elizabeth Samson, born in February 1904 or 1906—the handwriting is difficult to read. Their daughter Louise Gocha was an infant. Also living with them was Annie's nephew James Carpenter. He was three years old, born in 1907.

Elizabeth would have been just four years old when her mother married Joseph in December 1908. She was officially given his last name in 1911, when she and her half-sister Louise were baptized as Catholics at Notre Dame du Portage Church in Kenora.

Did Annie ever speak of Samson to Elizabeth? Did she hide the identity of the man she'd had five children with? Speaking of, what about those other children—Elizabeth's sisters and brothers?

Annie, a widow with five young children, must have been desperate and distraught. Was it just easier to be married to a white man? Was she trying to bring Elizabeth up as a white girl, to hide her and therefore protect her from the misogynistic and racial hatred she had experienced?

Is it fair to judge Annie?

Of her six children, one had died of illness as a young child. Liz we know about. But the others? Vanished. Gone. Apprehended. There are no words to describe how awful it must have been to live through the taking. And, like a genetic disease, it would happen again and again, spreading silently and viciously to all of Annie's descendants.

But by then, the evil of residential schools had given way to the child welfare system, which took children away as soon as the residential schools began to close in the 1950s and into the 1970s. We call this the "Sixties Scoop." The state either apprehended our children or it persuaded Indigenous mothers that the right thing to do was to give their children away for someone else to raise. The state knew best. This still occurs today.

I did not know I had a sister until I was in my mid-twenties. My mother was a teen when she had her. She was encouraged to give her up so another family could give her the life my mother clearly could not. My mother held her daughter in her arms for one year before she was taken and given to a white couple in Manitoba to raise.

When this sort of situation occurs and the records to track a family member are wrong—keep in mind that paperwork filled out by church officials and Indian agents have historically been the only records the Government of Canada would accept as reliable—a cascade of mistakes and missed truths is set in motion, of people not knowing who they are or who and where they came from. That is the devastation wrought by careless clerical errors. Our sense of "belonging" is ripped away officially in the eyes of the law.

Of course that begs the question, whose law? And an even bigger one: Why did our families follow it, unless they felt they had no choice?

FOR DECADES, UNCLE HANK and my grandmother, aunts and uncles and cousins and my mother spent their lives denied any "rights" or "privileges" as "Indians" in the eyes of the law or with their communities. Rusty had evaded Indian Affairs by living in the bush and had no status card. The children therefore grew up thinking they were never "Indian enough."

This left my uncle Hank incensed. He was a man who had served his country in the Second World War. A man who was literally imprisoned for months at a time in the Fort William Indian Hospital Sanatorium. I say "imprisoned" because not only was the care awful, but the more Indians an institution had, the more it was paid. It was just like residential schools: higher head counts meant more funding.

Uncle Hank would not stop trying to find out who his mother was or who his grandmother was. After countless phone calls and letters, he finally received his status card in 1995. But it wasn't through Annie or Elizabeth that he was at long last deemed "Indian enough"—it was through his father, Alphonse Piska. Or, in the English world of Canada, Russell Bowen.

When Hank was registered as a Status Indian, the rationale was, according to the April 19, 1995, letter sent to him from Indian and Northern Affairs, "One parent deemed entitled to be registered under section 6(1) of the Indian Act." The letter went on to outline registration particulars:

FATHER: *Russell Bowen (a.k.a. Alphonse Piskey), born on August 25, 1903, deemed entitled to be registered under section 6(1)c of the Indian Act.*

RATIONALE: *Omitted from the Indian Register due to non-Indian paternity. His mother, Mary Pishke (a.k.a. Piskey), whose brother Joseph Pishke was the father of William Piska of No. 248 Fort William Band, is deemed to be entitled to be registered under section 6(1)(a) of the Indian Act.*

REMARKS: *The applicant is affiliated with the (187) Fort William Registry Group.*

Uncle Hank, who officially is known as Joseph Rodgers Bowen, felt a conflicted brew of emotions after reading this letter. Anger. Happiness. Disgust. It was a bittersweet moment.

He, and all of his brothers and sisters, Elizabeth and Alphonse's children—including Mary, born in 1920, Liz born in 1922, Margaret (my grandmother) in 1925, Blanche in 1927, Russell in 1930, Connie in 1931, Bernice in 1932 and Sarah in 1946—were entitled to their status cards. They already knew they were born "Indians," but now they were officially counted.

But Canada still did not recognize Hank's mother as an Indian.

This letter of registration was an insult. It ignored Elizabeth entirely. She remained a non-Indian. A nonentity. The Government of Canada thus wiped from the rolls the birthright of all her descendants. They weren't allowed to be counted as Indians under the Indian Act. Not a single one of them—even though they were actual Indians. Instead, they continued to be condemned to live in a state of flux, feeling neither here nor there, not part of the proud First Nations communities of Fort Albany, Moose Factory, Mishkeegogamang and Fort William to which they were blood-related.

Uncle Hank quietly attended the Thunder Bay Indian Friendship Centre for years, knowing he belonged but, in the eyes of a law, not officially belonging. Canada's indifference gnawed at him.

He tried one last time. He wrote another letter. Indian and Northern Affairs replied that they had conducted another search of their records and had not been able to identify Annie Carpenter as ever having been registered as an Indian. They offered to review Uncle Hank's application if he could provide additional information such as the name of Annie's or her parents' band and band number, the names of any maternal relatives who had been registered as Indians, or "any other pertinent information that may be helpful in determining your mother's entitlement to registration as an Indian as defined by the Indian Act."

The letter concluded by pointing out that "it is the responsibility of the applicant to supply information concerning their Indian ancestors and identifying the names of the band or bands with which they may be associated. We verify the information provided in our records and determine what, if any, entitlement to registration a person may have based on this information. Ordinarily, information regarding a person's Indian ancestry is obtained from family members . . . Until such time as you can provide such information, I am unable to determine whether or not your mother has an entitlement to registration as an Indian defined by the Indian Act."

The letter dripped with condescension. If it were not so insulting, it would be laughable. Annie Carpenter and her daughters were at the signing of Treaty 9, which was negotiated by Duncan Campbell Scott himself, Canada's notorious architect of the genocidal laws—the legacies of which are all too apparent in this letter written nine decades later.

Treaty 9 opened up the province of Ontario in 1905. Without it, there would be no province. There would be no railway, there would be no Canada. *Annie witnessed the signing of that treaty.*

Uncle Hank, the man with the kind eyes and soft smile, who was born in 1924 and lived much of his life out in the bush, died on July 6, 2011, at the Hogarth Riverview Manor in Thunder Bay. On the wall of his room hung a massive dream catcher. Beside it, the beret worn as part of his soldier's uniform. On the nightstand stood a clear glass jar stuffed with terracotta-coloured two-dollar bills, many faces of the queen staring out from different angles.

Uncle Hank never banked any of the four-dollar treaty payments he finally began to receive as a registered Indian under the Indian Act. Four dollars annually is what the treaty payment has been since 1850, when the Robinson-Superior Treaty was signed. Uncle Hank kept every single last dollar, refusing to spend any of it. Canada had broken the treaty it had with him, with my family and all our relations, time and again.

My uncle Joseph "Hank" Bowen was a veteran of the Second World War and a proud member of Fort William First Nation. He assembled much of the research that became this book. (Talaga family handout)

AS OUR ELDERS pass and memories fade, the race against the clock to remember, to write down the meanings and proper pronunciations of names, to straighten out who was related to whom, is urgently under way in all our communities, among our family members. We do this as we wait for courts, governments, church leaders and politicians to do what was asked of them in the recommendations of the Truth and Reconciliation Commission: release all the records.

These are not just dusty old papers. Despite the errors they inevitably contain, these records, held on to by bureaucrats and church leaders and heads of hospitals, universities, museums and other institutions, hold vital clues about, and the names of, those we've lost. Facts about those who were taken and about those who we never knew existed in the first place.

Our gatherers and truth tellers, those tasked with finding the truth, have had to wait for a digital world and then demand, yell, scream and take everyone to court to get their hands on those records—to get them digitized, uploaded and available. Canadian authorities do not willingly just open their bureaucratic drawers, their office cabinets and basement archives. The churches do not, out of the goodness of their hearts, release what they have. I say that cynically, because we are under no illusion that much of what the churches had has been destroyed, either deliberately or through negligence. We have to fight for what records remain. In doing so, we aren't just fighting for dusty pieces of paper; we're fighting to acknowledge the very existence of our ancestors in the colonial form this country made us adhere to in the first place.

The word *available* clearly means different things to different people. Records of our missing loved ones, those who vanished at residential schools or at Indian hospitals, at asylums and in prisons, are hidden everywhere, sometimes even in plain sight. And, in typical Canadian fashion, the release of these records, in whatever form, is hampered by bureaucratic red tape, or by denials of their very existence. Or they are tucked away, sometimes even forgotten, in the basements of universities, hospitals, museums and diocese offices.

Go ask for your records. That is the first thing Kimberly Murray, the independent special interlocutor for missing children and unmarked graves and burial sites associated with Indian residential schools, told the first-ever National Gathering on Unmarked Burials, in Edmonton, in September 2022, sixteen months after the discovery of the 215 in Tk'emlúps. I was there, listening to Kim in a giant conference hall at the Westin hotel. Kim's office had asked me to be one of four rapporteurs, witnessing and recording what was discussed.

Myself and Kimberly Murray, executive oversight lead of the Survivors' Secretariat and member of the Kanesatake First Nation, at the Mohawk Institute. Murray went on to become the independent special interlocutor for missing children and unmarked graves and burial sites associated with Indian residential schools. (Photo by Tanya Talaga)

Murray, a member of Kanesatake First Nation, is a lawyer who led the Survivors' Secretariat at the Six Nations of the Grand River and was formerly the executive director of the Truth and Reconciliation Commission. In her last days at the secretariat, we met at the Mohawk Institute, and Kim showed me around the institution. She showed me the caverns of the building where children had been forced to fight each other in boxing matches—bizarrely a sport that was repeated at Kamloops and Shingwauk. We saw the old laundry room and the cafeteria, and she showed me where children used to scrape their names into the red bricks at the back of the Institute. When I visited, little brightly coloured triangle flags on wire stems marked the areas where the Survivors' Secretariat would soon be using ground-penetrating radar.

I did not know at the time that Annie's nephew Charles attended the Mohawk Institute as a young boy.

Murray's mandate as special interlocutor is to advise the government on how to proceed as more and more burial sites are found at former residential school sites across the country. (Thousands of possible gravesites have so far been identified.) The ask was huge—to consult widely and deliver a final report within two years—and she'd moved at lightning speed to set up this first national gathering.

Nearly three hundred of us assembled in the hotel's cavernous meeting spaces, deep in the heart of Treaty 6. Edmonton was a good place for the special interlocutor to begin her task: it is a meeting place of many Nations, being the traditional territory of the Nêhiyaw, Dene, Anishinaabe, Nakota Isga, Niitsitapi, the Métis and home to Inuit. It's also the sometimes left-leaning provincial capital (much to the chagrin of other parts of Alberta) and the proud home of the West Edmonton Mall, one Canada's biggest shopping malls, complete with an aquarium, skating rink and roller coaster.

The gathering hosted a sea of Survivors from the schools and their relations, Survivors of intergenerational trauma wearing orange shirts and colourful ribbon skirts, clutching satchels of tobacco and porcelain cups of stale Starbucks coffee prepared hours earlier and left to sit in giant silver vats outside the meeting room. The hotel had flat-screen TVs everywhere. This premiere gathering was taking place one week after the death of Queen Elizabeth II, the head of a country that had colonized this nation, affixing the royal seal to hundreds of treaties that the British never intended to honour. All of the dozens of TVs in the hotel's common spaces were tuned to the live coverage of the funeral procession as it made its way through the colonizers' home country.

Elizabeth was head of state for seventy years, and during that time, she silently presided over the decades-long residential school era. This was not lost on any of us who had to endure nonstop coverage of her funeral on seemingly endless loops.

During her time on the throne, her governments ignored broken treaties that stole away land from First Nations, not to mention the racist national policies that led to the running and maintenance of the so-called schools—along with all of the trauma left in their wake. While the funeral procession continued, we were also mindful that, in Treaty 6 Territory just weeks before, a murderous rampage had taken place on James Smith Cree Nation, leaving ten dead.

As always, a gathering of this size lets us reconnect with those we've not seen in years and meet others we've only known electronically. The years of Covid had kept us apart and prevented events such as this. Whenever anything of importance happens, the first thing we do is hold a gathering. We sit in giant circles of connection, and we meet to discuss. Always face to face.

The three-day gathering began with a sunrise ceremony at the site of the sacred fire outside Edmonton's city hall. We burn sacred fires for four days, and during that time, the fire is never extinguished, never left alone. Firekeepers silently tend to their duty, sitting close by, seeing to the needs of our ancestors who are called by the fire. The Firekeeper maintains and feeds the flames, sitting with it and with whoever comes to be beside it, to place tobacco—one of the sacred medicines—into the flames as an offering, to sit quietly and think. On the first day in Edmonton, Kim Murray, Saskatchewan lawyer Donald Worme, lawyer Julian Falconer, Dene National Chief Gerald Antoine and school Survivors met before dawn outside the front entrance of the hotel and walked to the site of the fire. After prayers were said to the Creator and to our summoned ancestors past, present and future, women and men separated, each going into their own tipi for a traditional Nêhiyaw pipe ceremony.

As the women entered our tipi, tobacco ties were offered as gifts to the Pipe Carrier, and we sat in a circle, in quiet contemplation as we made space for each other. The Pipe Carrier leads the ceremony, providing prayers to acknowledge the seven cardinal points: the four directions, the spirit world above, Mother Earth below, and the centre representing all living things. The Pipe Carrier smokes the pipe first, then passes it around the circle, each of the participants inhaling and exhaling. We were making a covenant to the spirit world and to each other to go forward in a good way, to listen and learn and care for one another.

After the ceremony, our hair and clothes smelling like sage and tobacco, we walked into the Westin to get to work.

Among us were leaders from three distinct Indigenous Peoples in Canada: Inuit Tapiriit Kanatami president Natan Obed, Métis National Council president Cassidy Caron, and Gerald Antoine, who was appointed by the Assembly of First Nations to head up the effort to find the missing children and unmarked graves. We were joined by Dr. Chile Eboe-Osuji, former president of the International Criminal Court, who told us that while what happened during the residential school period in Canada undoubtedly fit the definition of genocide, the court's jurisdiction limits it to events that occurred after 2002.

"The law is not justice," he said. "Often the law allows injustice to linger or the law itself can *be* the source of injustice, as in the system that allowed Indian Residential Schools to operate."[2] While he spoke, you could feel the air draining out of the room. The Survivors knew what had happened was an orchestrated national crime, and it hurt their hearts to be told what they had always known: there would be no criminal redress.

We also heard from Fredy Peccerelli, director of the Fundación de Antropología Forense de Guatemala, an organization that has extensive experience in finding graves and victims and how to go about seeking, exhuming and identifying remains and returning them to loved ones. He spoke of their work looking for loved ones who'd disappeared over the span of three decades of conflict. (The population of Guatemala is 50 per cent Maya.) He spoke of how cultural protocols and ceremonies guided their searching:

*When you think of a crime scene usually you think of a "do not cross"
tape. But here, families first need to perform a ceremony; they need
to act with a lot of ceremony and reverence when we are disturbing
Mother Earth.*

*The ceremonies are a permanent part of everything we do.
Normally, as a scientist and archaeologist, you look where you have
evidence—satellite images or soil removed. . . . But sometimes a loved
one will come to a family in a dream and the family will say, "they
told me they are buried over there by this tree" . . . so we will look by
the tree, we look there.*[3]

My counterparts as rapporteurs were journalist Brandi Morin from
Stony Plain First Nation; Koren Lightning-Earle, legal director of
Wahkohtowin Law and Governance Lodge at the University of Alberta;
and Janice Makokis, a lawyer from Saddle Lake Cree Nation, Treaty 6
Territory. Our job was to write down what we heard and then present
it to the entire assembly at the end of the gathering. Sessions included
"Search Technology: What Technology Exists, What Does It Do and
Not Do?"; "Investigations: Differences between Community, Coroner
and Police Processes"; and "Protecting and Accessing Residential Schools
and Other Sites: Practical Barriers, Jurisdictional Issues, Indigenous
Cultural Protocols and Laws, and Land Reclamation/Land Back."

I was assigned the session "Records and Archives: What Records
Are Out There, Where Are They, and How Do You Get Them?" Who
should own, control, access or possess the records and information about
missing children and unmarked burials? Barriers exist for those leading
searches in accessing relevant records in all levels of government and
in church archives. Those that hold the records continue to hold the
power. How do we, as families and communities, know that everything
is honestly and wholeheartedly being released? Why is it that the current
holders of records are the ones deciding what is relevant, what may be
disclosed to and seen by communities leading their own searches?

The meeting was held in a windowless brown-carpeted basement
room. Despite rows of brown chairs at least twenty deep, it was standing

room only to hear the presenters talk about what they'd experienced hunting for information on behalf of their communities. And no wonder. The topic was painfully relevant to us all. Squished in with the others, it occurred to me how much a gathering like this would have helped Uncle Hank.

All three presenters came with separate messages. The first message, from research lead Leah Redcrow of Saddle Creek First Nation, focused on the importance of locating records and doing whatever we need to get our hands on them.

Saddle Lake Cree Nation is in central Alberta, 180 kilometres northeast of Edmonton. Redcrow, an Intergenerational Survivor of Blue Quills residential school in St. Paul, Alberta, spoke of the experience of her community searching the Catholic boarding school that opened in 1891 at Lac la Biche. The school was torn down and moved several times. This complicates conducting a ground search: there is so much territory to examine. She spoke, too, of the practical realities of hunting for records. Catholic Indian missions in Redcrow's territory gave way to Catholic residential schools. Eventually, the schools moved off the reserves, but the Catholic missions remained. The parishioners own the church records and the church is the custodian of them, and as such they are guarded carefully, kept in locked vaults and safes so they won't be stolen or mishandled. All life events of residential school students were recorded and held by the parish, not the school. But if the students died, Indian Affairs should know and have a record.

At Saddle Creek, the parish, like many, maintains registries for births, baptisms, marriages and burials. The church, Redcrow explained, is not compelled or required to share anything from their files. So establishing good relations, sometimes called "reconciliation partnerships," is of the utmost importance if we want to get anywhere. Once again, we have to be kind to those who held us down, and be willing to look the other way if we actually want to get anything accomplished.

Meanwhile, the records, Redcrow stressed, must be safeguarded and kept. After the announcement of the findings of the 215, Le Estcwicwéy̓, grief and anger had been directed towards places of worship. In the two months after the announcement of the findings at the Kamloops Indian Residential School, sixty-eight Anglican, Protestant and Catholic churches across the Prairies were torched, desecrated and vandalized. Some First Nations, such as Kamloops, took to hiring security firms to make sure no harm came to their churches. (In Kamloops, the church is actually attached to the Indian residential school.) Redcrow called for the burnings of churches to stop. Original parish records, she cautioned, including crucial maps, blueprints, bulletins, classroom registries, student medical records, admission forms and more, go up in flames every time a church burns.

She reminded everyone that this work could be hard. "Of note, you have to be ready for what you might find, it is difficult to uncover, difficult to hear. You really have to prepare yourself as a lead investigator as you might find information about family members—things you may have not known. Take care of yourself. The information you will find is distressing."

The meeting's second message, from Charlene Belleau of Williams Lake First Nation, was to proceed in ceremony, to do things in a good way—whether we are searching for records or, as in her community, for yet more unmarked graves. It does not lessen the blows or stop the pain, but we must take back who we are as a people so we learn how to carry the pain forward.

Belleau went to St. Joseph's Mission residential school, outside Williams Lake First Nation in B.C., roughly five hundred kilometres northeast of Vancouver and a three-hour drive north of Kamloops on the rolling Cariboo Highway. The Missionary Oblates of Mary Immaculate, notorious for their operations of numerous residential schools, opened the mission in 1867. By 1891, they had raised the funds to open the St. Joseph's Indian residential school. It closed ninety years later, in 1981.

The school was rife with sexual abusers. In fact, what happened at St. Joseph's gave rise to some of the first charges and convictions against priests and religious brothers for abusing children in their care at residential schools. In 1989, Brother Harold McIntee pleaded guilty to abusing seventeen children, thirteen of them at the mission. In 1996, the school's former principal, Bishop Hubert O'Connor, was charged with six counts of sexual abuse from his time at the mission in the 1960s. He was convicted of rape and indecent assault on two young First Nations women. O'Connor resigned as a bishop in 1991 after he was charged with sex crimes, and he served six months in jail for the two convictions.[4] Brother Glen Doughty was charged with dozens of sexual offences against children at two residential schools, one of them St. Joseph's.[5] In 1991 he was convicted of four counts of gross indecency against children at St. Joseph's.

After the announcement in Kamloops, the stories began coming to the surface again in Williams Lake—it was a continuation of the horror experienced by those who had gone to the school. Survivors' testimony has led the search at Williams Lake from the beginning. The community search team has listened to everything, from remembrances of the murders and disappearances of children and infants, to stories of torture, starvation and the rape or sexual assault of children.[6] "Former students of the industrial school—ninety-two and ninety-four years old—are sitting with us and telling us their stories," Belleau told us. "Interviews with Survivors are very important for this work. We must remember that many Survivors are elderly, and time is of the essence."

Finding records can be near impossible if the name of a school has changed. In some cases, the schools themselves have been destroyed or moved. Another problem seen at many former residential school sites is that the land is now in private hands. "This brings a whole different layer of complexity and challenges—dealing with owners and getting access to burial sites," Belleau said, noting that 782 hectares around Williams Lake need to be examined and there is infrastructure to sift through, including building debris. Gaining permission to search on privately owned land is an issue for many communities. For example, in Brandon, Manitoba, children from the Brandon Indian Residential School are believed to be buried on what is now a privately owned RV and camp park.

The first phase of searching at Williams Lake focused on fourteen hectares of land and used ground-penetrating radar, magnetometry and terrestrial laser scanning. It turned up ninety-three anomalies, which the community calls "reflections." (Anomalies are areas that look different from their immediate surroundings.) During the second phase, searching eighteen hectares, another sixty-six were found.[7]

The third message, from Barbara Lavallee, was this: We are learning as we go.

Lavallee is from Cowessess First Nation. She is a Survivor of the Marieval Indian Residential School and lead researcher for her community. Cowessess is Saulteaux, Cree and Métis. Her people used to follow and hunt the bison throughout the Great Plains, well into Montana, before being put onto reserve lands after Chief Cowessess (or Ka-wezauce, Little Boy) signed Treaty 4 in September 1874. The community encompasses 21,488 hectares and is about 150 kilometres northeast of Regina in the Qu'Appelle Valley.

Marieval operated from 1898 until 1997. Barbara's team started their sacred work around June 2021. The first thing they did was make sure they were spiritually supported. They approached Chief Cadmus Delorme and asked for two Knowledge Keepers to walk side by side with them, always making sure the work they did was in ceremony.

They knew they would be unearthing something buried too long. Everyone had heard the stories connected with Marieval. As Survivor Edward Dutch Lerat told the conference, "In the 20s and 30s a lot of incidents happened [at the Marieval Indian Residential School] that were passed down through our oral history: who did what, who was where, who got murdered, who went for a walk and never came back. There were stories of murder within the School, stories of nuns throwing babies into furnaces, stories of priests coming to get the older boys to come and dig graves under the cover of darkness. So we know that there is more to this than meets the eye right now."[8]

When the Cowessess team started to search the vast area of the school, they had no case study or reference guide. Everything they did was trial and error. After all, who, in this community, would have had prior experience looking for the mass graves of little children?

They initially did three sweeps of the grounds, forty square metres each, using ground-penetrating radar, or GPR. Those three attempts revealed 751 anomalies several feet below the surface. After Kamloops, 751 anomalies was a huge number. The country recoiled, and the story of Marieval was headline news everywhere. Cowessess was besieged and needed to take a pause.

They also needed the time to build a more sophisticated search plan and team. That was because Lavallee and the team thought that the number of anomalies was inaccurate. The number 751 was horrifying. But they'd expected worse.

They paused their search for a little over a year, which allowed them time to process what they'd found and for the media attention to settle down. Meanwhile, they worked on obtaining a much more advanced GPR system than the one they had been using, with advanced programming, as well as finding a geospatial scientist and extra hands to do the expert work.

When they started up again, Lavallee explained, they began searching an "extremely sensitive" area, a livestock barn that was built when the Oblate nuns ran the school. The advanced GPR machine was brought in and the readings were off the charts. But there wasn't anything more the team could do. "We were told, 'Science has its limitations and this is as far as we go,'" she said. The team knew something was there, but they couldn't say what.

Lavallee refused to give up. Their next move came to her in a dream, after she attended Sundance, a traditional sacred ceremony that must be followed strictly for four years—a ceremony that was once illegal under the Indian Act. "My husband and I went to Sundance," Lavallee told the gathering, "and really prayed that the help we needed would be on the way. When we left, I fell asleep in the car and the answers came. When I woke up, I told my husband that we needed to use dogs, they will help us."

So the Cowessess team hired cadaver dogs, trained to sniff out the dead, from the Canadian Canine Search Corps and the Lloydminster Rescue Squad. The maximum depth such dogs can search is fifteen feet. Cowessess only needed the dogs' sense of smell to penetrate seven feet down. They would be used to ascertain whether human remains were present in four specific areas of interest on the grounds and in the barn.

When the dogs arrived, Lavallee was there to keep an eye on them as they moved across the site. The dogs seemed confused and were moving everywhere. "I was unsure of what was happening. I asked the handler to interpret the dogs' behaviour. The handler said: 'The dog does not know where to start because the human scent is so strong.' I nearly collapsed when I heard this," she said. She also felt her community, still reeling from news of the 751, could not handle information like this at that time. "We kept it to ourselves for a bit of time."

They took the new findings to the University of Saskatchewan and the University of Alberta. And they looked for an even more advanced GPR system, one that had the capacity to explore in 3D imagery, the type used to examine four-thousand-year-old Egyptian tombs. "We are learning as we go along with no documentation, no routine to follow," she told us. "We are creating our own way."

Integral to their search were records of what was once on the school grounds. To find these, they had to go to Université de Saint-Boniface, in Manitoba, where most of the Cowessess records are held. The team was after anything that might prove useful, including student admission and discharge forms and quarterly returns reports written by the priest in charge of the school. With these, they could build a timeline of who attended the school and when. This would help the searchers identify who might be in the graves.[9] Team members copied student medical records, nominal rolls, classroom registries, school newsletters—every piece of documentation they could find that was associated with the school.

"When you think a document may not be important," Lavallee told us, "take it anyway. Because further down the line you'll regret if you didn't. We experienced that and had to go back to it."

Part of the hunt for records involves Cowessess asking the National Centre for Truth and Reconciliation for a memorandum of understanding, or MOU, that would grant them full access to all documents relating to the Marieval school. An MOU is yet another layer of bureaucratic red tape communities need to wade through when trying to find out who went to the schools. The National Centre for Truth and Reconciliation was created out of the Truth and Reconciliation Commission. Housed on the University of Manitoba campus on the outskirts of Winnipeg, the NCTR "preserve[s] the record" of the human rights abuses committed against First Nations, Métis and Inuit who attended Indian residential schools. It is, in its own words, "the permanent, safe home for all statements, documents, and other materials gathered by the TRC."[10] Working with universities, churches and municipal, provincial and federal governments, the NCTR continues to expand its collection daily.

One of its goals is to decolonize the archive and hold the knowledge on the Seven Grandfather Teachings: the "principles of respect, honesty, wisdom, courage, humility, love and truth."[11] The Survivors' statements, documents and other materials collected throughout the commission's six-year existence, including the testimonies of nearly seven thousand TRC witnesses and Survivors, form the heart of the NCTR.

The NCTR continues the work begun by the Truth and Reconciliation Commission of Canada, which was launched as part of the Indian Residential Schools Settlement Agreement of 2006 by the courts. That agreement was reached between Survivors or their representatives, the Government of Canada, the Assembly of First Nations and Inuit representatives, and the church bodies that ran residential schools. The centre's goal is to continue to teach all here in Canada and around the world about the residential school system and its legacy.

Despite that goal, accessing records at the NCTR is not easy. The small but mighty staff of researchers is overwhelmed with requests and bound by access-to-information bureaucracy. The NCTR is now the keeper of so much more than the Survivors' statements. For instance, it holds the personal information of people who attended the schools, including the digitized death certificates of students who died at schools in British Columbia, Alberta and Ontario. If First Nations communities want to access records at the NCTR, Manitoba's privacy laws require the community to sign an MOU between the two parties. Provincial privacy laws therefore add another legal barrier preventing communities from quickly accessing information they need to conduct searches. Legislation was drawn up to negotiate around Manitoba's privacy laws and give the NCTR more leeway, but it is still proving to be cumbersome.

When Kim Murray was the head of the Survivors' Secretariat for the Mohawk Institute Residential School at Six Nations, it took eight months to finalize an MOU with the NCTR. Murray was Ontario's first-ever assistant deputy attorney general for Indigenous justice, from 2015 to 2021, working with communities to revitalize Indigenous laws and legal orders. Before that, she was the executive director of the TRC. If it took *her* eight months, imagine the time it would take others without her extensive legal background. In the end, she received access to five million records.

For Cowessess's purposes, in the Saint-Boniface trove of records, Lavallee was hunting specifically for blueprints of the livestock barn. She found them. The blueprints held a clue to why the dogs had gone wild: the Oblates had poured a concrete floor.

In the early fall of 2022, the Cowessess team began to search the barn once again.

ONE OF THE most powerful talks at that first gathering was given by a young Mohawk leader, Six Nations Chief Mark Hill. I heard frustration and the brimming anger of incredulity in his voice, present in every word.

He told a packed Westin ballroom that the amount of time it takes to secure agreements to gain access to government and church records is simply ridiculous. "Identified deaths related to the Mohawk Institute have doubled based on research and records we now have. Some of the challenges that we've gone through include putting the agreements and the MOUs in place with the National Centre for Truth and Reconciliation. We are looking at ways we can have more accessibility to the records that we need."[12] Those particular records are affiliated with the Anglican Church of Canada, the federal and provincial governments and the New England Company, the founder of the Mohawk Institute.

Barriers need to be taken down, wherever they are. And if the NCTR does not have the capacity to handle requests, it should be top of mind for the federal government and for all the provinces to make sure that is changed. The Indian agent should no longer control access to records of our people.

Nor should any other entity—especially not one overseas. The records for the New England Company are held—wait for it—in the U.K., in the London Metropolitan Archives. According to this proudly un-ironic post on the City of London website: "You might be surprised to learn that LMA holds items in the people languages of Algonquin and Mohawk. These are amongst the archive of the New England Company, the oldest English Protestant missionary society, founded in 1649 to convert the indigenous people of America to Christianity."[13]

At Six Nations, nearly 250 hectares needs to be searched. "We're searching through waters, we're searching through concrete. We're searching through buildings. The list goes on," Hill told us at the meeting. "So we're going to need the expertise and the dollars in order to do this properly. We went after $10 million to get the work started and that has to maintain on an ongoing basis. This can take years of work."[14]

Recognizing the importance of relationships, he said, is key to the search effort, and that includes the provincial chief coroner's office, the Ontario Provincial Police and all who have the authority to help Six Nations. "We have to work on those relationships. We are all relationship people."

When the discovery of the 215 was announced, Six Nations had knowledge of 52 deaths at the Mush Hole. After getting access to some key records, they've doubled that number to 104. But that number is likely to grow even more. "The majority of our docs are with the federal government and the New England Company overseas," Hill explained. Meanwhile, he said, "ground-penetrating radar work has begun, but only 2 per cent of six hundred acres have been searched to date."

Chief Hill made a plea for healing at the Edmonton gathering. He said all of us must walk a healing path. Survivors have been saying this for years, he added. "We need to be together. We have no choice but to be together. We have many missing children to bring home. The government wants to talk about reconciliation—I don't even know what the hell that word means anymore."

This is what the bathroom in the student residence at the Mohawk Institute looked like. The space is being restored by the Woodland Cultural Institute.
(Photo by Tanya Talaga)

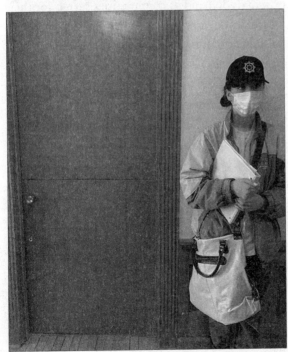

Natasha, my daughter, standing in a hallway inside the Mohawk Institute in May 2021.
(Photo by Tanya Talaga)

FAST-FORWARD TO ANOTHER Survivor gathering, nearly one year later in Toronto. I am sitting in the lobby of the Sheraton Centre. Dr. Kona Williams is trying to sit comfortably on a misshapen couch. It's awkward seating, in a busy lobby that has been jazzed up to look modern and sleek. Thousands commute in and out of this space daily. It's like a glorified bus terminal that sells wildly overpriced glasses of orange juice. A bank of escalators behind her continuously moves people up and down from conference rooms underground. Williams is here with her mother, Karen Jacobs-Williams, to attend a meeting of Kim Murray's Special Interlocutor's Office, which is taking place in conference rooms two flights down. This gathering has brought nearly five hundred Survivors and community leaders together to talk about Indigenous laws and protocols surrounding the search and recovery of missing children and other family members.

Dr. Williams is the only First Nations forensic pathologist I've ever met. The Kanien'kehá:ka (Mohawk) and Cree woman with long dark hair and a kind smile is in high demand as communities search for their lost loved ones. Many turn to her for help, for answers, for information on how to navigate their way forward in the hunt for the missing. This pause on the lumpy couch is her only respite between meetings. At the time, Dr. Williams effectively had three full-time jobs. She was the medical director of the Department of Laboratory Medicine and Pathology at Health Sciences North in Sudbury, a midsize city known for mining and its Big Nickel statue. She was on the National Advisory Committee on Residential Schools Missing Children and Unmarked Burials—a federally appointed panel that was created to help lead the recovery work happening across the country—alongside experts on archaeology, Indigenous law and criminal investigations. And she was involved in the reinvestigation of Indigenous deaths in Thunder Bay that were flagged in a provincial report as not having been investigated properly by the Thunder Bay police.

Her mom is a Survivor of Indian day schools. The school Karen attended was one of several at Kahnawà:ke, south of Montreal. Her dad, Gordon Williams, attended Birtle Indian Residential School, outside Brandon, Manitoba. "I can't even imagine what the average person would do," Dr. Williams admits to me as we talk in the lobby.[15] "It is mind-boggling to me. How would they even know where to begin? Myself, I don't know. There has got to be an easier process, there has to be.

"I can't do my job without knowing who we are looking for, without having some sort of history about how they died, because when you are dealing with bones you won't have a lot of physical evidence aside from the bones to work with. Having some idea: one, who the person is, and two, what happened around their death. I use that information to look at the physical evidence, the body, and see if it matches what I see.

"Does it match with what could have happened or am I seeing a completely different story than the more subjective information that I've been told? My job is to get the subjective information and compare it to the scientific and medical facts, the objective facts and information. If there is a disconnect, then those questions need to be answered."

Which brings us to the importance of having accurate records.

"If we don't have an idea of who this person might be in front of us, the trail of trying to find these kids is hard. The records are falsified, they are incomplete. They are lost or not being released. Those are all important for us to find people—to just identify somebody, we need to have an idea of who we are looking for. Who this person might be. To get the samples to be able to prepare family members to identify them. If we don't have that, all we have is human bones, and that is really all we've got.

"Human bones don't tell the whole story. There is a whole life story behind the bones. We get a small piece. There is a whole bigger piece around anyone who has died, but with bones, that part is small."

THE INCONSISTENCIES AND mistakes in the records we are left to work with, when we do find them—be it baptism, marriage or death records or residential school records—often mean we have to spend hours and days, months, years aimlessly hunting for grains of truth.

Along the James Bay coast, it is Paula Rickard who consistently helps us fill the voids with the people we've lost. On September 8, 2023, during the final editing of this book, Paula sent me an email: "Your great-uncle John Samson has been found! I found a death record for John Sampson. He died on May 13, 1905. The death record indicates his age is unknown, but we know he was born in 1892, making him about 13 years old when he died."

I felt sick reading this—he was so young, just a child, not even ready for high school.

Paula was more hopeful. She wrote, "Did John manage to escape the horrors of residential school? I hope he did, but, maybe he did later in his young life."

Again, the mistakes in the death record were pronounced. It was a miracle Paula had found him. John's last name, Samson, was misspelled with a *p*. His place of birth was listed as Moore Factory, not Moose Factory. There is no Moore Factory in Ontario.

His residence was listed as Biscotasing. The town of Bisco, as it was known by locals, sprung up just north of Sudbury in the 1880s. It started as a railway workers' town, an access point for the CPR train and the southern Great Lakes. In 1887, the HBC set up a store there and it became a hub for First Nations trappers and traders. Apparently, it was a rowdy place, with bars, brothels and lumber mills.

The death record indicated John was single and his occupation was labourer. What barely thirteen-year-old boy lives as a labourer?

No, this record contained only a fraction of a clue about John's hard, harrowing life, only a glimpse of the true story of what really happened to him. It left me with an even bigger hole in my heart—why wasn't he with his mother Annie? How did he wind up in a place time forgot, in a town now listed on ghost town websites?

Chapter Seven

ANNIE AND THE SIGNING OF TREATY 9

OUR EGGS HOLD OUR SECRETS. PASSED DOWN THROUGH OUR MOTHERS, THROUGH the womb, regenerating, carrying forward the lines of our families, whichever corners of the earth they come from. They also carry our lived experiences, our love and pain. Eggs travelling like beavers swimming in the rivers, moving gently but purposefully before stopping and deciding that this is where they should make their homes. When they have chosen carefully, they begin to fortify, to ensconce themselves in the place they have chosen to gather wood and make a sanctuary, a place of safety as they multiply.

Beavers represent one of the seven Anishinaabe Grandfather Teachings. These are teachings that the Anishinaabe have used to guide themselves since time immemorial. Many First Nations have their own versions of the seven teachings, passed down through the generations. Each carried by its own animal, they teach us how to lead a good life, mino-bimaadiziwin. The seven teachings are:

Zah-gi-di-win, or love: to know love is to know peace. This teaching is brought to us by the eagle, because the eagle has the strength to carry all the teachings on its back. Love is a force, it is fire, ensuring everything is possible.

Ma-na-ji-win: to honour all of creation is to have respect. The buffalo teaches us about respect, as the buffalo gives every part of itself to keep us alive—the skin, the fur, the meat, the bones. Honour the buffalo, honour yourself.

Aak-de-he-win: to face life with courage is to be brave. Bravery is represented by the black bear. Strong and protective, the bear protects its kin. The bear gives us strength to face our toughest enemy, ourselves. The bear gives us the spiritual strength and tools we need to survive.

Gwe-ya-kwaad-zi-win: to walk through life with integrity is to know honesty. Honesty is taught to us by the sabe, or sasquatch, a tall, animal-like being that lives in the forest, comfortable in its own skin, not pretending to be anyone else.

Dbaa-dem-diz-win: to accept yourself as a sacred part of creation is to know humility. Humility is the wolf. Being part of a pack ensures survival, and everyone in a pack has a role, knows their role and acts with humility.

Nbwaa-ka-win: to cherish knowledge is to know wisdom. The beaver teaches us wisdom, carrying the truths of the ages from their very beginnings. Wisdom comes from experience, it shows us the way.

Finally, debwewin: truth, the turtle. The turtle has been with us since the beginning of Creation and the turtle carries all of the teachings on its back.

To know these seven teachings is to know the truth.[1]

These seven grandfather teachings carry me forward on my journey to try to achieve mino-bimaadiziwin, or the good life. Not a life full of material things, of fancy clothes and cars, lots of money and fine wines, but a life that lives up to the teachings we have been given. A set of instructions from the Creator to nudge us along and remind us that we are part of a community. As an Anishinaabe, I am connected to the earth, the air, the sky and the water, to the four-leggeds and to the trees. We are all bound by the same circle. Our circle is community: everyone has a place, everyone has a role to keep the whole strong and intact. None are not worthy or not wanted. If our circle is broken, we all experience a spiritual break. The search for Annie is the reclamation of the circle.

IN FEBRUARY 2019, I gave the Pelham Edgar Lecture at Victoria University in the University of Toronto. It was a busy time. I was giving many talks around the country after the publication of my first two books. I had spent four years as a student scraping by at Vic with horrible grades, spending most of my time working on the campus newspapers, frustrated with my studies.

The Pelham Edgar Lecture sounded pompous. I knew Edgar's name but I couldn't quite figure out where from. It nagged me.

I walked into the Senior Common Room, a space that, as an anonymous student, I had never seen. There was a roaring fire, big leather chairs, lots of portraits of older, white faces, and one of the man himself: Oscar Pelham Edgar. Born in 1871, the same year as Annie, he had a distinguished career in education after earning a PhD from Johns Hopkins University. He started off as a teacher at the elite Toronto boys' school Upper Canada College and was a member of various writing clubs that, it is safe to say, did not have any Indigenous members: the Athenaeum Club of London, the Tennyson Club of Toronto and the Canadian Society of Authors, to name a few. Eventually, he became head of the Department of English at Victoria College. Ironically, I was about to give a lecture named after the man whose department I'd flunked out of because I could not wrap my head around what the major British authors were saying.

Also in the room, the only other Nish face, was Riley Yesno. I'd met Riley the spring before, when she was a high school student in Thunder Bay. She'd told me she was planning to study at U of T. As soon as she arrived for her first year, I hired her to be my assistant, and she accompanied me to many events just like this one.

As we stood glued together surrounded by the colonial haze that permeated the Ivy League room, a woman came over to us and took me by the hand. She held it, tears rolling down her face. She said she was Edgar's great-granddaughter and she apologized—a blanket apology for what her great-grandfather had been a part of by his very presence. I didn't know what she was talking about. She explained that he had been best friends with Duncan Campbell Scott, and that in 1906

he accompanied Scott as his secretary on a journey through northern Ontario. The purpose of the trip? Negotiating Treaty 9. Indeed,
Edgar's name is listed on the original treaty as the secretary. He wrote
it all down and witnessed what was negotiated. He was there, speaking
and listening, observing and recording vital historical facts that made
the country of Canada what it is today.

Still holding my hand, the woman said she had some things she
wanted to give me: photographs taken by Scott himself and letters, hundreds of them, that Edgar had written to his wife back in Toronto. He
loved her and missed her, so he wrote to her near every day, and sent the
letters in batches when he could. The woman said she'd been wanting to
donate these letters—they were tucked away in an old shoe box underneath her bed—but she wasn't sure who to give them to. She recognized
they were of historical significance, but she did not think it would be
right to give them to a museum or a university. She wanted to give them
back to the people, to the descendants of those in the photographs.

After reading *Seven Fallen Feathers*, my first book, about the deaths
of seven First Nations youth forced to move to Thunder Bay for a high
school education because there were no high schools for them in their
home communities, this woman decided she should give the letters to
me. She said these families in the Treaty 9 communities were the ones
who needed them.

The lives of those seven have resonated with people around the
world. (They were called the "seven fallen feathers" because Christian
Morrisseau, the father of one of the students, Kyle Morrisseau, was tired
of media calling his son one of the "seven dead students.") Five of the boys
died in and around the waters of Thunder Bay, and the other two died
in their boarding homes. Each of the seven was from Treaty 9 Territory.
Jethro Anderson, fifteen, was the first to be found, in the Kaministiquia
River on November 11, 2000, one month after Dennis Franklin Cromarty
High School, or DFC, opened in Thunder Bay. He was in Grade 9.
Curran Strang, a beautiful singer, was eighteen, from Pikangikum First
Nation, and his body was found in the McIntyre River on September 26,
2005. Paul Panacheese, from Mishkeegogamang First Nation, was

twenty-one and still trying to get his high school diploma—he had been in ten different boarding homes before his mother Maryanne decided to move to Thunder Bay and give him some stability. He died on November 11, 2006, of medically undetermined causes. Robyn Harper was eighteen; she had only been in Thunder Bay for three days before she died on January 13, 2007. Poplar Hill First Nation's Reggie Bushie was also fifteen years old and in Grade 9. He was at DFC with his older brother Ricky. His body was found in the McIntyre River on November 1, 2007. Kyle Morrisseau, a painter and grandson of the famed Ojibwe artist Norval Morrisseau, was seventeen. His body was found in the McIntyre River on November 10, 2009. Webequie First Nation's Jordan Wabasse, fifteen, also in Grade 9, was last seen on February 7, 2011, by his boarding parent. His body would be found in the Kam River on May 10.

The Thunder Bay Police Service was heavily criticized for its lack of investigation into every single one of these deaths. The seven became the focus of a provincial inquest that ended in 2016. The jury had 145 recommendations, many of them identical to the Truth and Reconciliation Commission's calls to action: calls for equity and basic human rights, including the right to a proper high school education. The coroner's inquest prompted another report, by an arm's-length agency of the Ontario Ministry of the Attorney General, that called for a reinvestigation of four of the seven deaths.

Riley and I were stunned by what Edgar's great-granddaughter had told us. There is so little record of what happened during the signing of Treaty 9 just over a hundred years ago. Besides their historical significance, these letters and pictures could potentially help in the ongoing litigation against Canada and Ontario over their failure to live up to the terms of the treaty. The Omushkego have long argued that there were oral components to the treaty that have never been fulfilled.

I told Edgar's great-granddaughter I knew exactly who needed to get those letters: my friend Alvin Fiddler, then Grand Chief of Nishnawbe Aski Nation. NAN is the political treaty organization that covers the vast area of northern Ontario: all of Treaty 9 and part of Treaty 5, stretching from the Manitoba border to Hudson Bay to James Bay. I'd gotten to know Alvin and NAN well when I wrote about the Seven Fallen Feathers. I invited Edgar's granddaughter to the Assembly of NAN Chiefs that was scheduled later that spring in Toronto so she could meet with them herself.

It was because of the lives of the seven and their story that I had been asked to give this lecture. The strength of their spirits is mighty, their individual life stories reaching out and leaving their mark on many. And there I was, standing with Riley, whose relation was one of the signatories of Treaty 9 in Eabametoong, or Fort Hope First Nation, along the Kistachowan. It felt somewhat fated that the news of those precious letters be given to us to take back to everyone else.

What I didn't know then was that Annie was also tied to this meeting. For Annie was present on July 12, 1905, for the original signing of Treaty 9 at Osnaburgh Post, an HBC trading post at Lake St. Joseph, where the Albany River begins. Annie's name is on the original paylist, a list of the very first annuity payments that went out in Treaty 9. She received sixteen dollars, eight for her and eight for her daughters. She and Christina would permanently be recorded as members of Osnaburgh's community, which would later revert to the name our people called this place: Mishkeegogamang, the swampy lands.

Two months after the lecture, Edgar's great-granddaughter attended the NAN Spring Assembly at the downtown Toronto Chelsea Hotel. (We call this hotel the Chelsea First Nation because so many northerners stay here.) She arrived with the precious letters and photographs tucked in a backpack slung over her shoulder. We began the meeting in ceremony. She stood with those pieces of our history in the upstairs ballroom in the presence of the NAN drum, with the Chiefs of forty-nine Nations standing around it in a large circle. The smells of tobacco wafted over all of us as the room was smudged by Elders.

The papers she held, not seen for over a hundred years, told of, and included images of, the ancestors of those standing in this very room, listening to the pound of the ceremonial drum, the welcome song, signalling the start of the gathering, cascading and echoing off the ballroom walls. The letters and photographs had come home.

=

THERE IS A picture of Duncan Campbell Scott sitting like royalty in the middle of a cedar-stripped canoe that I found one night in scholar John Long's incredibly detailed book about the signing of Treaty 9. His book, 624 pages long, is a treasure trove. Many Nish consider it the go-to for an accurate description of what happened when the treaty was signed. The copy I was riffling through was loaned to me by Alvin Fiddler, whose father Moses had witnessed the signing of the adhesion to Treaty 9 in 1929. The photograph shows eight Indians paddling while Scott is seated, enjoying the view. That picture was taken as he was being propelled up the river to negotiate and sign Treaty 9.

Scott, who was born in Ottawa to Scottish parents in 1862, had entered the federal bureaucracy when he was seventeen years old. The son of a Methodist preacher who worked with the Indians, Scott was a pianist, a romantic, a penny-pincher and an occasional drinker who loved an adventure.[2] He originally took a job in the bureaucracy, offered to him by Sir John A. Macdonald as a favour to his father, because he wanted to save money to attend medical school. Who could have predicted how he would flourish in the civil service, helping to build the infrastructure of genocide that ruined so many lives?

In 1894 he married Boston violinist Belle Warner Botsford. They had one child, Elizabeth, born in 1895, who would die at age twelve in Paris, one year after the work on the first phase of Treaty 9 was completed.

Working in the Department of Indian Affairs must have suited Scott's lust for life and fed his superiority complex. His friend Oscar Pelham Edgar wrote of him, "For many years he has been the formulating mind in the general policy of the Department, and his value was recognized by his appointment in October, 1913, to the rank of Deputy Superintendent General of Indian Affairs. He is thus, under the Minister, the permanent head of a great Government service."

Treaty 9 was the only treaty Scott orchestrated from start to finish. The treaty encompasses a vast area that is roughly twice the size of New York State. It brought ninety thousand square miles into the country now called Canada. His work getting the Anishinaabe and Cree into treaty, along with his highly regarded standing in Ottawa society—by

1899 he was a Fellow of the Royal Society of Canada—would serve him well. Eventually he'd serve as president of the RSC, and in 1927 he was awarded the Lorne Pierce Medal for merit in literature. The society still exists as a national council of distinguished Canadian scholars, humanists, scientists and artists (it is also known as the Academies of Arts, Humanities and Sciences of Canada). And back in the early twentieth century, it was exactly as exclusionary as it sounds, being described as a "closed white male club akin to those that operated in London, Oxford, and Edinburgh. In many respects, *who* Fellows knew was as important (if not more) than *what* they knew."[3]

Indeed, the RSC was the most influential think tank and gathering space for all federal leaders and Canadian captains of industry. Scott had immense power within the group. According to Carleton University history professor Ian Wereley, Scott "was one of the most active contributors to RSC discussions about race, colonialism, and Indigenous issues in Canada. Crucially, Scott's views about these topics were not confined to his poetry. Rather, Scott sought to influence conversations and policies on the ground." Scott's ambitions with regards to Indigenous Peoples went even further, Wereley reports: he wanted to count and record all the white and the Indian "races" in Canada and build ethnology museums showcasing them.[4]

Scott believed in imperial expansion, the rule of law and the superiority of his "race." He never questioned the methods used to civilize and Christianize the Indian because he thought the Indians lived in "squalor, dejectedness and intemperance" and that they needed to be fully enfranchised in the Canadian way of life.[5] He clearly subscribed to the belief that, to be fully effective, efforts to assimilate Indians had to start early so that every part of a child's former life was erased.

To ensure this happened, the Indian Act was amended in 1894 to give the department the power to commit children to industrial or residential schools. In 1920, under Scott's direction as the highest-ranking civil servant in charge of Indians, the act was further amended to require that all Indigenous children between the ages of seven and fifteen attend a residential school.[6] In 1924, to further strengthen these heartless laws,

Canada made it illegal for Indians to hire lawyers without the approval of the Department of Indian Affairs.[7]

Scott is infamous for uttering these often-quoted lines in 1920: "I want to get rid of the Indian problem. . . . Our object is to continue until there is not a single Indian in Canada that has not been absorbed into the body politic, and there is no Indian question, and no Indian Department, that is the whole object of this Bill."[8]

To Scott, Indians were pathetic creatures, part of a dying race and culture that would soon be swallowed up by history, "wandering between two worlds, one dead, / The other powerless to be born."[9]

Did Scott feel he was doing our Peoples a favour by bringing them the treaty, forcing them to conform to the British Canadian way of being? Teaching them how to have a stiff upper lip and to adapt to an "acceptable" way of life based on Christian truths and values? Is that what he told himself as he was helping to shape policies that would crush people's lives for generations? Did he know? Worse, did he care?

SCOTT NEGOTIATED ONLY one treaty in his career, and that was Treaty 9. He was definitely a man of his time, emboldened by his position representing King Edward VII and Canada. As has been outlined in this book and in his own writing, he thought of us as a dying race. His task was to take the land, the resources, everything he could get, claim it for Canada and do away with the Indians. By making treaty, he promised all Ojibwe, Cree and Oji-Cree who signed a paylist four dollars annually. It remains the same amount today.

Accompanying Scott were Indian Affairs commissioner Samuel Stewart and the Province of Ontario's representative, Daniel George MacMartin. Stewart was Presbyterian and Irish, and ten years older than Scott. He was the one with the neatest handwriting. (In 1906 he would be replaced by Oscar Pelham Edgar, the man whose granddaughter gave Nishnawbe Aski Nation those letters.) MacMartin was a miner and came from a family of British Loyalists.

All three were avid diarists who wrote endlessly about what it was like to travel up the rivers and meet with the Ojibwe and Cree. They rarely mentioned women or children, preferring to focus on the men they were meeting.[10] Scott, an amateur photographer, took hundreds of photographs of his journeys along Kistachowan in the summer of 1905. He used a No. 1 Folding Pocket Kodak Model C camera—state of the art at the time.[11]

There was also a young doctor travelling with them, Alexander George Meindl, and rounding out the party were two Dominion police officers. Everyone assembled in the bustling rail town of Dinorwic, northwest of Lake Superior, near modern-day Sioux Lookout, to begin their trek into the interior waterways to Kistachowan.

SHORTLY AFTER THE treaty party launched, they found themselves near Frenchman's Head at Lac Seul, a First Nation that is part of Treaty 3, negotiated in 1873. James Bunting, Annie's cousin and the council-lor in charge of the band, came out to meet the travellers, who were somewhat stuck in an area of rocky rapids.[12] (Dorcas Bunting, Annie's grandmother, had died of influenza in Frenchman's Head in 1899.) Noticing that Scott's party was having a difficult time, weighed down by supplies and baggage, Bunting offered the help of a dozen local Nishnawbe to help them over the Ishkaqua Portage.[13] This gave them the push they needed to reach Lac Seul's Hudson's Bay post on July 6. This is one of a couple of times my relations would come into direct contact with Scott.

Lac Seul's trading centre was a busy meeting point for many coming from the smaller HBC hubs in Mattawa, Minnitaki Lake, Frenchman's Head, Wabaskang and one near Savanne. The lake, Obishikokaang, meaning "pine-covered point," is deep, beautiful and dark. The French called it Lac Seul, "the lonely lake." By the time of Scott's arrival, the fur trade had begun to wane. Gold had been discovered beyond the lands allotted to Lac Seul after the signing of Treaty 3, and mining had started to gain a foothold in rugged land of thousands of lakes and pristine forests.

Today, Lac Seul is adjacent to Sioux Lookout, a town of four thousand frequented by American hunting tourists in the summer. It is a regional health-care centre, with many from surrounding First Nations coming down for doctors' appointments, to see a dentist or to access social services. Until 1998, the town was also the site of the Sioux Lookout Zone Hospital, previously known as the Sioux Lookout Indian Hospital, part of a racially segregated hospital system set up for Indigenous people only. Indian hospitals started off as tuberculosis sanatoriums or were attached to residential schools, but they soon became general hospitals. They were not opened out of concern for Indigenous people. In fact, the opposite was true. The federal government began the Indian hospital system in the 1930s out of fear: non-Indigenous Canada believed Indigenous people could be more infectious than others.[14] There were twenty fully functioning Indian hospitals in Canada by the 1960s, and they represented a form of apartheid. Indian hospitals were chronically underfunded and understaffed, and those who worked in them often did not have the same training as those hired by regular hospitals.

An incident occurred at Lac Seul that is worth noting as it demonstrates Scott's complete disregard of First Nations ceremony and how his experience fuelled his racist poetry and law-making. When Scott and the party arrived at Lac Seul, hardly anyone was there to greet them. Most everyone was at the community for a white dog feast. The practice of the Anishinaabe Midewiwin is eternal. The Midewiwin is, essentially, the grand medicine lodge in charge of ceremonies, the deep holders of our ways of life, language and songs. At the white dog feast, hand drums beat all night long. Sometimes a shaking tent ceremony, where we communicate with the spirit world and ancestors, is held. During this time, ceremonial rites are performed for days. The Midewiwin teach us how to live our lives according to our Seven Sacred Teachings, in order to achieve mino-bimaadiziwin, the right state of being, the ethical way to live as Anishinaabe.

Our ceremonies follow a series of laws and have been performed for thousands of years. But in those days, when Scott arrived, dancing and practising "pagan" ways was no longer allowed. Section 114 of the amended 1895 Indian Act outlawed ceremonial practices: "Every Indian or other person who engages in, or assists in celebrating or encourages either directly or indirectly another to celebrate, any Indian festival, dance or other ceremony . . . is guilty of an indictable offence and is liable to imprisonment for a term not exceeding six months and not less than two months."

Scott heard the drum, and that must have annoyed him. He got his team together, including the two police officers—one was waving a giant Union Jack—and they arrived where the ceremonies were taking place to find about twenty tipis and tents pitched.[15] Scott thought he could intimidate the Anishinaabe with the Union Jack and that the police would cause a "wholesome fear of the white man's law."[16]

The treaty party of commissioners, Duncan Campbell Scott, Samuel Stewart and D. George MacMartin, arriving at Long Lake. This is how they would have appeared arriving at Lake St. Joseph, Osnaburgh, in 1905. There were seven "white men" in the party—the three commissioners, two police constables, one doctor and the transportation officer—along with their Indigenous guides. (Duncan Campbell Scott fonds / C 275-2-0-1-S7640 / Archives of Ontario)

A well-known Chief and member of the Midewiwin, Pow-wa-sang, was pointed out to the party as one of the men in charge of the gathering. Scott lectured everyone there about how this type of behaviour was outlawed. He then ordered a feast at the HBC post. That evening, as everyone feasted, Scott suddenly came down with a violent illness and could not attend.[17] No one else was sick, just Scott.

Besides being a photographer, Scott was a poet, popular in his day and long revered as one of Canada's "Confederation Poets," whose personal biases came out clearly in his words. Some still see him as a literary giant and believe that he should be celebrated as a man who wrote eight volumes of verse. In 2017, while editing my story on the suicides of seven First Nations girls, a copy editor at the *Toronto Star* challenged my characterization of Scott as a genocidal bureaucrat, someone she knew as a "great Canadian poet" she'd studied while an English lit student. If you are Indigenous, you do not know Scott as a great poet. You know him as a racist, a classist and someone who willingly allowed thousands of First Nations children to die.

After Scott's time in Lac Seul, he wrote a poem, "Powassan's Drum," clearly based on the Midewiwin who was in charge of the ceremonies he'd called to a halt. To Scott, Pow-wa-sang was a threat to progress, a conjurer of things Scott could never understand and was repulsed by. In his eyes this was anti-civilization and anti-Christianity.

> *Is it the memory of hated things dead*
> *That he beats — famished —*
> *Or a menace of hated things to come*
> *That he beats — parched with anger*
> *And famished with hatred — ?*

Scott finishes the poem with an image of a headless Indian, which can be read as symbolic of the end of the "race" and, as such, the lack of all rational thought in the mind of who he considered an "Indian."

The next morning, Scott and his party left Lac Seul and headed out to the Albany River watershed.

═══

THERE IS A photograph on an Ontario government website that celebrates the story of Treaty 9, and it stopped me cold. It is a beautiful picture, capturing a large family in a white birchbark canoe on a body of water. The family looks surprised, wary. All eyes are on the person taking the photograph: Duncan Campbell Scott.

The photo shows Joseph Carpenter, Annie's oldest brother, with his wife and five children. We know this because Scott has labelled the photo "Joe Carpenter and family." Joseph has a brownish hat perched on his head, his paddle in the water on his left. His round-faced children stare at the photographer. All but one wear cloths or hats on their heads to protect them from the hot July sun.

Joseph met Scott and the three treaty canoes on their way to Osnaburgh. This was Scott's first stop on the signing tour, at the head of the mighty Kistachowan.

Samuel Stewart, the secretary, wrote in his journal about the meeting with the Carpenter family. "While taking lunch at noon on an island we were joined by Joe Carpenter, his wife and five children from Osnaburgh, who informed us that the Indians had been waiting for us at that place for the past three days, and that as they had little or no provisions he had come out to catch some fish to keep his family from starving."[18]

Joseph knew the river well. HBC records show that he'd followed in his father Jean-Baptiste's footsteps and worked for the company as a trapper. Joseph spoke Cree, Ojibwe and English. Scott recorded his name as Shabokeshick, meaning Through the Sky. Joseph's wife, Mary Maung, was Anishinaabe from Osnaburgh, and their children—including Joseph Jr., Clara and Josiah—were with them when they took Scott and his party on to Osnaburgh.

The "entertaining" Oombash would also have known the area well, as he, too, was from the Osnaburgh area, which comprised Lake St. Joseph and a community on Cat Lake.

"Osnaburgh was the first point at which treaty was to be made and we felt some little anxiety as to how the Indians would receive our proposals," Stewart wrote. They asked the Indians to appoint representatives to speak with the commissioners, and after they were selected,

Stewart said they asked many questions about whether they would be forced to stay on the reserve land set apart for them, and if their hunting and fishing rights would be harmed. Stewart said he assured them that "they could continue to live as they and their forefathers had done, and that they could make use of any lands not disposed of by the Govt."[19]

I couldn't believe it when I first saw this photo. It is of Annie's older brother, Joseph Carpenter, and family. Remarkably, it was taken by Duncan Campbell Scott, who was leading the Treaty-making party to then-named Osnaburgh, an HBC trading post. (Canada. Dept. of Indian Affairs and Northern Development / Library and Archives Canada / a059662-v8)

By the time Scott was canoed in to Lake St. Joseph, on the way to the shore at Osnaburgh, his policies would have already seen thousands of Indigenous kids being sent to their deaths at schools such as Kamloops, Cowessess, Île-à-la-Crosse and St. Anne's, their broken bodies and spirits filling shallow graves that we are only finding now.

THE OSNABURGH TRADING post was established by the HBC at the head of Kistachowan in 1786. It was built at the site of a large lake that had been a gathering place for the Anishinaabe for at least a thousand years.

Families moved in big hunting groups and would meet there. Before the fort, there wasn't a permanent settlement. When Scott arrived, it comprised several wooden houses separated by fences more than six feet tall and made of thick white birch trunks.

The families who had gathered at the post that summer had heard about the potential of treaty, and they were all there waiting for Scott. The men wore Western-style clothes: dark pants, white button-down shirts, felt fedoras, pageboy hats. A few also wore vests or jackets. The only thing Indian-looking about them were the moccasins on their feet and their long, black hair, tied back neatly.[20] Their appearance was something Scott would later comment on and commend them for.

Missabay, the spokesperson, was the kind of person who stood out in a crowd. He was a blind man and a dapper dresser with a confident stance. Photographs taken by Scott show him in a dark fedora, white shirt and dark business suit, his hair a perfect thick bob.

With the provisions brought by the commissioners, a feast was held inside the walls of the Osnaburgh fort. Scott's photo of the feast shows the bounty of food being prepared. There are piles of bannock—rounds of white bread easily made with flour, lard and water—and large metal pots with the lids off. Stewart noted in his diary that the bannock had raisins in it. He wrote that there was bacon, pork and tea, plus a supply of pipes and tobacco. Dr. Meindl described the assembled folks as being in very poor health, the men small, their upper bodies underdeveloped, evidence of malnourishment. Everyone had scabies, a pimple-like rash caused by mites burrowing under the skin. More than half of the Indians had lingering tuberculosis. This was all the result of the destruction wrought by the fur trade: the near extinction of the animals leading to the near extinction of the people.

In Scott's picture, all the families who came to listen to the terms of the treaty, with dapper Missabay in the middle, are gathered around, waiting patiently for the feast to begin. They are there in their Sunday best, seated up against the walls of the post and the surrounding fence. Men sit on the left, women on the right, in skirts, with children in their laps.

We know Annie Carpenter was among them, with her daughters Christina and possibly baby Lizzie (my great-grandmother), her brother Joseph and his family, and her sister-in-law Charlotte Carpenter, her brother Charles's wife, and their two school-age children, John and Sarah. They were all assembled because, on the morning of July 12, Chief Missabay said they had all decided that "it would be much to their advantage to enter into treaty."[21] After it was agreed on, the gratuity payments began. According to the records, 350 people were recorded and given their $8 payments, a $4 annual payment, plus an extra $4 for signing the Treaty.

Treaty paylists gave Paula and me an indication of who in our family was where in the early twentieth century, and they gave us clues as to what could have happened to others. For example, a notation on one later Treaty 9 paylist says that Charlotte Carpenter's daughter Sarah was believed dead for nearly five years but had turned up alive at the Washakada Home for Girls, part of the Elkhorn Indian Residential School near the Saskatchewan border. As such, Ottawa was commencing her annual treaty payments and providing back pay. The Anglican-run Elkhorn school comprised two facilities, Washakada and the Kasota Home for Boys. Many children at Elkhorn came from northern Manitoba, but others came from Alberta and northern Ontario.

Was Annie in the photograph Scott took before the feast? Is that her holding on to my great-grandmother as they wait patiently for something to eat? Is one of the little girls Christina?

Since we have no written account from Annie, no letters or diaries from her, we are left to piece together what we can of her life and that of her children and husband Samson. The census of 1901, four years earlier, shows Annie and Samson were living in the Matagama-Algoma area, south of Weeneebayko on the traditional Omushkego hunting grounds. The census shows them living in an area known as Pontiac, on the north shore of the wide Ottawa River. Directly down the centre of the river runs the Ontario-Quebec border. This area, now known as Outaouais, was named after an Odawa chief named Obwandiyag, or Pontiac, who led a revolt against British-held Fort Detroit in 1763 that touched off a larger pan-Indigenous rights movement.[22] That movement is credited with how the Royal Proclamation of 1763 was worded. With it, the British tried to gain Indigenous loyalty by saying that Indigenous People reserved all lands that were not ceded or taken from them.[23] The proclamation paved the way for the treaty arrangements that soon followed.

PAY-LIST of *Osnaberg*

Band No.	NAMES.	Men	Women	Boys	Girls	Total	Amount Paid.	Amount relapsed to Dept. for Absentees.	No. on previous Pay-List.
	Brought forward	13	12	14	11	50	392 00		8 00
95	Myginecootchageneno	1		1	1	3	24 00		
96	Satchekelau	1				1		8 00	
97	Ashayokiisie	1	1			2		16 00	
98	Okitick	1	1	3	3	8	64 00		
99	Achepegayenene	1	1		2	4	32 00		
100	Ouassowan		1			1	8 00		
101	Shaywaiskung	1	1			2	16 00		
102	David Skunk	1			2	3	24 00		
103	Clara do		1		1	2	16 00		
104	Simon do	1	1	4	3	9	72 00		
105	Thomas do	1	1		2	4	32 00		
106	Amelia Swampy		1			1	8 00		
107	Wassay Keesic	1	1	1	2	5	40 00		
108	George Waywanishkung	1	1		1	3	24 00		
109	Philip Skunk	1	1			2	16 00		
110	Wassaykeesic's Mother		1			1	8 00		
111	Papsay		1	1		2	16 00		
112	Moosewayass	1	1		2	4	32 00		
113	Winwaywaynughee		1			1	8 00		
114	Annie Samson		1		2	16 00			
116	Charlotte Carpenter	1	1	1		3	24 00		
		26	30	26	31	113	872 00	32 00	
	Dominion Indians	53	71	70	68	262	1736 00	360 00	
	Total	79	101	96	99	375	2608 00	392 00	
	Absentees deducted	13	17	9	10	49			
	Total	66	84	87	89	326	2608		

This paylist gave me a huge clue about Annie and her life. The Osnaburg Treaty paylist of 1905 identify who was recorded as a "Treaty Indian" for the first signing of Treaty 9. Annie Samson is here—by now she was using Samson's first name as her last name. Her sister-in-law Charlotte Carpenter is with her. (RG 1-273-5-2-1_006 / Archives of Ontario)

In the nineteenth century this area had been lively with traders, with both North West voyageurs and HBC traders moving along the river. The James Bay Cree's traditional hunting territory reached far south, down this river system, and in Annie's day there was a collection of "Indian" families who moved to and fro over the Quebec-Ontario border. It astounds me that Annie and Samson canoed and portaged through water systems and lakes, moving south hundreds of kilometres, with two small children.

Also on the 1901 census were Sarah, their daughter, who was six years old, and their son Johny, nine. Bizarrely, the French census taker recorded the children as being "Algonquine," while Annie and Samson were "Crie." These are two distinct Indigenous People—Algonquins are Anishinaabe, and the Cree are Ininiw. Algonquins live on a vast unceded territory that includes the Ottawa River Valley.

Paula had already found Johny's death record, dated 1905. He had died of pneumonia in Biscotasing, north of Sudbury, aged thirteen. And we know Samson died around 1905, though we didn't know how. But what happened to Sarah? Why wasn't she with Annie at the treaty signing? How come we can't find any trace of her after the 1901 census? And where was their other son, James? Did they drown on the fast-moving Ottawa River, the highway for the French fur traders from Montreal? Was it illness? Or had the children vanished into the residential school system?

It was Paula who found the Matagama census. It took her months, combing through Library and Archives Canada, ultimately finding them under another wildly incorrectly spelled last name. Samson and Annie Wemaystikosh were Samson and Anny Ewimistignish. The census said Sarah was born on the Abitibi River and brother Johny at Sucker Lake. Samson was listed as born in Moose Factory and Annie in Marten Falls, the first community up the Albany River. This might be true or it might not, but since she lived on the land with the Carpenter family, it is not out of the realm of possibility that that was where she was born.

But by 1905, Samson had died, and Annie must have been living by her wits, leaning on her eldest brother Joseph to survive. Of Samson and Annie's five children, two had died and two had vanished from the record; only the youngest was still with her. Annie would surely have been carrying the burden of their absence and, if they were at one of the schools, most likely feeling a constant, nearly unbearable worry over their well-being. She would know that other children in her community hadn't made it home from the schools. Did she suspect hers might not either?

What she did know, by this point in her life, was just what it meant when a white man became involved in the lives of her people. She had tasted it. She'd lived attempted assimilation and was still churning through it, figuring out how to survive. After all, she had grown up with a father who worked as a servant for the HBC. Now her existence was desperate, she was in total free fall, with two small girls. The treaty she'd been a part of, the four-dollar annuity she would receive from the government, wasn't going to fix that. Nor would it much improve the lives of anyone else in her community.

It wasn't supposed to. On the contrary. Duncan Campbell Scott, the man who'd been paddled to Osnaburgh like royalty, was one of the key government officials who would see to that. It was his job, and he believed in it wholeheartedly.

After the first signing of Treaty 9, the team left for Fort Hope, where they met others—including Riley Yesno's relation—who would argue against treaty but grudgingly agree to it.

Scott and Commissioner Stewart returned to Ottawa in October of 1905. The coming cold weather would make river travel impossible for the treaty party. Scott, along with Pelham Edgar as secretary, would return in 1906 to finish signing up communities. Over the next two years, the treaty commissioners travelled throughout Ontario's north.

As to what happened to Annie and her children, we have no idea until another record appears: a St. John's Mission record of her 1908 marriage to prospector Joseph Gauthier. A marriage record does not mention children, but where were they? Where were Elizabeth, James, John, Christina and Sarah?

TODAY, DINORWIC IS a blink-and-you-miss-it town. I've driven by it several times on my way to Sioux Lookout. It is little more than a road sign. But Dinorwic Lake was once home to an HBC trading post and bustling community called Wabigoon. There was a CPR station busy enough to have a night operator. Steam locomotives ran regularly along the line, on their way across the country to and from Montreal. There was a restaurant that doubled as a bar. When the National Transcontinental Railway line (later merged into the CNR) was being built, construction companies had their headquarters here.

This was also the place Annie Samson, by then a widow, listed as her home when she married Gauthier. Dinorwic is just north of Wabigoon Lake Ojibway Nation, on the shores of what is now called Dinorwic Lake. Witnesses to Annie's second marriage were from Wabigoon. The Wabigoon post had traders coming in from Fort Hope, Osnaburgh, Lac Seul and Savanne. All waterways were connected. A series of smaller rivers got you to Savanne, the last community in the southeast corner of Treaty 3 Territory. Beside Savanne was the rail community of Raith, on the traditional territory of Fort William First Nation, part of the Robinson-Superior Treaty that was signed in 1850 along with the Robinson-Huron Treaty.

A witness to Annie and Joseph's marriage was James McKenzie, a sixth-generation HBC trader and son-in-law to Jabez Williams, the chief HBC trader in charge of the Osnaburgh post who'd played host to Duncan Campbell Scott and his party there. McKenzie was a staunch supporter of the Church of England.

Annie listed her occupation as a domestic. She was starting her life over again at the age of thirty-eight in a marriage that, for her, might have been largely based on survival. At this time in newly colonized Canada, Annie would have been wise to her limited options as a widow with toddler Liz (and four other children of, possibly, unknown whereabouts). In early twentieth-century Canada, Indigenous women were the lowest of the low, with no rights and often treated like commodities. The "country wives" concept still held strong: women were scooped up by traders to act as wives on their journeys inland. They kept their houses and bore their children. Some men stayed, some did not. They often abandoned or disposed of their wives when they were done with them.

Annie did what she had to do for herself and for her daughter—the only child left, of six. She scratched out an existence, depending on her kin, on her brothers and sisters, nieces and nephews. Just like her, tens of thousands of other Indigenous women were doing the same. They have repeated these patterns of survival from long before the founding of Rupert's Land and for generations since.

ONE OF THE most disturbing accounts of the making of Treaty 9 comes from Duncan Campbell Scott himself. He wrote a lengthy article for *Scribner's Magazine* in 1906, supplying photographs to illustrate it.[24] In it, he let fly with all his classist and racist biases. The piece clearly states the dominant feelings of the British ruling class of Canada at the beginning of the twentieth century: "Indians" were a dying race and needed to be conquered, put into service for the rest of the country.

"In the early days the Indians were a real menace to the colonization of Canada," Scott's piece begins. "At that time there was a league between the Indians east and west of the River St. Clair, and a concerted movement upon the new settlements would have obliterated them as easily as a child wipes pictures from his slate. The Indian nature now seems like a fire that is waning, that is smouldering and dying away in ashes; then it was full of force and heat. It was ready to break out at any moment in savage dances, in wild and desperate orgies in which ancient superstitions were involved with European ideas but dimly understood and intensified by cunning imaginations inflamed with rum."[25]

He goes on to describe the treaty-making process as made up of laughable, "puerile negotiations" in which an alliance was based "on a childish system of presents." Gift giving has always been a part of the Anishinaabe way of life. It is a sign of respect, and it seals deals. Something lost on him.

Scott is most telling in his description of the signing of Treaty 9, describing it as an inevitable event: "When all the arguments against this view are exhausted it is still evident that he is but a slave, used by all traders alike as a tool to provide wealth, and therefore to be kept in good condition as cheaply as possible."[26]

Therein lies the essence of Canada: keep the Indians as slaves and make sure that they are assimilated, that they are schooled and kept in good condition. No mention here of partnership, of kindness or of a willingness for Canada and the Indigenous Peoples to engage together in a new, democratic dream of a country.

Scott knew he, and Canada, was swindling all those who agreed to sign the treaty. "What could they grasp of the pronouncement on the Indian tenure which had been delivered by the law lords of the Crown, what of the elaborate negotiations between a dominion and a province which had made a treaty possible, what of the sense of traditional policy which brooded over the whole?" he asked. "Nothing. So there was no basis for argument. The simple facts had to be stated and the parental idea developed that the King is the great father of the Indians, watchful over their interests, and ever compassionate."[27]

CHAPTER EIGHT

STEALING CHILDREN

NORTHWESTERN ONTARIO IN THE EARLY TWENTIETH CENTURY WAS FRONTIER wild, a lush land of clear-water lakes full of fish: muskie so big you could barely hold them in your hands, walleye, smallmouth bass. Prospectors had discovered the gold and other precious metals that lay beneath the ground from Sioux Lookout all the way to Kenora and through the Lake of the Woods. The discoveries caused a boom in the waning days of the fur trade. That meant working men were still coming up along the railway tracks and the rivers, looking for jobs, women and anything else they could get their hands on.

Everywhere you looked there were spruce trees and plenty of clean, fresh, sparkling water in deep lakes left behind by retreating glaciers. As Winnipeg, just a hundred kilometres west along the highway, began to prosper, the city turned to the Kenora area to meet its immense, endless thirst. As was the custom of the day, Canada ignored the terms of Treaty 3 with the First Nations in the area and signed a deal with Winnipeg to start siphoning the water away from Iskatewizaagegan, a community about seventy kilometres southwest of Kenora, home to Shoal Lake 39 and Shoal Lake 40, two Anishinaabe communities that had been established at and around the lake for thousands of years. It took six years, from 1913 to 1919, to construct an aqueduct to transport water 155 kilometres from Shoal Lake to Winnipeg, a city that we can now say built itself off that reliable source of clean, fresh water—water that's still used to mix Winnipeg's concrete, flush its residents' toilets and fill their swimming pools.

It sounds unreal but it's true. A century-old dirty secret.

Every single day, 220 million to 250 million litres of water—the equivalent of about 10 million water jugs used in office water coolers—are removed from the lake and sent to Winnipeg. No thought was given to what drainage meant: all the flooding due to construction, the effect of the canal and the dike and the changes to the surrounding shorelines. Water levels in the lake went down. The wild rice beds, the habitats where blueberries grew—entire ecosystems were changed. The constant siphoning of the lake, which has continued for more than a hundred years, has significantly altered life in the communities along its shores.

Shoal Lake 39 is still fighting, to this day, for some form of compensation. In 2011, the community started sending invoices to the City of Winnipeg for its water usage.[1] Shoal Lake 40 did sign a deal in 1989 regarding payment for the water, but their friends and relatives at Shoal Lake 39 were not part of that agreement.

It used to be a steamer could easily run between the mainland and Cecilia Jeffrey Indian Residential School, which was on its own island in the middle of Shoal Lake from 1901 until 1920. I have driven past the island where Cecilia Jeffrey once was, on the ice roads in the deep freeze of winter, when the full grey clouds were so low they looked like they were being held up by the tips of the tall spruce trees.

In 2019, I was in Iskatewizaagegan, researching for a podcast series I was writing called *Seven Truths*. I met Chief Jerry Lewis and attended a community meeting and feast. I was researching the teaching on honesty, about the failure of Canada, the City of Winnipeg and the Province of Ontario to live up to the Treaty 3 rights of the Anishinaabe. Treaty 3 was signed on October 3, 1873, and it encompassed 55,000 square miles from west of Thunder Bay, Ontario, over into Manitoba.

There were always issues with the steamer boats getting from the mainland to the school. Water levels in this area, where the channel narrowed, would fluctuate. Boats would break down. That meant labour and supplies—food, tools, equipment—didn't always get to the school when they were needed.

From 1908 to 1911, Presbyterian church officials exchanged a number of letters with Duncan Campbell Scott, the deputy minister of Indian Affairs, and the Department's secretary, J. D. McLean, about the water and discipline problems at Cecilia Jeffrey. In 1908 McLean sent over a rocket from Ottawa to the Presbyterian Reverend R. P. MacKay explaining that the location of the school was "badly chosen, it being difficult to reach at any season of the year. The site is low and impossible to drain, owing to the water in Lake of the Woods being raised by the heightening of the dam."[2] Further, he wrote, the school was cold, without reliable heat or running water.

Those weren't the only problems, McLean wrote. There were serious management issues and questions of the competency of the principal, Mr. Dodds. In his letter, McLean told MacKay that "the last inspection report on the Cecilia Jeffrey Boarding School does not leave a very favourable impression of this institution. The discipline is lax, the Principal being indulgent and disinclined to excite the hostility of parents, and, owing to his being overworked, cannot give effective supervision to the school." McLean went on to say the children were not "warmly clad, although there were ample supplies of unused clothing on hand furnished by the Woman's Foreign Missionary Society. The bedding was insufficient and not clean."

Beyond this, in 1917 the Shoal Lake band Chiefs had been trying to get rid of Dodds, informing the department that he was "incapable of running the school." None of the children wanted to go to Cecilia Jeffrey because of Dodds's viciousness.[3] The letters and complaint show the department was well aware of serious problems at Cecilia Jeffrey while it was under Presbyterian rule. The children were not well cared for and the letters describe consistent and brutal corporal punishment.

By mid-1917 Dodds had been removed, but the letters show that things did not improve at Cecelia Jeffrey.

When I was driving by the school with Chief Jerry Lewis, the snow crunching beneath our tires on the ice road, I didn't know that I had a great-great-aunt named Christina. I didn't know that Annie had lived close to this area, or even that she had any children from that time in her life. Driving on that cold winter's day past a grey island that once housed a school full of bad memories, I did not know one of Annie's children was likely a student there. I was so close, yet so far away from the ghost of her.

And I could never have guessed the legacy the Cecilia Jeffrey school—named after the first secretary in charge of "Indian work" at the Woman's Foreign Missionary Society in Kenora—would have over my extended family.[4] The imprint it would leave, the erasure.

Not only was it possible that Christina was connected here, but it is certain that her daughter Christina was a student there, and that her children were also students there. Unknown to me when I drove by, generations of my extended family attended Cecilia Jeffrey, a school made famous by Chanie Wenjack, a boy from Ogoki Post, Marten Falls First Nation, who died while running away from the school in October 1966.

Cecilia Jeffrey Indian Residential School, which three generations of my relations attended, was torn down in the 1970s. All that is left are the sidewalks that lead to nowhere. (Photo by Tanya Talaga)

In *Seven Fallen Feathers* I write extensively about the circumstances inside Cecilia Jeffrey during the period Chanie attended the school. I interviewed and spent time with many of Chanie's family members, including his sisters Pearl and Daisy Wenjack, as well as Chanie's cousin, Elder Sam Achneepineskum. I visited the site of the second school, which opened in 1929 on a sixty-eight hectare farm at Round Lake. That school was demolished years ago, and hardly any trace of the building remains.

A barbed wire fence surrounds the property. There is an area where a graveyard sits. The rolling ground slopes gently downwards. Worn and decaying wooden crosses popped up every so often. Towards the other end of the vast yard, near the lake, there is an old metal swing set, a baseball diamond and, farther along, a memorial stone to all the children who died at the school.

Besides the physical, mental and sexual abuse going on at the school, something else was happening. Something state-sanctioned and unconscionable: medical, nutritional and starvation experiments on children. Six schools were targeted for such experiments from the 1940s until 1952. Doctors wanted to see how children's bodies reacted to dietary changes, especially as they fought off viruses. Parents did not know about these experiments, and no consent was ever sought from them or from the children.[5]

THE SUMMER OF the start of the First World War, the principal of the Cecilia Jeffrey school was the Reverend F. T. Dodds. Letters in the Library and Archives Canada reveal students running away was a constant problem and that First Nations families in the area knew Dodds as a violent man who liked to whip the boys. They had begun refusing to send their children to the school.

The Department of Indian Affairs had to act. They enlisted one of their most formidable inspectors, Methodist missionary John Semmens, who was based in Winnipeg, to see what the problems were. Semmens, who was constantly seeking to expand enrolments at Church of England schools in Manitoba—and who had a special talent for finding children to bring to residential schools and keep them full—was only too eager to help.

A former minister from Cornwall, England, Semmens may have believed he was doing the work of God, but his actions ripped apart Indigenous lives in Manitoba and Ontario, tearing children away from their families forever. He'd immigrated to Canada with his mother and sister in 1860 and attended Victoria College in Cobourg. After being ordained in 1872, he left for northern Manitoba. He was a religious zealot who thrived on converting Cree and Ojibwe to Christianity.[6] Photographs capture Semmens as a man with light eyes, dark hair and an otherworldly gaze. A man who, with his first wife, Helen Kalista Behimer, was father to seven sons of his own.

On paper, to colonial governments of the day, Semmens was exceptionally qualified, just the kind of God-fearing man they were looking for. But he had developed a reputation throughout Indigenous communities as someone who stole children and took them away to school. And he would eventually become deeply entwined in the life of Annie's daughter, Christina Samson.

But long before that, in 1874, he opened a Methodist mission station at Nelson House, which he ran for two years, a time that he loved and fondly remembered, saying that his work there "resulted in the complete eradication of paganism and a purified society." He was known to do the same in Berens River, Poplar River, Little Grand Rapids, Fisher River and Pikangikum, spreading the word of the Lord to Indigenous people.[7] While posted at Berens River, teaching at the Methodist day school, he referred to the Saulteaux People as "hard" and full of the "viciousness of their heathen ways."[8]

He did not enjoy working in white settlements, as the pay was less. In 1884, he begged to be transferred to Norway House, where he could have a secure, regular salary and not rely on parish congregations to pay him. While he was at Norway House, he learned how to speak Cree. He worked with translator John Sinclair to transcribe two hundred hymns, as well as John Bunyan's *The Pilgrim's Progress.*[9]

In 1894, the Methodist Board of Missions recommended Semmens be appointed to the Department of Indian Affairs so he could become principal of the new Brandon Industrial School. Semmens studied how to be a headmaster by learning the ropes at Manitoba's Elkhorn Indian Residential School and Qu'Appelle Industrial School in Saskatchewan.

A note here about Elkhorn. The school was the grandiose vision of Methodist missionary Edward Wilson, a man who was already running the Shingwauk and Wawanosh Indian residential schools in Sault Ste. Marie. Elkhorn was a feeder school for Shingwauk and vice versa. Even though they were thousands of kilometres apart, their Anglican denomination tied them together. Like Semmens and the Cecilia Jeffrey school, Wilson had an impact on my family. My great-grandfather's two brothers spent their brief lives at Shingwauk: the residential school Wilson built would be the only "home" they ever knew.

Wilson's vision was to construct a series of schools across the country called "branch homes," including one in Banff and another in Sarnia.[10] He managed to gain support for his vision in the United States, in England, in Ottawa and in the Anglican Church. In 1885, he received a $1,000 donation from a businessman from Elkhorn, a George Roswell, to begin construction on his branch home for girls. The school was also funded by other Canadians who wished to aid in the assimilation process.[11]

These schools were placed far away from any First Nations or Métis community on purpose. Students couldn't run away—there was nowhere to run to. This made it easier to assimilate them into white farming families and society. Wilson was endlessly fundraising and was somewhat successful at convincing white folks they were doing the morally righteous thing in saving a class of people not at the same level as themselves. This was, he contended, the work of the Lord.

Also of note were the channels of mutual influence between Wilson and his friend Col. Richard Pratt, a Presbyterian American war hero who established the Carlisle Indian Industrial School in Carlisle, Pennsylvania. Pratt had served as an officer on the western frontier, helping to "settle" the West. He participated in two of the Indian Wars—the

Washita campaign of 1868–69 and the Red River War of 1874–75—and then helped run a prisoner-of-war camp. He was still on active military duty while he served as head of the Carlisle school from 1879 to 1904.

Wilson and Pratt shared an unfailing belief that Indigenous Peoples needed saving, and that they were the men to do it. Being a captain during the period of the ending of slavery, Pratt was not just invested in the "Indian problem"; he was seeing race and class divisions play out in front of him. His views, like Wilson's (and not unlike those of Duncan Campbell Scott), were widely shared, chiefly his belief that Indian education was a tool of "enforced participation" that would be "the supreme Americanizer."[12] His writings on the subject include arguments like this one: "These experiences plainly showed that, through forcing Negroes to live among us and become producers, slavery became a more humane and real civilizer, Americanizer, and promoter of usefulness for the Negro, than was our Indian system through its policy of tribally segregating them on reservations and denying this participation."[13]

At the time of Wilson and Pratt's friendship, there was mass Indigenous starvation across the prairies and the U.S. Plains. This was the result of a confluence of factors: the targeted killing of the buffalo by the United States government, the decline of the fur trade and the loss of big game due to overhunting by settlers around the Great Lakes. Indigenous ways of life were being obliterated with the destruction of the animal populations, thus feeding settlers' perceptions that Indigenous Peoples needed to be taken care of, shown the way—"civilized."

Ideologically, Wilson and Pratt were a match made in heaven. They regularly wrote letters to each other, comparing their schools and methods, and Wilson even went to Carlisle's school to see it first-hand. They both believed in forced participation of Indians at the schools, while neither believed in sending the children home in the summer. Instead, they were sent to work in settler homes.

From the writings of Pratt and Wilson and from the friendship that formed between the two men, we see, loud and clear, settler denialism. They convinced themselves and the public that they were doing a good thing—saving us from ourselves—with no input whatsoever from

Indigenous leadership. They were united in their goal of stealing the land and the children.

While the Brandon school was under construction in 1894, Semmens went about looking for students to recruit. By the time of the school's opening, he had "secured" thirty-eight Cree and Ojibwe children from Norway House, Brandon and surrounding communities.

How did he do it?

Children were stolen and recruited, parents were pressured and threatened in various ways all over Canada to populate the residential schools. There were pressures to fill the schools: the more students a school enrolled, the more funding it would receive from Ottawa. At the turn of the twentieth century, missionaries and their agents, including the North-West Mounted Police, roamed the land looking for school-aged children to recruit.

Money was used as an incentive to induce impoverished families to give their children up. If that didn't work, parents were threatened with having their treaty annuities withheld. Children were also often taken by force.

In 1894, changes were made to the Indian Act that gave truant officers the right to enter "any place where he has reason to believe there are Indian children between the ages of seven and fifteen years" and force them to school.[14] So now, under the Indian Act, missionaries and their agents could go into any home and apprehend children. It was terrifying.

Meanwhile, the NWMP ran loose in the West and in northern Ontario, upholding its own version of the law. It is interesting to note that its agents came from all over the British Empire. Take Francis Jeffrey Dickens, third son of the author Charles Dickens. He was a North-West Mounted Police inspector, receiving his commission in 1874. He reportedly had an "unspectacular career" that was "marked by recklessness, laziness and heavy drinking," and that could be "blamed for worsening relations between the Blackfoot and the NWMP."[15]

Implementation of the law regarding Indigenous children attending school went down like this, according to the RCMP's own report:

It is near the turn of the century. Indian agents, RCMP constables, and non-Native farmhands encircle a Manitoba Indian reserve. One of the Indian agents and an RCMP constable approach the house of an Indian family, bang on the door and loudly demand the parents give up their children to them. The Indian agent instructs the RCMP constable to break down the door. They rush into the house, pry the frightened, screaming children from their parents' arms and rush them to a holding area outside. The constable and agent go to the next house and the next and in the ensuing few days this scene is repeated many times on this reserve and on most reserves in Southern Manitoba. All children captured during the "Fall round-up" are marched to the nearest CPR station, assigned a number and unceremoniously herded into cattle cars for transport to the residential school at Winnipeg.[16]

For a family struggling to exist at a time of great social upheaval for our communities, the threat of fines, jail time or both for keeping children home and out of the hands of the Indian agents and the police drove many to go deep into the bush and not come out. They hid their children; they hid their identities out of fear. They did not want their children forcibly removed, which the state was entitled to do under amendments to the Indian Act that made it mandatory for children under sixteen to attend.

In Semmens's journal, "Notes on Personal History," he proudly details how he was able to "recruit" students for Brandon or Elkhorn. His entries on establishing the school begin with the difficulties of starting such an undertaking from scratch. "The year 1895 found me at Brandon with the duty before me of organizing an industrial school for Indian children. It goes without saying that this was no ordinary task even for one who has had some experience in this class of work."[17]

The beginning of construction was rough. "The farm was in very poor shape. The ground had not been cultivated for some time and most of it was soured bottom land covered with chameleons and lizards. . . . Windmills needed to be erected, sewage disposed of."[18] The

next line of his journal spoke to his greatest task. "The all important matter was to secure the pupils," he wrote, adding that no one
understood how difficult it was to find children and then get them to
the school from his "recruiting field" of Lake Winnipeg and Norway
House.[19] His journal speaks of how the *Winnipeg Free Press*, on July 6,
mentioned that he'd secured the thirty-eight children who would form
the first student population at Brandon. He'd brought the children
across Lake Winnipeg on a steamer ship, and he was annoyed that
the article didn't communicate how difficult it had been to collect and
travel with all those kids.

He wrote: "This item does not convey to the reader any idea of how
hard it was to secure parental consent in so many cases, neither does it
show the difficulties in the way of transporting and feeding and protecting such a crowd of youngsters of both sexes. There was no cabin
on the steamer and no bunks for us to sleep in. We were sheltered in
the freight hold, boys on one side, girls on the other, with a tarpaulin
between. I spent day and night with them to prevent any sense of loneli-
ness, to guard their conduct towards each other, to meet their small wants,
especially at night, and to prevent quarrelling and homesickness."[20]

He also wrote that the police sometimes got out of hand, men-
tioning his recruiting effort in Norway House as an example. "The officers left in charge were not always wise or kind in their dealings with
the children so that disagreements and misunderstandings arose which
had serious consequences of a wide reaching character," he wrote. There
was no elaboration on what had occurred or on the specific nature of the
"serious consequences."[21]

Besides saving souls, Semmens was hunting for students because
of the tuition money that came with them. "In the summer of 1896, I
again went north for more children so as to have the full number of one
hundred on the roll of the school. It was necessary to have our full count
of students because with a less number the income was not sufficient to
meet the expenditures."[22] He wrote of the dire straits the school would
be in were enrolment to dip. At the time, the per capita annual grant
from the Department of Indian Affairs was $110. So Semmens searched

for more children: "In order to remedy this [low enrolment], some Sioux children from Griswold [Brandon] were admitted. Another trip was made to the north and 17 more pupils were brought in. This gave us the desired number."[23]

No.

$ 4.00/100

August. 30ᵗʰ 1915.

Received *from* R. S. McKenzie.

Four. XXdollars 100

for my Annuity as No. 153, Osnaburgh Band Treaty 9. For 1915.

Witness, | *Signed in duplicate,*

John Semmens | Christina Sampson

No.

$ 24.00/100

August. 20th. 1915. 1915.

Received *from* R. S. McKenzie.

Twenty four. XXdollars 100

for arrears of my annuity for 1909 to 1914. both years inclusive, Dept Cheque No. 875, June 5. 1915. as No. 153. Osnaburgh Band Treaty No. 9.

Witness, | *Signed in duplicate,*

sgd, John Semmens, | sgd, Christina Sampson.

Why was Inspector of Indian Agencies John Semmens the witness to Christina Sampson's annuity payment on August 20, 1915? She was a member of the "Osnaburgh Band" or Mishkeegogamang, in Treaty 9. (Library and Archives Canada / RG 10, volume 6888, file 486/28-3 pt. 3)

Semmens had become so successful at keeping his schools full—in his letters he talks about rounding children up by horse and by train—that in 1905 he was promoted. He became the department's inspector of Indian agencies and schools. And that promotion is what eventually brought him to Cecilia Jeffreys and into the path of my relations.

THIS WAS A time of unprecedented growth in the Canadian residential and industrial school system. It was also the period during which Annie and her siblings were having their children. By virtue of where they lived, they found themselves in Semmens's orbit.

At this time, Ottawa had no systematic plan to construct schools across the Dominion. The "contract method," first suggested by Nicholas Flood Davin in an 1879 report, by which the government commissioned church entities to run the schools, was still in use. (Davin had been asked by Prime Minister Macdonald to conduct a study of U.S. and Canadian western industrial boarding schools to see whether similar schools could be set up in the North-West Territories. He was reportedly very impressed with the Carlisle school and how it used education to assimilate and "deconstruct" young Indians.)[24] In this context, according to scholar John Milloy, with the churches continuing to wield influence, the residential school system was growing, driven by hard lobbying by church officials in Ottawa and the "acquiescence" of the federal government.[25] Milloy points out, however, that this acquiescence wouldn't have happened without the enthusiasm of the senior staff at Indian Affairs, support that effectively gave the churches the freedom to teach Indians how to enter what government officials called a "circle of civilized conditions" via schooling.[26]

In 1879, just four federal residential schools existed, all of them in Ontario: Mount Elgin, the Mohawk Institute, Shingwauk and Wikwemikong. By 1880, the numbers had begun to grow by two to three commissioned schools per year, so that by 1904, nearly a quarter century later, there were 64 schools: 24 industrial and 40 boarding. By 1923, there were 71 schools, 16 industrial and 55 boarding, spread through every part of the country except Quebec and the Maritimes, with annual expenditures hitting $1.2 million.[27]

Not one of the boarding schools opened at this time was a departmental undertaking, and just six of the industrial schools were initiated by government officials. As described in a briefing to Superintendent General Charles Stewart in 1927, the churches were the "pioneers in the remote parts of the country, and with missionary funds have put up the buildings and induced the Department to provide funds for maintenance."[28]

The churches had a "plough and preacher" approach to education. To the missionaries, the road to civilization was through farming and learning about Western modes of agriculture. It was about learning how to become carpenters, blacksmiths, cooks and maids. It was never intended to provide enough education to become doctors or lawyers or politicians.

As the residential school system became widely established, Canada and the United States had opened their borders to European immigration to settle the Plains and grow the economy. Of course, the children of the settlers would have their own schools to attend—they would not be forced into missionary or residential schools.

In the summer of 1896, finding children to take to the Brandon school proved difficult. Semmens travelled to Norway House on a recruiting drive and found when he arrived that "stories had been circulated detrimental to recruiting." He wrote in his journal, "The missionary resident there had originated an active opposition" against taking the children away to Brandon.

Wherever Semmens seemed to go, the First Nations opposition was growing. The parents had lists of questions for him. He recorded some of those:

- Will the children return to us after their course at School?
- Is it the object of the Gov't to destroy our language and our tribal life?
- Is it the purpose to enslave our children and make money out of them?

- Can the children return at their own wish or at the wish of the parents before the term at School expires?
- . . . Will the Government keep this promise or break it as they have others made in like beautiful language? [29]

Semmens seemed to feel the parents' objections were a personal attack. But it fuelled him. Instead of "discouraging us," he wrote, "it nerved us to make a more extended canvass in the regions beyond."[30]

He went farther in his quest for children, on to Oxford House and God's Lake, "returning in due time with about twenty children."[31] He did not say how he managed to get the kids. But he did note that the journey itself was difficult. "Many stormy lakes had to be crossed and the portages were numerous and swampy. The weather was adverse and the mosquitoes intolerable."[32] It was hard, he wrote, to feed and care for the children in the wilderness with few supplies and no one around to help.

He also wrote that the children were excited when they saw the school in Brandon, which was located on an expansive 130 hectares: "Astonishment knew no bounds. The thought of such a palatial building becoming their future home was to their minds quite overwhelming."[33]

That is one way to describe how the children might have felt. Another could have been horror.

Eventually, the reach of the Brandon school would be vast, far greater than anyone could have predicted, especially First Nations leadership, who, when they'd negotiated Treaty 5 in Manitoba, had been led to believe they would be receiving schools in their home communities. Chief Jacob Berens, a practising Methodist in Berens River, on the east side of Lake Winnipeg, hundreds of kilometres from Brandon, was incensed when he learned where the school was being built. His community had not been notified of where the school would be located, and they were not part of the plans. That lack of consultation and communication went against the terms of the treaty, which stated that the government would "maintain schools for instruction in such reserves . . . whenever the Indians of the reserve shall desire it."[34]

Chief Berens protested, writing in August of 1891 to the secretary general of the Missionary Methodist Society to voice his outrage, imploring the church not to take the children so far away. "Our hearts are sad for we cannot think of sending our children away, such a long distance from their people and their homes . . . we love our children like the white man and are pleased to have them near us."[35]

When that letter did nothing—the society replied that the decision was already made and dismissed the community's concerns—Chief Berens went to the top: the inspector of Indian agencies in Ottawa. "We heard we were likely to get Indian industrial schools in this Agency, and we were glad and would have been willing to send our children to the Institution. But now we are informed that . . . only one is to be established and that at Brandon, we cannot really think of ever sending any of our children so far away from our reserves even for the purpose of getting an education."[36]

It was to no end. The Methodists wanted their own school, on farmlands, and they didn't want it located near any of the Anglican schools, which they viewed as competition.[37]

Everywhere Semmens went, he faced opposition from the Chiefs. No one wanted to send their children far away. The Methodists dismissed their concerns and, using the force of the law, took the children. And they didn't just do it in the province of Manitoba. They extended their search into Ontario—to Kenora, Sioux Lookout and communities stretching to the Manitoba border. Going west, they went all the way to central Saskatchewan to take children.

By 1900, one hundred students were enrolled at Brandon. However, when Norway House Indian Residential School opened in 1901, the numbers started to decline, and officials increasingly looked to northern Ontario for students. That same year, Semmens's wife, who had been paralyzed in a horse and buggy accident, died.

Meanwhile, Semmens's diary makes clear that his enrolment was dropping for other reasons as well: the children were dying of illness. He called these times "nights of anxious waiting and watching." And he said it was "sad beyond measure" that they had to bury the children so far from home. "Distress keen and trying was felt when in hours of extreme illness the dear children longed for their dusky mothers and their humble wigwam homes."[38]

Eventually, Brandon Indian Residential School earned such a bad reputation for harsh discipline and poor nutrition that, by the 1940s, Saskatchewan First Nations refused to send their children there. The school finally closed in 1972.[39] In June 2021, the Sioux Valley Dakota Nation announced that 104 potential unmarked graves had been discovered at three sites at the former school. Only 78 graves could be accounted for in the records. Since 2012, the Sioux Valley Nation has been looking for the lost and missing children who attended the school.[40]

Early in the twentieth century, though, John Semmens was still holding things together despite dropping enrolment at Brandon and the loss of students' lives to illnesses that could surely have been prevented. By the time he received an SOS call from Principal Dodds at Cecilia Jeffrey Indian Residential School in early 1914, he was a seasoned hand, not just at scooping up children and forcibly taking them away to residential schools, but at keeping those troubled, damaging institutions afloat.

SO, WHERE WAS Canada while all of this was happening? When Indigenous children were being "kidnapped"—the RCMP's words, not mine[41]—and transported out hundreds of kilometres away, even out of province, for school?

One of the most prominent female writers and social activists of the time was Emily Murphy. The daughter of a newspaperman, Emily was a national literary star who travelled the prairie with her family. She wrote magazine articles and books under the pen name of Janey Canuck. Her book *Janey Canuck in the West* was widely popular.

Murphy would go on to become a suffragette, one of the Famous Five who secured the right for women to be considered "persons" under the law. Well, some women—not Indigenous women. They were left out of the efforts by the Famous Five, women who are lauded all over Canada now as fighters for equality. There is a statue of the Five on Parliament Hill, and there is even a Famous 5 Foundation, which extols the Fives' virtues. On its website, the foundation does point out the "flaws" in some of the Fives' reasoning, including support of the forced sterilization of Indigenous women, but mostly they are celebrated as "champions of the rights and welfare of women and children." The site declares that "they worked hard and courageously in the face of the prejudices and resistance of the day. Together, they formed an unstoppable force that changed the world for women in Canada and in all Commonwealth countries."[42]

Emily Murphy spent some time at Elkhorn in 1902, at the request of Principal A. E. Wilson, the son of the school's Methodist founder, Edward. She did not have anything kind to say about the young Indigenous women she encountered there, calling them lazy and loose. "A freshly recruited girl from the Reserve is not always promising material, she is often taken from a hut or tepee . . . She is wretchedly ignorant of the simplest sanitary laws and the yoke of restraint lies heavily on her. Very often her vocabulary seems restricted to the words 'I dunno' or 'I won't.'"[43]

Reading instalments from *Janey Canuck in the West*, it's clear that Murphy's suffragette ideals were meant only for white people, including settlers from Europe. She saw nothing but destruction in the future of Indigenous Peoples. She believed they would someday become extinct. "Regarding his future, we may give ourselves little uneasiness," she wrote. "This question is solving itself. A few years hence there will be no Indians. They will exist for posterity only in waxwork figures and in a few scant pages of history. However brave and game they may be, there is nothing for them in the end but death. They have to reckon with invincibility."[44]

Emily Murphy, a believer in and supporter of eugenics—preventing Indigenous reproduction to control their population—was made an honorary senator by the Canadian Senate in 2009 for her work with the Famous Five in advancing the rights of women in Canada.[45]

It must be acknowledged that Murphy was merely reflecting the classist and racist beliefs of many who were now settling the Canadian

West. Newspapers of the day echoed Murphy's prejudices. A headline in the *Regina Standard* on November 26, 1896, atop an editorial decrying the amount of money spent on Indian education, read "A Sumptuous Indian Palace." The paper was referring to the $301,000 that had been allocated in the federal budget to cover the cost of "Indian education in the Territories." That sum was for fewer than a thousand Indian children. The paper was incensed. "It is a little hard to imagine how the education of Indian children can be made, legitimately, to average over three hundred dollars per head." That amounted to a dollar a day, it protested. "The Spectator does not wish to be misunderstood in the matter. It is quite content that our young Indian wards should be dealt with on lines of the broadest philanthropy; but there is such a thing as philanthropy run mad. There is an old aphorism which tells us to be just before we are generous; and another which says that charity begins at home."[46]

BY LATE 1915, there was a surge in the number of students being admitted to Kenora-area schools, including the Presbyterian Cecilia Jeffrey and its Catholic counterpart, the Kenora Boarding School, which was run by the Grey Nuns until 1911, when the Missionary Oblates of Mary Immaculate took over. That year, in a note to the Department of Indian Affairs, Indian Agent R. S. McKenzie wrote that he had received a letter requesting that the department increase its number of pupils to seventy, as the school had "ample room."[47] The former Rat Portage Boarding School opened in 1897 on the picturesque Lake of the Woods. In 1906 it was renamed the Kenora Boarding School. The Oblates owned just over twenty hectares of land adjacent to the Rat Portage Indian reserve, Wauzhushk Onigum. The Kenora school had another name change, to St. Anthony's, then another, to St. Mary's in 1938.

The children who came to the Kenora Boarding School did so not just from all over the Kenora area but from all the way to Thunder Bay and from farther afield: from down into southern Ontario; to Wikwemikong, or Manitoulin Island; to Temagami and Maniwaki in Quebec; and into Manitoba, all the way to the community of Sagkeeng

First Nation, on the banks of the Winnipeg River. Like the Methodists and the Anglicans, the Catholics would search far and wide to find and capture students for their school.

I do not know where Annie Carpenter's young daughter Elizabeth, born in 1904, went to residential school. But according to Uncle Hank's records, she was rebaptized as a Roman Catholic in 1911. Elizabeth had been baptized in the Anglican Church in 1907, when she was with her mother, Annie Samson, in Nipigon, an HBC hub northeast of Thunder Bay. In 1911, her name was changed to Gauthier. She and her younger sister Louise—Joseph Gauthier's daughter, born in 1911—were baptized by an Oblate priest.

Did Elizabeth attend the Kenora school? After searching the available attendance records from the school, we could not find her. We have two slim clues from her daughter Bernice, my great-aunt, who told me, "Mom used to say the nuns taught her how to bake bread." And: "She said she went to residential school in Kenora." Whatever happened to Liz at the schools, it was so awful she never spoke of it. But she came out of the system a staunch Catholic.

The Kenora school was large, three storeys high, with a semi-basement. It was imposing enough to be visible from the water. As with all residential schools, it was red brick, with a centre-hall design and steps leading up to the grand front doors like a tongue leading into a dark mouth. The school was famous for hockey. Many of the students played, taught by the young priests. St. Mary's is said to be the model for Anishinaabe author Richard Wagamese's St. Jerome's Indian residential school in his beloved novel *Indian Horse*.

The school also had a graveyard full of tiny white crosses, according to photographs of the grounds taken in the early twentieth century.[48] In December 1913, a couple of years before the Indian agent received the letter from Kenora asking for more pupils, the school had experienced a smallpox epidemic that saw the entire school under quarantine.[49]

The requested enrolment bump happened at Kenora even though the school had a history of violent and abusive treatment of the students. Several year later, in 1922, parents were complaining about the new principal, Father Hervé Kerbrat. Indian Agent McKenzie forwarded these complaints in a report to Scott. Boys in their late teens were running away because they were "afraid of being punished by the principal." Kerbrat, parents had said, "went to the Indian houses with a gun, and frightened them, that he carrie[d] a knotted bootlace with him for the purpose of hitting the pupils."[50] Other parents complained of girls being whipped and beaten by a priest, their hands and feet tied together and put in the cellar for hours at a time. "The chiefs grand child was shut up in the toilet (an outhouse) with her hands and feet tied together. And this kind of humiliation was continued for 4 days."[51]

This photograph of children standing in front of the Roman Catholic St. Mary's Indian Residential School in Kenora was taken in 1929. In early 2023 Wauzhushk Onigum Nation (Rat Portage) announced 171 possible anomalies were found on the grounds. (Société historique de Saint-Boniface, Oblats de Marie-Immaculée Province oblate du Manitoba / Délégation (0096), SHSB24377)

The parents complained but to no avail. Father Kerbrat denied any of this occurred.

According to the Truth and Reconciliation Commission, thirty-six children lost their lives at the school that is now mostly referred to as St. Mary's. Survivors of the institution have always maintained the number was far higher. From enrolment alone, that is plausible. Between 1897 and 1972, more than six thousand children passed through St. Mary's. In January 2023, 171 "plausible burials" were discovered on the former grounds. The graves were mostly unmarked except for five grave markers.[52]

Meanwhile, at Cecilia Jeffrey, the problem with Reverend Dodds resurfaced and caused Indian Agent McKenzie to ask for help once again. "I may say that there appears to be some friction between the Principal and Pupils, what it is I do not know," McKenzie to Scott in March 1917, "when I visited the school in January last in Company of Inspector Semmens, there was trouble then. A girl had ran away in the night, and a boy the next day, I got the two brought back and thought all was going to be well, but it did not stop there."[53] The older children kept running.

"There is sure something wrong out there," McKenzie continued, begging for Inspector Semmens to return and investigate. He added that if the children are returned to the school, "they should be transferred at once to the Elkhorn School."[54]

Government and church officials who were in positions of power could have stopped the abuse but they didn't. Instead, administrators such as Principal Dodds were protected, their actions explained away. One Indian Affairs inspector reported, "When the Principal enforced discipline he displayed considerable temper possibly forgetting his own strength, without realizing the subjects of correction were only children after all."[55] However, the inspector added that Dodds is a "godly man" and it is "hardly likely he would resort to corporal punishment."

The case of one young boy, Wilfred Redsky, was singled out. He ran away at the end of December 1916 because he had been punished by hand-strapping for writing a "suggestive" letter to a girl. A few weeks later, the boy's father brought him back to the school and lodged a complaint against the principal for cruelty.[56] The following August, before school started, Wilfred "ran into the woods and hid while the other children were being taken away," read the agent's report. But authorities took him back. "A week later the father returned and by force took the lad away in his canoe."

The report notes that Redsky was summoned to explain why he had taken his son. He said: "Because he did not want his children killed."

Like other parents, Annie would have had no authority to stop the transfer of her children to residential schools. She would have had no say regarding where they were sent. They would simply be taken.

Did John Semmens take Christina?

And what happened to Elizabeth?

BOOK THREE

Black

When we are grown into adulthood and in the fall of our lives, we sit in the western direction. The western door leads us away from our physical life, from these bodies of blood, skin and bone. Our spirit is readying for the journey onward.

Chapter Nine

CHRISTINA AND THE GONE GIRLS

IT IS NOT THAT PEOPLE DISAPPEAR IN MY FAMILY. THEY ARE JUST NOT THERE. They are never talked about. We never hear their names. It is like they were never born.

Sometimes, it's easier if we pretend someone never existed. It dulls the pain. I wonder: Is that what Annie and Liz did? Did they keep their thoughts shut away, deep inside their minds, as they kept moving, hunting, trapping, hiding in the bush? Were they exhausted, defeated by it all, just trying to survive while everything was changing around them? Annie, her brothers and sisters and all their children were born right in the thick of it, in the mouth of genocide, thrust from the land and their very ways of being, tossed into the fast-evolving, unfamiliar world of the settlers. Their life was upended. They were no longer in control of their movements. They were confined by the Indian Act—by white Indian agents, by church officials, by police officers, by those who made the foreign laws—forced to live by their wits.

Did Annie wonder where her children were? Did she mourn their loss with every step she took and every thought she had, so that it was hard to breathe?

Or did she soothe herself by hoping that gaining an education in the white man's ways would protect her children from the life she was living? Did she worry that once her children were trained in the language and customs of the settlers—how to dress like them and act like them—they might not want to come back to her and to their former way of life?

Maybe she took comfort in believing her children weren't hungry, that they'd found love, wore nice clothes and had fancy shoes, that one day they'd come home for a visit.

Likely she was too wise for this and knew that no amount of education could protect them from the oppression that had been her fate. Did she see the faces of her missing children—John, Sarah and James—in her dreams? Did she wake up screaming, terrified they didn't know who they were or where they were from? Was her worst fear that they would come to believe she'd forgotten them?

Late one night, I was poring over the family tree I'd put together over the past year, hand-drawn on big sheets of recycled paper. Looking at all the Jameses, Johns and Sarahs in the Carpenter family, a thought crept into my mind: What if I couldn't find John, Sarah and James because they weren't with Annie? What if they were with someone else in her family instead?

Kinship raising is common in First Nations families. Sometimes, communities raise children. My mother, Sheila, was raised by her grandmother Lizzie (Samson and Annie's child). Was Annie overwhelmed? Did she give John, James, Sarah and Christina to other family members to raise? And if she did, where did they go? Were they given different names? Will we ever find them?

There are so many questions I am unable to answer. I wonder if this is how Uncle Hank felt: that someday, decades from now, things might become clearer, as more records are unearthed or become easier to find. Or maybe they are gone forever.

I HAVE WRITTEN of Annie's daughter Christina Samson, but the fact is, I didn't know she existed until this book was well under way. I now know more about her than I do about my great-grandmother Liz: Christina became the child we've found out the most about. And what we've learned is not happy or hopeful.

She appears, along with her other Carpenter relations, on the 1915 Fort Albany paylist for Treaty 9. Christina's name is there, at the bottom, underneath Charlotte Carpenter, who had a son, John, born around 1897—and a daughter Sarah, who was born in 1902. Charlotte's son Tommy, who came along in 1905, is also there.

Charlotte and Annie were frequently together on the early Osnaburgh paylists and likewise in the Indian agents' letters regarding Treaty 9 Indians who had run away and left their James Bay homes to live in other parts of the province.

Before Paula found Christina, I'd had no idea that Annie had a third daughter. She was not in the records at St. Thomas' Anglican Church in Moose Factory. How come she didn't have baptismal records like her siblings? Then again, the lack of papers is not entirely surprising. Elizabeth also had no papers at Moose Factory.

Paula has studied the files and records at St. Thomas'. She can find no Christina born among Annie and Samson's other children. To find out more, Paula contacted Luke Hunter, a Treaty 9 expert with Nishnawbe Aski Nation. Everyone in NAN territory knows Luke Hunter as "the treaty guy." He is the keeper of the records. Luke holds much of the historical information for Nishnawbe Aski Nation at its Timmins, Ontario, office, including band treaty lists. Timmins is a hub community for many coming in from the James Bay coast to access services, health care, shops and restaurants.

Luke was able to clear up some, but not all, of the mystery. He told us via email that Annie and Charlotte were both widows at the time of the treaty signing in 1905. The 1905 treaty paylists for Osnaburgh, he explained, had two versions: one that listed "Dominion Indians" (those whose hunting territories lay outside Ontario's 1905 boundaries), the other "Ontario Indians" (those living inside provincial boundaries). This is because when Treaty 9 was drawn up, Ontario's boundary extended only to the south side of the Albany River. The north side of the river was still under the control of the federal (Dominion) government. It was still part of the Northwest Territory. "Indians that had hunting territory north of the Albany River (NWT) were taken to Treaty and paid under the Dominion pay list," Luke told us.[1] "This meant that Canada was responsible for those annuities. For those listed as Ontario Indians, the group had their hunting territory on the Ontario side of the Albany River and the annuities were the responsibility of the Ontario government." With regards to my relations, he had this to share: "Annie Samson appears on the Osnaburg 'Ontario Indians' Treaty paylist for 1905. It only shows one child: girl (Christina), no husband. Her ticket is #114." Charlotte Carpenter's ticket number was 116.

In those days, every Indian in Treaty 9 had a ticket, a slip of paper with their number on it. The ticket system was used to track people who were recorded on those very first treaty signings. When someone died, their number went with them. (The ticket system has since "modernized" into a ten-digit number and an Indian status card.) Luke can tell from the treaty records when Christina Samson was paid. By 1911, she had her own ticket: 153.

Annie's daughter Lizzie Samson, my great-grandmother, was not identified on the Osnaburgh paylist, but she appears for the first time in the 1911 census for the area of Thunder Bay and Rainy River as Liz Samson, the "half-daughter" of Joseph Gauthier, whom Annie had married in 1908.

Luke had a little more information for us: "Annie, Charlotte and Christina were paid in Lac Seul. It appears they moved there."

The census suggests that Charlotte and Annie left Osnaburgh quickly. It's almost as if it was a pit stop on their way to Frenchman's Head: Lac Seul First Nation. They would live in and around there for years. In fact, there were so many Treaty 9 Fort Albany Indians living in the area that for decades, the Kenora-area Indian agents complained about their constant presence, not understanding why they would not return to their original "reserves" on Treaty 9 lands. Censuses show that other James Bay coast families, such as the Wesleys and the Goodwins, were constant companions over generations.

Coincidently, Luke Hunter is also a relation of mine, something I learned during our correspondence about Christina. One day he wrote: "My great grand father was also named Charles Carpenter and had a daughter Sara, she married Abraham Hunter. This is from my dad's side. The Carpenters are listed in Fort Severn in census records, and Attawapiskat, Fort Albany and Winisk paylists. Sara's family end up at Lac Seul. We have family there including New Slate Falls."

Charles Carpenter, born in 1846, was Annie's uncle, her father Jean-Baptiste's brother. Sara was born in 1880 and married Abraham Hunter of the Hunter family in Winisk, home of Louis Bird, the Omushkego storyteller and historian whose story of Cha-ka-pesh begins this book.

The Indian agents had no true idea about the nature of our peoples, how they moved in large, interconnected circles and had done so for thousands of years. Of how we were in constant motion with the river, unaccustomed to paylist tickets and checking in with Indian agents annually so they could keep track of us. The agents were the evil hand, holding out the carrot of the treaty annuity payment while also holding, behind their backs, the big stick of the Indian Act, which they waited patiently to use. The agents insisted on keeping tabs on every single family. Every birth added an Indian to the roll, while every death took one off. And every marriage of a Native woman to a white man meant the woman lost her Indian status.

The agents' clear frustration with how difficult it was to keep track of us would be comical if it weren't so insulting. There is a whole digital reel in Library and Archives Canada containing documents about trying to keep track of all the Fort Albany Indians that were moving up and down the river. When I read through it, I was stunned to find both Christina's name and Annie's, to find Annie's sister Jane and her sister-in-law Charlotte—these Carpenter women and their whereabouts. After knowing nothing for decades, reading the Indian agents' letters about my family members, written to Ottawa and to the office of Duncan Campbell Scott himself, was like throwing a door open to the past.

This, from an exasperated R. S. McKenzie, the Kenora agent, in April 1912, to J. D. McLean, assistant deputy and secretary of the Department of Indian Affairs, regarding Treaty 9 Indians living in Lac Seul: "Would you kindly inform me if I am to pay the Fort Albany

Indians, now living at Lac Seul, as I have done the past two years or not?"[2]

Annie Samson in particular seemed to be giving him a headache.

Also Mrs. Carpenter, of the Osnaburgh band? There is another No. 114 of the Ontario Indians? Named Annie Sampson. This is supposed to be the Mother of the Girl we sent to Elkhorn School last summer, Christina Sampson. Now this Annie Sampson it appears has been drawing the girls money for a number of years, and has never done any thing for this girl, having left her with her Grand Father, and went off with some other man, so I am told.

Would it not be well, to have this girl place[d] on her own ticket and paid, instead of allowing this woman to draw the money."

Despite the letter's cranky tone, McKenzie signed off politely at the bottom with, "I have the honour to be, Sir, your obedient servant."

Who knows what Annie's reasons were for keeping Christina's money. For Indigenous women, options for making a living were limited: they could either become a domestic servant or get married. If Annie didn't know where her daughter was, had she given up hope? Was she keeping the money safe for her, hoping she'd come home? Maybe her husband, Joseph Gauthier, had demanded the money.

A few months later, evidently still awaiting instructions regarding Annie, McKenzie sent a telegram to McLean. It read: "Will I pay Fort Albany and Osnaburg Indians now living at Lac Seul or not if so what about Christina Sampson at Elkhorn school answer quick."[3] McLean's reply came by telegram just two days later: "Pay Treaty Nine Indians as usual and return Christina Sampson's money to Department."[4]

The word that screams out at me from this exchange is Elkhorn.

The Elkhorn Industrial School was in another province, near the Saskatchewan border, nine hundred kilometres away from Osnaburgh, the First Nations community Christina was recorded at on the 1905 paylist. The school was shockingly far from Lac Seul First Nation where many of the extended Carpenter family lived.

In that same reel, there is a further clue about Christina from three years later, in 1915, via a Treaty 9 paylist notation made by the ever-diligent McKenzie, who always accounted for every penny dispensed. He wrote in minuscule handwriting on the far right of the ledger that Christina was already paid her five years of back treaty pay, so she'd only receive four dollars for 1915. "This girl has been paid her arrears for 1909–1914. $24.00 Dept. cheque no. 875 of June 5th, 1915. Copy of her receipt is attached."[5]

McKenzie also made a note regarding Charlotte Carpenter's daughter, but gave no name for her. This must have been Sarah Carpenter, as they were first cousins, and they were both at Elkhorn.[6] McKenzie notes that this girl was also owed two years of back pay, in this case because the department had thought she was no longer alive. "Girl reported dead 1914," McKenzie writes, adding that this was an error and that she was, in fact, "No. 0188. At Elkhorn Industrial School."

Both girls, Sarah and Christina, would have been teens when this 1915 paperwork was completed. Which means they'd been taken away as little girls. Stolen by white men in suits or police uniforms, or maybe by those carrying crosses and preaching the word of God to children who would not have understood a damn thing they were saying.

Christina and Sarah would have arrived at Elkhorn, 105 kilometres west of Brandon, days after leaving home, to find they had left the bush and were at a functioning farm in the middle of the Prairies: fields as far as the eye could see. Were they frantic? Petrified? Crying for their mothers?

As told in the previous chapter, Elkhorn was founded by Methodist missionary and minister Reverend Edward Wilson, who was also the founder of the Shingwauk Indian Residential School in Sault Ste. Marie. Reverend Wilson was an eccentric thinker, an avid letter writer and doodler. He documented all that he did and drew constantly: simple, comical charcoal sketches of his travels, his ten children and, curiously, the floor plans of people's houses. Wilson was convinced that the only way to "solve" the "Indian problem" was through schooling.

He so believed in teaching the "word of the Lord" to Indians that he envisioned a system of residential schools built across the country on his own model. Elkhorn was part of that vision. Students there would be trained as farm workers and labourers, to grow crops and milk cows, to be carpenters. They were being groomed for a life of servitude. They toiled away on 260 hectares owned by the federal government, located about six kilometres away from the school buildings.[7] In 1944, four decades after Christina's and Sarah's arrival, an inspection found that 28 per cent of girls and 70 per cent of boys at Elkhorn were underweight and malnourished.

How did Christina and Sarah come to be taken out of one province and across another? Were these young girls threatened by authorities? Were their mothers?

And here is a question I can't help wishing I knew the answer to: Were they taken by John Semmens, the Methodist missionary and eventual Indian inspector who was so well practised at apprehending children in order to keep his schools full?

By the time Christina and Sarah were taken away to school, Semmens was a feature at Cecilia Jeffrey school in the Kenora area, having been brought in to deal with "problem" children there. One of his methods for helping deal with such children was to take them to Brandon or to Elkhorn, to prop up the numbers at those schools. Were Sarah and Christina problem children? Or where they just unlucky: girls with mothers but no fathers on the scene, making them easy pickings?

Did the girls travel to Elkhorn by car or truck? Or by train?

The Canadian Pacific Railway was hammered down through Canada over four years between 1881 and 1885, bursting through settlements, appropriating land. The hurry was fuelled by politicians' fear that the United States would begin to annex land north of its border, and by the belief that a transcontinental railway was an economic necessity for a young nation trying to establish itself—required for moving goods and people from one coast to the other.

But the CPR did more than simply connect a growing nation and buoy its economy; it was also a vector of disease, delivering smallpox, measles and influenza to populations in the north and west that were already struggling with tuberculosis and starvation. The train made it easier for fur traders and trappers to travel, so more of them came, which in turn led to a depletion of the big game animals that families and communities had relied on for centuries.[8]

The completion of the railway further crushed Indigenous Peoples. Treaties in the west were signed under duress because people were starving. As James Daschuk writes in his groundbreaking book *Clearing the Plains*, by 1885, when the railway was finished, the "subjugation of the treaty population was complete."[9] The stage was set for large-scale settlement and agrarian capitalism.

Besides driving colonization and spreading disease, the train was used to transport stolen children. The sight of the Canadian Pacific Railway trains—the iron horses that took them away from their families, homes and communities—must have filled children with fright. Ushered onto the trains, they would have had no idea where they were going, who was taking them or why. Some Survivors, in testimony before the Truth and Reconciliation Commission, referred to them as "trains of tears."[10] Here's how Larry Beardy described his first train trip, which took him 1,200 kilometres away from Churchill, Manitoba, to the Anglican school in Dauphin: "There was a lot of crying on that train. At every stop . . . children will get on the train, and then there'd be more crying, and everybody started crying, all the way to Dauphin, and that's how it was. That train I want to call that train of tears, and a lot [of] anger and frustration."[11]

Trains were used frequently in Nova Scotia to carry students to and from Shubenacadie, the only Indian residential school in the Maritimes. It operated outside Halifax, in the central part of the province, from 1930 until 1967. From the RCMP files in 1938: "Girl en route from Shubenacadie. Indian Agent requested that RCMP meet the girl at the train station and hold the girl for him. RCMP met the CNR train at Union Station and brought [the girl] to the Detachment. The Indian Agent picked up the girl at the Detachment and then drove her to Fredericton in the evening."[12]

In Nazi Germany trains were used to transport children and those being sent to forced labour and concentration camps. In Canada trains were used to transport Indigenous children forced to attend residential schools. Train conductors watched over children, RCMP files note, securing their transfers to secondary trains or other modes of transportation.[13]

Whether Christina and Sarah were taken by Semmens or another missionary or agent, whether they were sent by train or by other means—to me, it makes no difference. They were stolen.

The Indian Act sanctioned their kidnapping.

BEING STOLEN FROM her community and transported to another province to attend residential school irrevocably altered Christina's life—and also Sarah's. I do not know what happened to Sarah. Neither Paula nor I can find any records of Sarah's whereabouts beyond the dates in the documents mentioned earlier.

And the scant records we could find of Christina's whereabouts and movements throughout the rest of her life make this woefully clear: she was left to survive cut off from home, from family, and from who she was. She never managed to reclaim any of those essential things. She struggled alone, the most vulnerable of the vulnerable. I cannot help but feel that, through Christina's story, we see the seeds of the crisis of murdered and missing Indigenous women and girls: how First Nations women were targeted, used and abused by Canadian society. We see how it came to pass that tens of thousands of Indigenous women continue to be marginalized and forgotten.

By summer 1915, Christina had left Elkhorn. Indian Agent McKenzie wrote on June 15 of that year: "Christina Sampson left there on June 4th instant for Winnipeg by orders of Inspector Bunn, and is now at service at Stonewall, Man. But I do not know her proper address, but expect to get it any day now, when I will send her the cheque in question."[14] The cheque was for her treaty annuity.

Indian Inspector John Semmens signed a receipt, beside the signature of Christina Sampson, as witness that she was paid this money.[15] At the time, Semmens was serving as the Indian inspector for Lake Winnipeg and Rat Portage, and was living in the small limestone quarry town of Stonewall, Manitoba. This is the place Christina travelled to from Elkhorn. Why? Did Semmens have her working in the small settlement for a well-to-do family? Or was she "at service" for Semmens?

This marks the opening of a black hole as far as records go. Regarding what happened in the period after Christina's departure from the school, I have only a handful of clues.

Three years later, in 1918, Agent McKenzie in Kenora sent an angry letter to the Department of Indian Affairs enquiring about Christina's whereabouts. He wrote that she was supposed to show up in person to collect her treaty money. In another letter to the department, McKenzie reported that Christina was sick in hospital in Winnipeg.[16] Correspondence from Semmens to McKenzie reveals that she actually spent nearly a full year in Winnipeg's Misericordia Hospital. Writing that she was still not very strong and "in very poor circumstances," Semmens offered no explanation as to why she'd been hospitalized. He reported that she had secured a room with a woman named Mrs. Bennet.[17]

Around this time, Christina, who could not have been more than seventeen or eighteen years of age, gave birth to a baby girl. The child was also named Christina. I found the birth record for Christina thanks to the National Centre for Truth and Reconciliation in Manitoba, which has signed an agreement with the Manitoba Vital Statistics Branch to release the birth and death records of residential school children.[18]

Christina Sampson was born in Winnipeg on May 2, 1918. The birth record states that the mother was married at the time, but no father is listed.

Luke Hunter, NAN's treaty expert, told me that according to the Treaty 9 paylist records, Christina Samson was married only once in her life and that wasn't until the 1940s. So why does her daughter's birth record tell a different story? Is it simply wrong? Did she lie on the forms?

Sometimes threads end. I have not been able to find out anything else about what happened to Christina in Stonewall or what she did there. Whatever it was, her life would continue to free-fall. It would hit rock bottom years later, in Winnipeg, where records indicate she was living in 1924, receiving her treaty money in absentia.

THE 1924 TREATY paylist was the last to record Christina's mother Annie. It was also the last to include Annie's sister Jane Carpenter.

That year, Annie made a fateful error in writing a letter to the Indian agent to ask for her treaty money. She was no longer in Lac Seul or near Osnaburgh. She was living in the Ignace area. Since she was married to a white man, Joseph Gauthier—a fact that had clearly escaped the agent's attention for many years—she no longer counted as a Status Indian under the terms of the Indian Act.

Jane had done the same thing. She'd married a white man, Sam Morrow, in 1920.

Luke Hunter informed me that Annie's annuities were "commuted," meaning she lost her status and therefore her right to annuities, and received her last four-dollar annuity on August 30, 1924. "The paylist record shows no more treaty money was paid and by 1926, ticket #114 is deleted," he wrote to me.

It's worth pointing out that if Annie had been an Indian man who'd married a white woman, not only would she have kept her status, but her partner would have received status, even though she was white. This sexist provision of the Indian Act was not changed until 1985.

Annie Carpenter was no longer an Indian. She was disenfranchised, her entire personhood demeaned. But here is the kicker: to the bureaucrats, she was *elevated* by marrying a white man. She no longer needed any special status in the eyes of Canada. The Indian Act was doing what it was designed to do: get rid of Indians.

WHILE ANNIE WAS being punished by the bureaucracy for marrying a non-Indian, her daughter Christina was hundreds of kilometres away, struggling to survive in a city still lurching from the 1919 Winnipeg General Strike and the fallout from the years of Prohibition. From 1916 to 1923, when the sale of alcohol was illegal, Winnipeg became a hotbed of liquor running and petty crime. Then, by the mid-1920s, the Prairie metropolis, once known as "the Chicago of the North," was spiralling towards the Great Depression.

A letter from Indian Agent Frank Edwards to the Department of Indian Affairs in 1925 states that "#153 Christina Samson is somewhere in Winnipeg" and that her treaty money should be paid out to another Indian inspector, this time a Mr. Bunn, at the Winnipeg office.[19]

Four years later, on July 13, 1929, Agent Edwards sent a typed letter from his post in Kenora directly to Christina in Winnipeg. It reads,

You had better write to the Secretary Indian Department, Ottawa, for your Treaty money. Tell them your number #153 Osnaburgh Band, and the cheque will probably be sent direct to you.

Your daughter is at the new Cecilia Jeffrey School at Kenora, and you should make arrangements to come to see her.

Edwards then added, in handwriting, as if an afterthought, "Your mother is at Vermilion Bay."[20]

This letter says so much in so few lines. It also—as usual!—raises questions. The original Cecilia Jeffrey school at Shoal Lake had been shut down and moved to Round Lake, on the outskirts of Kenora. When the new school opened in 1929, its administration had switched from the United Church to the Presbyterian Church. Meanwhile, no records—no footprints or shreds of evidence at all—remain showing that Annie had seen her daughters Christina or Sarah since their disappearance to Elkhorn. The girls were taken at such a young age. Would Christina have known that her mother was at Vermilion Bay? Would they even have known where Vermilion Bay was? Was it normal practice for Agent Edwards to pay this close attention to everyone he provided treaty money to?

In contrast to the groups of families her mother lived among, families that stuck together in their regular movements along the river and in nearby communities, Christina was a young woman trying to make her way in a big, challenging city, with no family or close community around her that we know of—none of the intricate webs of support our peoples had woven among themselves for millennia. From what I can tell, Christina's only contact with her family consisted of these brief, cryptic messages from the Indian agent.

This particular message would be, so far as we know, the last time Christina heard anything at all about her mother. Edwards's scrawled afterthought is the last written record that anyone can find regarding Annie's movements—until her death.

THE 1931 CENSUS of Canada reports a Christina Simpson in the Manitoba provincial jail, in Portage la Prairie. She would have been in her early thirties at most, still so young.

The spiral of Christina's life stings.

How do we know this Christina Simpson is actually our Christina Samson? Because Luke Hunter was able to tell me that, according to the Treaty 9 paylist, Christina was single until 1943, when she married O. J. Arnold. And in the records, the woman who married O. J. Arnold was Christina Simpson. The last name is, once again, misspelled, but that is my auntie.

Why was she in prison? She couldn't have stayed there for long. During that same year, 1931, she was writing letters from her downtown Winnipeg address to the Indian agent, looking for her treaty payments.

Christina was, not surprisingly, having a hard time getting by in Winnipeg during the Depression. Her financial problems seem to have been constant. On October 16, 1931, Agent Edwards told her in a letter to go and see Inspector Bunn in downtown Winnipeg "and ask him to write to Ottawa for your treaty money."[21]

It's remarkable what these bits of correspondence from the Indian agents sometimes reveal. In that same letter, Edwards offers us a clue, an unexpected and significant one, about Christina Sampson's life: "Your Daughter Christina," he wrote, "is getting along all right at School and is keeping well."

Little Christina would have been thirteen years old. Nothing else is said about her, but that sentence reveals so much: Little Christina was in residential school, on track for the same fate as her mother.

When we next hear from the older Christina, she's clearly in dire financial straits. On February 23, 1933, she wrote a letter on a small sheet of paper to the Indian agent in Kenora. Tellingly, there was no familiarity, no direct address to Mr. Edwards or Mr. Bunn. The handwritten scrawl reads,

Dear Sir,

I wonder if you could sent me my money for 32 . . . and I would be very glad if you could sent me for this year 33, my number is 153, because I have a hard time to make my living here, and I been sick for 2 month so I cant work yet, and there is no work here to be found. . . . I hope to get a answer soon as possible.[22]

In March 2023, Paula Rickard sent me an email: "I searched for Christina Sampson in NewspaperArchive and found a few news articles. Christina was apparently dealing with the impacts of disconnection from family, residential schools, colonization, etc. It seems to me that she wasn't married to O. J. Arnold for long. I can't find anything on him. Is the photo her? You'll see.

"If it is her in these news articles, I would like to say, Christina, we found you and remember you."

My heart hit the floor.

Paula had sent me several news articles from the *Winnipeg Tribune*'s police brief section that tell the story of Christina's life up until the 1950s. It's wrenching reading. She was written about at different times for drinking and for stealing, for being intoxicated and for being a vagrant. In 1936, she was fined $200 or required to spend three months in jail for possessing liquor not bought from the provincial liquor commission. This may offer a clue to her earlier brief incarceration.

In another instance, the police responded after she was beaten with a stick by her husband. According to an article published on July 24, 1944, she was involved in an armed robbery with a J. Wolozub from Port Arthur. Alcohol was involved. She was fined fifty dollars or offered the alternative of spending two months in jail.[23]

That fall, on September 29—quite possibly shortly after her release from jail—the forty-five-year-old Mrs. Arnold ended up in the Winnipeg General Hospital requiring nine stitches after she was savagely beaten with a stick by sixty-two-year-old William Murray. She was found bleeding profusely at the bottom of the stairs in their home.[24]

According to the treaty paylist records, Christina is listed as Mrs. O. J. Arnold from 1943 until 1949. She continued to receive her treaty money during those years, but never in person. She was "issued a cheque and money order." Then, suddenly, in 1950, she drops off the treaty paylist.

The headline for one of the last news articles Paula found, published in the *Tribune* on February 22, 1951, reads "Crowded Block Condemned For Fire and Health Hazards."[25] The story reveals that Christina, by now blind, was living in a dilapidated rooming house in Winnipeg. A photograph of her accompanies the piece, in which she bears an almost regal air, perched on her bed, eyebrows arched, staring at the camera with near defiance. She is wearing a dark dress and galoshes with the zippers half-undone, one leg partly exposed. The room must have been cold; the article says it is "heated by a one burner hot plate." Long icicles can be seen through the window. A large can is near her feet and another on the bedside table beside her. The article reports that everyone living in the terrace houses had thirty days to leave the property. The reporter noted he had to read the eviction notice to her. According to the city health officer, there was a "great accumulation of filth in many rooms with rooms containing toilets and washing facilities covered with slime."

The next day, a bit of brightness. The headline reads "New Room Offered Terrace Resident." According to the piece, "After reading Wednesday's *Tribune*, in which blind pensioner Miss Christina Simpson was shown in her tiny $8 a month room, Mrs. W. R. Rhodes . . . offered a room in her suite for the elderly woman."

The kindness of strangers never ceases to amaze. I hope the remainder of Christina's life had a measure of peace. We can find no other trace of her.

WHERE NEXT?: Blind pensioner Miss Christina Simpson sits on the bed of her tiny room at 356 William Ave., after a Tribune reporter read her an eviction notice from city health authorities giving her 30 days to find new accommodation. Her room, heated by a one burner hot plate costs her $8 a month and is her second in six months in buildings condemned by health authorities.

Crowded Block Condemned For Fire and Health Hazards

This is the only photograph we have of Christina Sampson, who also went by the last name Simpson. It was taken by a *Winnipeg Tribune* photographer for an article on how her rooming house was condemned for being a fire and health hazard. (The University of Manitoba Archives & Special Collections, The Winnipeg Tribune fonds, A1981-012)

AS FOR LITTLE Christina, Christina's daughter, we know little more, other than that she was sent to Cecilia Jeffrey. By then she was going by the name Christine Sampson.

We do know (surprise, surprise) that there were ongoing problems at the school. Allegations were sent to Agent Edwards about Mr. A. Menzies, the principal from 1925 until 1929, being an "autocrat," unfriendly to the staff, refusing to let anyone but himself use the front door, and that his wife "had no sympathy for the work of the school," and that she was "the real head of the school."[26]

Cecilia Jeffrey's principal Egerton Byers, who took over in 1929, frequently called upon the RCMP to track down truant students and bring them back to school. By the authority of section 10 of the Indian Act, which made it a crime not to turn one's children over to schools, the RCMP were frequently used in Kenora and Winnipeg to find and return school runaways. And in the case of Cecilia Jeffrey, there were a lot of them.

Here is just one example from the period Christine was at the school. A report dated October 26, 1936, describes how Officer E. Stanley was dispatched to Northwest Angle in Lake of the Woods, outside Kenora, to bring children in. He went with Staff Const. J. Burns and Johnson Cutbeard. His detailed report speaks of visiting several islands by boat until they discovered Chief William Oshie, who was with two children, Bennie Oshie and Arnold Pinesse. Oshie told the officers he was unable to take the children back to school because he had been "ill" and was unable to get anyone else to take them. So the police did, along with Oshie's three-year-old grandson, Elvin Oshie. They took the three boys back to Kenora, hired a car and dropped them off with Principal Byers. The next day, the Chief was charged under section 10 of the Indian Act.[27]

Also during Christine's time at Cecilia Jeffrey, it was anonymously reported in a letter to Duncan Campbell Scott that the children were starving. This would have been quite a blow to the department after the successful opening of the new school in Round Lake, Kenora. The large red-brick school, built in the same shape and size as all other residential schools across Canada, was celebrated as "magnificent," and the opening made the news in local newspapers such as the *Kenora Miner & News* on November 9, 1929.[28]

The handwritten anonymous letter is five pages long and it is full of grievances against Mr. Byers and his wife. The letter sounds as if it were written by one of the staff. It starts off by saying, "One member of staff can testify that she served two suppers to the children consisting of one slice of dry bread and a cup of cold water. This in a Christian mission!"[29] The staff protested to Principal Byers about the "meagre food supply," with one woman staff member asking him to go to the dining room at mealtime "and hear them asking for food, and have none to give them." To this Byers replied: "Give them all they want, and let them make pigs of themselves."

The school building might have been new but the old attitudes prevailed. Three years later, in 1932, at age seventeen, Christine was married to Frank Shebahkeeseequab, eighteen, in Kenora. At some point Frank's surname in English became Churchill, according to the marriage record. Christine and Frank were both listed as Presbyterians and must have met as students at Cecilia Jeffrey. The records show they lived in Jaffray Township, which is the part of Kenora where the residential school was located. The two witnesses at their wedding were Cecilia Jeffrey Principal Byers and his wife.

Frank and Christine must have married because Christine was pregnant. She gave birth to a son, Donald, in 1933. The couple went on to have two more sons, Leonard and Harvey. The family eventually settled in Lac des Mille Lacs First Nation, or Nezaadiikaang, about an hour and a half outside Thunder Bay

Lac des Mille Lacs is a short drive from Graham, Ontario, where Annie's daughter Liz lived with Alphonse Piska and their children, hiding in the bush, away from Indian agents and residential schools. This proximity is, to me, remarkable. Liz and Alphonse lived here with their youngest daughter, Sarah, along with my mother Sheila. In the early 1950s, they would move to Raith, directly beside the community.

Like his parents before him, Donald Churchill attended Cecilia Jeffrey Indian Residential School as a child. If his grandmother Christina was also at Cecilia Jeffrey before being sent to Elkhorn, this would make him the third generation to attend this residential school.

However, in the mid-1940s, times were changing. If he could pass the entrance requirements, Donald would go to Kenora for high school. "Donald has applied himself well to his studies since my arrival," Cecilia Jeffrey principal T. P. Ross wrote on Donald's application to Indian Affairs for a tuition grant. "I believe that he can succeed in high school."[30] Listed as an Indian with Lac des Mille Lacs First Nation, he continued to live at Cecilia Jeffrey while attending Kenora High School. That was the way it worked: Indian Affairs paid Cecilia Jeffrey $100 a year per high school student.

But by the late 1940s, Principal Ross had other ideas. He proposed to the Kenora Indian inspector on August 8, 1949, that Indian students board with white families so they could learn how to "mix socially with white people." It was, he wrote, important for these older students to "escape from the 'institutional' atmosphere which of necessity permeates a residential school. They need to be allowed more freedom than can be permitted in a residential school containing younger children who must for obvious reasons be subjected to pretty rigid discipline. I believe that this can be done by allowing them to board in white homes."[31]

Thus, an idea began to form within the department: an extension of residential schools that involved paying white families to take in boarding students while they attended high school.

Did that happen to Donald?

I CANNOT END this chapter, after writing about Christina, the missing Sarah and Annie's granddaughter Christine, without sharing the story of Annie's great-niece, Doris Carpenter.

As I noted earlier, Annie's brother Charles and his wife Charlotte had a third child, named Tommy. He was born in 1905 in Osnaburgh. Tommy grew up and married Matilda Rooster, also from Osnaburgh. They had a daughter named Doris.

Doris's name jumped out at me when I started researching this book. I'd been speaking with James Cutfeet, who was working with Lac Seul First Nation Chief Clifford Bull on the search for the children who died at Pelican Falls Indian Residential School. Pelican is sandwiched between the Lac Seul community and Sioux Lookout.

I have been to Pelican for a Nishnawbe Aski Nation student awards dinner. Pelican still operates as a high school for students from northern Treaty 9 communities that don't have their own high schools. If parents there want their children to have a high school education, the right of every other child in Canada, they have no choice but to send their children away. Pelican is now run by the Northern Nishnawbe Education Council and funded by the federal government. It is not a residential school. There is no church involvement anymore.

Poplar Hill First Nation's Everett Bushie, the youngest brother of Reggie Bushie, one of the Seven Fallen Feathers, went to school at Pelican. The school has newer residences for students, like little townhouses, which are crowded and in need of repair. Students can also be billeted with families in Sioux Lookout, about ten kilometres away.

The Anglican-run school was originally built in 1925. Its setting is stunning, on the shores of Pelican Lake, nestled among the thick fir trees. The residential school building looked like every other residential school in Canada: hulking, three storeys high, with a centre-hall plan and wings on each side where the student dormitories were. It still lies between the Sturgeon and Vermilion Rivers, near the Pelican station on the mainline of the Canadian National Railway. Before the road came, the school was reached by boat or train. If students were sick, they could travel by motorboat into Sioux Lookout, where the Sioux Lookout Indian Hospital had opened in 1949. Later known as the Zone Hospital, it was the twenty-first racially segregated Indian hospital to open in Canada.[32]

The Pelican school did not normally take children under the age of six. But Doris Carpenter, who was born on November 26, 1932, died there on October 17, 1937. She did not make it to her fifth birthday. There is a little kindergarten building on the far end of the current Pelican high school site that was in existence when Doris went to school. It is now a girls' dorm and office space. Doris would have attended class in the building.

In the 1930s, when a child died at a residential school, there were protocols in place. Straight away, a Department of Indian Affairs form needed to be filed. The official policy read, in part, "When a pupil of an Indian Residential School dies, the Principal is required to inform the Indian Agent at once. On receipt of the Principal's notice the Indian Agent shall convene a Board of Inquiry, consisting of himself as Chairman, the Principal of the Residential School, and the Medical Officer who attended the deceased pupil. These members of the Board shall, in each other's presence, complete this memorandum, which shall then be forwarded to the Department of Indian Affairs, Ottawa, in one copy."[33] The board was required to assemble within forty-eight hours of a death, and the parents or guardians of the deceased pupil were to be given notice of the inquiry and permitted to attend or to send a representative. Parents were also allowed to make a statement, and that statement would be "attached to the report."

But according to letters from community members, it is clear that these policies were not being carried out at Pelican.

On February 14, 1937, a letter was sent to the Indian Affairs branch by Simon Wesley, a band councillor for Lac Seul. On a blank invoice from Patricia Stores Ltd., Fur Dealers and General Merchants, Wesley wrote, "I am writing to ask you if you could be good enough to arrange that parents be notified of any sickness or death of their children at Pelican School, while in attendance there. It is always through other sources that we find out of the children's welfare, and not by the school authorities—so I am wondering how they do not notify us."[34]

In response, Philip Phelan, chief of the Training Division at Indian

Affairs, sent a short letter from Ottawa to Pelican's principal, Fred Mayo, that read, "I would appreciate your advising to whom you write when a pupil dies in the Sioux Lookout School."[35]

Mayo replied, "In cases of death, of which I am sorry to say we have had three this past winter, we have also written letters notifying of death and condolence to the parents. Copies of these letters are on file here. . . . In a great many cases parents or guardians complain that they do not get their letters, that we are not able to help."[36]

The letters that I found in Library and Archives Canada files concerned the children Doris Carpenter, John Wapoos and Nancy Tooshenan. However, only John had died in the winter of 1936; Nancy and Doris died in fall 1937, after this exchange of letters. All three children were from the Osnaburgh band, or Mishkeegogamang.

Mayo made reference to other children dying that winter. He does not name the other children he referred to in his letters. However, a search of the NCTR database shows Maggie Cromarty died on October 27, 1936, and Thomas Wapoos, John's brother, died nearly a month later, on November 5. It quickly becomes clear that there was a crisis: so many children were dying in 1936 and 1937. The NCTR database shows students Daniel Masakeyash had passed away on February 3, 1936, and Lavina Beardy died February 24, 1936.[37]

The official forms Mayo filled out as acting principal of Pelican are telling—his notes are trite and dismissive, as if it were the children's own fault they'd died.

Of Nancy Tooshenan, Mayo wrote, "This child spent half her time last year in bed with a temperature, she was visited and examined by the doctor on each of his visits during the year." She died on October 19, 1937, of pneumonia. She was sent by boat to hospital in Sioux Lookout.[38]

Of John Wapoos, he wrote that the boy was sick on October 11, 1936, with "heavy measles rash," that he recovered, but then complained of an earache and a cold. He was put to bed. By early December, he had a second heavy measles rash, but appeared to be doing well until his neck became stiff on December 14. He was given a "mustard plaster" and "camphorated oil to his chest twice a day," plus "tonic and cod liver oil after meals." On December 15, he was taken to the train on a stretcher. "John had been a delicate child, his brother Thomas died here of tubercular on Nov. 5, 1936."[39]

SIOUX LOOKOUT INDIAN RESIDENTIAL SCHOOL.

Oct. 19, 1937.

Mr. Thomas Carpenter,
c/o Hudson Bay Co.,
Cat Lake, Ont.

Dear Mr. Carpenter:

We are very sorry to have to let you know that
Doris passed away early Sunday morning.

We are burying her in Sioux Lookout, Canon Sevier
is taking the service.

With sincer sympahty,

I remain,

Yours faithfully,

Fred A. Mayo,
Acting Principal.

This is the letter sent to Thomas Carpenter, Annie Carpenter's nephew, regarding the death of his daughter Doris at Pelican Falls Indian Residential School. The letter states Doris was to be buried in Sioux Lookout within days. It is unknown whether Thomas received the letter on time, or at all. (Library and Archives Canada, RG10, vol. 6216, file 470-23, part 1)

Of Doris Carpenter, Mayo recorded that she had "whooping cough Sept. 10, chicken pox Oct 2. Very severe burns suffered in her own home last November when she was brought by plane to Sioux Lookout Hospital. Four years old last March." She was treated with "camphorated oil, cod liver oil, cough medicine." She died in bed at the school.[40]

Indian Agent Frank Edwards did not show up to participate in the inquiries into these children's deaths, as was mandated by the department. He said it was "impossible" for him to attend. In his place he sent Ontario Provincial Police constable H. S. Johns.

On October 19, 1937, Mayo wrote to Doris's father, Thomas Carpenter, whom we know as Annie's nephew Tommy. His letter—which, as we know from earlier, Tommy may or may not have received—read,

> *We are very sorry to have to let you know that Doris passed away early Sunday morning.*
> *We are burying her in Sioux Lookout, Canon Sevier is taking the service.*
> *With sincere sympathy, I remain,*
> *Yours faithfully,*
> *Fred A. Mayo.*[41]

Thomas Carpenter was not given the option to attend the funeral or to take his daughter's body back home for burial.

The letter to Nancy's father, John "Toosehnan" (Mayo misspelled his name), was similarly short, with zero details and offering no family involvement in what would happen to Nancy's body. Dated October 20, 1937, it read:

> *We are very sorry to have to inform you of the death of your daughter Nancy in the Sioux Lookout Hospital. She passed away on Tuesday, Oct. 19 as a result of pulmonary pneumonia.*
> *Burial was made today in Sioux Lookout by Canon Sevier. Please be assured of our sincere sympathies.*[42]

John Tooshenan lived in Cat Lake, at least 180 kilometres northwest of Sioux Lookout. Just like Doris Carpenter's family, Nancy's family weren't given the time to make it to the funeral, held the day after death. Worse, school officials didn't even offer this as an option to families—as if never considering that they would want to say goodbye or take their children home.

CHAPTER TEN

IN THE MOUTH OF GENOCIDE

IN 1929, ANNIE GAUTHIER DISAPPEARS.

My mom, who was born in the decade after Annie vanished, says her aunties told her that Joseph Gauthier took Annie to the hospital in Thunder Bay and that, from there, she was sent to the provincial lunatic asylum in Toronto. "All she did was rock and sing to the children," my mother recalls. Somehow, that gave her husband licence to take her into Thunder Bay and leave her there. My mother leans over to whisper: "You know, I heard he might have had somebody else."

Family lore. There might be a grain of truth in that story, but after all this time, who really knows?

"Indians" were sent to asylums, especially Indian women, the ones men wanted to get rid of, to discard. Annie was dumped. Abandoned. Somebody signed off on her to be transferred to Toronto, 2,500 kilometres away. But who?

It wasn't just that husbands were implicitly given carte blanche to pack away unwanted wives. "Out of sight, out of mind" was the colonial practice of the day. Governments were constantly looking for ways to get rid of their "Indian problem," and committing Indigenous people was one tool at their disposal. By this point, both Canada and the United States had well-established track records of violently removing Indigenous Peoples from the land. Those who were seen as troublesome, especially those who were politically motivated or unwilling to cooperate with assimilation policies, were often shipped off to hospitals, mental institutions or prisons. Throwing Indians in asylums was the ultimate "othering."

However she wound up there, life inside the Mimico Asylum would have been horrendous for Annie. Psychiatric care of any kind a hundred years ago was the stuff of nightmares. More than that, white settler mentality imposed Western psychiatric and psychological norms on Indigenous Peoples, in large part because they thought us wild, untamed, a mystery. Power is truly central to Western psychiatry: labelling and categorizing people as mentally ill if they don't follow societal norms.

Annie was an Innino woman whose life coincided with an especially destructive period of colonial aggression. She'd already been stripped of her language, her way of life and the customs she had struggled to hang on to in an anglicizing, assimilating world. By the time she was sent from northern Ontario to the asylum, she would have lost absolutely everything near and dear to her. Her children, her spirituality, even her identity as a Cree had been stolen from her by the federal government and its Indian Act. She was being told, left and right, that she came from a dying culture and race, that she was worthless. She existed at the mercy of government policies designed to negate her being. The final place to which it all led? She was committed to an institution, from which she could not—would not—escape.

Annie was in the mouth of genocide.

RECORDS REGARDING WHERE Annie was in the years before she was sent to the asylum follow the pattern of paperwork connected to her life: they're rare, inconsistent, full of holes. More than provide answers, they raise questions.

The 1931 Census of Canada shows Annie to be a "patient" at the asylum. It says little else. I was able to see her counted there, as well as her daughter Christina in a Manitoba jail, during the final stages of writing this book in June 2023, when that census was released.

Earlier that spring, I'd filed freedom of information requests with the Ontario government, seeking Annie's patient records. What came back was laughable. Two redacted attendance records that revealed nothing other than her name. That was it. There was no trace of her in the files beyond that.

I wasn't all that surprised; my expectations had been low. As a journalist, I know how difficult it is to extract concrete information from governments via access requests. In fact, around this time, the newspaper I write for, the *Globe and Mail*, released an investigative series called "Secret Canada," the result of years' worth of work looking into Canada's broken freedom of information system, which revealed how government information that is supposed to be accessible to the public—that is supposed to be ours—is kept hidden by a bureaucratic system designed to keep it that way.[1]

At the same time, my search for Annie, and the lack of any documentation on what had happened to her—why she was placed into the asylum and how she was treated once there—only reinforced what I already knew: that, to Canada, an "Indian" woman's life was worthless.

I knew that, in that last decade before Annie was sent to the asylum, she was no longer receiving any treaty money. As noted in the previous chapter, those payments eventually ended when Indian Agent Frank Edwards discovered that she was married to a white man. And one of the last records I have of her, also noted in the previous chapter, is thanks to Agent Edwards himself, who'd jotted something extra at the bottom of a 1929 letter to Christina Sampson: the information that her mother was in Vermilion Bay.

Being taken to a hospital and abandoned meant that Annie would have lost any hope of further contact with Christina, and that she was also separated from her daughter Elizabeth, along with Liz's growing family, as well as from Louise, the one child she had with Joseph Gauthier. She was also now, if she hadn't been already, completely cut off from her other children: Sarah, John and James.

One blessing the Canadian colonial record keepers have given us is an account of who was where and with whom every ten years. Some census records are remarkably accurate. Then you've got records like the 1921 Port Arthur and Kenora census—the last one that records Annie before she turns up, in the 1931 census ten years later, in the asylum. That 1921 census was filled out by the one and only Indian Agent Frank Edwards. He must have been having a bad day. The census is illegible in spots, with big X marks drawn over sections and other lines rubbed out.

Annie appears in the 1921 census twice. It is an oddity that puzzles Paula and me, and that no one in my family can explain. It's possible she wasn't living with Joseph Gauthier at the time. Or that, if she was, she also kept another residence at Lac Seul First Nation with the rest of her family. Perhaps she had left Joe Gauthier.

She appears the first time as Annie Gauthier. By now, as we have learned from his correspondence over the years, Agent Edwards knows Annie well. He records her as head of her household, a one-room house, at Lac Seul First Nation, outside Sioux Lookout. I had never seen Annie declared the head of her household. No occupation is listed for her. The census indicates she has gone to school, that she is fifty years old, that she identifies as a member of the Church of England and that she is married.

The Lac Seul community included Frenchman's Head, the cere-monial grounds where the family of Annie's mother, Jane Bunting, had settled. That would put her near extended family. And according to the census, Annie had a lot of family living with her at the time. Their names are familiar, the same relations who've appeared alongside her over twenty years of paylist records and who've turned up in the Indian agents' letters. Their consistent presence speaks to the Cree concept of kinship, of families living together and staying together, of taking care of children—your own and whomever you pick up along the way.

Annie's mother, listed as Mrs. John Carpenter, is also in the house. Her eldest brother Joseph is living with her (the census calls him a lodger), as is his son, Joseph Jr., who's twenty-five, and another nephew, John Carpenter. Her oldest sister, Jane—who was a widow after her husband, a Mr. Jeffreys, died, and is now Mrs. Sam Morrow—is living with her, along with Jane's daughter, listed as Mrs. Grenier. Also in the household are a five-year-old girl named Jane McLean; fifteen-year-old William Moore, an orphan from Moose Factory they have been taking care of (he was somehow related to the Wemaystikosh family); and Alleyn (or Allan) Carpenter, who is Annie's little brother Henry's son. Allan is ten years old and identified as "Ojibway." His mother, Maggie, was from Lac Seul and also Ojibwe. He was living with his family in the previous census of 1911, but by the time the 1921 census was taken, his mom and dad had disappeared. We have not been able to locate them.

Tellingly, the Goodwin and the Wesley families are neighbours, as they have been since that first Fort Albany census I found of 1881. The Albany folks stuck together.

The second mention of Annie in the 1921 census shows her in Savanne, in the household of Joseph Gauthier, along with her daughters Lizzie Gauthier, who was around seventeen (not fourteen as the record indicates) and Louise, who was eleven.

Savanne is about three hours outside Lac Seul, in Lac des Mille Lacs territory, on the highway to Thunder Bay. It is where Liz and Alphonse "Rusty" Bowen would marry the following year. I know this because Uncle Hank had a copy of his parents' marriage certificate in his files. It contains a clue regarding Annie's marital situation. The bride's father is listed as Joseph "Gautier"; her mother is Annie Carpenter—not Gauthier. Miss Mary Louise Gauthier is named as a witness.

Was Annie no longer with Joseph and living in Savanne in the early 1920s, or did Joseph tell the census enumerator that his wife was temporarily absent? (It is not unheard of to have a home in community and also one outside of it, say in the city, especially if you are married to a white person.)

THERE IS A lot that is comical about that second census entry. I can't help but imagine that Frank Edwards must have been seething, having to deal with Annie and her family again. Starting in 1921, Edwards was the Indian agent in the Kenora area for twenty-one years. After reading so much of his correspondence with my family, and sensing his irritation over their refusal to stay put and be easily counted, I got curious. I looked into him. And what I discovered is food for thought.

Edwards was born in Lancashire, England, to well-off parents. He and his siblings grew up with a nurse, a cook and a waitress. His father was a trader who had business in Africa. But that line of work apparently didn't interest young Frank: he decided to move to Canada instead. In the early 1900s, he was a fur buyer and a general merchant in Dinorwic—the bustling rail town where Annie had married Joseph Gauthier in 1908. Did Edwards already know them, way back then?

Edwards must have done well for himself there. In 1912, he was appointed justice of the peace for the District of Kenora. He enlisted in the British Army in World War I, became a captain and fought at Ypres and Poelcappelle. While recuperating from a shrapnel wound in Britain, he met Winnifred Soper. They married in 1918 and returned to Sioux Lookout after the war. Two years later, in 1921, Edwards was appointed Indian agent for the Kenora district. He kept the post until his retirement in 1942.

The recently married Edwards couple appear in the 1921 census, living in a hotel on 2nd Street South in Kenora. They soon moved to a house adjoining the Indian Agent office on 1st Avenue South. They had one daughter, Nora, in 1924.

Edwards was a big deal in Kenora. He was president of both the legion and the Rotary Club, as well as a Boy Scout leader. After he retired, he moved to Toronto, and died there in 1945.[2]

British-born Kenora Indian agent Frank Edwards was a decorated veteran of the First World War. He had a "great interest in Indian folklore" and collected ceremonial pipes, jingle dresses, fire bags, cradle boards, stone tools, beaded jackets and much more. (The Muse—Lake of The Woods Museum. Detail of collection item 1976.25.1vv)

Here's the interesting part. According to the Kenora Great War Project website, Edwards collected a vast array of artifacts, mostly consisting of First Nations belongings, including "ceremonial pipes, jingle dresses, fire bags, head dresses, stone tools, beaded jackets, leggings, bandoliers, beaded belts, moccasins, wool bags, necklaces, games, cradle boards, birch bark baskets, Hudson's Bay Company axes and copper pots, fossils, flintlock guns, a powder horn, fish spears, fawn skin bags, gauntlets and a wide variety of books." Apparently, Edwards would loan out pieces from his collection for costume parties. Upon his death, he left his "native artifacts" to the Town of Kenora. For decades his trove made up the bulk of the collection in the Lake of the Woods Museum.

I wonder how he came to have such a "collection," and whether it contained any of my family's belongings. Edwards was apparently a "meticulous" man who kept "accurate reports and records," including a "small black notebook containing a catalogue of his collection." The black notebook is now lost, as are the journals he kept during his years with the Department of Indian Affairs.

ON THAT 1921 census with Joe Gauthier, Annie is identified as an Indian and, in contrast to her first entry, as a Catholic. Joseph is listed as French. Lizzie Gauthier is first identified as Scottish and her sister Louise as Irish, but Agent Edwards or someone else has crossed out both those entries and written "Indian" instead.

At this time, Liz had a daughter, my great-aunt Mary, who appears on the census as being five months old. There is also a lodger at their house named Agnes Gauthier. She is four years old. She speaks "Indian" only and is apparently Scotch. This has got to be wrong, but it begs the question: Who is Agnes? And was she an Indian? Was she Annie's child? Or the daughter of one of Annie's brothers or sisters?

It was eight years later, in 1929, that Agent Edwards would mention in his letter to Christina Sampson that her mother was "at Vermilion Bay," near Sioux Lookout. This is her last known location until the Mimico institution.

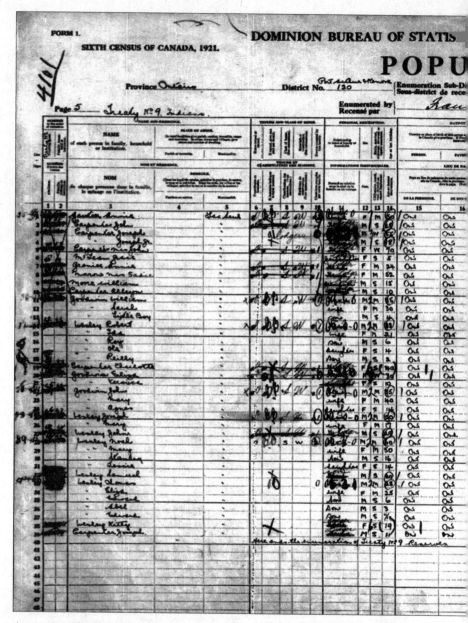

A page from the 1921 Census of Canada, recorded by Indian Agent Frank Edwards, shows Annie Gauthier (née Carpenter) as the head of her household in Lac Seul First Nation. Her older brother Joseph Carpenter lived with her, as did nephews John Carpenter and Joseph Jr., and her mother Mrs. John Carpenter (Jane Carpenter).

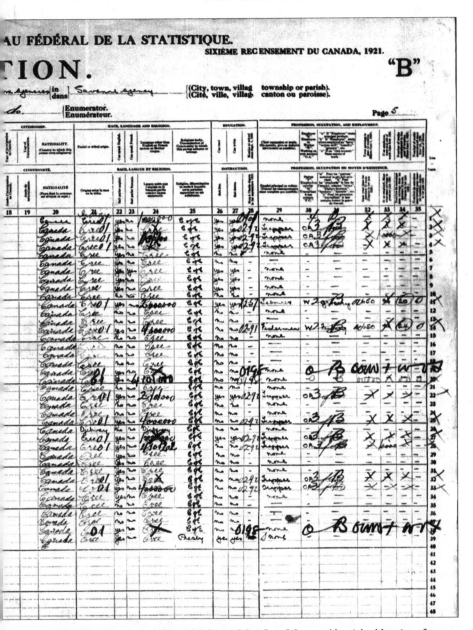

Also in the home were Grace McLean, Mrs. Sam Morrow (Annie's older sister Jane Carpenter) and Annie Grenier (Jane's daughter), along with orphan William Moore and Annie's nephew Alleyn (Allan) Carpenter. (Library and Archives Canada / RG31, Statistics Canada / item number 3289586)

THE MIMICO BRANCH of the Provincial Lunatic Asylum opened in 1890 as the Mimico Asylum. In 1919, at least a decade before Annie's committal, its name was changed to the Ontario Hospital (Mimico). The satellite campus west of the Toronto Asylum at 999 Queen Street West was held up as a model for its time, designed by the renowned Irish-born architect Kivas Tully. No expense was spared in its construction. The idea was to house patients by the lake, out in the fresh air, in a farm-like setting, with everyone living in scenic cottages. When it was nearly ready to open, about 112 men were moved from the Toronto Asylum to the new institution because they were needed to help finish the construction.[3]

Plans were also under way for a cemetery. Originally, ten hectares north of the asylum were set aside for burial plots, a considerable size, which might speak to the number of patients who were dying at the downtown Queen Street asylum. But that was quickly whittled down to four and a half hectares, due to the encroaching city. The cemetery is about four kilometres away from the Mimico Asylum.

Historically, asylum patients had been buried in a paupers' cemetery at the corner of Yonge and Bloor Streets, some distance away from the institution on Queen Street West. But as the city grew, that gravesite was dug up and moved to Mount Pleasant Cemetery on Bayview Avenue. Today known for the gravesites of wealthy Torontonians, among the cemetery's first inhabitants were those considered indigent, poor and insane. Institutions such as Mimico and 999 Queen Street West were not just "lunatic asylums." They provided a place to live for the elderly, the infirm and those without any family to care for them or means to support themselves.[4]

An on-site burial ground was desirable because the cost of burying bodies was going up. The Provincial Lunatic Asylum's medical superintendent Daniel Clark reported that the price had already doubled from two dollars a burial and would soon rise to six dollars. On May 8, 1890, in a letter to Ontario's inspector of prisons and public charities, Clark wrote, "Our own ground at Mimico is almost as near to us as Mount Pleasant Cemetery & no bodies need then to be brought into the city from our Mimico Branch as we have been obliged to do."[5]

By 1891, a year into the Mimico branch's operation, the hospital's administration wanted work on the burial ground to begin. People were dying at both the Mimico site and the downtown site, and the hospital was desperate for a place to bury them. The male patients who'd been brought in to help finish building the institution were also made to dig the graves. Forced labour was seen as a form of therapy at Mimico. Patients were not paid for the work they did.[6] Residential school children were also made to dig graves. At Sault Ste. Marie's Shingwauk, which my family members attended, children built the Anglican chapel and dug burial plots.

The 1891 annual report for the Toronto Asylum, the first to include the Mimico Branch, is riveting reading. With so little information about life at the Mimico asylum in the early twentieth century, it gives us a glimpse into what the facility was like and who was there. In that first year ending September 30, 1890, seventy-three patients died in Ontario's asylums. Causes of death included "Killed," "Suicide," "Exhaustion of mania," "Senile decay," "Cardiac disease" and "Dysentery."[7] Just like in residential schools, many others died of tuberculosis and malnourishment.

The report also lists patients' "callings and occupations," offering a glimpse of the types of people who were admitted to the hospital. That year, the patient roster included six carpenters, twenty-four domestic servants, forty-two housekeepers and twenty-seven labourers. (All of the housekeepers and domestic servants were women, while the labourers were all men.) Among the patients were also one farmer's daughter, an innkeeper, two male doctors and four teachers (two men and two women). Only eight had no occupation.[8]

The report tracks the reasons for admission, with causes classified as moral, physical, hereditary or congenital. The diagnoses within these categories are revealing, providing a picture of the many circumstances and afflictions that might be connected with "mental illness" at the time. Under "Moral," the reasons for a patient being committed include "Domestic troubles, including loss of relatives or friends," "Religious excitement," "Adverse circumstances, including business troubles," "Love affairs, including seduction," "Mental anxiety, 'worry'" and "Fright and nervous shocks." Under "Physical," patients were admitted for "Intemperance in drink," "Intemperance, sexual," "Venereal disease" and "Self-abuse, sexual," as well as overwork, sunstroke, fevers, pregnancy, lactation and "Uterine disorders." Also of concern: "Puberty and change of life."[9]

Gender and sexuality, as well as class, affected who was admitted to asylums and how they were diagnosed. According to Dr. Geoffrey Reaume, a professor of psychiatric history, promiscuous or headstrong behaviour among women who were seen as part of the lower classes led some to believe them mentally incompetent. And there was a general belief, his research shows, that "chronic insanity was highly related to membership in the lower classes." As criminality was also thought to be prevalent among the lower classes, locking up such folks would help preserve the social order.[10]

At Mimico, patients were put to work on the farm as well as in carpentry, tailoring, the bakery, kitchen and laundry. Seven male patients worked full-time on the "subway," a series of tunnels that connected the cottages.[11] Domestic jobs included mat making, quilting, sewing and making lampshades, curtains, shawls and even tea cozies.[12]

Somehow, I can't imagine Annie would have been sitting and crocheting tea cozies. I picture her assigned to harder labour, such as working in the kitchen or the laundry rooms. While Indigenous asylum patients in Canada weren't segregated into different races as they were in schools and hospitals, segregation did occur by class. If you had money and had a family to advocate for you, you were treated differently. The Queen Street site had sixteen wards, six of which were for paying patients. These private wards were well appointed and not crowded like the public wards.[13] That begs the question of how segregated the institutions were inside the walls: what wasn't recorded, and what the public could not see.

Annie had no one to advocate for her. Everything we know about that time points to a life inside the Mimico facility that, for a woman in her situation, would have been terrifying.

WHILE CANADA WAS infamous for having Indian tuberculosis hospitals that turned into general—and atrocious—hospital facilities, it did not segregate those in need of "mental health" care.

The United States did. In 1897, Senator Richard Pettigrew, who was chair of the Bureau of Indian Affairs, purchased land near the bustling frontier town of Canton, South Dakota, on which to build an insane asylum for Indians. He believed that Indians had "peculiar mental afflictions" and that to mix the "savages" with the white settler population would be counterproductive. In his own words: "Association with their ancient enemy has a harrowing effect on them."[14]

In 1903, the Canton Hospital for Insane Indians opened, the first American hospital designated for patients of a particular race.[15] Shaped like a giant Maltese cross, with two wings for men and two for women, it was built on forty hectares on the banks of the Big Sioux River. The facility was modern, with electric lights and steam radiators. A two-metre-high steel fence surrounded it.[16]

The first head of the institution was a local lawyer named Oscar Gifford—a person with no experience in mental health[17]—and its first patients came, under duress, from all over the U.S.[18] Just like with students in residential schools, as soon as patients were brought in, they were stripped, their clothes and belongings taken away. They were washed and their hair was cut.[19] They were then examined by strange white doctors, likely having no understanding of why they were being poked and prodded. None of them wanted to be locked up and confined. According to testimony from some staff members, the screams, and the constant singing and chanting, were unbearable.

Most of those admitted were under the age of thirty. Many had children at home. People were there because they'd refused to give up their ceremonies and ways of life, or because they'd refused to send their children to residential schools. Even though the population of inmates was fairly young, the death rate at the institution was high.[20]

Anyone sent to Canton was said to be "defective," and was sterilized so they could not reproduce.

In 1933, Canton was finally shut down, in part due to whistleblower

Dr. Samuel Silk, clinical director of St. Elizabeths psychiatric hospital in Washington, D.C., who'd been sent by the Department of the Interior to inspect the institution. He found that fifteen inmates at Canton were aged twenty or under, and four were under the age of six.[21] He also determined that, out of a population of ninety, less than one-third of the inmates actually needed to be in a psychiatric facility.

Indian agents in the U.S. had the power to admit Indians to asylums. Once inside, it would be up to whomever was running the place to decide whether that person was ever "well enough" to leave. Canton was built with a cemetery, of course, and there are reportedly 121 people buried there. The Hiawatha Golf Club now operates on the property.[22]

Annie's experience would not have been dissimilar to that of Native Americans, and it should be kept in mind that when she was incarcerated, Canada's control over the Indigenous population was at its height.

Everything about Annie would have been judged to be barbaric by the Western medical system at that time: her language, the food she ate, her lack of "civilized" ways of being, her poverty, and the way she lived her life with her family and extended family. Morally, she would have been called into question for her very being, and her circumstances would have been measured and judged against the myth of the "noble savage": the idea that Indigenous Peoples were just hanging around in loincloths, waiting for settlers to "save" them. Being an Ininiw woman in Canada in the early twentieth century placed Annie among the most vulnerable people on Turtle Island. Her treatment would be so far removed from the medicinal and spiritual holistic practices she knew as an Ininiw.

Little information is available about how Indigenous Peoples put into "asylums" were treated, how they got there or why. But one thing seems clear: committal was often a death sentence.

Canada and the Western medical system did not recognize the medicinal and health practices of the Anishinaabe and Omushkego. We had our own Medicine People and spiritual healers, our own methods and plant-based medicines. Traditional medicine cared for the entire body, including the mind. If one part of the body was sick, all of the body was treated, not just the one sick part. Early Canadian medical care dismissed our healers as silly or insane.

The Anishinaabe believe everyone belongs in life, that every spirit born into a physical body has a purpose. Before the arrival of the settlers, there are few recorded instances of Indigenous people who went "insane" or suffered from mental health issues. Even those with perceived oddities or who acted differently could be useful in keeping the community fed, well and whole.

One could surmise that, from the start, mental health diagnoses of Indigenous people were rooted in control and conformity. A study of Indigenous psychiatric patients in B.C. from 1879 to 1950, by Robert Menzies and Ted Palys, found that of the one hundred institutionalized cases they examined, the majority were younger men with an average age of thirty-seven, most individuals were childless and most had low levels of formal education. At least thirteen had been to residential school. The researchers also found very little documentation specific to Indigenous people and mental health. They write, "Apart from a few sporadic references and singular 'case studies' (such as that of the Canadian Métis leader Louis Riel), the psychiatric historical record is peculiarly silent on the important subject of Aboriginality."[23]

When Annie was admitted to the Ontario Hospital, she was sixty years old, had been to residential school, was married and had children, several of whom were missing. But psychiatric medicine, when it encountered an Indigenous woman like Annie, didn't consider the trauma she'd suffered due to genocide and all that fed into it: forced removal off the land, forced attendance at Indian residential school and the abuse suffered there, and the stealing of one's children, to list just a few.

It's impossible not to wonder: Was Annie simply a problem woman who needed to be moved out of the way?

THE MIMICO ASYLUM would have been a particularly miserable place during the Great Depression. Dr. Geoffrey Reaume points to severe provincial funding cutbacks during the 1930s and says that, ironically, while operating with tighter resources, the asylum would have been overcrowded with people struggling and breaking under the extreme pressures of life during that time. Annie, he says, "would have been confined in one of the grimmest periods in asylum history."

The Mimico site, with its cottage-based design, was meant to be more "humane" than most institutions of its ilk, with patients living in smaller buildings that didn't feel so alienating. On paper, sure, that makes sense. But in reality? "When you look at them, they are still big institutions," Reaume says. "When you think of cottages you think of the countryside. But these were nothing like that."

Mimico, which has since been repurposed and now houses part of the Lakeshore campus of Humber College, was full of horror. Look closely at some of the old photos and you see bars on the pretty windows.[24] You also see pristine lawns and well-kept buildings near Lake Ontario, but you don't see any patients outside getting air. They are all trapped indoors.

Don't forget the "subways," those tunnels that connected the cottages on the large campus. Reaume says they were notorious places where sexual assaults and abuse would occur, unseen. Patients were taken into the tunnels and tortured. (Even "ghost tours" of the tunnels used to be on offer.)

For Annie, resistance would have been pointless against her white Western medical captors. Think of her in that environment, and then ask: How many other Indigenous people would have been there with Annie? How many were from the James Bay region and spoke Omushkego? There would have been no translators, no one to have a conversation with. She must have felt extremely alienated and alone.

The nature of psychiatric treatment at the time is a whole other matter. The year of Annie's death, insulin shock treatment was used at Mimico on patients who were believed to have schizophrenia and on those who, Reaume explains, were seen to have a fighting chance of getting back to "reality." Ruefully, he adds, "Depending on how one defines reality."[25]

Insulin shock therapy was intense: large doses of insulin were injected into patients to put them into a coma. Of the 443 patients to first receive the "treatment," 74 per cent were diagnosed with schizophrenia, 21 per cent had manic depression, and 5 per cent had melancholia. Metrazol was an alternative shock-therapy drug mainly used in those with manic depression and melancholia. It caused convulsions and seizures, and fractures were a side effect.[26]

Did Annie receive either of these forms of shock treatments? I have no idea. Even if she didn't, though, women had their own issues once they were drawn into the web of psychiatric interventions: the puberty-menstruation-menopause triangle. By the end of the nineteenth century, it was common teaching in North America and England that problems in females' brains could be tied directly to the pelvis.[27] Women's "womb madness" and "hysteria" were considered psychiatric ailments. Hysterectomies or surgeries to remove ovaries and other female reproductive parts were sometimes "prescribed."

Without Annie's patient records, there is no way to tell if she was experimented on with these harmful treatments. But we do have one record: her death certificate. A photocopy, contained in Uncle Hank's brown folder, has been the strongest guiding piece of information I have had in the writing of this book. That one piece of paper is dark and hard to read. It contains so much, yet at the same time so little, information.

It shows that she died on March 20, 1937, after being confined at the asylum for seven years, eight months and twenty-eight days. This accounting, at the top of the form, is jarringly specific, considering how little else can be found in any records about Annie's time there.

The certificate states her place of birth as unknown, her age as unknown and the names of her mother and father as unknown. It does show her as married to Joseph Gauthier. For this, she's described as "French-Indian."

The coroner reports that she died of broncho-pneumonia, combined with acute peritonitis and gangrene of the intestines. A complicating factor in her death was chronic mania, which seems to be her only mental health diagnosis.

The Province of Ontario—Certificate of Registration of Death for Ann Gauthier (née Carpenter) shows that she spent seven years, eight months and twenty-eight days in the Ontario Hospital, then known as the Mimico Asylum. (Uncle Hank's folder)

I found it helpful to share the details of Annie's death certificate, such as they are, with Reaume. "Chronic mania," he says, was a catch-all psychiatric diagnosis that was applied when doctors couldn't identify a patient's psychological issue.

He also points out that how Annie died suggests poor hygienic conditions. Asylums would have been humid and musty, so they were horrible incubators of TB. He figures Annie was most likely assigned to work in the laundry. "Women were made to sew, work in the asylum laundry, no matter how old they were. You can't argue that this was therapeutic. Working in the laundry was not easy, with heavy irons and heat. There is no question that it was exploited labour. How could you call making someone in their eighties, who isn't even a hundred pounds, work in the laundry therapeutic?"[28]

When an asylum patient died, families had to specifically request that their loved ones be sent home. And if they did make such a request, they had to pay the cost of transporting the body.

Did Joseph Gauthier receive a call or a letter letting him know that Annie had died? Did he offer to pay for her to be sent home?

Colonization means more than the theft of land, the stealing of children and the imposition of British colonial rule. The otherness, the separation and segregation from the rest of the non-Indigenous settler population, all worked to steal something else from us: our minds.

CHAPTER ELEVEN

LOST, FOUND AND LOST AGAIN

ELIZABETH SAMSON WAS SMALL AND WIDE, WITH STRONG HANDS. SHE WORE horn-rimmed glasses and her thick, black hair framed her face. She did not wear it long. I remember her plaid dresses. She was soft to hug. The softness being at odds with who she was.

Was my great-grandmother raised by Annie? No one knows for sure. Like many women in my family, Liz shared little about her early life. She refused to speak about anything that had happened to her before she married Alphonse Bowen when she was eighteen. Their marriage took place in Savanne, Lac des Mille Lacs, on the shores of the Savanne River. Savanne is near the Arctic watershed, where all the waters on the continent divide and move either south or north. This is a spiritual, magical place, where the waters make a choice, turning up towards James Bay or south towards the urban cities.

Three treaties meet here: the eastern edge of Treaty 3, the southern tip of Treaty 9 and the northwestern edge of the Robinson-Superior Treaty, just north of Lake Superior.

Though we knew few details about Liz's early life, we know that in these treaty lands, during the time she was a child and beyond, the Indian agents and government officials would always have been circling in the background. Inspector John Semmens, Indian Agent Frank Edwards, Indian Agent R. S. McKenzie, Department of Indian Affairs assistant deputy and secretary J. D. McLean and even the department's deputy superintendent Duncan Campbell Scott himself would have been moving around the Carpenters and their children, carving up northern Ontario and assigning people to specific communities, making decisions about their lives like cruel stepfathers.

As we know by now, there was no shortage of letters between officials regarding Annie's movements—she wasn't easy for them to pin down. In one letter, Agent McKenzie writes to McLean to ask yet again about Annie Sampson of Osnaburgh and her movements outside of Treaty 9, this time wanting to know if he should pay her at Lac Seul and whether Annie "is alone" or has any "children."[1]

I can find no mention of Liz, or of any of Annie and Samson's other children, in these letters, aside from those regarding Christina, which I related in chapter 9. I can't help but feel Annie was doing her damnedest to keep her remaining daughters hidden in the bush. At this point, she had lost so much.

If that was the case, her efforts didn't entirely work. For the census records show that Liz was educated. She did indeed attend residential school—there was no choice. We just don't know which one. Yet her location and other clues put the following possibilities on the short list: St. Mary's in Kenora, St. Margaret's in Fort Frances, and the school her niece Christina Sampson attended, Cecilia Jeffrey.

According to the 1911 census, Joseph "Gocha," his wife Annie, his stepdaughter Elizabeth Samson, age eight, and "Leeweso" (Louise), age five months, along with Annie's three-year-old nephew James Carpenter, lived together in Rainy River, southeast of the picturesque Lake of the Woods and west of Savanne. Joseph, Annie and Elizabeth are identified as Presbyterian. The Presbyterians ran Cecilia Jeffrey. Was Liz, therefore, a student there, at the school whose remains I visited at Round Lake when I was writing *Seven Fallen Feathers*, when I went looking for Chanie Wenjack and spent time with the late Treaty 3 Elder Thomas White?

Maybe, maybe not.

Late in the writing of this book, Paula discovered an Anglican Church baptism record for Lizzie Sampson in Nipigon. It states her mother is Annie Sampson, and Lizzie's date of birth is given as February 3, 1907. In 1912, alongside her one-year-old sister Louise, Liz was rebaptized a Roman Catholic at Notre Dame du Portage in Kenora. From that moment on, as far as I can tell, she became Liz Gauthier, a name that would appear on all documents until her marriage. Does this mean that Liz was removed from one school run by Presbyterians and thrown into another that was run by Catholics?

Liz refused to speak about her childhood, or any aspect of her life before she married. She never told stories of growing up, never shared any memories of her mother. We all understood that her past was a no-go zone, as if it had never happened. But this is what her family did know of her: She loved Jesus Christ and insisted on eating fish on Fridays. She believed everything Indian was dirty, and she loved the royal family. Her pride and joy was a silver tea set, her ownership of which was a longstanding mystery: no one knew how she'd gotten the money to pay for it.

Liz would not allow her husband Alphonse, or Rusty, to speak Anishinabemowin in the house, and as far as we know she did not speak Ininímowin. But Liz couldn't escape who she was. She could use a slingshot on a partridge like nobody else, she could quickly harvest a moose and she could skin a beaver effortlessly. She was a midwife, married to a trapper, who lived her life with him in the bush, birthing many babies in the communities they frequented along the railway line: in Graham, up in Treaty 9, where Alphonse often worked as a labourer on the CPR tracks, and in Raith, a small settlement of Fort William First Nation families. Liz knew which plants were medicinal and which were not. She used them on her children. Her pantry was stocked with blueberries, cranberries and wild rice. And she made everyone's clothes.

For decades, Uncle Hank searched far and wide for records on where his mother went to school. Now we know he was looking for her under the wrong surname. Her last name was Samson or Wemaystikosh or Chapish. He didn't know this because she'd never told him, or anyone else in the family. Did she prefer being known as the daughter of a white man, or was Joseph Gauthier simply the only father she'd known and loved?

Father Cornelius O'Dwyer, the priest who presided over Liz's 1912 baptism, was a member of the Missionary Oblates of Mary Immaculate, the group that ran St. Mary's Indian Residential School. This new baptism offers us a big clue: it suggests that Liz was enrolled there. It was not uncommon for children to be rebaptized to match the denomination of the residential school to which they were being sent.[2] Was Annie trying to protect her daughter? Or did she have another reason for wanting Liz to have a French surname? Was she still trying to keep her daughter—the only child of Samson's she had left—out of residential school and hidden from the Indian agents?

MY MOTHER SAYS she has had this dream only twice. The first time was before her beloved aunt Sarah Bowen died. Sarah was Elizabeth's youngest child. She and my mother were raised together like sisters. The second time was the night before I visited St. Mary's Indian Residential School in Kenora in the summer of 2021.

In the dream, my mother is a little girl. She is at home in the bush. She is maybe five or six years old, dancing and laughing in the tall grass. She walks inside the "big house," the wood-framed cabin they lived in when she was a child. The door to Grandma Liz's bedroom is open; she is lying on her side, her face away from the door. My mother quietly walks into the room, creeping around the side of the bed, watching her sleep. Suddenly, Liz's eyes fly open, wide with fright.

Both times, my mother has awakened from this dream terrified, her heart racing.

I did not know about my mother's two dreams until I called her from Kenora as I drove away from the former St. Mary's site. I had been in Kenora during the early stages of shooting a documentary film about the Anicinabe Park Occupation. In the summer of 1974, a group of young First Nations residential school Survivors held one of the very first land back occupations in Canada, right in the heart of Kenora, in the town's main public park. The armed occupation, which lasted just over a month, was led by the charismatic Louis Cameron, a Survivor who'd persuaded dozens of Anishinaabe young men and women—all of them tired of police brutality and a lack of government services—to stand up and say "Enough."

After I'd interviewed Lynn Skead, Louis's former partner, in Wauzhushk Onigum—what the English call Rat Portage—I drove to the former St. Mary's site. Lynn and her husband Lucien had suggested I buy some candy and leave it as offerings for the children's spirits. On my way, I came upon a small trailer with a neon Open sign and colourful lights. I threw the door open and walked in. As soon as I did, I realized I was in the wrong place. Drug paraphernalia, oils and weed lined the shelves. I laughed and I said, "I think this is the wrong kind of candy ..." The store owners chuckled and told me to try the gas bar across from the community centre.

I did, and purchased a handful of hard candies, brightly coloured suckers and sour keys. I walked past the gas pumps and up a slight hill to a newly constructed pavilion, beneath which granite blocks were arranged as benches around a circular monument made of heavy square stones. It reminded me of a firepit. In the centre, a flat circle with this inscription: "St. Mary's Indian Residential School Site. In Honour Of All The Children 1897–1972."

In the back of my mind, I'd always wondered if this was where Liz had gone to school. I wanted to see where the school had been, to feel it—and to see how I felt, standing there. The day I finally did was three months after the Kamloops discovery of the 215. As was happening at sites all over the country that summer, pairs of little shoes had been carefully arranged around the monument: bright pink new running shoes that still had the tags on them, grey rubber summer slides, orange and blue flip-flops, rubber boots, purple sandals. Orange tobacco ties were wrapped around the four posts that held up the pavilion's metal roof.

I placed some of my candies in the spaces between the monument's square stones. Over by one of the benches, someone had left a collection of tiny tipis made of wooden sticks and white fabric. I counted nearly twenty of them, and whoever had made them had gone to a lot of trouble. They were falling over in the wind. I stood them upright, huddling them together.

Then I saw it, the only physical part of the school that remained: the concrete base of the incinerator stack. Lynn had told me to look out for it. Some schools had incinerators for various purposes. During the TRC hearings, many Survivors told of seeing babies born to students being thrown into the incinerators. I wondered if that had happened here. I was overwhelmed at the thought. I bent down and put the remaining candy deep in the earth at the base of the incinerator.

In the grass, a few metres away, I saw a discarded orange T-shirt. I picked it up. It was a child's shirt that read, in black and white letters, "Every child matters." I shook it out and placed it on a stick, leaned it against the crumbling stack.

I spoke to my mother on the drive back into Kenora. I told her where I'd been. There was silence on the other end.

The women in my family have always been able to see things in their dreams. It doesn't happen frequently, and it happens for some more often than for others, but it is there. When the dreams come, I have learned the hard way to pay attention.

"I wonder if she is trying to tell us she went to St. Mary's," my mother said from her home far away in Scarborough.

But I have not been able to find any proof of that. I've spent many nights trying to navigate and search through the digitized files of Library and Archives Canada and through what is available on the NCTR website.

In January 2023, while I was writing this book, it was announced that Wauzhushk Onigum had used ground-penetrating radar and detected 170 anomalies where St. Mary's once stood. Before this discovery, the NCTR had said that, according to available records, thirty-six children had died at the school.[3] Work is now under way to search for answers.

Despite Liz's rebaptism, we have no idea whether she wound up in the hands of the Oblates at St. Mary's or somewhere else, such as at

St. Margaret's in Rainy River or somewhere even farther afield. It seems that no matter how hard we look, we always come to an end beyond which there are still questions. Or the answers we do find are devastating. Sometimes the search for Annie and her children has been too much to bear: too frustrating, the lack of records and the years of not knowing where to go for help. I spent many months parking it, setting aside that brown folder.

It was during one of those times, in 2022, that I was scheduled to travel to Sault Ste. Marie to give a talk about *Seven Fallen Feathers* at Algoma University. Because Algoma is on the site of the former Shingwauk Residential School, I thought it would be a good idea, before heading north, to punch that name into the NCTR database.

How could I have known that this simple search would lead me down a lengthy trail connected to another side of my family—or that it would lead to fresh, unexpected heartache?

LIZ'S HUSBAND, ALPHONSE "Rusty" Bowen, was Anishinaabe, a Piska from Fort William First Nation, which falls under the Robinson-Superior Treaty. Alphonse came from a long line of Piskas, a large family that, according to Elder David Chippewow Thompson, was directly related to Ininway, or Chief John L'Illinois, one of the Chiefs who, along with Chief Peau de Chat, made treaty at Robinson-Superior.[4] Chief L'Illinois was of the Kingfisher Clan, oh-geesh-kih-muh-nih-see. Treaty records depict him as an older man who liked to talk a lot. In fact, when he stood up to speak, often he did not stop.

Anishinaabe families are formed within a Clan-based system that comes from the environment around us, the earth, the sky and the water. The Clan system is how the Anishinaabe communities kept a social order (as well, you could not marry within your Clan). Birds like the kingfisher are of the earth and of the sky; they hold a special place as the carrier of messages and teachings from the spirit world to the human world. They communicate through song. Feathers from birds hold power. The gift of a feather is sacred. We hold our feathers when we speak our truths.

The second Robinson treaty, the Robinson-Huron, partly came to pass because of Chief Shingwaukonse of Garden River First Nation at the south end of Lake Superior, who wrote to the government after settlers began appearing in droves in his territory. Chief Shingwaukonse was ahead of his time. Just like Chief Louis in Kamloops, he saw what was coming. They both knew the onslaught of colonization would not stop, so getting in front of it, trying to ensure longevity and rights for their people, was their primary goal.

Chief Shingwaukonse dreamed of a place where Anishinaabe children could learn their language and ways of life alongside those of the new settlers who were swarming over the borders from the United States and coming off the ships from England. He envisioned teaching wigwams, and in 1832 he led a delegation to York (Toronto) to meet with Lieutenant Governor Colborne, with the aim of hiring teachers for Garden River. Anglican missionary William McMurray answered the call and soon established a mission at nearby Sault Ste. Marie. A small schoolhouse was opened in 1833.[5]

Around the same time, the Jesuits were inviting many to settle in the area of Fort William, trying to turn the people there into Catholics and farmers. Their mission was initially farther south, at Pigeon River, but they moved it to the Kaministiquia River, to Fort William. (The Jesuits often acted as translators, whispering into the ears of Chief Peau de Chat when the treaty was being made.)

Over a decade later, Chief Shingwaukonse, at the southern end of Lake Superior, noticed provincial surveyors examining the land. He was not pleased. In June 1846, he wrote a letter to the "central government" and to the governor general. In the letter, he mentioned his service to the British in the War of 1812. The deal, he said, was that he and his people would be allowed to remain "unmolested forever" by the settlers. But that was not happening. The settlers were coming. And if other Nations were gaining annuities, he and his people wanted them as well, for what was "found on [his] lands."[6]

Four years later, the Robinson-Superior Treaty was signed, clearing the way for the coming railway around the Great Lakes and eventually leading to the creation of the city of Thunder Bay. That treaty saw 57,000 square kilometres of land exchanged for annual payments of four dollars and a reserve of 207 square kilometres. Nothing about this was a fair exchange.

But Chief Shingwaukonse held out and refused to sign. Other Lake Huron–area bands followed suit. He wanted more than four dollars a head as an annuity: he thought ten dollars was more fair. He also tried to secure land for "half breeds" at one hundred acres per head, but the lead negotiator, William Robinson, refused, saying he'd only treaty with Indians and threatening to take his money back and leave. Chief Shingwaukonse and the other Chiefs came to the decision to abandon their stance. On September 9, 1850, they signed the Robinson-Huron Treaty.[7]

These two agreements essentially gave Canada what it wanted most: control of the Lake Huron and Lake Superior shorelines.

Chief Shingwaukonse died in 1854, four years after the treaty was signed, but his sons, including Chief Buhkwujjenene, kept trying to raise money for a proper school. Buhkwujjenene even travelled to London, England, in 1872 with Rev. E. F. Wilson to raise money for a boarding school. Reverend Wilson is the man behind the Elkhorn school, the one with the unflagging belief in the need to "save" Indigenous people through assimilation-by-education. Wilson's work with Buhkwujjenene would be transformative for the overzealous missionary, unleashing his desires to spread the word of God to all the Indians in the area.

The fundraising trip was a success. They came back and constructed an industrial school right in Chief Shingwaukonse's home community of Garden River. It had a dining hall and dormitories to house thirty boarding students. But six days after it opened in 1873, the school burned to the ground.

Reverend Wilson was not deterred. He picked out a new plot of land, thirty-six hectares along the St. Mary's River, which runs along what is now the border between the U.S. and Canada. It was the perfect spot, with a harbour that could accommodate ship traffic. Children could be dropped off by boat from across Lake Superior. The new school opened in 1875.

Meanwhile, as this was going on across the greatest of the Great Lakes, Mary Piska, my great-great-grandmother, was born in Fort William First Nation, on the banks of the thick, powerful, meandering Kaministiquia River. Where she was born had been a meeting place for the Ojibwe for as long as anyone could remember and, with the rise of the fur trade, it likewise became important in the fast-changing colonial economy. The first fur-trading post in the area, Fort Caministigoyan, was established along the banks of the river in 1683. The North West Company renamed it New Fort and then, in 1807, Fort William.

Mary Piska's records, like so many others I've dug through, offer a variety of different spellings of her name: sometimes it is Pisky or Piskey. Mary was born in 1870, one year before Annie Carpenter. She was Anishinaabe; Annie was Ininiw. Two women born at the birth of Canada who would experience the seismic shift of colonization, of suddenly having their worth and their rights diminished under its yoke.

Just as with Annie, little is known about Mary. Her parents were Joseph and Isabella. The 1881 census shows that Joseph was a trader, his racial origin "Indian." Mary had an older brother also named Joseph, an older sister Elizabeth and two younger siblings, Margaret and Paul. Mary met a man named Samuel Skelliter, an English labourer and trader, and with him bore five children: Marianne (which sometimes was written Marion), Margaret, Thomas, Samuel and John. Even though their father was white, the children were identified in the 1911 census as both "Indian" and "Canadian." My great-grandfather Rusty (Alphonse)—I've always known him as Gramps—was born last, in 1902, to an unknown father who we've been told was named John Bowen. Some in my family say that the name was picked out of a hat, or that Mary gave her son the last name Bowen out of spite for the man who'd fathered him. I can find no trace of a John Bowen in the area during that time.

By the time Gramps was born, his two older brothers, Thomas and Samuel Skelliter, had been taken away to the Shingwauk Indian Residential School. It is fair to say he never met them.

Samuel Skelliter, my great-uncle, is believed to be in this photograph of "Ojibway children: Pupils of the Shingwauk and Wawanosh Homes." None of the children are labelled in the picture. (Courtesy of Shingwauk Residential Schools Centre, Algoma University)

BY THE TIME Thomas and Samuel were sent to Shingwauk, the school was well established. Thomas arrived in 1900, when he was just six years old. Samuel was even younger, only four, when he came in 1902, the year my Gramps was born. The school must have looked absolutely daunting to them both. It was three storeys high and built of stone, which gave it a whitish hue. Shutters flanked its windows.

On my first visit to Shingwauk, I was shown around the later-built red-brick school, now home to Algoma University, by Jenna Lemay, one of the university's digital archive technicians who was instrumental in helping me find my Shingwauk family. Exceptionally smart and passionate about genealogy, Jenna spends her days sifting through and cataloguing the extensive papers, books, photographs and objects that form the collection of the Shingwauk Residential School Centre.

Jenna took me to see the chapel, the only original Shingwauk building still standing. She told me that the extraordinary carpentry work inside—the pews hand-carved with care, the ornate altar area—was done by Wilson and the students of Shingwauk. Before it was built, Wilson would march the children several miles into town every Sunday to attend service at the nearest church. He had grown tired of the walk.

I found it difficult to walk in through the oversized heavy oak door that is rounded at the top. I could not help but think about how many times my great-great-uncles Thomas and Samuel had walked inside.

Over the door's archway, set inside the sandstone face of the Gothic- and Tudor-style chapel, are two black-painted wooden beams that form an X. On them is inscribed: "Bishop Fauquier Memorial Chapel 1883." Inside, arched stained glass windows line the sides, light filtering through them in reds, greens and golds. The ceiling is particularly impressive: dark oak runs in a herringbone pattern to the church's peak. It is remarkable to think that students built this.

What did the Skelliter boys think the first time they saw the chapel? Was it a place of refuge or did it scare them? The red carpets and the Latin carved into the walls. The celebrant's chair that resembles a throne, its back intricately carved in wooden lace patterns, its stitched green seat bearing a red star. In all caps over a stained glass window etched with crosses are the words "CHRIST DIED FOR OUR SINS."

ACCORDING TO THE Shingwauk annual report for 1902, Samuel and Thomas were sponsored by James Meek, Esq., the city clerk of Port Arthur, Ontario, who donated $125 to help cover their costs.[8] In the early twentieth century, that was a significant sum. Records show that Meek sponsored the boys for as long as they were at Shingwauk.

The federal stipend of sixty dollars per child was not nearly enough to pay for a student's food, lodging, clothing and the expenses incurred in running a school. Churches actively sought sponsorship for students' tuition, and it was not uncommon for members of the Anglican Church either here in Canada or in the United Kingdom to answer the call. And answer they did. People like Meek, people from congregations all over Ontario and even into Quebec and the Maritimes. There was even an Algoma Association in England. It is hard to read the list of donors. These are churches most of us would recognize in the centres of most big cities and little towns. It seems as though every single Anglican church and Sunday school in Ontario, plus a surprising number of them farther east, sent money to keep the children imprisoned: St. Stephen, All Saints and the Church of the Redeemer in Toronto; St. George's in Montreal; St. John's in Lunenburg, Nova Scotia; All Saints in Windsor, Ontario. Those are just a few examples.[9]

Census records also show that Sam Skelliter Sr., living in the small settlement of Raith, about an hour and a half's drive along the railway tracks outside of Thunder Bay, died in about 1899. Was this why the boys were sent to Shingwauk? Because their mother couldn't care for them on her own, on top of two daughters, Marianne and the very young Margaret, who was born in 1900, after the death of her father? Margaret would eventually be sent to St. Joseph's Indian Residential School in Fort William. Was Meek sponsoring the boys because he felt sorry for them, with their father dead? Had he been friends with Sam Skelliter and promised to take care of them?

The children at Shingwauk were not called students in the 1911 federal census for Algoma. It is a stomach-churning census to read. Thomas "Skilliter" is the very first student listed. He is fifteen years old, an "Indian" by race and an "inmate" of the school. The thirty-six other Shingwauk students listed after him are also "inmates."

For its first twenty years, before the Skelliter brothers' time, Reverend Wilson served as the principal. He was wildly enthusiastic about the work being done at Shingwauk to turn the children into good Christian British subjects. Wilson's mind never turned off. He was constantly busy, planning and scheming, especially for ways to make money.

He had a printing press on hand at the school, which he used to produce a pamphlet full of his ideas and drawings. Called *Our Forest Children, And What We Want to Do with Them*, it was part newspaper, part diary—a kind of nineteenth-century zine. Wilson sold copies for a modest fee. He had a second publication, *Canadian Indian*, which he edited, and he also sold postcards featuring portraits of Indigenous students from the school.[10]

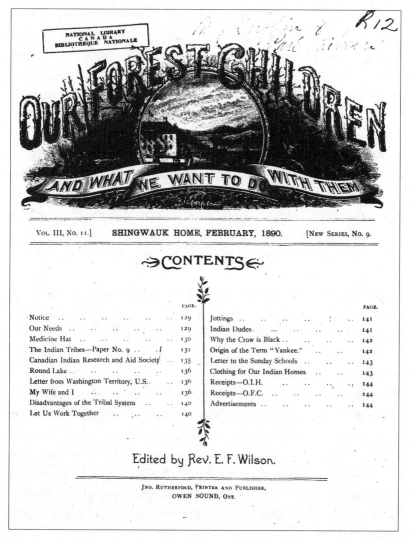

This promotional pamphlet *Our Forest Children, And What We Want to Do with Them* was created in 1887 by Rev. E. F. Wilson to advertise what was happening at the Shingwauk Home. (Courtesy of Shingwauk Residential Schools Centre, Algoma University)

The July 1889 edition of *Our Forest Children* begins with a long-winded feature on who the Cherokee Indians are, according to Wilson. He talks about how they were the "Eastern mountaineers of America," how devoted they were to the land and their expulsion. He even adds his own illustrations. On the first page of the zine he has drawn a tomahawk in the top left corner, and on another page he's drawn dancing Cherokee, dressed in jail-striped uniforms, with the caption "Cherokee Prison." Wilson was also an obsessive amateur linguist. He'd try to collect words from every "new" Indian he met. In his zine, he lists pages of Cherokee words, explaining how personal pronouns are properly used and including a list of phrases.[11]

The pamphlet offers a useful glimpse inside of the mind of the man who was head of the school for two decades. For instance, he lovingly recounts a class trip to Montreal. In 1887, "thirty of our Indians" joined the queen's Golden Jubilee celebrations.[12] In a photograph of the group, Wilson stands in the middle, sporting a Rasputin-type beard. He is wearing a dark suit and has a somewhat wild look on his face. He's surrounded by students, including Etukitsin, one of two Blackfoot boys that he brought back to Shingwauk from Manitoba around the time of the North-West Rebellion. The other, Appikokia, was also on the Montreal trip—he is the tall boy on the far left in the back row. Appikokia stayed at Shingwauk only for one year. As soon as he was old enough to leave, he went back home to Alberta.

So how did two Blackfoot boys from Manitoba wind up at Wilson's Shingwauk? It wasn't just that Wilson's efforts to find students for his various schools spread far and wide. He took a particular interest in the fallout from the 1885 rebellion, an uprising led by Métis leader Louis Riel during the period when the Canadian government had been starving the Indigenous Peoples off the prairies. The government was aided in its cause by severe drought and the settler-caused decline of the buffalo population.

In retaliation for their part in the rebellion, eight Cree warriors were publicly hanged in Battleford, Saskatchewan, on November 27, 1885. The day of the hangings, in an inhumane and cruel act, all the students at the

Battleford Industrial School were taken out of class to watch the men die. Those men, since known as the Battleford Eight, may have been the students' relations, members of their families. The message to the students was clear: don't disobey the Crown.[13]

Wilson was a voracious letter writer, and in a letter to the *Mail* after these events, he seems to show sympathy towards the cause. "Would it not have been better to have been less eager about the immediate possession of those vast hunting grounds, and to have limited for a score of years or so the progress of the surveyor with his chain? Would it not have been better gradually to have drawn those 50,000 roaming Indians within the coils of civilization instead of shutting them up suddenly onto Reserve lands like prison houses and compelling them to farm or die?"[14]

Wilson was convinced he could help the children of the men hanged in Battleford. That summer, he wrote, he wanted to "go and bring down from the North West some 30-40 of those young braves whose fathers and uncles have taken up weapons against us—because poor fellows they are feeling the pangs of starvation, and in their ignorance imagine that they can stay the tide of immigration which is depriving them of their homes and hunting grounds."[15]

He felt the schools were the only way to separate the students from their parents, from everything that made them Indian. "I maintain, and I think I have common sense, justice, and wisdom on my side, that the only way to deal with the Indians is to take their children while still young and train them up in the path of Christianity and civilization."[16]

That is why Shingwauk had two Blackfoot students. Wilson stole them.

ETUKITSIN DIED IN 1888. I know this because in Reverend Wilson's zine, he spoke of his trip westward to visit a man named Crowfoot, who lived about fifteen kilometres outside Gleichen, in southeast Alberta, adjacent to the Siksika Nation. On the Prairie trail, as he described it, he passed many colourfully dressed "Indians" on their way to Crowfoot's, where a Sundance ceremony would take place. Once there, they encountered the "angry uncle" of Etukitsin. Unsure of what he wanted, Wilson agreed to see him. He wrote that the uncle presented him with a beautifully beaded bag and said, "I wish to give this to you that you may know Etukitsin's relations have no ill-feeling towards you; show it to your friends when you get home and tell them so."[17] The uncle told Wilson he did not blame him for Etukitsin's death. (The seventeen-year-old had died of tuberculosis on April 23, 1888.) His proper name is listed on the NCTR memorial banner as David Etukitsininani.[18]

Also on that trip, Wilson said he would not take any other Blackfoot boys back that year, but he said the next year, he "should want twenty."[19]

REVEREND WILSON'S DELUSIONS of creating a grand interconnected system of residential schools did not start and end in Canada. As described in chapter 8, he'd befriended U.S. colonel Richard Pratt of the Carlisle Indian Industrial School in Pennsylvania, which opened its doors in 1879. Colonel Pratt was still on active duty while he was head of the Carlisle school, and the two learned from one another. The boys at Shingwauk wore military-style uniforms—navy blue suits with brass buttons—just like the uniforms at Carlisle.

Many of the U.S. schools that came after Carlisle were modelled on it. Just like in Canada, American education policy was a removal tactic. The boarding school program was initially run by the War Department. The president had the authority to delegate members of the army to act as Indian agents, and the government empowered the secretary of war to repurpose former army barracks as boarding schools.

It made perfect sense, after President Andrew Jackson's extermination policies, to sic the War Department on the Indians. It was all about assimilation by destroying ways of life and violently separating the people from the land. The language around the schools' purpose was nearly the same on both sides of the border. As the birthing United States started to expand westward, "federal policy toward the Indian was based on the desire to dispossess him of his land. Education policy was a function of our land policy."[20]

In 2022, the secretary of the interior, Deb Haaland, the first-ever Native American to serve in this role, released a groundbreaking investigation entitled *Federal Indian Boarding School Initiative Investigative Report*. Work on the report had started after the discovery of the 215 in Kamloops, and the report was released in May 2022. For the first time, America had quantified the existence of boarding schools: where they were, when they opened and closed. It found that between 1819 and 1969, there were 408 boarding schools across thirty-seven states. There were at least fifty-three burial sites at these institutions.[21] Just as in Canada, there were also day schools, asylums, Indian hospitals, sanatoriums and orphanages that offered segregated care. In fact, there were nearly one thousand such federal and nonfederal institutions. Of the federal boarding schools, about 50 per cent had a religious affiliation.

The U.S. program "deployed systemic militarized and identity-alteration methodologies" to assimilate Indigenous kids. The education system was used to rename children, giving them English names and identities; their hair was cut; the use of Indigenous language, spiritual and cultural practices was forbidden and the children were often organized into "units" to perform military drills.[22]

In 1889, ten years after the Carlisle school opened, Reverend Wilson and his wife travelled to Carlisle to meet Captain Pratt, the man in charge. Wilson wrote about the visit in his zine. The school complex, he wrote, looked like military barracks (which they had been). He described Pratt as a powerfully built man, about fifty years old, who lived in an opulent home. There was, he observed, "plenty of room in America," declaring that it took quite a time to walk across the bedroom in Pratt's house, where Wilson and his wife were staying. It had "three doors leading out in three directions and four large windows."[23] The drawing room was full of "curiosities and ornaments" such as Pueblo pottery and brightly coloured Navajo blankets. On one wall hung a collection of "curious Indian weapons and articles of bead-work, forming quite a trophy, and from the corner of a bookcase hung suspended a splendid Sioux head-dress."

Regarding the school, Wilson wrote that six hundred pupils were enrolled, with some out on the farm and about 150 "placed out temporarily as apprentices" to white people. The oldest pupil was sixty-five years old, an Arapaho Chief, and the youngest was an Apache baby, seven months old and "born on the premisis."

The Wilsons stayed for a few days and were treated to a performance of songs, readings, recitations and speeches delivered by the schoolchildren. At the end, General Pratt went on stage and "spoke rather low, but very clearly."

Pratt and Wilson continued to correspond about sending students between the institutions. It is unclear from the letters whether that actually happened.

The Carlisle Indian Industrial School operated for thirty-nine years, closing in 1918. During its lifetime, students from more than 140 tribes were forced to attend. There are 186 known graves of children who died at Carlisle.[24]

IT'S FAIR TO say Rusty never met his brothers Thomas or Samuel, because once the boys were taken, they never went home. Not once. The school's principal, George King, did not believe in allowing Indian children to go back home during summer vacations. He felt that if the children mixed again with their Indian parents, the work done on them throughout the year would be undone. Thomas and Samuel were essentially imprisoned at the school, across the lake from their family and their home.

Rusty, by contrast, had no formal education. He was a runner. His children say he attended St. Joseph's Indian Residential School for not more than a nanosecond before he ran home to Fort William First Nation, which was across the Kaministiquia River. His mother Mary, he told us, had no interest in raising him, so he was passed over to his aunties. He used to say, "I was not raised. I was dragged up."

His sisters Margaret and Marianne were at St. Joseph's. It is unknown whether Mary raised the girls at all, or if they went to St. Joseph's as orphans. That's because, before it was a residential school, St. Joseph's was an orphanage.

The school's history definitely has some twists and turns. St. Joseph's was originally the school on the Mission Indian Reserve, near Fort William. In 1905, the land it occupied was expropriated by the Grand Trunk Railway: the school had to go, as did the Anishinaabe who lived there. With the money they received from the railway, the Sisters of St. Joseph built a new school and a church on a picturesque spot known as Squaw Bay. ("Squaw" is a derogatory term for "Indian wife.") They also built a church.

Eventually, that school had to close because of lack of funds, so the nuns combined the school with an orphanage they owned on Franklin Street in Fort William.[25] It was a red-brick monstrosity, four storeys high, with a little green hedge around it, perfectly trimmed. When the new school opened in 1907, Margaret and Marianne were already living with the Sisters of St. Joseph's, but whether as students or as orphans, we don't know.

While many of the children at St. Joseph's did not have parents, some came from the homes of sick or destitute parents. The school was constantly in need of money. The nuns often begged for food, clothing and provisions. Around the beginning of the twentieth century, sickness plagued the school, particularly typhoid fever and measles. There was no money for a doctor.[26]

The school had half a day of academics. The rest of the day went to learning domestic chores: the girls were taught sewing, cooking and cleaning—how to be a good worker. Indeed, Margaret Skelliter would go on to be a domestic. She lived for a time on Machar Avenue on the Port Arthur side of Thunder Bay. I have friends who live on the same short street. I never knew that Margaret had lived there too.

My mother has a photo of her, sitting on the grass in Graham, with my grandmother Margaret and Uncle Hank sitting at her feet. They look like goofy toddlers. Margaret has a half smile on her face. She looks gaunt, and wears a sweater around her frail shoulders, over her summer dress. She's with Louise Gauthier, who is much taller and healthier looking. Margaret died of pulmonary tuberculosis at the Thunder Bay General Hospital in 1934. She was thirty-four years old.

THE TRUTH IS, until recently, before I stumbled on them, no one in my family knew Thomas or Sam Skelliter existed. Not one single person. Or if someone did, they'd never said a word.

It fills me with shame to say it. To acknowledge it. As they have for many other families, residential schools and racist policies such as the Indian Act and the Sixties Scoop have combined to nearly crush us. Even today, you never know when someone new is going to show up. Alive or dead.

Truth is, I know more about a man named Rev. Edward Wilson—his passions, what he looked like, what books he liked to read and what he liked to draw—than about Uncle Hank's own uncles. It is as if Samuel and Thomas didn't matter. Were not as important as a man who was the creator and principal of two residential schools—Elkhorn and Shingwauk—that have dominated my family's history. In death, the reach of such men and their life's work continues, attempting to rub us out. This book disrupts that narrative as I try to reclaim our own—to take our story back.

I found the boys quite by accident, that night I'd decided, before travelling to Sault Ste. Marie to give my talk at Algoma University, to do a search on Shingwauk in the vast trove of the National Centre for Truth and Reconciliation website. In some cases, their records contain every detail you could possibly imagine, from school general account ledgers to shopping lists to attendance rosters. It can be overwhelming. There is an intense amount of information, some of it pertinent to a search and some not, but you don't really know until you get in there, dig around and try to find something, anything, about your missing or barely known relation.

Each school has a landing page featuring brief highlights of its history, such as which denomination ran the school, when it opened and when it closed. Also on each school's page is a memorial list of the children known to have died there. No other schools in Canada feature a roll call of dead children on their websites.[27]

Shingwauk was not on my research radar when I began to write this book. It was only that impending trip to Algoma that led me to punch the name into the NCTR search box. Within minutes of opening the Shingwauk page, while skimming the memorial list, I saw the names Thomas Skilliter and Sara Skilliter. As soon as I saw them, I knew. Immediately, I felt I was going to vomit.

It was almost the exact same surname as that of my great-grandfather's brother John Skelliter and his sisters Marianne and Margaret. The name is unusual in Indian country. Years ago I had been to Manitoulin Island with my mom, Grandma Margaret and all my aunties to attend a Bowen-Skelliter family reunion for those who remained of Mary Piska's descendants. But no one at that reunion had talked about these children. Did they know?

Suddenly, another layer of truth was being revealed. I knew in my gut that these were my relations. I contacted the Shingwauk Residential Schools Centre for help, and was lucky that archivist Jenna Lemay promptly answered my email. Jenna got to work combing through records. Since Shingwauk closed in 1970, the Survivors have been locating, gathering and organizing archival materials, which has led to a collection that was decades in the making. All of those connected to the school are in their debt. Without their work, I doubt we would have such complete records of the school's history.

Jenna found a Samuel "Skilliter" and a Thomas "Skilliter" from Fort William, nine hundred kilometres away from the school. So it was Sam, not "Sara," and even though children weren't supposed to be admitted before age ten or eleven, Sam was just four when he arrived at Shingwauk. Thomas had arrived two years earlier, when he was six. They were to be trained in the trades: carpentry, blacksmithing, farming.

The boys' father was clearly identified as Sam Skelliter, but their mother was simply listed as Mary. As with so many First Nations women, her documentation is inconsistent or lacking. But one school record is more detailed: Thomas was born to a Mary Alicuing. Despite an extensive search, no Mary Alicuing could be found. It is believed this is actually Mary Piska.

══

DID THOMAS AND Samuel have any love in their lives? Did anyone show them an ounce of kindness?

In the 1902 annual report of the Shingwauk and Wawanosh homes, the students are described by George Thorneloe, the bishop of Algoma, in his introductory letter, as animals who need to be tamed: "With animalism in their nature well developed, and with strong passionate inclinations to do only what pleases them best and yet with natures sensitive to a degree if crossed or sharply reprimanded, our task is not an easy one, and calls for the greatest tact and patience."[28]

That year there were forty-one girls and fifteen boys at the institution, representing mostly "Ojibway and Delaware tribes." Some were motherless, some fatherless, some orphans, but the majority had families. The bishop wasn't brief on the subject of their natures and the difficult work of improving them. His letter carries on: "From the moment the new arrival enters the Home, he must be watched closely in school and out, and with systematic perseverance the old shiftless ways and dirty habits must be eradicated."

In photographs in the Shingwauk Centre's archives, the children look miserable in their uniforms. In the NCTR database, there's a photo of Frank, Edward, Frederick, William, Lila and Ruby Day—said to be "orphans." The oldest can't be more than ten. The two smallest girls, Lila and Ruby, wear dresses and are seated on the ground in front of their brothers, who look like little British soldiers of misery.

Jenna and I have not found any definitive photographs of Thomas or Sam, so I do not know what they looked like. Were their eyes black like mine with thick lashes? Were they small in stature like Alphonse, or super tall like John Skelliter? Did they have that same crooked smile? Every time I look through the photographs in the Shingwauk collection, I scan the faces of the boys, wondering if I'll recognize a trace of myself.

A researcher I have come to know, Edward Sadowski, a retired Algoma professor who has become a staunch advocate of the Shingwauk Survivors, sent me some other photographs. We met for coffee in Sault Ste. Marie one morning. He told me about his quest to find information about two nameless boys who had drowned in a pond. Their bodies were never recovered, and the pond was later filled in by the city.

The boys drowned between 1914 and 1915, the same time as Thomas was at Shingwauk. He must have known them. The boys' deaths were recorded by the principal, but he did not bother to make note of who they were or where they were from, or whether their families were notified.[29]

Edward sent me copies of photographs that once belonged to Rev. Benjamin Fuller, who was Shingwauk's principal from 1910 until 1929. Thomas died during his tenure. I opened the file and read, on its first page: "Rev. Fuller Photo Album, Shingwauk & Wawanosh IRS, Shingwauk Project Archive."

The photographs are haunting. Picture after picture of children with mostly dour looks on their faces. There are no names. All are black-and-white. In the very first photograph, twelve girls of various ages pose in front of the school's sandstone walls. They are wearing white formal dresses. Some of the younger ones—they look about three or four years old—are sitting on the grass. On the left, four boys are seated beside the girls. They are wearing the military-style uniforms, with the caps and the shiny brass buttons. No one is smiling. Not one single child.

Another photograph is of four teenage boys, all wearing dark, ill-fitting suits and leather lace-up boots. They are gaunt, their faces downcast. Someone has scrawled in black marker on the bottom of the picture "Shingwauk boys making good." Could one of them be Thomas?

There is a photograph of a little guy in his brass-button uniform, so young his long socks are tucked into his short pants. His right hand rests on a large toy horse. Two smaller toy horses stand below it. He looks like he is about to cry. My mind races. Is this Sam?

It is the graveyard photographs that undo me.

The first one is of Reverend Fuller in his white minister's robes. They are flowing as he walks ahead of six teenage boys carrying a wooden coffin. They appear distraught. Behind them, the younger students follow in a long line, two by two. Everyone is dressed in black. It looks to be fall. The boys must be carrying a classmate. The students, or inmates, at

Shingwauk not only dug the school's graves, they made the coffins and carried their friends to be buried in the cold ground.

CHILDREN CAME TO Shingwauk from all over Ontario, from the Prairies and from the East Coast. But an overwhelming number of children at Shingwauk were from Walpole Island, a First Nations reserve between Ontario and Michigan. Thomas and Sam seem to be the only two children at Shingwauk from Fort William. They were never entered on the paylist for the band. Was that because their father was English? The 1911 census lists Thomas as "Indian." The distinction isn't clear.

Thomas and Sam would have lived inside the big, damp Shingwauk building, the first one they saw when they walked up the lawn from the boat that took them across Lake Superior. The building faced the river. There was no plumbing, no electricity.

The first Shingwauk Indian Residential School building was situated along the St. Mary's River. It opened on August 2, 1875, as a home for boys. The girls had a separate school called Wawanosh Home, which was in the Sault Ste. Marie area. (Courtesy of Shingwauk Residential Schools Centre, Algoma University)

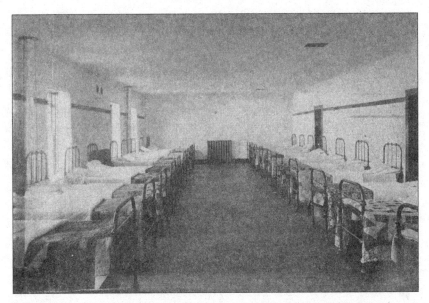

The Shingwauk boys' dormitory in 1903. (Courtesy of Shingwauk Residential Schools Centre, Algoma University)

As at many schools, students attended classes only for half a day. For the other half, they were sent to learn labour skills. The boys went to work in the carpentry shop or in the fields, while the girls were taught domestic chores such as sewing, cooking and laundry. (The Wawanosh Home school for girls had been relocated to the Shingwauk site in 1900.)

It's curious, then, that the 1905 annual report notes that Thomas went to school in the morning after daily church service and in the afternoon was on "gang" duty with Solomon Jacobs and Elijah Argustine. There is no explanation as to what type of work this was, but it is listed directly after "laundry." Thomas would have been eleven at this time. Did he toil away in the laundry, scrubbing the clothes and linens, hauling the water in a possibly windowless room filled with hot steam?

I can find few mentions of Thomas or Sam in the school records. No words of kindness by the teachers or anyone in authority at the supposed school. Nothing. Just that one item concerning the work Thomas was assigned, and finally, records of each of their deaths. Even those were written chillingly. They were "discharged."

It seemed there was always illness at Shingwauk. Sickness and death stalked the poorly ventilated, crowded facilities. Fevers and infections spread quickly. About five years before Thomas arrived, several girls at the nearby Wawanosh Home became infected with erysipelas, a strep A skin infection common where there's poor sewage drainage. In 1897, Sault Ste. Marie's board of health visited the school after complaints about the home's next-door neighbour: a slaughterhouse. Principal George King called the slaughterhouse "filthy and abominable." It was horrific to see, he reported: "offal, heads of animals, blood, bones and manure . . . littered about all over the place, rotting. In a pond of stagnant water close by is a quantity of putrid offal, the stench from which is unbearable."[30]

Sam was just seven years old when he died, on December 9, 1905, of a "rupturing bowel in Typhoid." Typhoid is a bacterial infection related to poor sanitation, frequently water contaminated with fecal material. After an intense fever and abdominal pain lasting nearly a week, the bowel can break down, causing sepsis that leads to death. Sam must have been in unbearable pain. I can't imagine how frightened he was. Did anyone hold his hand? Did his mother know he was dying? Was Thomas allowed to visit his little brother?

According to the school's annual reports, Thomas was an average student. But we don't know if he ever played sports or liked to draw or if he ever fell in love. We know he was assigned to work in the laundry room during his later teen years—not carpentry or the farm, but the hot, steamy, dank laundry room. And we know he spent four months in hospital in Sault Ste. Marie before dying of tuberculosis. We know that detail only because the Indian agent was trying to figure out where to send his hospital bill. He was eighteen years old when he passed away on July 12, 1913, barely a man

Reading how both boys lived, and how they died, makes me seethe. The utter cruelty of the Indian residential school is perfectly illustrated in the lives and deaths of Thomas and Samuel Skelliter.

THE FIRST TIME I went to Shingwauk, I visited Jenna, the archivist who'd helped me find Thomas and Samuel. That was in October 2022. We walked through the grounds, into the cemetery beside a thicket of tall maples, the green of their leaves fading to bright yellow. I wondered if the boys had walked here, had seen these trees. This cemetery has always been here at Shingwauk.

A waist-high wire fence surrounds the oldest part of the graveyard. Visitors have placed tobacco ties on the wires. Someone had left a pair of tiny moccasins. There is a monument, a pillar, about a metre high that has sweetgrass braided on the top. The sweetgrass ensures safe travels. The inscription reads: "In loving memory of pupils & staff of the Shingwauk Indian Residential School buried in this cemetery; Erected by former pupils, staff and friends. Shingwauk Reunion 1981. Names recorded in the Bishop Fauquier Memorial Chapel."

Supposedly, Thomas and Sam were buried here, somewhere beneath my feet. I took my tobacco out and I walked to each of the four directions, pressing tobacco into the wet earth to the east, to the west, to the north and to the south. As I did this, I whispered to the boys, starting by introducing myself in Anishinabemowin. "Booshoo, Ka-musko pimojijet pinaysheesh, ndiznikas." I told them my name is Little Bird with Big Wings Who Carries a Heavy Burden. "We have not forgotten you. We know you are here. You are not alone." Finally, in the southern direction, I knelt, placed my hands on the cold ground, and wept.

In April 2023, I went to visit Tom and Sam again. This time I went with Garden River First Nation's Darrell Boissoneau, a walking encyclopedia of local history. With us was my cousin Gary Holford. Thomas and Samuel are his great-uncles. Alphonse was his grandfather. Gary lives in Massey, about an hour outside Sault Ste. Marie. He wanted to come to see where the boys are.

Boissoneau is a treasure for all in Garden River who know him. He has devoted the latter part of his life to ensuring Shingwauk's original vision—of a school that was kind, and that would teach the children both their own ways of life and those of the settlers—is actually achieved and followed. He has sat with Shingwauk's grandchildren, listening to their stories first-hand. One of his favourites is this: Chief Shingwaukonse fought alongside General Brock in the War of 1812. He was given a sword and a red uniform jacket. He was shot several times but unharmed. Afterwards, he apparently stood on the battleground and shook his jacket—and the lead bullets fell out.

Boissoneau was instrumental in bringing together Algoma University and the Shingwauk Education Trust to establish the Shingwauk Kinoomaage Gamig, or SKG Teaching Lodge. He spent years quietly hounding politicians to secure more than $10 million for building the school, which now sits across the street from Shingwauk. He also made sure the Anishinaabe education plan the school created was accredited by the World Indigenous Nations Higher Education Consortium. Of this he is especially proud: that they were recognized by their peers.

We trudged through the thick ice-covered snow, past the maple trees now brightly coloured with blue buckets to catch the running sap. No one knows for certain where the boys are. They do not have grave markers, and whether they even had coffins is unknown. Someone had left an orange-painted rock at the base of a tree in the centre of the space that said "215."

The orange rock, nestled in the snow, immediately took me back to those heady days after the world discovered the Kamloops Indian Residential School children, Le Estcwicwéy̓, buried in the apple orchard by the powwow arbour. It was the children's spirits that called to us, shook us awake and mobilized us to get out there and start looking for our lost family members. They had already waited too long. I did not know when I was standing on the front steps of the residential school at Kamloops that the power of those spirits would lead me to find Thomas and Sam here, buried somewhere in Shingwauk's frozen back field. I didn't know that it would be my role to tell all of our extended family that these two lost boys were ours, and they had been found. I was there to tell their spirits it was time to go home.

Chapter Twelve

TRAIN SCHOOLS

THE VOICE ON THE RADIO DECLARED, "THEY WERE KNOWN AS SCHOOL CARS AND schools on wheels. Trains that brought the classroom to children in the most isolated communities of northern Ontario."

I was listening to the introduction to an hour-long CBC *Ideas* feature on train schools, a program that would explore "remote education home schooling and nation building."

Home schooling? Nation building? Was this for real?

My friend Alvin Fiddler, then Grand Chief of Nishnawbe Aski Nation and the leader who'd pushed for the inquest into the deaths of the seven, had called to tell me about the radio doc. He'd been driving around in his truck in Thunder Bay after a Tim Hortons tea run when he heard the episode. He said, "You need to listen to this."

Setting aside my work, I played the episode on my computer. It kicked off with a romantic locomotive sound. "It began with two chugging school car locomotives, school car number 1 and school car number 2 . . . It was an unprecedented collaboration between Ontario's then Ministry of Education and the railways." The schools took in a "diverse group," some from "families with long roots in northern Ontario."[1] The children's diversity would mean they were First Nations, Métis and European.

The more I heard, the more I felt sick to my stomach. Who did they think those isolated "trappers and hunters" were?

My mother went to school on a train. She remembers little about it. Memory does that. Blocks things out, makes them go away because your body can't handle the truth of what happened. It is a classic trauma response.

Though her silence is not as extreme as that of my great-grandmother Liz, my mother rarely talks about her childhood. It only comes out in dribs and drabs. You can't predict when she'll have one of those days where she is overcome. The emotion, the memories, are all too much, making her heart skip beats and pulse with irregular rhythms. Interruptions of the circle, the drum, the beat of the heart.

"Some things I will never tell you, I will take to my grave," she tells me, stifling a sob as she picks up dirty dishes and carries them to the sink. My mother is always cleaning, cooking, trying to make things right, trying to help me make a home. Without her, my children would be lost, there would be no second parent. William and Natasha's father, David, died suddenly when they were young. My mom and her husband Alfred, a wonderful man who immigrated from Guyana in the 1960s, have been rocks for my children and me.

My great-aunt Bernice remembers her dad, Rusty, saying, "If anyone tries to take my children away, I'll shoot them between the eyes." Remarkably, none of Liz and Rusty's nine children went to residential school. That is nearly unheard of. The 1931 census for Port Arthur–Thunder Bay lists every single one of their children as "Indians." Alphonse's job is "fur trapping wild animals." They were living in Graham when caught on that census, north of Ignace, in a small rail settlement beside what the English called Graham Lake.

This is Treaty 9 territory, deep in the dense boreal forest of thick, tall cedars and white birch. The rocky land is full of small, deep, clear lakes, countless beaver dams and moose. At one point, according to a faded sign on Graham Road that tells us to be mindful of their habitat, caribou were here, but I have never seen them. This is where I have gone hunting with students from Treaty 9 territory who attend school in Thunder Bay. The hunting trips are put on by NAN staff members to get the students out on the land, to remind them of home. These trips were a recommendation from the seven youth inquest, to remind kids of who they are.

Margaret, my grandmother, remembers watching Liz skin beavers outside the house. She's told me of the hides being stretched and tanned, and of the minks Rusty kept in cages. He used a dogsled to check his traplines outside of Graham. The family always had dogs. Rocky, a German shepherd, was a favourite.

Liz's daughter Connie's son Gary remembers a story of the good times. "There is a story I overheard when I was little that Uncle Dick"—Bernice's husband—"retold, God I miss his stories, about driving down the 1960s Trans-Canada and coming upon a traffic stoppage. Gramps, Hank and Dick got out to investigate and found a moose in the ditch feeding. Families had stopped and were oohing and aahing about this magnificent beast and taking photographs. Gramps or Hank suddenly shot the animal dead. Babies and children started bawling and their parents were horrified by these savages."

There was a small rail station in Graham, a post office and, at one point, a one-room schoolhouse. From the 1931 census, it looks as though the Bowens were one of the only local families, of about a dozen, who were "Indians." How did they all escape the Indian agents?

Mostly by hiding in the bush. Life wasn't easy. My great-grandma made all her children's clothes and she was also a midwife. She did not want to raise any of her grandchildren. She was done. But Gramps wanted to keep my mother, as a playmate for his youngest, Sarah. They were just two years apart.

"Gramps wouldn't let anyone cut my hair," my mother says, running her hands through it, remembering the weight of what used to be there. Her once brown-black thick, thick hair shines silver-white. She wears it in a bob just above her shoulders.

Despite Rusty's determination, he wasn't able to protect all the family from the authorities. By the 1940s, things had changed. Their daughter, Liz, had a son who is also named Rusty, a little boy with bright blue eyes. He disappeared into the provincial children's aid system and then to residential school.

Children's Aid's appetite for Indigenous children started to grow in the mid-twentieth century. It is the monster that grew out of residential schools. We know it as the Sixties Scoop, but the scooping of Indian children from their mothers was happening well before the 1960s and it continued long afterwards—it goes on even to this day. The state didn't just take the children; they also convinced First Nations women who were struggling under the weight of colonialism that they weren't fit to be mothers in the first place—that they should hand their children over to those who could do a better job.

Remarkably, during the writing of this book, we were reunited with the family of another child who was gone from us, adopted out in 1948. His name was Donald and he was the younger Rusty's brother. No one knew Great-Aunt Liz—Grandma Liz's daughter—had two sons. Well, I shouldn't say no one. The women in our family keep their secrets close.

My mother's times with Sarah are some of the only truly happy memories of her girlhood. When my mother was about seven, the Bowens moved from Graham to Raith, a loose collection of families living on the western edge of the Robinson-Superior Treaty area, about an hour and a half's drive from Thunder Bay. Rusty's cousins the Plummers also lived in Raith.

Sheila and Sarah were always getting into mischief, doing little things like hauling a big wooden bucket to the well to get water. There was no running water in their home, which was more of a plywood-and-log shack near the railway tracks. "We were both so tiny," my mother laughs, "and we had to drag this big bucket so far to get the water. We couldn't lift it. And in the dead of winter. Sometimes we almost fell in."

On my fridge is a picture of my mother with my great-aunt Sarah. It was taken in the 1980s. It is night. My mother is holding a long shotgun aimed at the sky. Sarah is laughing on one side of her and Sarah's husband, Chuck Amirault, is on the other. It's New Year's Eve. They were shooting at the stars.

Sarah lived in Raith into adulthood, in the house her parents moved to after they left Graham. Liz and Alphonse lived there too. After Liz died in 1974, Alphonse stayed on with Sarah and Chuck. Sarah worked at a truck stop down the highway. She looked exactly like her mom.

Sarah was as tall as she was wide and famous for her apple pie, her quietness. Her silence. She always had a cigarette in her hand.

Sarah went to school on the train with my mother.

IN THE EARLY 1990s, there was a devastating fire at the house in Raith. Of course, there was no fire response unit. Sarah and Chuck were not hurt, but everything, including the house, burned to the ground. All the paperwork, correspondence, certificates of anything official, photographs, clothes—everything that had marked Liz and Rusty's life was destroyed.

Uncle Hank felt the blow of those lost records as he hunted for the truth about our family, and now I feel it too. Given the difficulty of finding official documents about our relations, and the continuing resistance of some institutions to release them, the loss of the paperwork in the fire— the answers it might have held, about Sarah and my mother attending the train school and so much more—hardly bears thinking about.

Still, there had to be more records somewhere, I just knew it. In a country obsessed with paperwork when it comes to Indigenous Peoples, there had to be more—hidden away in federal and provincial government offices, in hospital and university basements.

Raymond Frogner, who is the NCTR's head of research and archives, agrees. I called him after meeting him briefly at the National Gathering on Unmarked Burials in Toronto in March 2023. Frogner, whose maternal family is from Duncan's First Nation in west-central Alberta, wisely puts into context the records mess Canada finds itself in. He says what we're facing when it comes to archives and Indigenous history in this country is the legacy of a 150-year program of colonial assimilation and genocide that never, ever had a detailed structure or defined policy for the collection and storage of records. The records were everywhere, hidden in plain sight—but there were no framework or rules for how they should be organized and stored.

Frogner has the formidable job of hunting for pieces of our lost families all over the country. He is the person everyone turns to. He has also been the only person of First Nations descent to visit the Oblate General

Archives in Vatican City.

In the 1930s and 1940s, he tells me, millions of records were destroyed. At that time, the status of Indian Affairs had been reduced to an office—it was no longer a ministry. "That speaks volumes, or a lot, to what rules and what authority the people operating in that office had regarding the control, the collection and preservation of records," he says. In that time, almost two million records on the topics of residential schools and children were lost. "The value placed on those records tells you the value placed on those children. It was a tremendous loss."[2]

He further explains that the war effort, which saw Indian Affairs documents reused to save on paper, and a lack of coordinated record-keeping, didn't help. Frogner refers to this as a "central explosion," when everything went flying off in various directions.

The TRC did not have sufficient time and funding to track down information from thousands of Survivors. They did not have an archivist working with them. They visited over two hundred communities to collect testimony, but gathering testimony is a different task than acquiring records. "For finding records themselves, the TRC struggled with private institutions and federal and provincial governments," Frogner tells me. "When I began to work at the NCTR archives in 2017, only two provincial sets of vital stats were in the hands of the NCTR, and that is after seven or eight years of the TRC's operation. I'll be blunt about it—what the hell happened there?"

Vital statistics include birth and death records, and the situation Frogner describes is finally changing. In 2023 Manitoba announced its vital stats will go to the NCTR, Ontario announced it would transfer 1800 death records of Indigenous children in 2021, and as of 2023 the NCTR was in negotiations with Quebec, Saskatchewan and the Northwest Territories. Filling another records gap is currently in the hands of provincial coroners. (In the TRC's final report, in 2015, Call to Action 71 was for chief coroners and provincial vital statistics agencies to release to the NCTR all records they had on Indigenous children who had died at residential schools.) A national conference of coroners put out a public statement to say they'd turn over their reports of children lost at residential schools, but Frogner says that so far, "none of the provinces actually ponied up and produced the records they said they would." The NCTR is now trying to individually track them all down. TRC Call to Action 77 asks that provinces transfer all records that document residential school histories.

The NCTR is also walking through every single federal ministry, working with assistant deputy ministers to find and identify all records relating to residential schools, including photographs, maps, building plans, attendance records and quarterly reports. "It is estimated to be approximately thirteen million records," says Frogner. "Four times what the TRC acquired. We are still picking up pieces here."

There are 141 schools on the NCTR site now, and it holds nearly three million records. Their goal, which might sound modest but would actually be a near-superhuman accomplishment, is to put 5 to 10 per cent of each school's records online.

I ask Frogner who speaks for Christina Sampson, who was stolen away to Elkhorn, Manitoba, from Ontario. I tell him about Inspector John Semmens, who used to sign the treaty annuity receipts received by Sampson in Winnipeg. The NCTR supports the concept that the community where the residential school was located should have access to the records, but, Frogner says, "the problem is the schools pulled in children from thirty or forty or more communities, often undocumented." So, he asks, when one community is coming to the NCTR for records, what about the thirty-nine other communities who had children at that school too? To further complicate the dynamics, the concept of First Nations communities run by band councils is colonial, a system constructed and dictated by the Indian Act. Frogner sighs and says, "It just never ends." Some challenges are hard to navigate—record-keeping varies by provinces and some may not include a child's Indigenous name or where they went to school. Currently, there are 4,127 children on the NCTR's national memorial registry of those who never made it home. We know that number is still climbing.

And these are all the reasons why Uncle Hank carried around a file folder. Hunting for what was lost.

HOW DO WE find out more about the circumstances forced upon our family members when those circumstances—such as the train school my mother and Great-Aunt Sarah attended—don't fit neatly into the categories now being created regarding the finding, retrieval of, storage of and access to records?

One thing is certain: In large measure, even now, amid all their talk of reconciliation, governments and institutions are not always willing or forthcoming. So we must do the work ourselves. We must impose that willingness upon them. Survivors and their families continue to be at the forefront of holding Canada accountable. The 2006 Indian Residential Schools Settlement Agreement and, more recently, the 2021 Indian Residential Schools Day Scholars settlement agreement, have used the courts to force Canada to confront the past.

The IRSSA is one of the largest class-action settlements ever seen in Canada. All eligible former students were entitled to a structured payment, and a fund was set up to pay Survivors of sexual or serious physical abuse who filed an Independent Assessment Process claim.

The IRSSA is not perfect or all-encompassing. There were hundreds of institutions, federally, provincially and privately run, aimed at assimilating children. However, under the terms of the IRSSA, Canada "recognized" only 139 former Indian residential schools.[3]

The IRSSA set in place a mechanism for individuals or organizations to request that an "unrecognized" institution be added to the list of "recognized" schools. Consequently, the court-approved Newfoundland and Labrador Residential Schools Settlement Agreement of 2016 added five institutions to the list.[4] However, a significant number of other institutions that Indigenous children were forced to attend, and where they experienced mistreatment and abuse, remain unrecognized under the IRSSA. In fact, as of 2019, it was reported that nearly ten thousand people had asked for another 1,531 "distinct institutions" to be added to the agreement. But only seven more schools have so far met the government's criteria for recognition.[5]

For children who attended an Indian residential school during the day but were allowed to go home at night, a class action was launched in 2009 by Survivor Garry McLean from Lake Manitoba First Nation. He attended the Dog Creek Day School. It took so long to wind its way through the courts that unfortunately Garry, who passed away in 2019, never got to see the Federal Indian Day Schools settlement take effect in early 2020. With a $1.4-billion settlement fund, it covered 699 schools.[6]

Like other settlements with the government, the day schools settlement has its flaws. It has a tiered compensation structure for Survivors. Level one compensation is given to those who can prove they attended a day school. Another level of compensation is decided based on the severity of abuse suffered, which is ranked on a scale of 2 to 5. This requires documentary proof, which is difficult, if not impossible, to find, as the Anishinabek Nation argued in a letter of protest to David Lametti, then the attorney general of Canada, in 2022: "It is hardly surprising that the abusers at these government-sanctioned institutions did not document the abuses of Indigenous children. Further, the production of this proof also causes traumatization for the individuals who have already suffered such immense harms."[7] The Anishinabek Nation represents thirty-nine First Nations in Ontario, including Fort William First Nation. It is the oldest political organization in the province and can trace its roots back to the Confederacy of Three Fires, which existed long before European contact.

The Chiefs of Ontario, the organization representing all of Ontario's First Nations communities, also protested, in its own letter to Lametti and the parties of the day school settlement, how the claims process for Survivors would work. Their letter reads in part: "Everyone needs to be realistic about what records are going to be there, or not be there. Records about abuse are unlikely to have been made in the first place, let alone kept. We know that the schools largely condoned abuse, and did not report it or treat it as criminal, so why would we expect records?"[8]

The unrealistic requirement for proof was one thing. But what about the schools that didn't count—that weren't accepted under either the day schools or the residential schools agreements?

Some schools aren't covered because they were provincially run or because they were considered private institutions. In Saskatchewan, there are two well-known examples: the Île-à-la-Crosse Boarding School, which operated from 1860 until 1976, and Timber Bay Children's Home, near Lac La Ronge, which ran from 1952 until 1994. Students from both remain uncounted. Both schools were run by the Northern Canada Evangelical Mission and later the Brethren in Christ Church. Many Métis students attended these two schools.[9]

Currently, a memorandum of understanding has been entered into between Canada and the Métis students who attended the Île-à-la-Crosse school, but Métis students who attended Timber Bay are still working to appeal the dismissal of their class-action certification.[10]

Other schools are lost through time, legal neglect and the fading memories of Survivors, coupled with a lack of adequate proof or documentation of what went on inside the institutions. On top of all that, the Canadian government remains reluctant to acknowledge that genocide has had a longer reach, with far more tentacles than it would care to admit.

AMONG THOSE SCHOOLS that have fallen through the cracks are nearly all the stops on the train school routes. The only train stop that is so far part of the Indian Day Schools settlement is the one at Nakina. (A rail school operated in Aroland, on the National Transcontinental Rail line twenty kilometres from Nakina, between 1949 and 1979.)[11] However, there were fourteen other stops in the province, including the one at Graham that my mother and Sarah attended. Those stops don't count because the Province of Ontario was in charge of them, not the federal government in concert with a religious entity. (As I write this, a number of individual claims have been filed by former First Nations students who attended the train schools. Some are from my home community, Fort William First Nation.)

Train schools were exactly what they sound like: railcars that stopped in rural areas so children could attend school on them. "They looked like coach cars," my mother says, "but inside there were little wooden desks." The cars were owned by the railways, but the schools were operated by Ontario. From 1926 until 1967, the trains would pull into a stop for one week and then disappear for three or four weeks as the railcar kept going along the line. One train school travelled from Thunder Bay and stopped at Larson, Graham—where my mother and Sarah attended classes—Tannin, Watcomb and Umfreville. On the Sioux Lookout line, the train school stopped at McDougall Mills, Ghost River, Allan Water, Armstrong, Ferland, Nakina, Foleyet and Capreol, then a small town just north of Sudbury. There was a line that ran from North Bay to Kirkland Lake, and another that ran from Thunder Bay to Fort Frances, with stops in Huronian, Kawene, Atikokan, Flanders and Farrington.[12]

Each day started with "God Save the King," followed by the Lord's Prayer. The students were expected to be washed and clean, with their hair done neatly, and dressed in their "Sunday best." The British flag would be raised at the back of the car. Then the lessons started. There was no instruction in Indigenous language, customs or culture.

In everything I've read, the train schools—which taught children from all kinds of families living remotely, not all of them Indigenous—are hailed as "progressive." They are seen as romantic, clever tools for remote learning. That was certainly the tone of the *Ideas* documentary I listened to. For some Canadians they were seen as "nation building."

But for my family and for others, the trains were further instruments of colonization and abuse, not unlike residential schools and Indian hospitals, TB sanatoriums and asylums, and the child welfare system. The net was vast and it was tight. The message during those many decades was very clear: assimilate or we'll do it for you.

For some Indigenous families, including my own, the train schools served as one more instrument of erasure.

IN THE EARLY and mid-twentieth century, the men settling the north, building the roads and railways, setting up industry in order to mine the rich resources there, were English. The "foreigners" who were brought north to help extract the resources, and the "Indians" who'd been there all along, needed to be anglicized, made to fit into Canada.

Like the Hudson's Bay Company, the Canadian Pacific and Canadian

National railways were instruments of colonization. The language of the train schools, of needing to "civilize" and "assimilate" those who lived and worked in the bush along the railway lines, sounds exactly like the language used to justify residential schools.

It is no surprise that the early education "pioneers" of northern Ontario did not give a second thought to the Anishinaabe, the people actually working and living on the land. The Anishinaabe and Métis were all over the north; not all lived on reserves. Many, like my own family, hid in the bush.

James MacDougall, described as a man who always wore a dark three-piece suit and carried a large pocket watch, was one of two educators from Queen's University who tried to devise an education plan for the north for the Ontario government. A Presbyterian who was born in Scotland, MacDougall believed non-English-speaking people who did not have British ideals were a problem, a menace to society that needed to be tamed. In 1919 he took on the role of northern education inspector, reporting to the Ontario government.[13] He believed that through hard labour, the souls of the people living and working in the north would be transformed.[14]

As he wrote in his poem "Builders of the North,"

And build ye a race, toil-bred sons of the Northland,
As your stately pines straight, as your granite hills strong,
Thew-knit, supple sinewed, soul and body puissant.
Britain's vanguard in right, and her bulwark 'gainst wrong.[15]

MacDougall is credited with being the first person to publicly suggest that a school be put on the rails, travelling to remote communities.[16]

THE ONTARIO INSTITUTE for Studies in Education has a large file on train schools. It is full of photographs and articles extolling the virtues of the schools. On a cold late-December day, when most of OISE was on winter break, I was up in the stacks, staring at the photographs inside the files.

One picture that really caught my attention shows the inside of a railcar. Instead of the usual train seats, there are small wooden desks, arranged neatly in long rows, facing the front of the car, just like my mom described. There is a large wooden teacher's desk with a hand bell on one side and a globe on the other. A large Union Jack covers the ceiling of the train. A man in a suit is seated at the desk, writing. Behind him, written in cursive in white chalk on a wood-framed blackboard, are the words "C.P.R. School Car No. 1, Cartier to Chapleau. W. H. McNally. Teacher." The teachers—and their families, if they had them—had separate living quarters on the trains.

My mom went to school on a train in Graham, Ontario, just like this one. The mobile school had stops along the CNR line, teaching both Indigenous and non-Indigenous students how to be good British citizens. (Ontario Institute for Studies in Education)

My mother does not remember who her teacher was. She attended the train school for only a year, when she was six or seven years old, before the family moved away from Graham. She remembers going to the dentist on the train. (Sometimes the trains provided dental care, a rarity in the north.) It's not a happy memory: eight of her teeth were pulled out, all of her molars gone. Afterwards, she walked home, alone and bleeding, in the middle of winter. When she stumbled in the door, her grandmother Liz nearly passed out. "She thought I was almost dead," she recalls. Fever came, then infection. Liz nursed her back to health.

My mom, Sheila Bowen, and her aunt Sarah Bowen attended the train school at the stop in Graham, Ontario, where she was being raised by Annie's daughter Liz. We do not have a photo of her at the train school. (Ontario Institute for Studies in Education)

Her other memory of going to school on the train is even more unsettling. "I was put outside the train, in between the cars. In between the doors. There is a little pathway to walk through. In the other car were living quarters," she says quietly. "That is when it goes blank."

The only other detail my mother can recall is that Sarah never had to leave her desk. It was just my mother: she was the one repeatedly taken out of the classroom car and taken between the cars.

I asked Murray Sinclair, the former chair of the TRC, if anyone spoke of the train schools during the commission's six years of hearing testimony. He told me he'd never heard of them. However, the existence of the train schools did not surprise him.

The refurbished railcar would stop along the CNR line for weeks at a time. Students came to the school daily and went home at night. A separate train compartment was home for the teacher. (Ontario Institute for Studies in Education)

All the schools that were part of the TRC, Murray pointed out, were federally funded and recognized. "When Sir John A. Macdonald started out in 1867, he started out with a huge population of Indigenous People," he said. "They were willing to be in a partnership with the white colonizers. But our people couldn't see the fraud being perpetrated upon them." He gave me his take on Macdonald's policies: "Colonization was the way to go. All these little brown children were all going to disappear because we'll turn them into white children." That approach was popular among settlers, he said, because they were coming from places that already had other people in control. The ones who came here were tired of being dominated; they wanted to be in charge. "White kids came to believe in the superiority of their civilizations, so they believed they had the right to do and take whatever they wanted."

As we've seen in this book, and as is gradually becoming more widely recognized, the railway has a complicated history in Canada. It blew through First Nations and Métis communities, expropriating land in order to build an economically viable national tool. The train was used to take the missionaries across the country and the train took our children, by the carload, to residential school—and if they ran away, it sometimes took them back, passing them like batons between RCMP officers and Indian agents onward down the line. If there was a death on the train or on the railway's lands, the railway could conduct its own investigation. That is still the law, within five hundred metres of the tracks, though local police forces are now more likely to conduct investigations.

Our people are still trying, still determined to have those documents released. In 2021, Six Nations Chief Mark Hill wrote a letter to Jean-Jacques Ruest, then president and chief executive officer of CN, regarding the company's archives of its death investigations. Hill begins by reminding Ruest of the finding of the 215 at Tk'emlúps te Secwépemc. He then tells him about Six Nations' own needs as they search the grounds of the Mohawk Institute Residential School: "We are now in the process of locating and recovering all our disappeared children across these lands, so that they can be properly cared for in accordance with our own cultures and traditions. This painful process requires the assistance of all of Canada," he writes. "Many of the Indian Residential Schools were erected near railway lines. The TRC documented several deaths near or on railway tracks."

Hill asks that CN search its archives for records relating to investigations of children who were injured, killed or died near or on railway tracks, and ensure that all such records are preserved and protected. He asks CN to provide copies of any records related to investigations within a one-hundred-kilometre radius of the Mohawk Institute "to assist with our recovery efforts of our children that were forced to attend this deathly institute."

His letter continues, "Our people have many unanswered questions about what happened to our children while being forced to attend Indian Residential Schools. The work that the TRC commenced to identify those that died needs to continue. As the former Chair of the Truth and Reconciliation Commission of Canada said, 'reconciliation is going to take hard work—people of all walks of life and at all levels of society will need to be willing to engage.' Today, we urge you to engage and assist us in recovering and honouring our disappeared children."

MY MOTHER WAS born in 1944, at the end of the Second World War, to my grandmother Margaret, an unwed young Cree and Anishinaabe woman. At the time, Margaret could not handle caring for my mother, so she left her with her parents. My great-grandparents desperately tried to fit in with colonial society: Grandma Liz didn't want whatever it was that she'd lived through to happen to her daughters or sons, or to my mother.

But you can't escape the circumstances you are born into, even though you do not ask for them. My mother's beloved daughter Donna was adopted by a white family from Manitoba when she was just one year old. My mother, one of the most whip-smart people I've ever known, was suddenly on her own, without a high school education. She had nothing but her wits. She married my father, David Talaga, and put herself, when she was in her 30s and against my father's wishes and without a penny of his support, through high school and then she went to Seneca College. For years she worked at a grocery store as a cashier and in her spare time, she sold Tupperware. She wanted to be able to find a good job, lift herself out. I know every choice she made was for her remaining children, my brother and me. Every choice was about survival. My mother, with her beautiful 1,000-watt smile, is the face of bravery.

When I was a girl, before she told my brother and me that we had a sister, I never knew why she cried herself to sleep at night. She had copies of *Half-Breed* by Maria Campbell and *In Search of April Raintree* by Beatrice Culleton Mosionier stashed under her bed. For a significant portion of her life, she never told anyone she was an Indian: her grandmother told her not to, that she had to fit in with Canadian society. My father wouldn't stand for it either. If she ever tried to be herself, he'd put a stop to it, calling her names, violently belittling her existence.

We lost Donna for decades. She didn't return to our family until she searched for my mother in the mid-1990s. Around the same time, my mother's brothers Bill and Maurice, who were also part of the Sixties Scoop, found Margaret. They came back to the family. (Their third brother, Alvie, never made it home.)

When this all happened, my mother left my father. I was in my early twenties, just graduating from university. The silence was broken. Her other daughter and remaining brothers were back.

We were Indian again.

BOOK FOUR

White

The last stage of adulthood is not the end, it's a time full of wisdom and truth as the winter comes, the cold season when everything takes a pause before life begins again. The end is the beginning.

CHAPTER THIRTEEN

ROME AND AN APOLOGY

I SLITHERED INTO A MONTREAL AIRPORT LOUNGE CHAIR, PUTTING MY BLACK backpack on the empty chair beside me. Feeling uneasy, with not a bone in my body wanting to get on that flight to Rome, I was hoping to go unnoticed. The majority of the folks coming to the gate on this late Saturday afternoon in March were part of an Indigenous delegation chosen by Métis, First Nations and Inuit leaders in Canada to attend a historic visit to Vatican City in search of that elusive apology nearly seven years after it was demanded in one of the TRC's calls to action. As always, the onus was on Indigenous Peoples to keep the pressure on, demanding this simple but powerful gesture be fulfilled.

A couple of men in dark suit jackets with white collars and crosses around their necks walked past me. That was when it dawned on me that the entire contingent would be travelling over on the same plane. This was something I had not quite thought of, even though it had been mentioned, during one of the briefings from the Canadian Conference of Catholic Bishops, or CCCB, that six Canadian bishops would be accompanying the delegation.

The weeks leading up to the trip were a blur. I had been scrambling to get my Vatican press accreditation—every time I filled out the online forms, the site crashed—and figure out my travel. I was not part of the official delegation of thirty-two Indigenous Elders, Survivors, youth and

Knowledge Keepers who were being sponsored by the CCCB. I had paid for my flights, hotel and other travel costs myself. I wanted to be a witness to this historic event and not be beholden to anyone. It meant too much to me.

For more than a decade, all of my work and my writing—my two books, including my CBC Massey Lectures that had taken me across Canada, and the documentary film I wrote, directed and produced, essentially the entire world as I understood it as a First Nations journalist—had been shaped by the colonial vise grip of the Indian Act and the Indian residential school system in Canada. Nothing was untouched by the policies of assimilation I struggled to contend with, in my mind and with my pen. The deaths of the seven students in Thunder Bay. The death of twenty-two-year-old Colten Boushie at the hands of Gerald Stanley, a white Saskatchewan farmer, who was acquitted of any crime. The murder of fifteen-year-old Tina Fontaine, whose body was found in the Red River, wrapped in a tarp, after she'd travelled to Winnipeg in search of her mother. Pedophile and former Anglican minister Ralph Rowe. The seemingly endless number of suicides and attempted suicides in so many of our communities, starting with the first death I covered in-depth, that of Nellie Trapper's son Thomas, aged seventeen, in 2009. That story, which I worked hard to convince the *Toronto Star* I needed to cover, took me to Moosonee. Thomas was one of thirteen teenagers in the region, along both the James Bay and Hudson Bay coasts, who took their lives that year. The youngest was fourteen.[1]

Every time I stood on a stage and gave a speech and told audiences what I was reporting, what I was seeing, I was pulled right back to the catastrophic harm caused by residential schools. It was one of the root causes of the pain. The Catholic Church was a main instigator. That's not me being anti-Catholic; it is just a fact. The church ran 60 per cent of the residential schools in Canada.[2]

When I was sitting in the airport that day, dreading the trip to Rome, my search for Annie had just begun. I hadn't yet met my cousin Paula Rickard, the keeper of the James Bay family trees. I was writing this book on residential schools, but I didn't know it would take a turn and begin to focus on Annie and the Carpenter branch of my family. I did not know about the existence of the Skelliter boys, or that they had been at Shingwauk. I didn't know that Annie had more children, or that four of them had seemingly vanished into thin air. I did not know how deep my family's connection was to the James Bay coast, or exactly how Christianity, the fur trade and the policies of a growing Canada had held us, for generations, in a vise. I wondered what kind of God, what kind of country, would let any of this happen. Who would allow this othering of us?

I had no faith in any apology from the pope bringing forward any absolution. Maybe this was arrogance speaking or maybe my mistrust came from my years as a journalist. A hard shell had formed around me. I had been writing stories for three decades. Sitting in that airport lounge, I told myself that I was going to Rome for everyone else.

But that wasn't necessarily true, was it? I was part of this story too. That's the reality of being an Indigenous journalist. We *are* part of the story: there is no escaping it. Our families have already lived through the apocalypse, the end of the world as we knew it: the taking of the lands we'd lived on for millennia, the destruction of our ways of life, the crushing of our spirits, the stealing of our children. The Survivors and Intergenerational Survivors have the scars to prove it.

I was going for Annie Carpenter, for Elizabeth Bowen, and for my mom, for what she'd endured as a child and the struggles she'd had as a woman. I was going for my late sister Donna and all she'd lived through. I was going for Uncle Maurice, for Uncle Bill, for Uncle Alvie, for all the years they were gone and all the tears they'd shed. I was going for Elder Sam Achneepineskum, a Survivor of three of some of the most notorious residential schools in the country—Cecilia Jeffrey, McIntosh and St. Anne's—and I was going for his grandson Aaron Loon, who died outside a motel in Thunder Bay and whose death was not adequately investigated by the Thunder Bay Police. I was going for all the Survivors I knew. I was going to witness.

This trip to seek an apology from the pontiff was contentious in Indian Country. There were many Survivors who did not want to go, could not bring themselves to do it. The pope, they felt, should have come to us without us having to beg.

There was nothing fun about stepping onto a plane to head to Vatican City, to hear words from a pope that may or may not be sincere or trustworthy. These were generational wrongs that had started at contact. After all this time, what would an apology mean?

All of this ran through my mind as I sat in that lounge, watching everyone arrive at the gate for the overnight flight. The strangeness of this journey overwhelmed me. And even though our flight was packed, the delegation all decided on, because so many hadn't wanted to come, it felt as though we were not all there. To me, our Indigenous delegation seemed half full.

But maybe I was missing something. Others around me looked joyful. Members of the Métis delegation kept springing up from their seats every time someone new came to join the group. They hugged, they laughed, they rejoiced in being there together. Their circle grew and grew.

Indigenous and non-Indigenous TV networks milled about, trying to capture the scenes unfolding before them. The Métis were a big draw. They were the only truly lively ones. Documentary film crews hustled for position. Lisa LaFlamme, the chief anchor for *CTV National News*, gracefully swanned in like a goddess. People parted to clear a path for her.

I couldn't help but notice the First Nations crowd seemed a bit different. We mostly sat quietly in our chairs, observing, squirming, a bit suspicious.

Grand Chief Wilton Littlechild, who'd been one of the commissioners of the TRC, slowly passed by me, his wife pushing his wheelchair. He wore his white cowboy hat and looked so frail and thin. That was a moment. After all this time, after asking—for forty long years—for an apology, Chief Littlechild, a member of Ermineskin Cree Nation and former Grand Chief of the Confederacy of Treaty Six First Nations, was on his way to Rome. Finally, after all the Cree lawyer and Survivor had been through and had heard. In 2015, after six years of listening to and absorbing the pain of the Survivors of 139 Indian residential schools—nearly 6,500 witnesses—Chief Littlechild, along with his fellow commissioners, former Canadian senator and TRC chair Murray Sinclair and journalist Marie Wilson, had completed the final report of the Truth and Reconciliation Commission of Canada, which contained ninety-four calls to action. That document was a roadmap, if you will, for how Canada could begin to heal from all that entrenched trauma. This trip was being undertaken in response to the TRC's call to action number 58, which asked the head of the Catholic Church to come to Canada within one year to apologize on Canadian soil.

Here we were, seven years later, still hunting for that apology.

Then it happened. I was spotted. St. Anne's Survivor Viv Timmins and her husband were standing in front of me. She grabbed my hand and said how happy she was to see me—the last time had been at the Na-Me-Res Covid vaccination clinic in downtown Toronto. She was on this trip as a healer, part of a team of spiritual healers brought on by the Assembly of First Nations. (Yes, we took our own spiritual leaders with us to Rome.) She had a stunned look in her eyes, as if she couldn't believe she was standing in the middle of this bizarre, surreal scene.

I mentioned the happiness I was seeing around us and told her I felt none of that, just a hollowness, a sadness. She said she felt it too, that this was going to be hard, and then she squeezed my arm and whispered, "You know, I'm here for all of our people, everyone with us. Come find me if you need me."

Boarding the plane was not as easy as it sounds, and it wasn't just me. Elder Fred Kelly, a member of the Midewiwin and another spiritual advisor on the trip, was having a hard time getting his more than three-hundred-year-old peace pipe on board. In fact, all spiritual items were nearly prevented from leaving Canada because of one of those Canadian law changes that officials think make sense but that can have damning repercussions for Indigenous Peoples. This one was courtesy of Heritage Canada, the federal department in charge of Canadian cultural items and identity. A change made to the Cultural Property Export and

Import Act in 2022 meant that artifacts more than fifty years old and worth more than $3,000 were no longer able to leave the country.

This posed a problem for a First Nations delegation carrying sacred ceremonial items to Rome. How does one put a price tag on a pipe, or on handmade drums? Such objects, once outlawed by the Canadian government under the Indian Act, are priceless to us. Indigenous ceremonies and all their associated cultural objects were banned for almost seventy years, our sacred possessions confiscated or destroyed, but now the Canadian government saw these very objects as so important, they had to prevent them from leaving the country. This was a strange turn of events.

Back in Ottawa, days before we left, the AFN had been forced to go on an offensive against Heritage Canada. The AFN demanded an exception, otherwise none of the objects needed for ceremony in Rome would be allowed to be transported—the things First Nations people would need to practise our own spirituality, the very thing the Catholic Church had taken away from us through residential schools, would be unavailable at a time when our peoples needed them the most. In the end, the AFN won—and Elder Kelly did manage to board the plane with his peace pipe—but the symbolism was striking.

Our plane was full—a collection of beads and bundles, long black hair and buckskin vests. You could tell who the church contingent were: the slightly uncomfortable-looking, conservatively dressed folks. As our plane rose, none of us really knew what to expect, what was about to unfurl. The delegation would be split into four one-hour audiences with the pope inside an ornate, palatial room. Would Pope Francis apologize to the Métis at the first audience on Monday morning, or perhaps to the Inuit delegation later that morning? Or would he do it on Thursday, when the AFN's delegation, the largest of the three, had its turn? Another scenario could be that he'd apologize on Friday, when all three delegations convened for one giant audience with the pope—an apology jamboree, if you will, at the end of a packed week.

Or would he not apologize at all?

LEONARDO DA VINCI–FIUMICINO Airport was chaotic. The Survivors, their families, bishops, and media people had to find our way to a train that would take us to another terminal where we would collect our bags. Then we boarded the large white coaches that would take us to the Best Western Plus Hotel Universo. A small-statured older woman with short orange-dyed hair took to the mic at the front of the bus and introduced herself. She was a tour guide of sorts, hired by the church to be an ambassador, show us around, take us on a couple of tours: a day-trip to Assisi, the birthplace of St. Francis, and a visit to the Vatican Museums and the Sistine Chapel. She spoke to us as if this was a vacation, sharing interesting facts such as that Rome was built on seven hills. I noticed that we passed Via Cristoforo Colombo. (For real.) It felt like we'd all signed up for a European package tour.

Our guide told us the hotel would call everyone at five thirty so we wouldn't miss out on the first mass of the trip. "Six p.m. mass, then an early supper," she announced. "You are in Italy so you are getting lots of pasta." She told us how well everyone would eat: the pasta, the seafood, the incredible daily breakfasts of pastries, eggs and ham. How great it was going to be at the hotel. She told us the rooms in European hotels were smaller than they were in North America, but she assured us that they were "much better," with "nice white crisp ironed sheets and clean bathrooms."

I couldn't believe what I was hearing. I wondered if the tour guide had been properly briefed for her assignment. Did she know she was speaking to residential school Survivors whose psyches carried the deep scars of going without nutritious food for years, of near starvation, of being made to eat their own vomit if they didn't like that particular day's gruel? How our children were medically experimented on in order to make nutritious food supplements for non-Indigenous children? Did she realize that being put up in accommodations by the Catholic Church might be traumatic for some members of the delegation, those who'd been kept in residential schools like prisoners, unable to say goodnight to Mom or Dad or to hang on to their favourite toy or teddy bear?

The papal buses swerved through the maze of streets outside beyond Termini, the main train station in the heart of Rome. Our guide told us that Rome is a walkable city, that everything we'd want to see was truly not that far. She then warned us about Roman drivers. "The drivers here are crazy but totally good," she said, laughing. "Stop signs are just suggestions."

We passed a green statue of Pope John Paul, the Polish pontiff, a reminder to me of whose city we were in. It made me feel queasy. There was a giant white Red Cross tent set up to handle the influx of Ukrainian refugees who had streamed into the city within the first few weeks of the war. Around the corner was the delegation's hotel.

The guide explained that the Universo was on a one-way street and the bus could not stop in front of the entrance. We were going to have to walk, while the bus would pull around the back to unload our bags. She assured us our bags would eventually be brought to our rooms, rooms that were not yet ready as we'd come on an overnight flight and it was still early on Sunday morning.

Soon the marble lobby of the hotel was crowded with Indigenous people, mingling and mixing, looking for the bathrooms, jostling for a seat on one of the lime-green or black leather couches. It occurred to me that there was something quite extraordinary in the fact that the CCCB had booked the Indigenous delegation into a Best Western. Many of our communities lie in rural areas or far-flung small towns. The only hotel for miles around is often a Best Western or a Super 8, chain hotels known for basic, comfortable rooms, plenty of parking and—most important for the Indigenous road warrior—an all-you-can eat breakfast, which usually consists of boxed cereal, stale bagels, a waffle maker, a toaster and, if you are lucky, real scrambled eggs.

Even if this Best Western was a slicked-out Euro version of what we knew, had someone from the CCCB done their research and figured that the best place to stick a bunch of Indigenous People was a hotel that we were already familiar with? Had booking us here been a stroke of genius?

Or—conversely—was it a massive slight?

Why, after all, weren't the delegates housed in one of the finest hotels of Rome, overlooking the Spanish Steps? Or, better yet, why were they not housed in Vatican City, as honoured guests of a church that was supposedly working hard to earn redemption from people they'd nearly papal-bulled into oblivion?

ON SUNDAY EVENING, I had a long-awaited dinner with Natan Obed, the president of the Inuit Tapiriit Kanatami, or ITK, the organization representing the sixty-five thousand Inuit in Inuit Nunangat, the homeland of the Inuit in northern Canada. The territory stretches over four northern Canadian Arctic regions: the Inuvialuit Settlement Region (in Yukon and Northwest Territories), the territory of Nunavut, Nunavik (in northern Quebec) and Nunatsiavut (in northern Labrador). The residential school and federal hostel system, combined with forced relocation of the Inuit off the land, has left a long legacy. About 75 per cent of Inuit kids aged 6 to 15 were enrolled in the institutions by 1964.

I hadn't seen Obed in nearly three years, since the start of the pandemic. He's one of my favourite people. He leads with kindness, never anger. The first time I heard him speak, at a medical conference in Ottawa, I was impressed by how he commanded his audience, and I was embarrassed by the lack of knowledge I had about Inuit. I approached him after his speech and told him so. We've been friends ever since.

We had lots to talk about as we walked the streets of Rome, jet-lagged and bleary-eyed. After nearly two hours, we were ravenous and walked into the first restaurant we saw. We missed the clue in the restaurant's window: pasta dishes encased in plastic. It was basically the Olive Garden of Rome.

Obed was leading an Inuit delegation of seven (one of their delegates had missed the trip because of bad weather in the Arctic). As we spoke that night at the restaurant, he outlined what he would say to the pope.

He also shared a worry: his luggage hadn't made it to Rome. That was a major concern, as it contained the traditional ceremonial dress he was planning to wear to see the pope less than two days later. Clothing, our ceremonial wear, proudly worn after decades of intolerance, ignorance and hate, is like our armour, reminding us who we are and where we are from. When children went to residential school, they were stripped of their clothes and any items they brought with them from home. Their belongings were taken by the church and destroyed. To put these clothes on again and stand in front of the leader of the Catholic Church holds meaning. It protects us.

Still, Obed was focused on his main reason for coming to Rome: he needed the Vatican's help in bringing former priest Johannes Rivoire to Canada. His ultimate goal was not an apology. It was justice. He would tell one of the most powerful men in the world that harm was inflicted by the Catholic Church's schools through cultural oppression; through the erosion of language, spirituality and culture; and by physical and sexual brutality. He would tell him the church continued to harm Inuit by refusing to act in good faith and fulfill its obligations under the 2006 Indian Residential Schools Settlement Agreement.

And he would tell the pontiff that harm was inflicted by sexual predators within the church who used their power and position to prey upon and sexually abuse Inuit. While many priests and members of the church abused children in Nunangat, the actions of three men in particular were on Obed's mind: Oblate clerics Lucien Parent, Eric Dejaeger and Johannes Rivoire.

This was why Obed wanted to be in the presence of the pope. He wanted him to understand what had happened in these cases, and to get him onside to bring some kind of peace to the many victims those men had.

SOME HISTORY ABOUT this endless quest for justice. Let's start with Brother Parent. Lucien Parent taught at the Oblate-run Sir Joseph Bernier Federal Day School in Chesterfield Inlet, on the western shore of Hudson Bay. He was a dorm supervisor at the school's Turquetil Hall. He used candy to lure young boys into his room, then he sexually abused them. Parent died by suicide in Hull, Quebec, in 1979.[3]

As for Eric Dejaeger, I had spent an evening at home in Toronto reading the 2014 Nunavut Court of Justice judgment against him by Mr. Justice Robert Kilpatrick. It was revolting. Many times I had to put the judgment down, get up from my desk and walk around. The allegations against him, laid out over 212 pages, are sickening and disturbing, but it is important to state plainly here exactly what some Survivors were forced to live through, and then to live with, for the rest of their lives.

The judgment revealed eighty alleged offences, committed between 1976 and 1982, against Inuit males and females ranging in age from four to twenty. The charges included indecent assault, unlawful confinement, rape, sexual assault, assault, acts of gross indecency, threatening, buggery and three counts of bestiality with a dog.[4] Most of the alleged offences were committed when Dejaeger was posted in the community of Igloolik, Nunavut, at various locations, including a shed adjacent to the Roman Catholic mission and at several isolated hunting camps, one near Igloolik, another in Baker Lake and another in Pelly Bay.

The allegations included taping a young girl's legs—she was between five and ten years old—to metal bed posts and anally raping her; the fondling of boys' and girls' genitals over their pants while they sat on his lap; anally raping a young teen (named LKC in the judgment), then forcing her to bring her little sister up to his room; and lining children up to watch him perform bestiality on a large grey dog.[5]

The complainant identified as LKC testified that the abuse started when she was fourteen, beginning at the mission when she and other youths were there cleaning the building. It continued for four years.[6] At fifteen she became pregnant. The court documents do not mention the child again or who the father was. When she tried to tell her mother what had happened, her mother became angry and told her, "Priests are gods. They are healers." Then, LKC testified, her mother beat her for suggesting anything had happened. Another complainant, identified as TI, was a young girl when, she said, Dejaeger lay on top of her and "it [felt] like her vagina [was] being ripped open." She blacked out and remembered nothing else until her mom came to get her the next day. Afterwards Dejaeger threatened her, warning that if she told anyone, "Jesus would not love her anymore and she would go to hell."[7]

In 1990, Dejaeger had been sentenced in the Northwest Territories Supreme Court to five years in prison for nine sexual offences involving children in Baker Lake, Nunavut.[8] The judge said he was "not satisfied" that Dejaeger was a pedophile. Rather, he was just "a lonely man who had normal sexual urges, which he repressed for many years because of his calling no doubt and who satisfied those sexual urges, not by approaching adults who were old enough or mature enough to say no to him, but by befriending or seducing young children who did not know enough, or were not courageous enough, to say no to him."[9] This, to me, was a stunning statement by a sitting Canadian judge.

Dejaeger was released after serving part of his sentence, and while the RCMP were investigating further allegations, this time into his activities in Igloolik, he fled Canada for his native Belgium, where he lived in a small Oblate villa in Blanden.[10] Reportedly, he worked as a tour guide for school groups for a number of years.

In 1995, after a two-year investigation, the RCMP laid charges and issued warrants for his arrest. Warrants were issued again in 2002, and Interpol issued an international alert in 2001. It did so again in 2010 and 2011. Dejaeger was finally extradited back to Canada to face the additional charges outlined by Justice Kilpatrick in his 2014 judgment.

Out of the eighty sex-related offences he was charged with, Dejaeger was sentenced in 2015 on thirty-two charges, for indecent assault, unlawful confinement, buggery, unlawful sexual intercourse, sexual assault and bestiality. Of these charges, he had pleaded guilty to eight and not guilty to twenty-four. Justice Kilpatrick sentenced him to nineteen years in prison. He was paroled on June 6, 2022.[11] However, almost exactly a year later he was arrested in Kingston on fresh charges of sexual abuse in Igloolik during the late 1970s and early 1980s, in this case eight offences allegedly committed against six individuals. He was taken into custody in Iqaluit.[12]

The third Oblate priest of particular concern to Obed and the Inuit delegation was Johannes Rivoire, who worked in several remote northern communities, including Igluligarjuk (Chesterfield Inlet), Arviat,

Naujaat (Repulse Bay), Baker Lake and Rankin Inlet, in the 1960s and 1970s.[13] From 1952 until 1969, the Oblates ran Sir Joseph Bernier Federal Day School in Chesterfield Inlet, one of Rivoire's posts and where Lucien Parent had also taught. Rivoire also managed the co-op store in Chesterfield Inlet.

Marius Tungilik, who for many years was the lead spokesperson for the Survivors of Sir Joseph Bernier, attended the school in the 1960s and was one of the first to talk about the abuse he suffered there at the hands of both Rivoire and Parent. His voice spurred many others to speak out, to report what happened to them. Their complaints led to the holding of a Royal Commission on Aboriginal Peoples hearing in Rankin Inlet in 1991.[14]

In July 1995, the RCMP and the government of the Northwest Territories released the results of an investigation into allegations of widespread physical and sexual abuse at Bernier. In its report, the RCMP said there were allegations of various forms of abuse and crimes against children, but due to the passage of time and the dimming of memories, the national police service would not be pursuing any criminal charges.[15] By the time that investigation wound up, Rivoire was living in France; he'd fled Canada in 1993. *Le Monde* has since reported that Rivoire denies ever abusing children and says that he left Canada in order to care for his ailing parents.[16] Despite their initial decision not to proceed with charges, two years later, in 1997, the RCMP did lay charges against Rivoire related to four complaints of sexual interference and rape of a child under the age of fourteen during his time in Naujaat and Arviat, between 1968 and 1970. Despite this warrant, wrote the *Nunatsiaq News*, "nothing was done to find him."[17]

In 2013, the RCMP issued a Canada-wide arrest warrant for Rivoire. An RCMP spokesperson said this warrant stemmed directly from those 1997 charges. The RCMP also said that no international warrant for Rivoire's arrest had been issued.[18] The numerous charges laid in 1997 were stayed in 2017 because the prosecution felt there was no longer a possibility of conviction.[19] One new charge, concerning indecent assault on a female child during the period 1974–79, was laid in 2022, and a request was made for Rivoire's extradition from France.

For decades, meanwhile, Inuit Survivors of the schools, their family members, politicians and activists had demanded the federal government bring Rivoire to justice, but their demands had consistently fallen on the deaf ears of successive Canadian governments.[20]

Tungilik's brave decision to speak publicly about the abuse he suffered at Bernier did have results. It led to a public apology in Igloolik in 1996 from Bishop Reynald Rouleau to the Survivors of Sir Joseph Bernier, an event Tungilik welcomed as a "historic" acknowledgement of what had taken place.

That acknowledgement, however, didn't change the fact that Tungilik lived his life haunted by the stinging abuse he'd endured. A father and public servant, Tungilik had a lifelong career working for people in the governments of Nunavut, Canada and the Northwest Territories. But his past never left him. Tungilik took his life on December 16, 2012. He was fifty-five years old.[21]

Rivoire, until his death, lived in a nursing home in Lyon, France. He had not spent one second behind bars for the litany of sexual abuse allegations against him and, over the last several decades, it is fair to say there had been only half-hearted efforts to bring him to justice.

AS OBED AND I ate our dinner and sipped our bottles of Coca-Cola, he said he was frustrated by the lack of justice his people have experienced when it comes to these men. Perpetrators remain unpursued, charges are dropped, or offenders are given slaps on the wrist for destroying people's lives.

Rivoire's victims would not let this die. In 2022, the RCMP laid the new charges against Rivoire as a result of a fifty-two-year-old Inuk woman who said Rivoire started abusing her after mass on Sundays when she was just six years old—abuse that went on for six years. She first tried to get the RCMP to take her statement against the priest in 1983.

Though she had no luck, she kept trying. She told the *Globe and Mail* that every time she tried to speak to police, they told her there wasn't enough evidence. Refusing to give up, she went back to the Mounties in 2021. This time, an officer took her statement.[22] That allegation led to an actual call for the extradition of Rivoire from France.

And that was a call that Obed was taking all the way to Rome. He was determined to bring Rivoire back. Obed hoped against hope that this time things would be different and the pope would use his immense power and influence to return Rivoire to Canada.

When we got back to the hotel, Obed's suitcase had magically appeared.

OUR SEARCH FOR justice is long and hard. It thumps in our chests, in the backs of our minds. What was done to us, to those we love. Like a baton being passed from one generation to the next, we do not forget.

Back in 1995, Inuit Survivors, overwhelmingly dissatisfied with the lack of any police action against the perpetrators of abuse at residential schools, began organizing to campaign for the legal system to take notice and act. Present at one of those early meetings was Phil Fontaine, who had, in 1990, been one of the first to speak publicly about the abuse he'd suffered at residential school.

It was a pivotal moment when Fontaine first spoke out, at an Assembly of First Nations meeting in Whitehorse, about what had happened to him as a student—that he was sexually abused at Fort Alexander Indian Residential School, which was run by the Oblates at Sagkeeng First Nation. At the time, Fontaine was the Manitoba Regional Chief of the AFN. The news made the front pages of most newspapers. This was one of the first times mainstream Canada had heard the truth about the schools from a political leader. And suddenly there was national publicity surrounding one of the greatest open secrets never talked about in many Indigenous communities until then.

After Fontaine broke his silence, others began to do the same.

Fontaine was with us on this journey to Rome. I ran into him outside the Best Western. I recognized him instantly. Those deep-set dark eyes, the silver hair swept back. By this time in his life, I knew, Fontaine had served three terms as the National Chief of the AFN, played a key role in negotiating the IRRSA and effectively spent more than forty years trying to get the Catholic Church to apologize and live up to its obligations as a result of widespread abuse at the schools.

And he was still hoping truth and fairness might prevail. Before travelling to Rome, he'd spoken to the CBC from his home in Calgary, telling them, "I have a long history of the residential school experiences in my family. There were ten of us. Eight boys, two girls that attended residential schools, some of my brothers [attended] two schools as I did. Our mother and father were both students at the Fort Alexander Indian Residential School. My grandmother on my father's side was a student at the St. Boniface Industrial School, where a lot of students perished."[23]

I had met him only once before, in 1997, when I was covering the Red River flood for the *Toronto Star*. Fontaine and I met in the town of Morris, the only place in southern Manitoba that had a ring dike around it, which was holding steady. I had flown in on a helicopter with photographer Ken Faught. It was one of the most thrilling and terrifying assignments I'd ever had. At one point, the flood was forty kilometres wide by seventy-five kilometres long. From the air it looked as if someone had spilled a glass of water on a table. Luckily, Fontaine and I had found ourselves on the right side of the dike. I introduced myself to him in a local restaurant and told him about my grandmother Margaret, who lived in Brandon at that time. I thanked him for all he had done for our people.

Standing on the streets of Rome, I shook his frail hand again and reminded him of our meeting during the Red River flood. I wasn't sure if he remembered me, but he did tell me he'd read both of my books and that he followed my columns. He told me to keep going, to not stop telling our stories.

I ran into Phil Fontaine in Rome. A former National Chief of the Assembly of First Nations, Fontaine was one of the first to publicly speak out about the sexual abuse he suffered at residential school. He was in Rome with the AFN delegation, seeking an apology from the Catholic Church. (Photo by Tanya Talaga)

EARLY MONDAY MORNING, the buoyant Métis delegation gathered in the lobby, everyone dressed in their traditional red sashes, beaded vests and finery. I watched them leave, on their way to their "appointment," the very first Indigenous delegation to meet with the pope in his private library inside Vatican City, led by Métis National Council president Cassidy Caron.

I'd met Caron the morning we arrived, in the hotel's busy lobby— which had instantly become the ultimate meeting place. Talking with her, I could see where the Métis got their vigour. Caron is a force, an absolute breath of fresh air. She's a young woman with a friendly, wide smile and a direct gaze. She has survived and thrived in the hard world of Métis and Indigenous politics, while at the same time bringing folks together and battling colonialism every step of the way.

Once the group left the hotel, I made my way down to St. Peter's Square. The Canadian media were already there, setting up their cameras in front of St. Peter's. It was the perfect visual of one of the most photographed and recognizable places in the world. As we waited for the delegation to come out, suddenly we heard the lyrical, heart-lifting sound of fiddles. And there the Métis were, coming out of St. Peter's behind two young fiddlers, Brianna Lizotte and Alex Kusturok, who led them out with song. One of the Elders from Alberta, Angie Crerar, was in a wheelchair, her feet tapping and her arms swaying. (She'd spent her youth at St. Joseph's Indian Residential School in Fort Resolution, Northwest Territories.)

Caron walked respectfully with her delegation of seven Survivors—some had attended Île-à-la-Crosse Boarding School—and their families. Then she stood in front of the microphones. This was the first address by an Indigenous leader from Canada—a twenty-nine-year-old woman at that—after the delegation's historic meeting with Pope Francis. The moment was not lost on any of us. I was full of pride.

"Truth, justice, healing, reconciliation, that is why we came here today," Caron said, a natural in front of the cameras. "This morning Pope Francis heard from just three of many, three of the many stories and truths that our Métis residential school Survivors carry." (While Métis are not included in the Indian Act, Métis children were sent to the schools). "However, untold numbers have left us without having their truths heard and their pain acknowledged. Without ever receiving the basic humanity and healing they so rightfully deserve."[24] She called this a travesty of both justice and conscience, and said it was never too late for the church to do the right thing. Tourists who were at St. Peter's crowded around, wondering who we were and what we were doing.

The Métis, Caron said, had done the hard work of preparing for their journey and for a conversation with the pope. Now it was his turn to reciprocate. "So today we invited Pope Francis and Catholics all around the world to join us, the Métis nation, on our pathway of truth, justice and healing. And we hope that in committing to us, committing to real action, the church can finally begin its own pathway to meaningful and lasting reconciliation."

She added that although the Métis delegation might appear joyous, they were not celebrating their meeting with the pope. They were celebrating "being here together as one nation, in partnership with our First Nation and Inuit delegates as well. That is what we are celebrating, our resilience, and that is why we are here today."

Watching Caron from the sidelines was Louise Simard, a member of the Métis delegation who had been in the room with the pope. She was wearing a stunning brilliant, royal blue wool cape, decorated with colourful vines and flowers, created using a special technique called felting. Simard is a descendant of a member of Louis Riel's provisional government and has, as a member of the Legislative Assembly of Saskatchewan, broken numerous political glass ceilings. Her face was full of hard-to-place emotion.

I asked her if she'd felt the pope was listening, and I asked the other question on everyone's minds: Had he apologized?

"He was listening closely," she told me. "He didn't say, 'I apologize.'" However, she pointed out that an apology needed to happen on Canadian soil, Métis homeland.

Then I asked her how she felt, now that the highly anticipated meeting was over.

Simard started to weep. "It has been a long road," she said. "It has been a long road."

"Yes," I told her quietly. "We all feel that."

Cassidy Caron's tenacity served as a force of unity among all the delegations. She had set the tone. Each delegation would take her lead and hold an impromptu press conference in St. Peter's Square after their audience with the pope. The fiddlers danced for us all.

THE INUIT DELEGATION was up next, later that same morning.

Each delegate had two minutes each to speak one-on-one to the pope. It felt quick. Obed told me afterwards that the pontiff had listened to every one of the delegates and that he was responsive, sincere. The Survivors invited him to Iqaluit.

After the Inuit delegation's public appearance in St. Peter's square, the organizers and delegates held a full press conference in the hotel's basement, where a Catholic mass was held each morning. The event was being broadcast live on CBC back in Canada, and members of the Canadian press were in attendance, including CTV's Lisa LaFlamme and Donna Sound and the *Globe and Mail*'s Willow Fiddler, Tavia Grant and Eric Reguly. The room was packed with seated spectators, with some reporters typing madly at the back of the room, trying to meet their North American deadlines.

Obed sat up front, at the table of speakers, beside Survivor Martha Greig from Kuujjuaq, a former HBC outpost on Ungava Bay; Bishop William McGrattan of Calgary; and Richard Gagnon, the archbishop of Winnipeg. Their backdrop was a giant poster that read "WALKING TOGETHER" and, in smaller letters underneath, "Toward Healing & Reconciliation." Neil MacCarthy, communications director for the Archdiocese of Toronto and seconded to the CCCB for the Rome trip, was the emcee, standing at a podium to their left.

Obed was measured, careful with his words. He told everyone he was "very pleased" with the meeting and that the delegation had spoken to the pope of faith, residential schools and intergenerational trauma.

I was sitting several rows back, with Obed's good friend Max FineDay, from Sweetgrass First Nation in Saskatchewan. We exchanged glances, thinking of all the people watching back home, knowing how important this moment was for Obed, and for Canada.

Obed paused and then spoke frankly, and with resolve. He brought up the Indian Residential Schools Settlement Agreement and the Catholic Church's obligation to pay $25 million in restitution and healing funds to victims of the schools. He reminded those listening that only $3 million had been paid so far, while the church said it was trying to "fundraise" the rest.[25]

Obed said he reminded the pope that it would be a sign of good faith for the Catholic Church to become a full partner in helping to locate the missing children. "It is not just records, or compliance with the IRSSA," Obed said. The church must use its vast resources to help families find closure, and to recognize the "gross human rights abuses" that had taken place.

He then said that he had asked the pope to intervene in the Johannes Rivoire case, in fact to speak to Rivoire directly and demand that he return to Canada to face charges. If Rivoire would not do this, then the pontiff should work with France to ensure that Rivoire could be tried there. "We want this new relationship of reconciliation to be based on action and mutually shared ambition," he said, and sighed. "It is a heartbreaking reality that some people who should have been brought to justice decades ago have not seen justice, and those who have been abused and were victims have sometimes died before they have seen justice."

Max and I could sense his frustration with the merry-go-round of pomp and circumstance. Obed is not a person who would have been in danger of losing sight of why he was there.

I was surprised by what came next. Bishop McGrattan, the vicechair of the CCCB, spoke. What he said made me catch my breath. Could there actually be some movement here? Was the Catholic Church truly ready to reconcile?

It is important to put on record the words that were spoken by a representative of the Catholic Church at that Monday, March 28, press conference, for the readers of this book, if no one else, to understand the intentions of what was spoken and what was not. Was there real intention behind Bishop McGrattan's remarks? Or was his intention simply to placate?

Bishop McGrattan told those gathered that he had been in the room when "President Obed made the request of the Holy Father." He continued, "I think I would begin by saying, any situation of sexual abuse, the church needs to take responsibility and, as we heard, justice and truth are important in this path of reconciliation."[26]

That sounded promising. Then he said that Bishop Anthony Krótki of Churchill–Hudson Bay had "expressed his commitment on behalf of the church" to assist Obed. Everyone in the room was listening intently.

"Personally," McGrattan continued, "the Holy Father, I think, heard that this is important. We need to continue to state the church needs to address this in a forthright manner. I know the Oblates have also reached out to President Obed and he'll have an opportunity to meet with them this week and discuss issues related to this case as well. I think these are concrete ways to . . . assist in this act of justice."

Had the Catholic Church just acknowledged that Rivoire was a predator and, further, suggested that it would use its considerable power to help bring him to justice?

Right away, more troubling thoughts crowded into my mind: What about the others—all the other priests who are accused of sexual abuse, who are still alive and well and in retirement? It is such a rarity for journalists to be able to confront the princes of the church like this, demanding answers for centuries of complicit behaviour.

It was a Cree reporter, her white beaded earrings gleaming, who asked whether it would just be Rivoire who is extradited. "We do have a case in Quebec as well and it was just ten years ago," she said. "We find out that priest is stationed somewhere else. They are just being moved around. It is the same thing. We want justice as well. I don't want to take your story away but, you know, can we look at other cases too as well and not just this particular one? Again, no disrespect to you. Miigwech."

Obed told the reporter he wanted all the accused offenders found and brought before the courts. "In no way did I intend or did ITK"—Inuit Tapiriit Kanatami—"intend to make this about one particular case when we know there are other scenarios. This particular case is one we've been trying to work on for decades. The same principles apply to all."

Bishop McGrattan's response was encouraging but noncommittal: "This is not just one isolated case. So I believe what I am stating is the church wants to work with the relevant justice authorities, whether they be international or Canadian. And if there are allegations that someone has committed these abuses, they need to be brought to justice and the church not stand in the way but assist those who have been victims to seek justice and healing. This is but one way the church can continue to do that."

I noticed he didn't offer to pay the rest of the $25 million. It wasn't as if the church didn't have the money. A 2021 *Globe and Mail* investigation, led by my colleague Tavia Grant, procured tax filings from the Canada Revenue Agency for thousands of Catholic Church organizations in an effort to find out how much the church in Canada collects in donations, as well as the value of its assets. The Catholic Church is the biggest registered charity in Canada, and the investigation found that, in 2019, 3,446 registered Catholic Church charities, dioceses and parishes received a total of $886 million in donations. And what the church owns is equally astounding. Its 2019 net assets—including property, cash and investments—amounted to $4.1 billion.[27]

The next reporter, from the Catholic News Service, asked if there'd been an exchange of gifts at the meeting. Obed stifled a bit of a laugh, remarking that he hoped there were pictures of the pope wearing his new sealskin fur stole. The Inuit delegation also gave the pontiff two stone carvings and a sealskin rosary case. Some delegates also gave the pope personal messages, written carefully on folded pieces of paper.

Pope Francis had given the delegation a gift of a velvet case that contained a large gold medal of the Virgin Mary holding the baby Jesus. It reminded me of the medals given to Olympic athletes.

That was a welcome moment of levity. The press conference was long, and people were tired, those from North America fighting both jet lag and the emotions of the day.

Then a reporter asked Inuit residential school Survivor Martha Greig about forgiveness. She said in a calm, pleasant voice, "I personally, as a former residential student, that would mean a lot to me myself . . . When we got to the school we learned to be 'white persons,' which we cannot be. We are Inuit, we are First Nations, we are Métis. We have to learn to live with one another and also be given the right to live the way we want to live our life. To be in respect with each other. What I am trying to say is we have to work together on this. So, an apology is the first step and the forgiveness will hopefully follow through."[28]

The press conference was wrapping up. But before it was over, Obed struck, delivering his final, uncompromising message with a smile. "We are incredibly resilient and great at forgiving, as Martha has talked about, but we are still in search of lasting respect and the right to self-determination and the acknowledgement of that right by institutions that harmed us. This is where we are at this moment and look forward to this new path and we'll hold people accountable to the path that we say we have a shared ambition to walk."

Bishop McGrattan was one of the last to speak. "This truth is coming out, maybe in ways some of us are still trying to understand. But by dialoguing and listening, as President Obed has said, I think we are better able to understand the truth, and from that truth, the path of reconciliation and hopefully healing and forgiveness. But we have to begin those steps in order to have people realize this is something that God wants, a real sense of forgiveness and reconciliation."

Something that God wants.

To my ears, this was the first and only time in the press conference that someone had mentioned the word *God*. And it was in the final moments. I wondered yet again what kind of God would leave us here, in this place. And if, after all this, the church does nothing—if all this is just bluster—what next?

THREE DAYS AFTER we arrived in Rome, a black bus pulled up outside the Best Western. None of the delegations were scheduled to meet the pope that day, so the CCCB had planned a trip to the Sistine Chapel in the Vatican Museums, the site of one of the most storied art collections in the world. The bishops told us something special was in the works, something that was not on the official program: a visit to the Anima Mundi, the Vatican museum of ethnological art and artifacts that includes eighty thousand pieces of Indigenous art from around the world. They told us we would see items from Canada that were not usually displayed for public view.

This was an event many delegates had hoped for, and the real reason for the excitement that morning in the Best Western breakfast room. It wasn't that we were going to see Michelangelo's masterpiece, though many people looked forward to that as well. No. We were going to see the objects taken from Turtle Island and kept in the Vatican's secret vault. The Catholic Church has obtained countless precious items from Indigenous Peoples all across the world. Its collection is of great interest to scholars, but few have been given admittance.

After breakfast we piled onto the bus. As it started rolling through the streets of Rome, Anishinaabe Elder Fred Kelly, one of the spiritual leaders on the trip and a residential school Survivor from Kenora, stood up in the aisle, leaned his tall frame against a seat for balance and started to speak.

In a sombre tone, he reminded everyone on the bus why they had come to Rome. They weren't on vacation: they'd flown all this way to ask Pope Francis for an apology for what the Catholic Church had done to our peoples for nearly five hundred years. He reminded us it was important to remember all of the children and youth lost, those who'd died and could not be here today. He told us to remember the Survivors of the schools, the murdered and missing Indigenous women and girls, and the Sixties Scoop kids. "I ask the Creator, over the next couple of minutes, for each one of you, in your spiritual identity, who you are and what you are, and what the Creator meant us to be, that we are going to get there with resiliency, and we have the hope and courage of our young people to see ourselves [through]." Then he asked us to spend a moment in silence to remember all the Survivors who did not make it here to Rome.[29]

Elder Fred's message was a dose of reality. He was right: this was not anything like *Indians on Vacation*, Thomas King's comedic novel about an old Indian couple on a tour through Europe. And we weren't being hosted by our "friends." We were here to seek an apology from Pope Francis for a genocide.

The opulence of the Vatican Museums is mind-blowing. I found myself face to face with the riches of the Catholic Church: long, ornate marble corridors; priceless Roman statues, busts and vases; gilded ceilings. The Raphaels, the Botticellis, the countless tapestries and the endless maps of Italy. If there was ever any doubt, the Vatican Museums are a strong reminder of the power of the Holy See. I found the excessive grandeur hard to stomach, especially when I walked through those halls with Indian residential school Survivors—when I knew that just a couple of marble busts could easily be sold so the church could pay the remainder of the $25 million it owes to Survivors. For that matter, why hadn't the Vatican sold a painting or two to feed the children in the schools, the thousands who went hungry? What about buying warm clothes or fixing the furnaces, repairing the grossly inadequate plumbing?

Our guide held high a stick with a flag so we wouldn't get lost. She walked us down the halls towards the Sistine Chapel. It was absolutely packed. Wall-to-wall people. Our group made its way through the crowds to stare at one of the most exquisite examples of High Renaissance art, painted by Michelangelo from 1508 to 1512. Several frescoes depict scenes from the Old Testament, such as Noah and the flood. The one I couldn't stop staring at was *The Last Judgment*, which dwarfs the papal chapel's altar with its torrid and frightening images. This is all about the end of life, about those who become immortal, living with the Almighty in heaven, and those judged to spend an eternity in damnation. I wondered how those who harmed our children were judged? Did all those clerics and believers wind up with the smiling God they believed in, or—if he was indeed a just God—had he punished them with eternal damnation?

These incredible paintings by the devout Michelangelo were being devised and completed just after contact, when our people were confronting European explorers wielding Christianity and the papal bulls in all their fifteenth-century power and might. The vicious crimes of Christopher Columbus in what we now know as Haiti, the deaths of millions, were playing out. Judgment Day was upon Indigenous Peoples, wrought by European men on the hunt for riches and glory.

We pushed on, following our guide's flag towards our next stop: the Anima Mundi ethnological museum. The Anima Mundi—which means "soul of the world"—houses an incredible, vast collection of Indigenous belongings. The collection, which was accumulated as Christian missionaries around the world acquired objects and sent them to the Vatican, is second to none. As the museum's web page describes it, the collection contains "thousands of prehistoric artefacts from all over the world and dating from over two million years ago, to the gifts given to the current Pontiff; from evidence of the great Asian spiritual traditions, to those of the pre-Columbian and Islamic civilisations; from the work of African populations to that of the inhabitants of Oceania and Australia, and the indigenous peoples of America."[30]

To protect and conserve the artifacts, the Vatican displays only a certain number of objects at once. The rest of the items are kept in the Vatican's vaults. As Indigenous people, we were highly skeptical about how each of the objects wound up in those vaults in the first place.

Walking through the wide entrance of the normally closed-off section of Anima Mundi, we were greeted, on our left-hand side, from behind glass, by a Haudenosaunee white-feathered headdress. It was clearly being repaired by museum staff. A small title card beside it said, "Gifted to John Paul II (1978–2005) in Rome, 1980." Past the headdress, the Vatican curators had set up tables laid with white cloths down a long, warehouse-like room. Museum staff had placed certain objects from their "collection" on the tables.

My breath caught in my throat. The entire Indigenous delegation was quiet, approaching the tables that held the objects, their phones in hand, ready to record the moment. There were beautifully beaded moccasins from British Columbia, a peace pipe, a stove pipe from Ontario, intricate soapstone carvings, Haida Gwaii face masks. A wampum belt, more than a metre long, was encased in glass. It had been made in late 1831, at the Lake of Two Mountains, today called Oka Kanehsatà:ke, near Montreal. It represented Algonquin, Nipissing, Mohawks; every purple and white shell used in its design held meaning. According to the text beside it, the belt had been a gift from the three Nations to Pope Gregory XVI. Other items—it was impossible to tell how they'd got here. A menacing-looking "miniature ball-headed club" was identified as "Great Lakes region, first half of 19th century."

Looking down the tables, I felt sick. None of the "objects" were being treated properly in accordance with Indigenous protocols. For the Anishinaabe, we call what the Vatican has in its collection our grandmothers and grandfathers. Meant to be used in ceremony, before their "acquisition" by the Vatican they would rarely have been seen on Turtle Island. Every object has a story behind it—each has its own meaning and proper use. There are protocols regarding when to take them out. For instance, a pipe can't be put on someone's mantel. It holds power and spirit, so it comes out only in ceremony. The grandmothers and grandfathers are certainly not put out on display tables.

The ceremonies for which these grandmothers and grandfathers had been made had been outlawed for decades: no Sweat Lodges or Potlatches. And during that dark time, all of our relations for such ceremonies were taken away, destroyed, saved as "souvenirs" or put inside museums such as this one. The fact that Elder Fred Kelly had a three-hundred-year-old pipe that had been hidden away from the church and settlers for all that time is remarkable. I do not know how the pipe survived.

I wondered whether some of the objects that were poorly tagged were from the James Bay or Hudson Bay regions. Were they ever in the presence of Annie, her brothers or sisters, nieces and nephews?

Among the artifacts was an Inuit kayak, about a century old, from Inuvialuit. The kayak was part of the original 1925 exhibition of nearly a hundred thousand objects, and was apparently "gifted" to the church. The kayak does not show signs of wear and tear. After touring the exhibit, Natan Obed met with the museum's curator, Nicola Mapelli, to discuss repatriating the kayak and other objects. Obed said the curator was "quite open" to any scenario the Inuit proposed to reclaim their belongings.[31]

Standing beside a carved black "Ojibwe stove pipe," a small head the size of a fist, chiselled from rock, I sent a text message to Elder Sam Achneepineskum to tell him what I was seeing. Elder Sam is an Anishinaabe Knowledge Keeper, a holder of ceremonies and a member of the Midewiwin lodge. He told me to make sure people spoke in their language to all the objects they were seeing on the tables. The artifacts needed to know that we saw them, that we knew they were there.

Nearby, large round tables, also covered in white cloths, had been arranged with place settings. I couldn't believe it: The Vatican officials were going to serve us lunch amongst our captive grandmothers and grandfathers.

The Vatican's Anima Mundi museum, where Indigenous "artifacts" from all over the world are kept and rarely on display. Items include moccasins, masks from B.C., a peace pipe and a wampum belt. Two reporters and I were asked to leave the area when the Indigenous delegation from Canada was on a special visit to the museum. (Photo by Tanya Talaga)

Just as I was finishing texting with Sam, I noticed Neil MacCarthy coming towards me with a determined look on his face. Some priests were with him. Neil began with an apology. He said he felt bad, "But I'm going to have to ask you to leave the museum."

I couldn't believe my ears. Tavia Grant, one of the four *Globe* reporters, stood beside me, looking inquisitive. Tavia's reporting might is unparalleled. She leaned in on our conversation, looking defiant, as did Marie-Laure Josselin, a Radio-Canada journalist. We were the few reporters who had come inside with the official delegation. The rest of the reporters had been asked to not come in. No explanation had been given as to why the media were not permitted. Tavia, Josselin and I had walked in with Obed.

When I asked Neil why I was being told to leave, he said I wasn't supposed to be there. I told him I was a First Nations citizen and as such I had every right to be there. He told me that this was an event only for delegates and not for the media, so as members of the media, my two colleagues and I were not welcome. He added that some of our colleagues outside were protesting our presence, saying it was unfair that we'd been allowed to stay with the delegation while they were not.

I disagreed. I told him his request was outrageous, that as a First Nations person I should be allowed to be here, looking at these objects.

He was unmovable and said I had two choices. I could either go quietly or be removed.

I couldn't believe his audacity. Tavia, beside me, was also protesting. Suddenly time seemed to disappear. Tavia and I had gone to the same elementary school, and it felt like we were girls again, back in the playground together, facing off against bullies. But this time we were standing our ground against the Catholic Church.

I felt it was clear that for whatever reason, MacCarthy wanted us out of the museum. We told him we'd go. I also told him that they couldn't pay me to sit there and have lunch with all our stolen things. It made me want to vomit.

My heart was pounding as we three expelled journalists made our way out the door of the museum and onto one of the Vatican's sunny, green, well-manicured lawns.

"Did that just happen?" Tavia asked.

I was incensed and felt somewhat powerless. But I was not. I took out my phone and I started a Twitter thread. Luckily I had taken plenty of photos of the objects on the tables.

My post went viral. The major TV news networks in Canada were soon calling, asking me to come on live to explain why it was that I'd been kicked out of the Anima Mundi.

I had no explanation.

═══

AFTER LISTENING TO Cassidy Caron speak in St. Peter's Square after the Métis delegation had met with the pope, I'd asked her if she would meet with me. I knew that I wanted to write a *Globe* column about her. It was clear that, like Natan Obed, Caron was in Rome with a mission. She represented hope in a desperate hour.

Of course, we met in the lobby of the Universo. Sitting on the already familiar lime-green couch, Caron told me that one of her primary purposes for being on this trip was to meet with the Vatican insiders who held sway over the entire Catholic machine.

Métis representatives had reached out to the CCCB before travelling to Rome, and Caron had a list of cardinals her delegation wanted to meet with. "This is very much a business trip for me," she said. "I need to make sure I'm getting our message across to as many people as possible and not just the pope. We only had an hour with the pope and we spent that time elevating the voices of Survivors."[32]

Even though the Métis are recognized as an Indigenous group in the Constitution Act of 1982, Métis Survivors and their families have largely been excluded from the IRSSA, because it was limited to federally funded schools. As I mentioned earlier, the Saskatchewan residential schools that many Métis children attended—for example, Île-à-la-Crosse and Timber Bay—were left out. (While the Catholic Church played a role in administering Île-à-la-Crosse from time to time, it was not involved with Timber Bay.) But funding these institutions was not cut-and-dried; it was complicated. Sometimes funding would flip between the provinces and Ottawa and church entities.

Caron had been on the go since she and the Métis delegation arrived. She knows the Catholic Church is a giant political organization and that she and her team needed to get into the system to start working it. As part of that, she'd also arrived in Rome with a request to see the Indigenous—specifically Métis—objects held in the Vatican Museums. She wanted a list of what was there.

The CCCB chose not to step up and help Caron arrange meetings between the Métis delegation and church leaders. Undeterred, she told me she turned to the Canadian ambassador to the Holy See, who said he was more than happy to help.

Their first scheduled meeting was with Cardinal Luis Ladaria Ferrer, who is in charge of the Dicastery for the Doctrine of the Faith, making him, effectively, the Vatican's minister of justice. He is assisted by a board of cardinals, bishops, priests and lawyers. Caron sought this meeting in order to talk about amending canon law—essentially the Catholic Church's legal system—to make it clear there would be consequences for denying the horrors of the residential school system or for saying the schools represented a positive experience for Indigenous Peoples. The Métis also wanted to tell Cardinal Ladaria that the Catholic Church needed to stop shielding perpetrators of crimes against children.

The meeting, however, never took place. "We showed up and his secretary said he 'fell ill' today," Caron told me. "That was slightly disappointing." They left with no possibility of rescheduling. "But," she said, with her characteristic determination, "we will be following up with a letter."[33]

Caron had another important meeting—and this one actually did take place—with Father Louis Lougen, the superior general of the Oblates, to talk about access to the Oblates' vast records. When he asked her why she wanted such access, she told him a story. "I told him we went to the Vatican Museums the other day and everyone was talking about how proud they were that they could tell their stories and they are fully documented. I told him we didn't have the opportunity to do that. Our people didn't document our history in the same way that theirs did, but their people documented our histories in different ways. The Oblates would write their journals, record everything." She said he got it, he understood, and he then promised to open up the records the Oblates have in Rome.

"I told him it is going to be a process—we want to send our people, our archivists to identify what is here. Then we can find out what is missing. What is still in church basements that we don't have access to? They are going to connect me to the provincial oblate in Ottawa."[34]

Caron was pleased with the outcome. "One of our Elders always says, 'Relationships are built over a hundred cups of tea.'"

EVERY MORNING, TWO services were held in the basement of the Hotel Universo. One was a Catholic mass, the other a traditional sunrise ceremony. The room that held the Catholic mass could fit more than a hundred people. All were invited.

The sunrise ceremony, on the other hand, was usually held in a room the size of a small storage room. Like the Catholic mass, all were invited. But we couldn't believe the room's size. It felt like a closet. Nevertheless, this was where we gathered each morning to welcome the day and give thanks to the Creator, many of the delegates and their family members cramming in before the sun rose—not that we could tell when that was, since there were no windows in the basement. As far as I could tell, only Indigenous people came to the sunrise ceremony. A few media members with TV cameras would squish in too, trying not to pile on top of us.

One morning, Chief Wilton Littlechild offered the morning prayer. Littlechild is a slight man with a kind heart. All of us gathered around him in a circle. Wearing his headdress, he laid out a prayer cloth and some objects, explaining what each was for and what it meant. He told the news cameras they could record this. He wanted to teach.

He started by showing us the fasting pipe in his hands. Its bowl, he said, was made of stone from the mountains and filled with tobacco for prayer. He said the pipestem is always straight, and the teaching in that is honesty: to be straight in what you do. He held up a feather and explained that it represents the brothers and sisters, the four-leggeds, because they die so we can live. Lastly, he brought our attention to the sweetgrass, long blades of sweet-smelling grass braided together. "Treaties should last as long as the sun shines, the waters flow and the grasses grow," Chief Littlechild said. "Doesn't matter how strong you are, you'll never be able to break this. But if you unravel it, it comes apart. That teaches the three of us, First Nations, Métis and Inuit, to be together. When we are together in unity, no one can stop us. My prayer for you, wherever you came before, on your journey, is that you will be blessed with this on our journey home."

One of the best parts of staying at the Universo was the breakfast buffet. Every morning, after the basement sunrise ceremony, we'd all head upstairs to eat. We were all there, First Nations, Métis and Inuit Survivors and their families, members of the media and all who had come to support the delegates. We navigated our way around a central table heaped with Roman pastries. We made toast and helped ourselves to a variety of meats and cheeses. These were precious times of coming together, digesting what had happened the day before and talking about what was to come.

For the first few days of the AFN delegation to Rome, Elder Fred Kelly held a sunrise ceremony in a small room of the basement of the delegation's hotel. Chief Wilton Littlechild is in the background. (Photo by Tanya Talaga)

On the Thursday morning, as members of the First Nations delegation were getting ready for their audience with Pope Francis, I had breakfast with Norman Yakeleya, a former Dene National Chief. The Dene Nation is a political territorial organization in Denendeh, the Land of the People, in the Northwest Territories, but the Nation covers a vast area, from Alaska to southern North America.

I had not met Yakeleya before, but I'd seen him around. He'd also given some press interviews after seeing the traditional objects held inside the Anima Mundi, particularly the ceremonial pipe. "I've been told by some Elders that it's not for show," Yakeleya had said. "It was there on display, and it was something that I didn't feel good about." Yakeleya had told reporters that the grandmothers and grandfathers should be given back to the people. The Vatican could "make plastic models" of them if they wanted, but, "For God's sakes, give them back to our people."[35]

I told him that I'd been thrown out of the Anima Mundi. He chuckled. It seemed that everyone had heard what happened.

As we ate and talked, members of the First Nations delegation were flooding into the breakfast room. Everyone was in their ceremonial dress: ribbon skirts, beautiful buckskin vests, dangling beaded earrings. Folks holding hand drums were jostling around the tables, making sure they had something to eat before they met the pope.

Suddenly, Norman put down his fork and pulled up his dress shirt to show me a large scar across his abdomen. "Seventeen stitches," he said. "They cut me. I do not know why."[36] Yakeleya is a Survivor of Grollier Hall in Inuvik, Northwest Territories. It was first established as part of a federal plan to create youth hostels.[37] There was Grollier Hall, a residence run by the Catholics, and, Stringer Hall, run by the Anglicans.[38] Combined, they could house five hundred students, First Nations and Inuit children who stayed at the halls while attending Sir Alexander Mackenzie Day School.

The TRC reported that it could not find any residential school that had policies or regulations related to preventing the sexual abuse of students.[39] But by 1960 the Anglican Church must have realized it had to do something. That's the year it required principals to report on why staff members quit. Also, the church kept a confidential list of the names of those who should never be hired again for a "lack of suitability on moral grounds."[40]

Grollier was a hideous place that employed four men who sexually terrorized children for decades: Joseph Jean Louis Comeau, Martin Houston, George Maczynski and Paul Leroux. It did not close until

1997. In 1962, a lawyer prosecuting an abuse case at Grollier Hall recommended the RCMP do a background check on every single man and woman given any authority over children.[41] But it is unclear whether anyone ever did a background check on those four men. What *is* clear to me is that in many such cases, the Catholic Church knew what was going on and took great pains to protect the perpetrators, often moving them to other schools, where their crimes continued.

Yakeleya told me it's estimated that between 1959 and 1997, when the hostel finally closed, nearly 450 children were abused at Grollier. The motto of Grollier, drummed into him by the priests, was "Don't talk. Don't trust. Don't feel."

Norman was never called by his first name. At Grollier, he was simply known by a number: 153.

Yakeleya told me he hadn't wanted to come to Rome and didn't care to hear an apology from the head of the Catholic Church. He told me he felt sick about it, but he wasn't there for himself. He was there for his mother, Laura Lennie.

His words resonated with me. So many of us were in Rome for others, the people we carry with us. Everyone who came to Rome came with others on their minds: fathers, mothers, grandparents, friends, Survivors both here on earth and those who had passed. We thought of all those we've lost.

Yakeleya told me that decades later, when he finally found the courage to tell his mother what had happened to him at Grollier, she told him that she had also been sexually abused at residential school, in her case at Fort Simpson in the Northwest Territories, another Catholic institution.

Burning in my mind, as I heard him tell his story, was the question of forgiveness. We were here for an apology. Were we ready to forgive?

I asked him, "What does it mean to forgive?"

"Being in the presence of forgiveness," said Yakeleya, "means you acknowledge the pain and the anger. You walk softly on it. That is what our Elders say—keep our language soft—walk on the forgiveness, allow it to happen."[42]

Forgiveness is a long journey many of us struggle to walk.

AFN staff started calling out that the bus taking them to St. Peter's was parked down the street. Norman got up and joined the rest of the group as they left the hotel. I followed them outside.

Of all the moments in Rome, for me this was one of the most poignant: The entire First Nations delegation—it was the largest, at nearly thirty people—out on the streets of Rome in all their finery. The Chiefs wore their white-feathered headdresses, and those with hand drums beat them. Cars halted, mopeds and Vespas braked to let us pass. Onlookers gasped from the sidewalk and pointed. Yes, we're real, I thought as I watched the spectators. What I wanted to do was scream: "We are *real* live Indians and guess what? We survived! And we aren't going anywhere!"

Maybe this was what Rome was truly about.

I WAS STANDING in the Vatican press office when Pope Francis, in the final meeting with all three delegations, on Friday, April 1, finally apologized to the Survivors in Rome.

"I also feel shame," the pontiff said, in Italian.

I'm saying it now and I'm repeating it. Sorrow and shame for the role that a number of Catholics, particularly those with educational responsibilities, have had in all these things that wounded you, and the abuses you suffered and the lack of respect shown for your identity, your culture and even your spiritual values.

All these things are contrary to the Gospel of Jesus Christ. For the deplorable conduct of these members of the Catholic Church, I ask for God's forgiveness. And I want to say to you with all my heart, I am very sorry.

And I join my brothers, the Canadian bishops, in asking your pardon. Clearly, the content of the faith cannot be transmitted in a way contrary to the faith itself. Jesus taught us to welcome, love, serve and not judge. It is a frightening thing then when precisely in the name of the faith counterwitness is rendered to the Gospel.

Your experiences have made me ponder anew these ever timely questions that the Creator addresses to mankind. In the first pages of the Bible, after the first sin, He asks "Where are you?" Then a few pages later He asks another question inseparable from the first, "Where is your brother?" Where are you? Where is your brother? These are questions we should never stop asking. They are the essential questions raised by our conscience lest we ever forget we are here on this Earth as guardians of the sacredness of life. And as guardians of our brothers and sisters and of all brother peoples.[43]

CHAPTER FOURTEEN

THE PRIME MINISTER AND A POPE

IT IS JUST AFTER NEW YEAR'S DAY 2022. I AM SITTING WITH ANNIE CARPENTER'S granddaughter, my grandmother Margaret, in her hospice bed, holding her hand, trying to soak in these last moments with her. My mother is here, floating around the room, straightening books, checking out the laundry situation. She is keeping busy.

It won't be long now. Margaret's ninety-seven-year-old body won't let her stay. She is half sitting but mostly lying in her easy chair, her stuffed Dachshunds around her, a remembrance of her precious dog Babe. We'd taken this trip out to Glenboro, Manitoba, because Aunt Cheryl, my mother's younger sister, had called to tell us it was time. Cheryl, like the other women in my family, sees things. Her dreams are vivid and real. She has been Grandma's constant companion, making sure she is ushered out of this life properly.

This is the last time my mother and I will be with her. Three generations stitched together in one room, memories held together by Elvis Presley, mincemeat tarts, long car rides, endless amounts of laughter and grief topped off with a bit of midnight glow-in-the-dark bowling.

Grandma was our link to Annie. She was the one who remembered her, who told me about her soft singing, about her rocking in her chair before she was gone.

Grandma's dark eyes twinkle when she looks at me. She is all there, still as sharp as a tack. I hold her hand, stare at her long fingers still full of grace, including her one right index finger that has always been odd, the nailbed like a tiny claw. I know this is the last time I'll see these hands, hold them.

I whisper in her ear that we have found Annie, after all this time. Of how her spirit has made a return. Grandma's eyes widen, eyebrows raised. "Albany," I whisper. "She was from Fort Albany." Grandma manages a smile, her eyes round with wonder. Margaret has lived her entire life, nearly one hundred years, without knowing exactly where her mother and her grandmother were from, or that she herself could say with certainty and without doubt that she was half Ininiw. "Annie came up the Albany River," I tell her. "All the way from James Bay. She really was Cree."

Turns out, I tell her, when Aunt Connie and Aunt Bernice took the Polar Express to Moose Factory one summer, with no idea what to do or where to go other than try to find their relations, they were on to something.

I imagine a younger Connie and Bernice, my grandmother's joined-at-the-hip little sisters, wandering through Moose Factory graveyards, trying to find their grandparents' family, their aunties and uncles, having nothing but vague clues as to who they were looking for. It was so typical of them, so typical of us. We are constantly flying on a wing and a prayer.

The three of us laugh, one of those laughs that you can only truly have with the women who have raised you. We are laughing because that was always the big rumour in the family, that Annie and Liz were Cree, yet the Government of Canada told us Annie and Liz didn't exist, let alone exist as Indians. But the paperwork was there all along. That's the joke of it: it was in their own damn records, hiding in plain sight, not to be found until the magic of the internet revealed the truth, in digitized census records.

The Knowing.

═══

IN MAY 2022, exactly one year after the finding of the 215 and five months after my kokum's death, I was standing in the powwow arbour, watching a blanket ceremony. Tk'emlúps language and culture manager Ted Gottfriedson was being draped in the bright-coloured wool blanket and given an eagle feather. The blanket holds him close with thanks from his community for all he has done, all he has given. The eagle feather is a gift of knowledge and wisdom, a sign of respect.

I first met Ted in Rome, in—of course!—the lobby of the Universo hotel. He has a long, white braid and wears glasses. Ted is a guiding hand in his community.

At the ceremony that day, he reminded everyone gathered where the name Le Estcwicwéy̓, the missing, came from. He said the community's Secwepemctsín speakers were tired of hearing the students found in the apple orchard referred to as the "215." It was so disrespectful, as many of the kids at Kamloops had their names taken away and were referred to only as a number.

It was clear his community loved him. The announcer at the powwow arbour told the crowd that Ted did not take one single day off after the discovery of the children. He worked straight through, never leaving the children untended. He was emotionally and spiritually working fourteen hours a day, seven days a week. "On many occasions," the announcer told us, "Ted felt so much trauma, criticism and blatant racism from very religious people who did not believe the atrocities of the church and the finding of the missing children and the graves."

After the discovery of the missing, residential school denialism hit Ted with full force. A landslide of hateful emails. It can be overwhelming, the hate.

But Ted remains undeterred. And he knows he can't leave the children out there in the apple orchard all on their own. Every Friday, he and his team stand before the orchard and they sing to Le Estcwicwéy̓. He never forgets.

Dignitaries had travelled here for the one-year commemoration. Canada's Inuit governor general, Mary Simon, was here. So was Prime Minister Justin Trudeau, who in his second term took a beating over

Indigenous relations—fulfilling all ninety-four of the TRC's calls to action being one big overpromise. It has proved to be a struggle. But that promise was starry-eyed. We knew as soon as he said it that he could not do it. How could he change the very fabric of Canada so quickly? Answering the calls would mean, just for starters, bringing clean water and proper education to every single First Nations community, and revamping the justice system to stop the over-incarceration of our people. Who could accomplish even one of these in four short years?

Kúkpi7 Rosanne Casimir introduced Trudeau to the crowd. His presence here could be seen as brave, considering that the year before he skipped out on his invitation to come to Kamloops for the very first National Day for Truth and Reconciliation, September 30, 2021, the holiday that's known by most people as Orange Shirt Day.

Trudeau had declined Kúkpi7 Rosanne's invitation to come to Kamloops that day to mourn the children in the unmarked graves here, and to remember Survivors. Instead, he went to Tofino, one of the most beautiful beaches on Vancouver Island, to spend the day with his family.[1] That was a serious political miscalculation. As a result, he ended up having to make a special trip to Kamloops the following month to apologize to the community in person.

"We all know that earlier . . . Prime Minister Trudeau apologized for missing the first day of TRC," said Casimir in the arbour. "He reached out, he owned that. He paid his respects to the unmarked graves and listened to our people's truths throughout the nation. I recognize that as a good start. I know it takes strong, strong leadership to work towards a better future for all of us." She then spoke about the need for the federal government to fund an Elders' building and a healing lodge for Survivors.

Trudeau, beside her onstage, looked contrite. As Casimir began to introduce him, a male voice shouted, "You are not welcome here!" Unfazed, Trudeau started speaking. "Today, we are here to remember Le Estcwicwéy̓, we are here to honour them." But the belligerent man wouldn't let up. Trudeau paused, used to dealing with protestors. He countered by saying, "I had the opportunity earlier to speak to a number of Elders and I know it is something they wanted to hear—my reflections. I hear your anger towards me and that is fine, but I'd ask you to respect your Elders. I'm sorry for your anger. Thank you." He paused again and then added: "If it makes anyone feel a little bit better to shout at me, then please, they should. This community needs and deserves healing."

Tk'emlúps te Secwépemc Kúkpi7 Rosanne Casimir stands on the front field of the Kamloops Indian Residential School in May 2021, shortly after news of the two hundred possible gravesites of children broke. (Photo by Tanya Talaga)

That seemed to work. He continued uninterrupted, calling what happened at Kamloops "unthinkable" and saying how "today is about the children and it is about the healing" and that he was in Kamloops with a single message: "We are here for you."[2] He left the stage and was immediately treated like a rock star.

Our people are remarkable. Trudeau can be chastised by the entire country one day for missing the very first Orange Shirt Day—and the next day he can be fully embraced as if nothing happened. He was swarmed by onlookers as he tried to wade past them on his way to the media scrum. Everyone wanted a selfie. As he wormed his way through the crowd, he ran up a hill to get across a parking lot. In that time he managed to throw an orange Frisbee to a child and kiss a newborn baby before handing the infant back to the wee one's mother.

Luella Jules, sixty-one, a third-generation Kamloops Survivor, was watching the scene unfold. She held up her iPad, filming it all. She proudly showed me a selfie with the PM. Luella told me she'd been very ill with Covid-19 and was in intensive care for forty days. The intubation scar was clearly visible on her throat. "Trauma can affect you in so many different ways," she said to me. "All of our communities, we need healing plans. What are our healing plans?"

As she spoke, the skies opened up and a torrential rain was unleashed.

I was in Kamloops with a small crew of two: Ramsay Bourquin, a Tahltan sound recordist, and Rodrigo Michelangeli, my director of photography. We were filming the gathering for a documentary series based on this book. We ran together to the building where the scrum was being held. As water poured from the sky, we followed the national media crew towards the front doors of the cultural centre, where they were ushered in. However, security stopped the three of us. They ordered us to stand in a line in front of the building. We couldn't move on until the RCMP checked our gear with their sniffer dog. *Globe and Mail* photographer Melissa Tait came out to see what was going on and piped up, "Oh, I haven't been searched yet either! Should I stand here?" She placed her camera bag on the ground.

"No, ma'am. You are good to go," the RCMP officer said. Melissa looked surprised, but stepped aside. As the rain poured on our heads, Rodrigo, Ramsay and I exchanged glances that said, "Are we getting special treatment here?"

The RCMP dog, a fierce-looking and wet German shepherd, started on Rodrigo first and cleared him. Ramsay leaned down to open up his sound case, which he was trying to shield from the rain, so the dog could sniff. The dog ran right towards Ramsay as he bent his head down. I cringed, thinking the dog was going in for the attack. But instead, the dog lurched towards Ramsay and began to lick his face. Everyone cracked up—even the RCMP. We were cleared by security and made our way into the basement of the cultural centre.

The scrum began with Trudeau thanking Kúkpi7 Rosanne for her "extraordinary leadership" over "a very difficult year." He made some statements about how hard the past year had been for Survivors and their families. He added that it was a difficult year for Canadians as well, "as we came to grips with our history." He spoke of the legacy of inter-generational trauma and the need for Canada to "fully come to grips" with the "dark legacy of our colonial past." He acknowledged that these issues linger in the present and said he had assured Kúkpi7 Rosanne that Ottawa would be there as "partners" on this journey.

Sometimes politicians don't even realize when they sound insincere. All the catchphrases get used. Because they've been repeated so many times, they ring hollow.

Canadian Prime Minister Justin Trudeau speaks during the memorial ceremony marking the one-year anniversary of the discovery of two hundred potential graves, at Tk'emlúps Powwow Arbour in Kamloops, B.C., on May 23, 2022. (Photo by Mert Alper Dervis/Anadolu Agency via Getty Images)

A CBC Kamloops reporter asked Trudeau about the records. "The last time you were here, you said all the paperwork, attendance records, were already handed over, and that turned out not to be true. What efforts are being made now to expedite them?"

Trudeau never truly knows what to say about records. When he was here in October, he said all the records Canada has had been turned over to the NCTR in Winnipeg. Turns out that wasn't true.[3] After that visit, Donald Worme, the former TRC counsel and former lawyer for Tk'emlúps, told me in an interview that if Survivors agreed, all records would be released to the TRC so they could be held by the National Centre for Truth and Reconciliation at the University of Manitoba—even the set of private records that contained the Survivors' testimonies and were used to provide individual compensation through the Independent Assessment Process.[4]

And now, those testimonies are at risk of being destroyed. Why? Because in 2017, the Supreme Court of Canada ruled that thirty-eight thousand stories would be kept for fifteen years, during which time Survivors could consent to having their records preserved if they wanted. The Government of Canada challenged this ruling at the Supreme Court, arguing that the IAP documents are "under the control of a government institution" according to the Access to Information Act, the Privacy Act and Library and Archives Canada, and that the lower court had no jurisdiction to order the records' destruction. The government lost the appeal. The Supreme Court's judgment said that during the fifteen-year retention period, claimants could choose to preserve and archive their IAPs. The court acknowledged this order could be inconsistent with the wishes of claimants who had died and were never given the option to preserve their records, but "the destruction of records that some claimants would have preferred to have preserved works a lesser injustice than the disclosure of records that most expected never to be shared."[5]

So, if living Survivors do not speak up, the records would be destroyed in light of privacy concerns. That is a backwards way to run consent over records. As Worme said, "Where in the civilized world do historical records get destroyed?"

Beyond the Survivors' statements given for the IAP, there are still unrecovered residential records in various federal and provincial government departments and agencies that Survivors, families and communities are still desperately trying to locate.

During a press conference in Kamloops on October 18, 2021, Trudeau was wrong when he said all records that were in the possession of the Government of Canada had been released. Truthfully, this would be near impossible to say with certainty given the volume of records out there and the size of various levels of government bureaucracies.

After Trudeau made this statement, the NCTR could not stay quiet. They put out a press release that declared, "At present, we are still waiting for Canada to provide the final versions of school narratives and supporting documents used in the Independent Assessment Process to the NCTR."[6] That wasn't all that was missing. The NCTR also called for the release of "various Library and Archives Canada quality records and records from provincial governments, most of whom have not yet produced vital statistics, including death certificates for children lost at schools or coroners' reports." They were also still waiting for access to Indian hospital records, federal health records and day school records.

This press release ended with a slap: "If the Prime Minister is telling all Canadians and Indigenous Peoples that the NCTR holds all records, it is time for that to be true."

But at the scrum in Kamloops, seven months later at the one-year anniversary of the discovery of the missing, Trudeau reiterated to reporters, "My understanding is everything we have has been handed over to the NCTR in Winnipeg, that is the central repository for all the archives the government has, as well as many of the religious archives as well. We continue to look through records, we look for copies we have of religious order records, but our understanding is just about everything we have has been handed over to the NCTR."

It was my turn to ask a question. I was both nervous and drenched. Standing among the pool of reporters, I was willing to bet I was the only reporter there who was Indigenous, let alone Anishinaabe. I asked my question as the great-granddaughter of Liz Samson, a woman who the Government of Canada said did not exist and whose residential school records appear to have been destroyed and lost.

"I know that Kúkpi7 Rosanne was asking for records the last time you were here," I began. "And also we went to the Vatican looking for records, we know the Oblates have records. Is Canada helping whatso-ever to try to get those records over here? So many schools, I'm thinking of St. Anne's and here, so many schools, we need to see those records, they have been hidden for so long."

When the prime minister responded, he avoided looking at me in the eyes. Instead, he looked at the floor in front of him. "As I said, to the best of my understanding the federal government has made all of its records available to the National Centre for Truth and Reconciliation in Winnipeg"—he looked up at me briefly before returning his gaze to the floor—"which is a repository for those archives. We continue to look carefully to see if there are others we have and that we can give because we keep finding more"—he looked up again briefly, then back to the floor—"in various places and we are going to continue to deliver all we possibly can and all we find. I have also directly spoken with leaders of various religious institutions to encourage them to share their full records as well. It is something that has long been asked to a number of church groups and hopefully they'll continue to do that. The federal government can facilitate that and we are looking to do that."[7]

It was a perfect non-answer. He might not have realized it, but it was insulting to me, to Annie and to all her descendants. For the rest of our exchange he spent a lot of time looking at the floor.

I was allowed to ask a second question. I asked if there were any updates on the extradition of Johannes Rivoire and other priests who are accused of committing crimes against children.

This was the prime minister's response: "Our justice minister takes that as he must, extremely seriously. We have a rigorous process around that, an impartial justice system where politicians don't get to decide who needs to get extradited on what. There is a legal process around that but I can reassure you that yes, that legal process is being looked at with all the attention the Justice Ministry can focus on."[8]

His answer said nothing. It was a polite smackdown. He had just schooled me in front of the national press on how Canada's justice sys-tem is impartial. The smile he gave me said it all. It was half-hearted, devoid of any meaning. In a way, it said absolutely everything about

Ottawa's inability to take this issue, to seize it with both hands, and make things right.

Then a local CTV reporter went for the jugular. He asked: What is Canada doing to combat the record number of children placed in state care in child welfare? Trudeau said his government had been working on this issue for years, with Indigenous leadership and the passing of Bill C-92, child welfare legislation that he said will safeguard children from being taken away from their communities, language and culture.

I rolled my eyes and looked away from the scrum. On camera.

But this reporter was not done. "As you made your way into the arbour today you obviously heard the drumming and singing that followed you. There was some visceral anger from some of the people there. One of the chants was, 'All of this Canada is stolen Indian land.' Do you believe this country exists on stolen Indigenous land?"[9]

I couldn't believe my ears, and suddenly I was proud of the tenacity of my colleagues.

Trudeau was flummoxed. "Canada is a country that consists of Indigenous people who have been here for millennia," he said, "who welcomed in settlers in some cases and were overrun by settlers in others. But we are a country that exists today with a commitment to always learn from the past and always do better.

"There's no question that we can go back to the past and see all sorts of terrible things that happened or we can look at the present and see there is a lot we need to improve, right now on who we are and where we are moving forward. Informed by the past but also committed to learning from each other, respecting each other and building a stronger future. I understand the anger and frustration out there, there is so much trauma people continue to live with. We just have to continue to be there, keep partnering. . . . For many people today was a positive step forward. . . . The story of Canada is the story of people coming together to build a better future for themselves and for their kids than they could have imagined a generation before."

With that, the press conference was over.

=

THE NEXT DAY I sat down with Ted Gottfriedson in front of the apple orchard, beside the powwow arbour. There were security guards on the grounds, there to keep out the nosy onlookers. "This is a tough story that no twisted mind could make up," Ted said. And then he gave me a bit of advice on writing my book. "I'm not a writer, but I'd say, tell the truth. It doesn't matter how painful it is or how embarrassing it is . . . telling the truth is probably going to be hard to hear." He pointed towards the orchard. "But I think we owe it to these guys to tell the absolute truth."[10]

Gottfriedson is a jovial man, always smiling. It was the Tk'emlúps te Secwépemc language and culture department, where he worked, that had applied for funding to get a path maintained on the former school grounds. But that was the winter Covid hit. Suddenly, everyone was on lockdown and they couldn't find any contractors to hire. They asked their funders if they could do something else with the money, and the answer was yes. So they asked some of the Elders what they should do with the funds. One of the Elders said, "Let's go find the kids."

"We all grew up knowing this," Gottfriedson said, referring to the missing. "It is just something we heard and that we knew. Once we decided to do it, we were like, 'now what?'" He joked that his only experience with archaeology was watching Indiana Jones.

They got in touch with Dr. Eldon Yellowhorn, a professor of Indigenous studies at Simon Fraser University, who recommended they speak with Dr. Sarah Beaulieu, an archaeologist and assistant professor at the School of Culture, Media and Society at the University of the Fraser Valley. "It was a heck of a ride for various reasons," Gottfriedson told me. "There was so much that happened here in the past year for our community and our little language and culture team."

But the missing children consumed them all; they were their top priority. How could they not be? Gottfriedson said that before they began, he'd never heard of ground-penetrating radar. "We had no idea what to do." Now he jokes that Sarah's machine "looks like a lawn mower." And it does: it rolls slowly over the grass, searching for any anomalies.

But how did they know where to look? Do you just pick a spot and start rolling? That was where Western science and the knowledge of Kamloops Survivors converged. Gottfriedson explained how the Survivors had always spoken about Brother Joseph's orchard. "It wasn't just a shot in the dark. We had an idea in the stories from our Elders."

Brother Joseph, Gottfriedson explained, was a "fixture" at Kamloops. One of the Elders remembers that the students at Kamloops were always hungry, and as a child she once crept down to the orchard to find an apple to eat. But when she got there, Brother Joseph let his two big black dogs loose on her. She was bitten. "Brother Joseph was the caretaker of this area and in charge of keeping the secret here," Gottfriedson said. "He seemed to cover it up, until now."

We paused for a moment, and then I asked Gottfriedson about Catholicism. I told him I continued to wrestle with how some Indigenous people can be strong Catholics. Ted answered that he did not consider himself to be a Catholic. "The only thing left of my Catholicism is, I hope they are burning in hell," he said. He added that Christianity is a story—it isn't a better story just because someone wrote it down.

The Tk'emlúps people, he told me, have their own word for the truths, the stories, that pass between them. "We call them Stsepetkwll," said Gottfriedson. "That means legend or story [that teaches]. But it is a gross mistranslation to call them a story. They instruct, they entertain, but they also contain our laws. Everything about who we are as Tk'emlúps—anything you would want to know—is all in there."

Then he told me a Stsepetkwll on how to free the salmon: There was a big logjam in the river of ice and it was the coyote who freed the logjam and let the salmon run. Scientists now realize there was an ice jam down the river and it did break. So the Stsepetkwll might not be written down, but they are fairly accurate.

I asked Gottfriedson to take me back to the day when the world changed—when he found out about the missing.

"Our Elder was here," he recalled. "She called me and said, 'There are 215 kids down here, Ted,' and I said, 'What?' I had to repeat it, '2-1-5?' And she said, 'Yes.' It took a long time to process that. I wanted to be optimistic. I wanted the story, in my own crazy way, not to be true. And if it was, five or ten kids, at worst. So that was really hard to hear. It is still hard to think about and talk about."

Then he began to speak about his mother, who was a Survivor of Kamloops. "She had that mentality—don't you cry in front of anyone. It is a weakness." His mom was the first person he called after the Elder told him about the 215. "From that moment, everything changed for her, for us. My dad, he is kind of rough. We are horse people. We are drawn to horses. My dad was a rough cowboy type. So my dad went into rodeos. They don't cry for a whole other set of reasons. But for my mom, she has been able to cry in front of us." It took this long. "That was hard to see, for all her kids and grandkids. She never let us see her cry."

Gottfriedson says he was reflecting a lot on intergenerational trauma. "As an IG Survivor, you don't realize it—it is just life. Life is like this because that is the way it is. . . . My trip to Rome was special because, on the day I left, it was the first time my mom hugged me—in fifty-three years. And what she said was, 'Come home safe. Do good over there.' I never once was hugged. That was hard and amazing. The trip was worthwhile because of that. I got back and said, 'Mom, you hugged me.' She said, 'Yep. One day I'll tell you I love you too.'

"This damn place. It keeps on giving. All-consuming. Full of hate and cruelty. I can't stress it enough, but those people are evil."

He did not blame his mom for not telling him or her other children more about what had happened, what she had experienced. "Two women I know, and who I respect, had to throw their babies in the incinerator," he said quietly. "One here and one in Williams Lake. Evil. They were impregnated by priests, and then aborted." And that, he said, wasn't even the worst part. The worst part was this: "They made someone's little sister go and watch. Both times. They were just girls, thirteen or fourteen. And you make a little kid go and watch? What the hell is wrong with these people?"

IN THE DEAD heat of July on the Prairies, I found myself and my film crew on the road from Edmonton to Maskwacis, Alberta. The road is about a hundred kilometres long and it seemed endless. As we neared Maskwacis, a community made up of four Treaty 6 Cree First Nations— Ermineskin Cree Nation, Samson Cree Nation, Louis Bull Tribe and Montana First Nation—suddenly the highway became incredibly smooth. It had been freshly paved, lickety-split for $20 million, paid for by the Alberta government before Pope Francis's visit to Canada. Apparently, the papal team who scouted out exactly where the pontiff would give his historic apology had said the roads needed to be redone. The eighty-year-old leader of the largest church in the world is frail. He would require something less bumpy.

That is ironic. All levels of government can't seem to get it together to bring fresh, clean water to the communities who have been living without this necessity of life, yet they can pave roads in the blink of an eye to give the pope a smooth ride. Even Marc Miller, then minister of Crown-Indigenous relations, criticized this move. "It shouldn't take the visit [from the] Pope to actually get the road paved. That's a reactionary approach to things," he said.[11]

Why pave the highway for the pope? Wouldn't it have been more of a reality check for him to see the four communities as they truly are—pockmarked by colonialism with potholes so big that they swallow you up?

There was a joke among those who live in Maskwacis, that as soon as the papal tour left, the roads would be ripped up and gone with him.

The papal apology tour touched down in Canada on July 24, 2022, after four intense months of planning, mostly organized by the Canadian Conference of Catholic Bishops. In Rome we'd heard a lot about how his visit would be a partnership. The pope's tour was to be planned in consultation with the Métis, First Nations and Inuit communities that would be receiving him. But then National Chief of the Assembly of First Nations RoseAnne Archibald said they had no control over the planning process, and the AFN "expressed disappointment over the unilateral decision-making on site choices and other logistics."[12]

Pope Francis visited only one Indian residential school site on his five-day visit to Canada. Only one of the 139 institutions included in the work of the Truth and Reconciliation Commission. That school was the Ermineskin Indian Residential School. Ermineskin operated for eighty years, from 1895 until 1975, one of the largest in Canada and located in Alberta, the province with the most residential schools in the country. And the pope didn't actually visit the school itself, since the building was torn down years ago. The pope's event was taking place at the Maskwacis powwow arbour, which was specially outfitted to receive him and the tens of thousands of worshippers from across Turtle Island who were expected to come to see him. Hundreds of overflow chairs were set up in perfect neat rows outside the arbour. White event tents were scattered around for dignitaries.

To be clear: TRC call to action 58 was a call upon the pope for an apology modelled after the 2010 papal apology to Irish victims of abuse: it was to be issued within one year of the commission's report, and on Canadian soil. Pope Benedict XVI had apologized, within a year and in a seven-page letter, for years of physical and sexual abuse children in Ireland suffered at the hands of priests.[13]

In Canada, it took seven years for the call to be answered. And this apology in Canada, when it finally came, seemed a lot shorter than seven pages.

Pope Francis was scheduled to be in Maskwacis for just the morning, to make his historic and long-awaited apology on Canadian soil before returning to Edmonton to visit the Sacred Heart Church of the First Peoples and then continuing on to Lac Ste. Anne.

Too early that morning, I'd dragged myself out of my Edmonton hotel bed and taken a taxi to meet up with the CBC TV crew. It was 3:30 a.m. We had to leave promptly to be at the Ermineskin site, set up and be ready to go for the arrival of the pope. I was with Adrienne Arsenault, an anchor for CBC's *The National*, and her team. I'd opted to forgo their offer of makeup and hair at two thirty. I'd wanted the extra hour of sleep.

The network had asked me to be Adrienne's "anchor buddy," commenting live on TV for the three-hour news special on this historic day.

This was a huge honour, but it also left me terrified. How could I put into context five hundred years of conquest and oppression, along with all the emotion and pain of the day, on the spot, on live television? I felt sick as I wondered what the hell I was going to say.

To help me through the day, I wore a beaded medallion. Stó:lō author Lee Maracle's voice was in my head as I put it on that morning. We were in a car once, driving back to Toronto from an event we'd both attended. I was telling her about how I was going to write a book on residential schools. From the passenger seat, she gave me the eye, and then told me to always wear a medallion. She cautioned that I was collecting so many stories, so much evil, I needed to protect my own spirit from the bad.

The first thing I said on air that morning was, "This is a tough day." That was exactly what I felt. So many of us had mixed emotions, remembering our families, all those who were lost in our communities. I thought of Annie and Liz. "What possibly is he going to say, and will it be enough? Will it ever be enough?"

I looked down at the TV monitors on our set and noticed the overflowing and zealous crowds of faithful had not arrived in the numbers expected. Empty white chairs were peppered throughout the Ermineskin field.

Inuit Tapiriit Kanatami president Natan Obed was in Maskwacis, waiting for the pope as part of the official Canadian delegation. A CBC reporter spoke to him outside the powwow arbour, and Adrienne and I watched him on the monitor. It was Tuesday, but in a few days, on Friday, the pontiff would land in Iqaluit for a few hours, the last stop on what we reporters were calling the "apology tour." Arseneault asked Obed if he had confidence the pope would hold abusers to account. Obed reiterated what he'd said in Rome: they wanted Johannes Rivoire brought back to Canada. "When we went to Rome, we had a number of clear positions from Canadian Inuit. One was to hold abusers accountable, particularly Johannes Rivoire. . . . We asked the pope to directly intervene, to speak with him and compel him to come to Canada. To our understanding," Obed said, "that hasn't happened yet."[14]

The ITK did work with Canada's then justice minister, David Lametti, and they tried to speak to the French government about returning Rivoire, whom the Oblates by then had expelled from their order. However, the ITK were unsuccessful.

This begs the question: Did the pope ever intervene, as Obed requested? We will never truly know.

In October 2022, three months after the pope's visit to Canada, the Public Prosecution Service of Canada would report that France had refused to extradite Rivoire on the grounds that, even though it had an extradition treaty with Canada, under French law it cannot extradite its own citizens and that "too much time" had elapsed between the event and the charge.[15] The best Canada could do was hope Rivoire left France for another country, and one with an extradition treaty, so he could be arrested and sent back here.[16]

At the time of the writing of this book, the Missionary Oblates of Mary Immaculate were supposedly set to produce a list of priests who had a history of offences against children. The Jesuits of Canada had already done so. On March 23, 2023, the Jesuits published a list containing the names of twenty-seven priests "credibly accused of abuse of a minor." The list was compiled by a private investigator hired by the Jesuits. The order said it had been working on the list since 2019, and blamed Covid for the slow rollout.

When they released their list, the Jesuits, in their own way, seemed to admit there had been a serious moral failure. Their statement read: "Over the past three or more decades, revelations of grievous abuse by clergy dating back many generations have come to light, and the Church has been slow to respond. Moving through phases of outright denial, victim blaming, and moral incompetence, the Church has begun to respond justly. All of this has undermined the credibility of an institution that, according to its own raison d'être, should have been a witness to all that contributes to the promotion of the moral dignity of each human person, rather than their humiliation."[17]

The Jesuits said they were aware that revealing names could retraumatize Survivors, but the head of the Jesuits in Canada, Erik

Oland, said it was important to make it public. Oland also pointed out that not all on the list had been criminally or civilly tried. Nearly all of the men on the list are now dead.[18]

An important aspect of the Jesuit list is that it includes all the places where each man lived and worked. For example, one of the twenty-seven, Robert MacDougall, was born in 1924, ordained in 1961 and died in 2004. His pastoral assignments included Loyola College, Montreal; St. Mary's University, Halifax; St. Paul College, Winnipeg; St. Ignatius Parish, Winnipeg; John Bosco Residence for Boys, Orillia, Ontario; 100 Huntley Street, Toronto; St. Brigid Church, Parrsboro, Nova Scotia; St. Francis of Assisi Church, Wolfville, Nova Scotia; "Food For Life" Television Ministry; Manresa Retreat House, Pickering, Ontario; and Xavier House, Toronto.[19]

At the time of writing, Survivors in Canada were still waiting for the Missionary Oblates of Mary Immaculate to release their own list. And in late February 2024, the Vatican announced it would not expel Rivoire from the Oblate order even though the Oblates in Canada and in France supported the move. When I asked Obed about how he felt about this, he did not hold back: "This is the truth about how the Catholic Church responds to sexual misconduct within its own institution—protecting a predator and turning away."[20]

POPE FRANCIS ROLLED into Maskwacis in his own car, a tiny white Fiat 500 with a papal flag on it, over the fresh pavement and past the five white tipis set up on the grounds.

The first four tipis each represented one of the Cree communities that make up Maskwacis. The fifth represented the former residential school. Before the pope entered the arbour, he spent a moment at Our Lady of Seven Sorrows cemetery, praying at the graves—both marked and unmarked—of the children who died at Ermineskin Residential School.

The First Nations leaders carried eagle staffs, they wore their head-dresses or war bonnets, and they danced into the powwow arbour to the sound of the drum. Among them were Natan Obed, Assembly of

First Nations National Chief RoseAnne Archibald and Métis National Council president Cassidy Caron. Along with the dignitaries was my friend Sol Mamakwa, a residential school Survivor and an Ontario NDP MPP. He was with NDP leader Jagmeet Singh. Then came in the rest of the Survivors.

Here it was, this moment many had waited for their entire lives.

They came in wearing the clothes that this church had banned in all of its so-called schools. The emcee of the procession was proudly speaking in Cree, the language of the land that the schools had also banned. And the drum—the drum that is such a large part of healing and life—the drum beat loudly. It was beautiful.

Then the National Centre for Truth and Reconciliation's fifty-metre-long red banner containing the names of children who died at the residential schools, was carried in. This was a moment in a day full of moments. If anyone had, for a second, forgotten why we were here, this was it. The children who never came home because of the policies championed and supported by the Catholic Church, the Canadian government and a society that stood back and did nothing as children suffered from illness, malnutrition, neglect and abuse.

My throat caught. They were here, the children. Including the names of my relatives: Samuel Skelliter, Thomas Skelliter, Charles Carpenter, Doris Carpenter. They were with us all, here in front of the pope.

"It catches my heart when I see that," I said on air. "Those are just the names of the children we know of. We have not forgotten them. They are with us."

They were with me.

The emcee spoke of the number four, of the four directions, the four stages of life: the sun rising from the east; from the south, the thunder birds fly; on the west side is the wind and the oxygen we breathe, and on the north side we have Mother Earth. Grass dancers and fancy dancers, in beautiful brightly coloured ribbons, jingles and feathers, began to dance in each of the four directions of the circle as the red banner encircled them.

"Who we are, Mother Earth, is the plant life, the mother of all insect life, Mother Earth is the mother of all animals on the ground, in the water and air. Mother Earth is of course, the mother of all humanity. Mother Earth is who she is. We are the children; we are the people of Mother Earth. Hiy hiy."[20]

Chief Wilton Littlechild then officially welcomed the pope, addressing him with his Nêhiyawêwin name, White Eagle. He thanked him for travelling such a long way, for the personal effort he'd made to be on "our land" and he extended him a most heartfelt welcome.

"I was a student at the Ermineskin Indian Residential School," he said, and noted that for today, this school represented all of the schools across the country. He welcomed Prime Minister Trudeau and Governor General Mary Simon. Chief Littlechild said he personally had heard nearly seven thousand testimonies from former students of residential schools. And he acknowledged that the pope had also listened to stories of abuse from the Survivors who had travelled to Rome, stories of how our languages were suppressed, our culture taken away and our "spirituality denigrated." "You have heard the devastation that followed in the way our families were torn apart. The words you spoke to us in response clearly came from the depths of your heart," he said.[21]

Pope Francis then spoke, in Spanish, his native language, translated into English by CBC translators. "Here, from this place associated with painful memories, I would like to begin what I consider a penitential pilgrimage. I have come to your native lands to tell you in person of my sorrow, to implore God's forgiveness, healing and reconciliation, to express my closeness and to pray with you and for you."[22]

He recalled the meetings in Rome, four short months earlier. He spoke of the little moccasins he was given by Okanese Chief Marie-Anne Day Walker-Pelletier. How he was asked to return the moccasins. He said he was doing so today.

He said he felt sorrow, indignation and shame—and the moccasins were a reminder. "The memory of those children is indeed painful. . . . At the same time, those moccasins also speak to us of a path to follow. . . .

We want to walk together, to pray together and to work together, so the suffering of the past can lead to a future of justice, healing and reconciliation."

The pope acknowledged that the policies of assimilation and enfranchisement systematically marginalized Indigenous Peoples; that, through the system of residential schools, languages and cultures were denigrated and suppressed, and children suffered physical, psychological and spiritual abuse; that children were taken away at a young age and how that ruined generations of families. He thanked the Survivors for sharing their "bitter memories" with him.

"Today I am here, in this land that, along with its ancient memories, preserves the scars of still open wounds. I am here because the first step of my penitential pilgrimage among you is that of again asking forgiveness, of telling you once more that I am deeply sorry." To that, the crowd applauded. Some whistled and howled.

He continued: "Sorry for the ways in which, regrettably, many Christians supported the colonizing mentality of the powers that oppressed the indigenous peoples. I am sorry." To this, more applause. "I ask forgiveness, in particular, for the ways in which many members of the Church and of religious communities cooperated, not least through their indifference, in projects of cultural destruction and forced assimilation promoted by the governments of that time, which culminated in the system of residential schools." He called it a "disastrous error" and a "deplorable evil," and he said in the face of this, the church knelt before God to ask forgiveness.

Okanese Chief Day Walker-Pelletier walked up the white steps towards the pontiff, and his aide gave her back the little moccasins, covered in an orange cloth. She smiled and, after a moment of silence, they spoke quietly.

Next was another moment in a day full of them, a song sung in Nêhiyawêwin with a lone drummer. Chief Littlechild stood up with a headdress in his hands and he carefully faced each of the four directions. Then he slowly walked up the steps and put the headdress on the pope's head. The two men held hands. The pope cracked a huge, toothy smile. As we watched the war bonnet being placed on the pope's head, there was applause, and then near-dead silence in the arbour.

I was stunned. As a commentator on live TV, what could I say to Chief Littlechild's act? Was it for me to say anything? He had been one of the commissioners of the TRC and was a Survivor himself. Struggling for words as I watched this happen, I explained that this act was Littlechild's personal choice, a gift he believed needed to be given. (Later on, after Chief Littlechild faced public criticism for this gift, he clarified that the decision to gift a headdress was a mixture of both community involvement and a personal family decision.)[23]

After Pope Francis apologized to residential school Survivors in a large ceremony in Maskwacis, Alberta, he was gifted a headdress from Chief Wilton Littlechild, one of the three commissioners of the Truth and Reconciliation Commission. (*Edmonton Journal*, photo by Patrick T. Fallon/AFP via Getty Images)

Suddenly, the silence was broken by the long, loud, mournful cry of a woman, singing in Nêhiyawêwin to the tune of "O Canada." Her face was soaked with tears. The entire audience fell silent as she belted out her song and raised her right hand like a warrior.

It was a masterful, perfect foil. Pope Francis stood up and smiled at her awkwardly, uncertain what to do.

Then she let him have it. She was crying with rage in Cree. Full on. Someone in the audience yelled out, "Repudiate the Doctrine of Discovery!"

Clearly the pope had stood up because he thought she was singing the national anthem. But she was not. We found out later that the woman was Si Pih Ko, or Trina Francois. She said later that she was singing in response to the headdress being put on the pope's head. She said she could not remain silent. She was singing of the land, asking the Creator to keep it sacred. And when she was finished singing, these were the words she directed at the bewildered pope: "You are hereby served spoken law. We, the daughters of the Great Spirit and our tribal sovereign members, cannot be coerced into any law, any treaty, that is not the Great Law."[24]

The last words of that historic day, televised around the world, belonged to a Cree woman crying out defiantly in pain.

MASKWACIS WAS THE one and only time Pope Francis truly fulfilled TRC call to action 58. He did not apologize profusely at every single stop in each of the three cities he travelled to—something I believe he should have done.

The next morning the pope held a giant open-air mass at Commonwealth Stadium in Edmonton. This was the big public event of the tour, and many pilgrims were expected here from across North America. The stadium can seat nearly sixty thousand, but there were many empty seats in the sweltering arena.

The homily was disappointing. On reflection, what were we expecting? That things would miraculously change overnight? That the *Titanic* of religion would turn around and the pontiff would direct all of his flock to start being more respectful of the Indigenous cultures throughout Turtle Island? We had hoped the homily would give clear instructions that things must change after the apology. Instead, the whole event was a near-regular Catholic mass. Communion was given by members of the church, who could be found under orange rain umbrellas. The smell of sage that burned at the beginning of the service in certain pockets of the arena was muted as the mass hit full swing.

We saw the same thing time and time again. From Lac Ste. Anne to Quebec City to the historic shrine of Sainte-Anne-de-Beaupré, so many First Nations, Métis and Inuit Survivors and their families came to the events—but they only heard the pope apologize one more time, in Iqaluit. It was clear that the rest of the events were exactly what the pope had said this trip was: a pilgrimage. This was a trip for the faithful to come and be healed by the leader of the Catholic Church in the manner Catholicism intended. The papal apology was nothing more than a circus passing through town.

Forgiveness is personal. Do we need others to heal? Do we need some kind of acknowledgement from the institutions and churches that hurt us, or is healing a journey we do within ourselves and with those in our communities?

I RAN INTO Natan Obed by the departure gate at the Edmonton airport. He was on his way to Iqaluit to prepare for the papal visit there.

Obed is an Intergenerational Survivor. His father went to a school in Newfoundland named St. Anthony. There were five boarding schools in Newfoundland and Labrador, all of them left out of both Prime Minister Stephen Harper's official apology to residential school Survivors in 2008 and the IRSSA. Run by the Moravian Church and the International Grenfell Association, the schools were in North West River, Cartwright, Makkovik, Nain and St. Anthony. Survivors started a class-action lawsuit against Ottawa, and when Justin Trudeau came to power, the federal government assumed responsibility for the schools. In 2017, Trudeau apologized to the former students of the Newfoundland and Labrador residential schools.[25]

Obed's father was seven years old when his family was relocated from northern Labrador and, shortly afterwards, his mother died from food poisoning. That's when he was taken away to residential school. He was at St. Anthony for eleven years, until he turned eighteen. His younger brother also went to the school. They lost their father while they were there. "I know this because he wrote about it," said Obed.[26]

Then, Obed cried.

"It might not have been a Catholic school," he told me, "but I think the solidarity we have as Intergenerational Survivors, it remains essential to our ability to work on these issues together. I may not know exactly what people in Maskwacis went through, but I can understand its effects on children and grandchildren."

As Indigenous Peoples, all our lives have been irrecoverably shaped by the residential school system. "That is a truth," Obed said. "And the church's part in that is central to this reality."

Sometimes he feels religious institutions do not accept and fully understand that basic truth. How deep it is. "An apology can help on everyone's path. But if you don't even get to the place where you understand how impactful residential school is to all of us . . ." That, he said, is why we saw and heard the frustration in how the official apology was received.

Obed said they'd been told early on that the official apology on Canadian soil would happen at Maskwacis, so he wasn't surprised when it wasn't said again during the tour. In order not to miss it, Inuit Survivors came down to Maskwacis. "The apology itself was detailed," he said. "I felt the humanity of it from the pope. But it was also very particular, and in particular language that left out some very big things, especially the consideration for sexual abuse. There was talk of, I think the pope said violence? But I don't recall him ever touching on the subject that has plagued this institution and the residential school system."

Pope Francis did not speak of violence. What he did acknowledge was "how children suffered physical, verbal, psychological and spiritual abuse."[27]

It wasn't until Thursday, at the Notre-Dame de Québec Basilica-Cathedral in Quebec City, that Pope Francis acknowledged the church's role in sexual abuse. But he did not directly say the abuse was committed inside residential schools by the clergy. Instead, he spoke of "the evil perpetrated by some of [the church's] sons and daughters," and "I think in particular of the sexual abuse of minors and vulnerable people, crimes that require firm action and an irreversible commitment."

This was, as the *National Catholic Reporter* described, more of a "blanket apology" for all sexual abuse against minors and vulnerable people, as the pope did not single out Indigenous victims.[28]

However, in Maskwacis, this was a huge hole in the apology, and not something to be skated around, especially when you think about the TRC, about the seven thousand Survivors and witnesses telling their stories, testifying. Sexual abuse was a recurring theme, and it has left a profound generational impact. The pope had nothing to offer those Survivors. He did not directly address it.

Obed told me he was surprised by the amount of proselytizing being done at the events. "I didn't expect that a condition of hearing an apology would mean that I would be, and that everyone listening would be, subjected to a sermon or a Catholic spiritual event. I recognize this is the pope and he is a holy person whose entire life is dedicated to the Church ... but I may have been naive to think the institution could come here and find the strength to apologize in the fullest capacity it possibly can without the accompanying religious element that ultimately is at odds with the very purpose of the visit. The pope has talked about being on a penitential pilgrimage, but it has felt like he has been a missionary. Those are two very different things."

This tour was tightly controlled by the Catholic organizers. Going along with it was a gamble for Indigenous leaders, who put themselves out there to take part. What if it had been a disaster? Politically, it could have been devastating.

As for the Iqaluit part of the "tour," Natan told me it would be a success if Inuit Survivors and their families were able to speak freely to the pope.

In Iqaluit, the pope did apologize one more time. He apologized in Inuktitut, in front of the Nakasuk Elementary School, after a private audience inside the school with Inuit Survivors, who included victims of abuse at Sir Joseph Bernier Day School in Chesterfield Inlet.

I was standing in front of the school with Inuit writer and filmmaker Nadia Mike, listening to the throat singing and a drum dance by Bernier Survivor Piita Irniq. Mike had recognized me; she was a fan of my books and had seen me on TV. I stood with her and her beautiful family, who were all wearing traditional ceremonial clothing, and we listened as the pontiff sat on the stage set up in front of the school.

"I want to tell you how very sorry I am and to ask forgiveness for the evil perpetrated by not a few Catholics who contributed to the policies of cultural assimilation and enfranchisement in those schools," he said.[29]

The pope continued speaking, but many in the audience—we were all standing outside—began to leave. By the time he left the stage, the crowd had thinned. Pope Francis was whisked away to board his plane and head back home to Rome.

I SPOTTED DENE National Chief Gerald Antoine, the Northwest Territories Regional Chief for the Assembly of First Nations, sitting alone on the return flight to Montreal. Chief Antoine was the AFN lead in Rome, and he had been ever-present on the tour. He is a spiritual, thoughtful man, and it shows in everything he does.

After our flight took off, I asked him if I could get his impressions after the six-day tour. Specifically, I wanted to know from Chief Antoine what we need in order to heal.

He told me we must look to each other, to look inward. Every single family must begin the healing process themselves. "We need to restore our house because our house was uprooted. And our responsibilities got relocated. So we need to share those responsibilities with all the members of our family. And also the functions of our families got displaced so we need to delegate those functions," he explained.[30] He carried with him a brown leather notebook. He had been jotting down his thoughts throughout the tour.

"I see today a change in seasons," he told me. "Look at it right now, we are in the middle of summer. But in the morning, it is getting cooler. You can hear the birds chattering. There is a conversation happening naturally. This season of the genocide, of the traumatic experiences of these residential schools, we are just coming to the end of it. We need to look at how we are going to get ready for the next growing season as a family."

He was speaking of the Medicine Wheel. "If you look at the next season, winter, it is a day of rest and reflection. There is a crackling of the fire right in the middle of our home, our home fires. You are going to see people coming together, there will be a ceremony of togetherness as a family, then you will hear all of these stories, all these different things people are sharing."

There is a rolling thunder of our peoples' voices across the land right now, he said. You can feel it: we are beginning to come together. "I am hopeful for us."

He told me we need to connect our families back to the land. And that together, we must join as families. He was not just talking about First Nations; he was speaking of all Indigenous Peoples. "It is the land that connects us. Every one of us is here because the land has a special connection to all of us. It has been like that since the world was new. We live in family communities, allowing each other our privacy. Whatever gathering that we are having, at times like this, it is a ceremony of togetherness. This is our home and we belong here, all of us. There is a miracle that is put into motion by the opening ceremonies of our families. Inviting others into the ceremony, into the circle, no matter what language you speak, will help bring all of us home."

Chief Antoine said he was thankful for that togetherness. "Taking care of things as a family is the very best work of all. Taking community, taking the family to raise a child, means all the spirits working together. That human family, all of us, we owe it to each other to respect and honour that. There is this trust that begins to slowly strengthen."

The spiritual by-product of innocence is learning. This, he said, brings us closer to truth. It is multidimensional. After the apology, he said, it is time to reflect, provide ourselves with space and time to understand each other and the situation, and to recognize that we need to work on ourselves from the inside out. "It will take perseverance and commitment. Being here, gathering together, it is evidence we all have that quality to change and to enhance this process. There is a needed quality."

Then Chief Antoine surprised me. He told me his old friend the late Ojibwe author Richard Wagamese had taught him these things through his own words. "These are some of the words he has been using. I'm just rephrasing it as things unfold here," he said. "There is a needed quality. In Ojibwe there is a word, 'you got to want it.'"

Chief Antoine told me that this was what he was reflecting on at the end of the papal apology tour.

I asked him, "Do you believe Christianity is good for our people?"

He answered, "Prayer is good for us. It is time to put the shame and the fear away."

Chapter Fifteen

QUIET NO MORE

IS IT POSSIBLE THAT, AS WE CONTINUE TO MOVE IN THE SAME REALM AS OTHERS, our ancestors play with us, while keeping us together, holding us close? Do they watch us, from the trees or in the gaze of four-leggeds who catch our eyes from the sides of the road? Is there a master plan that keeps drawing us back into the circle? One that makes sure our spirits keep intertwining? Over the years, the decades, time and space don't really matter. You are born into a giant weave of sweetgrass, to generations of families, of people, whose spirits keep returning over and over.

The Anishinaabe believe we are all spirits, spending time in our physical bodies together before disappearing again, back to the land. We always return to the land, back to where we breathed and loved and sat by the fire before memories were remembered.

Does this give our ancestors comfort, the ones who pass through the western door and enter the spirit world?

Mishkeegogamang is about a six-hour drive northwest of Thunder Bay. I visited here many times before I had any idea of my connection to this rugged, stunning place—full of Canadian Shield rock covered in moss, a place where the smell of fresh pine needles dances in your nose, where the great thunder birds roam, where the American eagles build their large nests at the tops of hydro poles and trees.

Mish used to be called Osnaburgh, or Oz, after the Hudson's Bay

Company trading post that was established here in 1786 by John Best, who'd been sent by the HBC into the interior of what is now Ontario to look for a good place to trade. He picked the right spot, what the English called Lake St. Joseph, at the head of Kistachowan, the fast water. For thousands of years, it had been a gathering place for large hunting groups of families, including my own.

It was also the place where Treaty 9 was signed in 1905, and the very first paylist in the treaty documented. That list includes Annie Samson, along with her daughter, her sister-in-law Charlotte Carpenter and the Panacheese and Skunk families.[1]

It was actually the Panacheese family that first brought me to Oz, long before I knew that Annie and her family had been here. I came to visit Maryanne Panacheese, one of the mothers of the Seven Fallen Feathers. Maryanne is a smart, quiet, considered person. I went to see her to talk about her late son, Paul. He was one of the seven students who had died in Thunder Bay between 2000 and 2011 after moving there to attend high school.

Maryanne told me Paul had lived in ten different boarding homes while trying to complete high school. She was so concerned for his well-being that she had moved from Oz to rent a home in Thunder Bay herself, so she could give him some stability. She loved him so much. Tall and lanky, with little round glasses and short black hair, he was the light of her life.

While visiting Maryanne, I stayed overnight in the Mish women's centre. There is no hotel in the community, so the Chief at the time, Connie Gray-McKay, suggested I stay in the safe house. Every single First Nations community should have a safe house like Mish's. It is staffed and secure, twenty-four hours a day, seven days a week, for women and children in crisis. They even take Elders who need a safe haven if things get a little rough at home.

During that first visit, I heard not just about Paul but about all the local missing and murdered. Gone from this community of nearly one thousand people are nearly a dozen women and men, mothers, brothers, sons and daughters. Maryanne told me about her sister Sarah Skunk, a

Survivor from the Mohawk Institute in Brantford. The names of others who are gone include Viola Panacheese and her nephew Paul Panacheese, Rena Fox, Lena Lawson, Evelyn and Sophia Wassaykeesic, Jemima Mulholland, Thomas Lyons, Mariah Wesley and Charnelle Masakeyash. I learned all these names, not yet knowing my own kin, Annie, had been a member of this community. This is the place she was originally registered with the Government of Canada as a Treaty 9 Indian. According to Ottawa, Annie was ticket number 114 on the Osnaburgh paylist. Her daughter Christina had number 153. Both women were stolen by the state and incarcerated, Annie in an asylum, Christina in a residential school. And Annie's great-niece Doris Carpenter, also from Mish, died at Pelican in 1937.

In the 1881 census for Albany Fort, the first time we see Annie, when she was ten years old, her race was classified as "Indian." Her father Jean-Baptiste and mother Jane were also classified as "Indians," and so were their children. However, that changed in later census records. The 1901 Matagama census lists Annie, her husband Samson and their children Johny and Sarah as all "Crie." In 1921, the census at Lac Seul again lists Annie as "Cree." So why were Annie, her brother Joseph and her sister-in-law Charlotte at Osnaburgh at the signing of Treaty 9, surrounded by nearly all whose race is classified as Ojibwe, or, as we call ourselves, Anishinaabe. The Anishinaabe are found all around the Great Lakes Basin and they include the Chippewa, Odawa, Potawatomi, Algonquin, Saulteaux, Nipissing and Mississauga First Nations. Some Oji-Cree and Métis also identify as Anishinaabe.[2]

Again, the mixing of the Anishinaabe and the Ininiw speaks to the movement of our families up and down the highways of the time, the rivers and lakes. If you worked with the Hudson's Bay Company as a trapper, trader or labourer, you often moved from post to post. When the treaty was signed, Joseph Carpenter was working with the HBC.

Now, eight years after I'd first visited, but the first time since I'd come to fully understand my connection to the place, I was returning to Mish. This time, I was making the drive in the dead of winter with my friend Sol Mamakwa and a small documentary film crew. Originally this was purely Sol's trip, something we had planned for years. We were on our way north of Mish, to Stirland Lake Indian Residential School, where Sol was a student in the 1980s. He wanted—no, he needed—to go back. He needed to see it, once more, in order to heal. To see the buildings, to walk the halls—as someone untouchable to them now.

For most of his adult life, Sol hadn't admitted to anyone, not even to himself, that he was a Survivor. It wasn't until 2018, while I was writing my second book, *All Our Relations*, about why First Nations youth are taking their lives in record numbers, that Sol told me he was a Survivor. I'll never forget it. Once he said the words, once he admitted it, it became real to him. He started to think about it more. He also started to grow his hair. He had worn it short ever since it was cut off at school.

Sol wanted to stop in Mish on the way to visit the band council. A politician, he is always in high demand in communities. Everyone, especially leadership, wants to talk to Sol. But now there was another reason for the stop, and it had to do with me. I had told Sol about Annie, and about her being in Oz for the treaty signing. He said it was important that we visit, that I bring what I'd learned to the community. Elder Sam Achneepineskum said the same. He told me I needed to tell Annie's story.

We had two buckets of Kentucky Fried Chicken in the truck and a dozen doughnuts from Tim Hortons. You always bring gifts when you go to community, it is de rigueur and KFC is much appreciated. We dropped in to see Chief David Masakeyash and Elder Ronnie Roundhead, whom Elder Sam had urged me to contact before we arrived. We met in the band council office, where a few community members joined us. Connie, who had been Chief the first time I'd visited, also came to listen.

It was time to share what I'd learned about Annie and her brother Joseph Carpenter, who had been one of the Chiefs of Mishkeegogamang nearly a hundred years ago. It was nerve-racking. I didn't want them to think I was a pretender, some weird woman from the south who suddenly appears and says she is a long-lost relative. There are too many "pretendians" all over Turtle Island. It is somewhat of a bizarre phenomenon: people who claim to be First Nations or Métis because they apparently have one relative, born in the 1600s or 1700s, who was an

Indian. Sadly, these fraudsters are taking opportunity away from real Indigenous people by falsely using an Indigenous alias to receive government grants, scholarships and awards and to apply for positions created specifically for Indigenous people. These pretenders—hence the term *pretendians*—harm people actually of Indigenous descent who were displaced and removed from their communities due to residential school, the Sixties Scoop and enfranchisement.

The Mish councillors and community members sat and listened and chatted with us. I nervously told them who I was, where my mother was from, that I lived in Toronto and was a writer. Then I told them about the Carpenters and about Annie. We talked about the old HBC trading post and how it was still there, but a long snowmobile ride away. They said I should come back in the summer. No one seemed surprised by my family being here from down the river all those years ago.

I should have known they would be welcoming. Chief Masakeyash said that this was the great meeting place: everyone came from somewhere. Then I took a selfie with the Chief and we departed, the buckets of chicken claimed and gone.

AFTER WE LEFT the council chambers, we drove up to the Missabay Community School, named after the very first Chief of Mishkeegogamang at the signing of the treaty. The school, on the banks of the lake, stands out starkly in snow, long and blue and peaked at the top. I have been here before, to speak with Daisy Wenjack, Chanie Wenjack's sister. Chanie was the twelve-year-old boy who died on his way home after running away from Cecilia Jeffrey Indian Residential School in 1966. But home was in Ogoki Post, Marten Falls First Nation, hundreds of kilometres away from the school in Kenora. Chanie was made famous by Gord Downie, the beloved lead singer of the Tragically Hip, who died of a brain tumour in 2017. Downie made educating Canada about residential schools by telling Chanie's story one of his last great acts.

There is an atrium in the middle of the school. The floor is the Medicine Wheel. Above, flags are hung around the circle: the white

Nishnawbe Aski Nation flag, one commemorating the hundredth anniversary of Treaty 9, and a few others. In the centre of the circle, poster-size and hanging in a place of honour, are about a dozen historical photos from the signing of Treaty 9. Among them are pictures that were taken by Duncan Campbell Scott in July 1905—when Annie and Christina were here, and quite possibly Lizzie, too. Others were taken a decade earlier, when Missabay was younger. These photographs tell the story of the origins of this community, Mish, of this province, Ontario, and of the country of Canada.

Standing in the atrium, in the circle, scanning the pictures, I saw it: the photograph of Joseph Carpenter and all his kids in the canoe on Lake St. Joseph. It's one of the pictures Scott took. I quickly walked over to it. I couldn't believe my eyes. I reached my hand out and touched the face of Joe Carpenter. There they were, my family. Sol came and stood beside me, stunned. What were the chances that they were here, in a photograph taken by Duncan Campbell Scott, all this time?

A little boy stands in the frame at the signing of Treaty 9. Behind him, one of the treaty party members tries to direct human traffic. (Library and Archives Canada / Treaty No. 9 fonds / 3367608)

I walked around, looking at the other photos, the nameless faces, wondering who among them were my relations.

Afterwards, while Sol waited in the truck, I trudged through the dense, thick white snow toward the lake, the head of the Albany River. It was bone cold. I held tobacco in my left hand, an offering to the frozen water. The snow was so thick and high, it was impossible to tell where the shore and the river met. I pulled my moosehide mitts off, mitts that my grandmother had on her hands before she died. She loved the soft rabbit fur on the cuffs, the beading on each mitt in the shape of a bear paw. I knelt down and touched the snow with my bare hands. I released the tobacco and told Kistachowan that I was home.

SOL MAMAKWA IS in his old classroom, back at Wahbon Bay Academy, also known as Stirland Lake Indian Residential School. He is quiet, pensive, sitting among the dusty old 1980s-era typewriters, projectors and textbooks piled on shelves and in corners.

Earlier that morning, we had left Pickle Lake, a small town north of Mish, after we overnighted at the Pickle Lake Hotel. It was minus forty. We packed the truck with a thermos of coffee and bags of potato chips bought at the Pickle Lake gas station—Tomahawk Chips, made by a First Nations company. Stirland is about ninety minutes north of Pickle Lake, which is at the end of Ontario's most northern highway, the 599. We travelled up on the winter roads—nothing but snow and ice and hope.

Sol is my age, in his early fifties. We've been friends for years, since he worked with Alvin Fiddler at Nishnawbe Aski Nation, in the health department. I was a journalist for the *Toronto Star* at the time, telling stories about the lack of basic health care—no doctors, not enough nurses, no clinics—in many remote northern communities. I was reporting on how these nonexistent health systems, coupled with a lack of clean running water, have led to frequent public health disasters, from skin conditions to infectious disease outbreaks to mental health issues such as suicide. Sol became a source and a good friend.

He is now the only sitting Ontario member of provincial parliament who was born in an Indian hospital, the old Sioux Lookout Zone

Hospital, and is both a residential school and day school Survivor. He went to the Kamisquabika federal day school from kindergarten to Grade 8. His first language is Anisininew. Until he went to "school" he lived in his community, Kingfisher Lake First Nation. He had three brothers, a sister and two loving parents. They moved with the seasons, out on the land. It is where he is most comfortable, where he is home.

But he ran for provincial politics to make a difference. He hoped he could. And he is a beloved member of the Treaty 9 and Treaty 3 communities in northern Ontario. He's also become a beloved member of the legislature who has, on the front lawn of Queen's Park, plucked and prepared a goose he shot during the spring hunt. It was a teachable moment, he says with a smirk. Sol is a father of five, a grandfather and a social media hound, posting on all platforms, all the time. He is extremely accessible to his constituents—he has his morning coffee on Facebook live—and he is always on the move. If he is not in the provincial legislature, he is often flying off to one of the northern First Nations. Sol never sits still. He is often the first one to show up when a fly-in community has had a devastating fire and lives have been lost. And when there is a community celebration or the need for a meeting regarding Ontario government treaty infringements, the first call the north makes is usually to Sol.

Stirland was run by Northern Youth Programs, which was affiliated with the Mennonite Northern Light Gospel Mission. It opened in 1971 and operated as a boys' school until 1986, when it merged with Cristal Lake High School, a girls' school about forty minutes closer to town.

At a time when many residential schools were closing in Ontario, the Mennonites were opening schools. Besides Stirland and Cristal Lake, they also ran the Poplar Hill Development School in northwestern Ontario. Mennonites say they opened the schools because some community members asked them to. The Poplar Hill school got into trouble with the First Nations communities over the use of corporal punishment. In 1989, funding ended for Poplar Hill.[3] Reportedly, a police investigation into physical abuse ended in 1991 after the student refused to press charges and because, according to a retrospective story on the Mennonite Church's involvement in residential schools, there is a section in the Criminal Code "that protects adults in authority if they used corporal punishment."[4]

Stirland was one of the residential schools situated far outside of an urban area. The nearest large town was Sioux Lookout, 275 kilometres south. Located on a lake, you could get to Stirland only via a floatplane or winter road.[5] The campus comprised a series of wooden cottages, each of which was a dormitory for the boys. Teachers had their own lodgings, and the principal had a house. There was a main school building that looked a bit like a ski lodge and there was another building that housed a gymnasium.

The bedroom at Stirland Lake Indian Residential School where four boys slept, including former student Sol Mamakwa. (Photo by Tanya Talaga)

The school was infamous for being the site of the "Quiet Riot." Sol is the one who told me about it. The Quiet Riot was named after the popular 1980s heavy metal band whose music was outlawed at Stirland. All rock music, in fact, was banned at Stirland. The teachers said it was

"Devil's music." Students were allowed to listen only to church-sanctioned music such as Mennonite hymns.

The Quiet Riot, one of the few physical revolts in a residential school, took place on March 2, 1987. Students wielded hockey sticks, table legs and, the TRC heard, pieces of firewood against the staff to stop them from taking a student away for a violent beating. Such beatings were common, and the students were not going to take it anymore.[6] One staff member had his cheekbone broken and six others were treated for cuts and bruises. Police arrested sixteen students, who faced a variety of charges. One student pleaded guilty to assault causing bodily harm.

Sol had already left the school by the time the riot occurred. But he proudly talks and jokes about it with his friends who were there at the time. On our trip to Stirland, he spoke to many former students on his cell phone about what had happened there.

On the drive up, other memories began to seep into Sol's mind. Things he had forgotten about completely. Like this: The school administrators told the boys if they wanted to visit the girls at Cristal Lake, they would have to participate in a marathon. The run was a straight shot fifty kilometres down the road from Stirland. Sol remembers he made it to the rest station before collapsing. Afterwards, his legs ached.

Sol remembers that road well. He used to walk it when he was feeling lonely at school. It made him think about going home. He missed home. He didn't want to be at Stirland.

We arrived at Stirland around lunchtime and went straight to the principal's cabin. Meeting us were two members of Weagamow First Nation, or North Caribou. Weagamow purchased the residential school after it closed. The council wants to refurbish it and use it as a culture and language camp.

We parked our truck and headed into the wood cabin. The fresh snow was everywhere, giant banks of it, making the scene look beautiful. But when we walked inside, things got weird. We were greeted by Dwayne, a former gym teacher and dorm supervisor when Sol was a student there.

Dwayne now lives and works at Stirland with his family. Practising Mennonites, Dwayne's wife and daughter both wore kerchiefs on their heads, almost like bonnets, and long skirts. They had three teen children with them, who were being home-schooled. A slight man with a soft way about him, Dwayne greeted us warmly. His wife told us she had fixed some lunch: moose stew and homemade bannock. To any Nish, that is a delicacy.

The two councillors from Weagamow were already there, sitting in the small living room—which had taxidermy animals on the walls—sipping their coffee. The children, near adults, hovered. It was like we were visiting with old friends, not one of Sol's former residential school captors.

As we had our coffee, Dwayne, with a big smile on his face, said, "Here you go, Sol, I have a present for you." He handed Sol two Stirland Lake yearbooks, one for 1984 and the other for 1985.

Sol, surprised, handed back the 1985 yearbook. "Thank you," he said, "but I was only here for one year."

Dwayne shook his head. "No, Sol, you were here for two years."

Sol laughed and told him that he must be wrong.

Dwayne said no, he wasn't wrong. Then he opened the 1985 yearbook. Sol's photos were everywhere. He was even on the student council.

Sol was stunned. "How could I forget an entire year of my life?" he asked. "Why don't I have any memories of being here?"

A Stirland Lake Indian Residential School yearbook photo of Solomon Mamakwa, who is said to be a "diligent worker" and "athletically inclined." (handout)

Sol flipped through the yearbooks. There were large photographs of each of the students on the first few pages. He lingered over their faces. There were about twenty boys, all teens, living at Stirland when he was there. Sol remarked that he'd thought there were more of them. And then he said, quietly, "Oh, he has died, and him, and him." So many of his classmates had died at such young ages. That was not lost on any of us in the room.

Sol handed the yearbooks to me and spoke to the Weagamow councillors, who were quietly watching me.

I flipped through the yearbooks, looking at the faces of young teenagers with thick black hair, plaid shirts and jeans. They looked so youthful and strong, their faces bright and full. What had happened to them? And what had happened to Sol? How had he lost a year of his life?

Then I saw a photograph that stopped me cold. I snapped out of the trance I had fallen into as I sat in this cozy living room, sipping coffee and about to eat moose stew with such a friendly family.

At the back of the yearbook, on the page labelled "Friends of the School," there was a black-and-white photograph of Ralph Rowe, the flying Anglican priest, Boy Scout leader and sexual predator of young teen men. He used to fly in to Stirland Lake. There, in the chapel on the second floor of the schoolhouse, he held services for the boys he knew from the fly-in communities he ministered to. There is no known evidence to suggest Rowe was abusive to the students while at Stirland. We simply do not know, and some of the students who attended are no longer alive.

I touched Sol on the arm and showed him the page.

AFTER THAT STRAINED lunch, we went on a tour of Stirland with Dwayne. The first stop was Sol's dormitory home. A white two-storey house with a balcony, it's built on the side of a hill leading down to the lake. We went in the front door. As we did so, Sol told us they were never allowed to use the front door. They always entered and exited through the basement.

A framed handmade sign above the doorway read "Home of the '7' Dwarfs." The kitchen had that 1970s wood-veneer vibe. The home was rundown. In spots, the ceiling was caving in. We went down the stairs to the basement, where Sol had lived in a tiny bedroom with three other boys. The seventies-era fake wood panelling was here too. Old white-and-blue-plaid curtains hung on the window and the green carpet was still on sections of the floor. It was hard to imagine four teenage boys crammed in here. The wood chest of drawers the students used was still in the room. Sol said everyone had their own drawer. He pulled his open to look inside.

He paused, standing in this house where he had lived during Grade 9. He seemed rattled. He showed me the basement walk-out. There were wooden hooks to the left of the door where the boys used to hang their coats.

We moved on to the second house. This was where he lived for Grade 10—the lost year. It looked nearly identical to the home we were just in, same footprint. But the kitchen in this house still had the lino-leum floor. And a dead grey bird was lying on the table by an old dusty calendar. Sol walked into a bedroom here. The same green carpet was on the floor. He looked stunned. He remembered nothing.

"The first year I think I remember most things. When we went to the second building, I don't remember. I don't even remember where I stayed . . . And I don't know why I can't remember that year. I don't know why. I am in the pictures, I am in some of them, but I don't know why I can't remember, why I've blocked them."

Maybe those memories will come back later, I told him.

We moved on, to the schoolhouse. We walked up the steps and through the big double doors. On the right-hand side of the wall was a mail slot. That was where you were supposed to put your letters home, Sol explained. Then he opened the office door. He wanted to go inside, see where the administrator sat when he or she read through all the students' letters. For Sol now knows that each letter was checked by the staff before being sent on to the boy's parents. If the boys wrote negatively about the school or an experience they'd had, that was redacted. They didn't want parents showing up to Stirland to take their kids back home.

"We didn't know our letters were being screened. I don't know, what was there to hide?"

They couldn't tell the true story of what was happening here. Their parents never knew.

I SIT WITH Sol in his former classroom. The curtains are falling down. Everything is covered in dust. Old library books are stacked along the floors. I ask my friend how he's doing.

"I feel a lot of mixed emotions," he says quietly. "It was hard for me, at first. At the beginning, I was very anxious about coming here. But it was something I had to do. It is like a filing cabinet of the years that I was here that I never spoke about. That I never thought about. We never talked about. It is like a hidden history, something that was blocked off. This is something I have to do as part of my journey.

"It was emotional at the beginning. I actually almost started crying. I don't cry. Even the drive over, it was emotional, too."

He holds the 1984 yearbook. "This is the first year I was here. When I looked through it, I thought there were more of us, but there weren't many of us." He looks at the photos and he starts to cry. I've known Sol for ten years. As he said, he never outwardly displays emotion. "They aren't here anymore. What happened to them? I don't know what their journey was. I don't know the circumstances of why they aren't here anymore.

"As a person who was here as a kid, I remember being very lonely, very homesick. But also wanting to go back home. And there were others who wanted to go back. But we couldn't, because of the censorship," he said. The parents never knew how badly their kids wanted to come home.

"One of the things I notice is how small this place is. I always thought it was so big."

WE'D MOVED FROM the main schoolhouse and walked through the snow to get to the domed gymnasium. The gym floor was well maintained.

There was a stage. On the walls were metal bars for strength tests and ropes for climbing.

It was getting late. We were going to have to hit the road. As it was, we'd be driving the winter roads in darkness.

Suddenly, as we stood in the gym, Sol asked Dwayne outright about the strapping of the children.

Mild-mannered Dwayne said, "It was a dark spot in the history."[7]

"I don't know what they did to get strapped," Sol said to him. "I don't know."

Dwayne seemed to agree with him, and said quickly, "I know, why?"

I jumped in, knowing that we had to take this moment with Dwayne. When do residential school Survivors ever get to confront people from their past? I asked him, "Do you ever feel guilty yourself, for knowing but not knowing? Were you afraid to ask?"

Dwayne replied that he hadn't known what was going on. "I was never there to see, I just thought they were getting spanked. I didn't realize that it was so severe that they couldn't sit down afterwards, that part I didn't know . . . The extreme part, I don't think I was totally aware of it."

I wasn't finished. I asked Dwayne, "Do you ever think you should have said something more?"

Dwayne looked uneasy. He hadn't expected this. But then, neither had we.

He said, "Knowing what I knew then, I didn't know that [is what happened]. I am sorry it happened to them, but to feel guilty for something I didn't really know . . . I do apologize and I'm quick to say I'm sorry for what they had to go through. They were my friends."

I took that in. Dwayne thought the students were his friends. Did he not know of the power he held over them?

I felt overwhelmed by the vast disconnect between us, First Nations people, and those who thought they were doing something good for us, helping us via religion and education, when all that resulted was harm. As I stood in a school that was run by those who believed they were living their lives according to the principles of Christianity, I just had to ask: "Do you ever think about the role that God plays in places like this? . . . Why would they do that to the boys if they were God-fearing people?"

Dwayne said he believed the administrators didn't see that what they were doing was wrong. "I think at the time, that they thought they were disciplining them, and they probably didn't realize how terrible the repercussions would be for the other person. That is just speaking for myself.

"Because we loved the kids. They are my boys, I look forward to seeing them. Their children are like my grandchildren." At sixty, Dwayne is not that much older than Sol.

We had a moment of silence, unsure what to say next. Then Sol said, "First Nations people can't always be the only ones trying to reconcile."

Dwayne said the school's former administrator knows it, and that he is flying to reserves and visiting the former students of the school.

I wondered if he was looking for forgiveness.

SOL AND I left a spirit plate out for the ancestors, to remember those who had been through this place and those who've passed early due to addictions, trauma, violence, suicide. Elder Sam had told us that we could not forget to do this. So we had bought a plate at Walmart, some buns, strawberries and a can of Klik. We joked that the spirits would like that. Klik is a northern delicacy: luncheon meat in a can.

Sol wanted to leave the plate in the garage that is attached to the school. We moved quickly in the dark, trudging through the snow, using our cell phones as flashlights. We found a place on a shelf against the wall.

We drove back to Pickle Lake in pitch-darkness, the truck roaring along the ice roads. Sol was lost in thought. He told me he was glad the documentary crew was with him, that he wanted it documented, recorded. He wanted to tell the world what happened at Stirland, get more community members talking about it. But first he needed time to reflect on what had happened.

Sol Mamakwa, from Kingfisher Lake First Nation, poses just like he did for the Stirland Lake Indian Residential School yearbook. (Photo by Tanya Talaga)

Sol told me he wanted all levels of government to start acknowledging what was done here, how far the tentacles of assimilation reached, and for how long. "They should start the process of acknowledging what the schools did to people in the north. It is time for Survivors and Intergenerational Survivors to have that dialogue, start talking about it. To become strong nations, you must be able to come out of it as nations," he said. "I am here on a journey to acknowledge the two years I was here. Seeing things, being here, will take some time. I need to remember those two full years I was here."

Sol continues to reckon with his past, his memory still searching for what was lost. He took a brave step towards reclaiming himself on September 28 in the Ontario legislature. He was given five minutes to address the house before Question Period began. He was asked to speak about the upcoming Orange Shirt Day, a day for Canada to honour Survivors and reflect on the legacy of Indian residential schools.

Sol rose from his seat as deputy leader of the Opposition and told everyone that he is a Survivor of a colonial system. "I was born in Sioux Lookout, the Indian Hospital. The Zone Hospital was a segregated hospital for Indigenous people. By the 1960s, there were twenty fully functioning Indian hospitals in Canada—places that delivered substandard care, you know it was a form of apartheid," he said.[7]

He told his colleagues that his parents raised him in the bush, that his first language is Anisininew, that he lived with the seasons, peacefully on the land, but when it was time to go to elementary school, he was sent to an Indian day school, one of over six hundred run by the churches but funded by Ottawa. "I had no choice, I had to go."

He said that when he was ready for high school, again, he had no choice but to attend an Indian residential school, at Stirland Lake. He told the house about his tiny room that he shared with three other boys, of his one drawer in a chest of drawers for all his belongings. He told them that the older boys used to be heavily punished, beaten, strapped until the backs of their legs were black and blue. "I have no memory of Grade 10. I see my photo in the yearbook. It is as if the entire year has disappeared from my life. The pictures in the yearbook say I was there, but I remember nothing."

He told them of the photograph of convicted pedophile Ralph Rowe in the yearbook, of how he used to fly to the school on his float plane. Sol said when he flipped through the yearbook, many of those he saw staring up at him have since died, have left too young for the spirit world through violent deaths, suicides, addiction.

"Why have so many left us?" Sol asked.

Their spirits were broken, he said, they could not carry on because of the schools—because of abuse, violence and the demons imposed on them. He said that all over Canada we see the horrors of a history that this country has largely chosen to ignore.

He told the house we are still searching for our lost family members, how they are in shallow graves outside of old churches, residential schools, on what is now private property and in the lands surrounding old Indian hospitals, sanatoriums and asylums.

At this point, more than ten thousand suspected remains—anomalies—have been discovered all over Turtle Island. Yet people still deny it is true, Sol said. Deniers, he said, have websites and make posts on social media that have become an acceptable form of hate, and this had to stop. Since Ontario was complicit in sending children to residential schools in the first place, since it was part of the system, he said it must do its part to combat denialism.

He asked, "Where is Ontario's public advertisement campaign about residential schools, admitting to the harms and fighting against those who deny our history? Where is the Province of Ontario's reformed education curriculum, one that makes it mandatory—not a choice—to teach all children in Ontario schools from kindergarten to Grade 8 that Indian residential schools happened? That our children, our loved ones, never came home from these institutions?"

Ontario premier Doug Ford was in his seat across from Sol.

He told Premier Ford and the legislature that Ontario can do its part. It can wake from its slumber and open its eyes to our true history.

Only then, he said, can we walk forward, together.

THE CLOSER I get to Annie, to retracing her steps, the more alive she becomes to me, her reality, along with those of my great-grandmother Liz, my grandmother Margaret, my mother. I see the weave of their lives—the immense ground they covered, the adversity they faced to make sure their children did not live through what they did. They survived to make sure the next seven generations thrive.

I see a similar strength in all Survivors and Intergenerational Survivors that I meet. We all share parts of the same story.

Chapter Sixteen

ANNIE FOUND

SPEAK TO ME IN THE LANGUAGE OF THIS LAND.

Wrap me in your story.

No word spoken, sung or whispered is ever unheard.

Each sound, each song and cry travels through atmosphere, pinging between the stars, bouncing off the light.

Once our words are formed and our stories are told, they become alive.

They touch the spirit world and mingle with all around us—the four-leggeds, the tree spirits, the water creatures. All are connected, all are part of the unbreakable circle.

Listen carefully to the voices that come to you from the place before memories are remembered.

Every sound, every beat, has a purpose, a meaning. Everything reverberates: it is heard and it lives, never leaving space and time.

We do not disappear. When we die, we become the aki, the earth. Our spirits travel on the soundwaves, in beams of brightness and through the bodies of the children we leave behind. Inside of them are traces of us, who we were, what we thought, what we saw and why we cried. Pieces of us slip into the next generation, swimming silently through the wombs of our mothers, possessing one single purpose: survival.

MY PLANE HAS just landed in Thunder Bay. The smoke from eighty-seven Alberta wildfires, one-quarter of them burning out of control, has reached across the country. The haze is with us, a reminder of the sickness of Mother Earth. I race to get my rental car and head to the NorWester Hotel, another Best Western, this one on the edge of Fort William First Nation. An Indian residential schools Survivors meeting is planned, and Elder Sam Achneepineskum has ordered me to attend. "Time for you to tell your story."

He wants me to tell them about Annie.

I head upstairs to the small conference room where the Survivors and Elders have gathered. They've just finished lunch. Nishnawbe Aski Nation's Rachel Kakegamic greets me. She's NAN's director of reclamation and healing. She is holding her lunch plate in her hands and manoeuvring around the tables. She gives me a big smile and tells me my timing is great. The agenda for the afternoon is light, so I'm it.

I drop my bags next to where Sam is sitting. His tall frame is folded into his seat, his long silver hair tied back in a braid. He greets me with a bemused smirk, happy to see me, but he also knows that I'm about to face my toughest audience: community. I excuse myself for a minute. Before I address the Survivors, I need to change into my ribbon skirt. The skirt I chose to wear today is dark grey with light yellow ribbons on the bottom and beautiful black satin spruce trees that cut through the ribbons. This skirt was made for me by Anishinaabe author Patty Krawec.

I know many of the Survivors in the room. NAN's Ocean Moberly and Rachel both work with the Survivors, discussing processes and protocols surrounding unmarked graves and missing children. They meet to discuss reclamation and how to go about finding and reclaiming lost relations. Among the small but mighty crowd is Sam, who attended three Indian residential schools: St. Anne's, McIntosh and Cecilia Jeffrey. Fort Albany's Evelyn Korkmaz is here—she went to St. Anne's. There is Peter Sackaney, who also went to St. Anne's, as well as St. Joseph's here in Thunder Bay. I see Stella Schimmens, who went to both Bishop Horden Hall and Shingwauk, and Darlene Angeconeb, who survived

Pelican Falls. Some of them I've known for years; others I've just met recently. But knowing that Annie's nieces, nephews, cousins and children and their children went to the same schools, are from the same line of survival, changes my connection to them. I feel a kinship with these Survivors now. Knowledge is a powerful thing. It can bring us together, or it can tear us apart—depending on how it is used.

I begin to tell the story of Annie, of her birth in 1871 in Fort Albany, before the 1905 treaty was signed, before there was a Fort Albany First Nation. I tell them about the families who travelled together since time began, the Wesleys, the Louttits, the Goodwins, the Rickards, the Buntings and the Carpenters. I tell them about Annie's travels along Kistachowan, the fast-moving river. Of how we pushed our way up it, into the interior, away from the coast. Of how we stopped in Eabametoong, or Fort Hope, how we stopped in Marten Falls, in Mishkeegogamang or Osnaburgh. Of how Mish was the land of meeting, of all of us coming together in the summertime. I tell them about Duncan Campbell Scott and his camera, capturing pictures of my relation Joseph Carpenter in his canoe. About how Annie was present at the signing of Treaty 9, and on that original paylist for Osnaburgh. I apologize for Uncle Joseph failing to take one for the team and pushing Scott into the river. That gets a bit of a laugh.

I tell them about the number of Treaty 9 Indians who lived at Lac Seul First Nation, in Treaty 3 territory, and how it used to make the Indian agents crazy that our descendants didn't return to the reserve they were assigned at treaty-making time.

I speak of all the children lost, Annie's children: George, John, James, Sarah, Christina. I tell them about Liz and Louise, the two who were saved. But at what cost? We will never know the full story of what happened to that family after the unbearable fissure of losing Samson Wemaystikosh, Annie's husband. We don't know what happened to him. All we know is that afterwards, Annie and her children were in free fall, surviving by their wits, their instincts, being tossed around without thought or care. Without dignity. We see traces of this struggle in the records left behind by those who controlled them.

Then I tell them about what happened to Annie. How I wondered if one of the Indian agents who'd plagued her throughout her life played a role in getting her sent to downtown Toronto, to the Provincial Lunatic Asylum—but not before first stripping her of her status, of her very identity as an Ininiw woman.

A muted cry comes out from the audience. It is Victor Chapais, my newfound cousin. We had met earlier that year, at the National Gathering on Unmarked Burials in Toronto—after a lifetime apart. I stop speaking and apologize. I need to be more mindful. This is not just my story. It is his too. His grandfather Jobb Chapais, born in the late 1860s, was my great-great-grandfather Samson Wemaystikosh's brother. Tears are rolling down Victor's cheeks. He cries, "I am just thinking about all we have lost. All the family. So much time gone."

Our families were broken apart for decades by everything outlined in this book. But we are putting ourselves back together again. That is the power of our ancestors rising through us to tell our stories.

The Knowing.

THE KNOWING is a story of reclamation and of outlasting. Yes, outlasting.

We do not disappear in a legacy of brutalism, genocidal policies and faulty records written by an angry man left in a forgotten box in some bureaucratic office, only to be digitized later and found on websites.

All of our peoples, our children, did not die in the schools. They scraped through life—torn and battered, but they made it. And they kept going, not for themselves but for the ones they carried inside, for the next seven generations.

My family has lived through seven generations of the Indian Act, an act that came into power when Annie and Samson were children.

There were no "Indians" on Turtle Island before the Europeans came here. They imposed that label on us. We never called ourselves "Indians." We were Anishinaabe. Ininiw. Nêhiyaw. Haudenosaunee. The Indian Act works to take who we call ourselves out of our own control, further taking away our language and making us subjects, making us wards of the state, othering us, making us second-class citizens. Never seen as equals.

The record that is left of Annie's life and the lives of her descendants is imperfect. In parts, it's clearly wrong. What was left of her life was not written by her. It was written by those operating the machinery designed to grind us into submission.

Section 51 of the present-day Indian Act is titled "Mentally Incompetent Indians." This section states, from the start, that the "Minister" has exclusive powers over "all jurisdiction and authority in relation to the property of mentally incompetent Indians."[1] Further, the minister may use that power to appoint a person to administer the estates of "mentally incompetent Indians" and "order that any property of a mentally incompetent Indian shall be sold, leased, alienated, mortgaged, disposed of or otherwise dealt with for the purpose of paying his debts or engagements, discharging encumbrances on his property, paying debts or expenses incurred for his maintenance or otherwise for his benefit, or paying or providing for the expenses of future maintenance."

Who is a "mentally incompetent Indian?" Whose definition is in play here? And who decides to whom that label should be applied?

It is only now, during the time I have been writing this book, that legislation has begun making its way through the Parliament of Canada. Bill C-38, introduced in 2022, seeks to further address the fundamental discrimination and inequities remaining in the Indian Act. These proposed changes primarily address the inequity of enfranchisement—of taking away a woman's status because she married a non-Indian man, and the generational fallout that happens as a result.[2] The bill seeks to eliminate "sex-based inequities" in defining membership provisions, and it removes some outdated and offensive language in the Indian Act, such as calling someone a "mentally incompetent Indian."

The bill also makes it easier for some descendants of women whose status was taken away to apply for their Indian status cards or to register as Indians under the Indian Act. And the changes allow women who were automatically transferred to their husbands' band to seek reaffiliation with their natal band. Their direct descendants may also apply.

It only skims the surface when it comes to derogatory language concerning Indigenous women. The bill does not challenge the word "Indian," outdated language still used in the Indian Act. And it also does not challenge the term "voluntary enfranchisement," even though most women did not have a choice when their status was taken away. The Native Women's Association of Canada, a national political body representing First Nations, Métis and Inuit women since 1974, says the language around enfranchisement should change to "coerced enfranchisement," as that is the reality most women lived. First Nations women's equal rights and liberties were constrained by residential schools and the Indian Act, which amounted to force by the state, since they were given little choice to exercise their own freedoms and powers to live their lives, NWAC says.[3]

As well, many women and their children who were forcibly removed from the act suffered discrimination and have lost much—a lack of membership can result in feelings of loss, unworthiness and a lack of belonging from being shunned from community. This can affect women and their descendants for a lifetime. As we've seen in this book, it affected my family.

An apology from Canada to all the women enfranchised and the generations of children that then went unrecognized would be the right thing to do. Financial compensation runs a distant second to saying sorry.

The bill also falls short in addressing the issue of the "second generation cut-off." Children with only one parent eligible for status are given what is called 6(2) status, which means their children will be ineligible to be registered as Indians. This ignores the First Nations concept of seven generations or community inclusion, and it cuts children out of our Nations. Our communities alone should be the only ones with the power to determine who belongs and who does not.[4]

This book has illustrated Canada's ongoing policies of erasure.

We are still fighting to remove them, but this bill offers a small step forward.

===

MY MOTHER IS complaining about the crack in my windshield. "Haven't you got that fixed yet? How am I supposed to see *anything*?" she says dramatically. We're on the QEW, heading to the corner of Evans Avenue and Horner Avenue, just south of the giant IKEA.

My daughter, Natasha, is in the back seat, her headphones on, blasting away the music so she doesn't have to hear us nattering. Natasha has just turned nineteen. Both she and her brother, William, have grown up listening to my mother and me speak about our family, the stories, the unknowns. They were close to their own great-grandmother, Margaret. Every year, at the end of August, we held a birthday party for Natasha and me. We share the same birthday, but Grandma always insisted we each have our own cake. Natasha knows today is an emotional one and that Nanny—the name my kids have affectionately called my mother since they were toddlers—will be in tears. The loss of Margaret lingers.

We were lucky to have her for so long. My children had Margaret, their chapan—in Ininímowin this means "the child I pull behind me"—in their lives until they became young adults. The women in our family outlast; we raise the children when the men die, disappear or get kicked to the curb. The kids joke sometimes that their parents are me and Nanny. Margaret was the only living great-grandparent they have known.

This makes today even more special. Annie was one of us, she was my Anasko-chapan, one of the grandmothers.

We are driving to meet Edward Janiszewski and the team of volunteers who, with him, care for the gravesites at the Lakeshore Psychiatric Hospital Cemetery. We are going to meet Annie.

WE FOUND ED online, through a story he had written about the cemetery for the *York Pioneer* community newspaper, with an advertisement for a biannual cleanup of the grounds. I sent him an email and he answered. It was that simple. Then the unfolding began. He told me the remarkable story of the cemetery and his role in maintaining it.

Ed Janiszewski is the one who stumbled on the existence of this neglected and abandoned graveyard. A kind, soft-spoken man, he had worked at the Lakeshore Psychiatric Hospital from 1974 until 1979 as a vocational instructor to the patients. He would be the perfect instructor, calm and patient. While he was working at Lakeshore, Ed joined the Museum of Mental Health Services, an archives-based group. That was when he found the blueprints of the Mimico building. They showed a graveyard. Records revealed 1,511 burials in the asylum cemetery, the last one in 1974. But none of Ed's former colleagues knew of such a cemetery. He was stunned.

The gates at the Lakeshore Psychiatric Hospital Cemetery, used by the Ontario Hospital until it closed in 1974. The cemetery was discovered and then maintained by Edward Janiszewski, a former employee of what is now the Centre for Addiction and Mental Health. (Photo by Tanya Talaga)

In 2003, Ed went looking for the cemetery on the Lakeshore site, and it was not hard to find. The archives said it was at the corner of Horner and Evans Avenues, and it was. It was overgrown with brush, weeds and fallen trees. It had been completely neglected for three decades.

For nearly seventy-five years, patients with unknown family, or those whose families were too far away, were buried in this cemetery. Neither the hospital nor any authority, it seemed, would pay to ship the bodies of those who'd died in the asylum back to their families. Like students at Shingwauk, and at so many other residential schools, the "patients" of Lakeshore both dug the graves and made the wooden coffins for their deceased fellow inmates.

Incensed, Ed knew he had to make it right. He started a database of the names of those buried at the cemetery. He wanted them to be remembered. He wanted to inform, educate and remind future generations of all ancestors, regardless of how they may have been perceived at the time. When he started this, he wasn't thinking about who was from where or what colour or race they were. He was just trying to do the right thing by remembering those who were lost, one person at a time. One Canadian at a time.

By chance, Ed met professor of psychiatric history Geoffrey Reaume at an art gallery opening around that time. The focus of the exhibit was on the two asylums, Lakeshore and Queen Street. Ed asked him to come with him and see the cemetery. Reaume couldn't believe it. "We were amazed. It was in such bad shape." So he said, "Let's start doing something about it." And they did.

Ed started calling local and provincial politicians. The pair formed the Lakeshore Asylum Cemetery Project and in 2005 organized a march to bring awareness to the forgotten cemetery. About 150 people walked through the streets near the cemetery and gave out information flyers to cars stopped at the intersection. Bright-coloured plastic flowers were laid on the ground. Another York University professor, Gary Bunch, who had a disability awareness group, raised money to put a large sign up at the corner of Evans and Horner, to let people know there was a graveyard there. Two days after the sign went up, it was stolen.

Ed got in touch with Laurel Broten, then the member of provincial parliament for the riding of Etobicoke-Lakeshore and a cabinet minister. She got involved, and eventually the land was properly cleared and an unmovable sign was placed at the corner, along with a tall black wrought-iron fence around the graveyard.

There is a new sign here now, arching over the wrought-iron gates. It was put up in 2012 thanks to Ed and company's tireless activism. It reads: "Lakeshore Psychiatric Hospital Cemetery 1890–1979."

A historical plaque on the black iron gate says this: "For 84 years, the cemetery at Mimico was used to bury patients who had no family or lacked sufficient funds to make other arrangements."

Annie had a family. We just didn't know where she was.

If there are any heroes in Annie's story, they are Ed Janiszewski and Geoffrey Reaume and all the volunteers and psychiatric survivors who took part in the Lakeshore Asylum Cemetery Project. Two decades earlier, they had sprung into action and demanded Ontario help restore the cemetery. This is what allyship looks like.

And this is what reconciliation in Canada could be. Regular citizens, coming together, each and every one of us, to do the right thing—to demand we are all treated with respect and dignity as human beings.

THE TRAFFIC IS light as we whip down the highway. There is nervous energy in the car. I've got a bundle of sage with me, and the eagle feather I was given after being a witness at Canada's National Inquiry into Missing and Murdered Indigenous Women and Girls, which began to be organized shortly after the TRC wrapped up in 2015. The inquiry ran from 2017 until 2019, travelling the country, interviewing nearly seven thousand family members, Survivors and witnesses. I've got my smudge bowl and a lighter. We are going to hold ceremony for Annie when we meet her.

We call Aunt Bernice from the road. She is ninety years old and, since my kokum's death in January—Margaret was her older sister—the last of the Bowen sisters to be with us physically on this earth. Aunt Bernice has just moved from her condo to an assisted living apartment.

"We have something to tell you," my mother half yells into the phone. "We are going to visit Annie today, your grandmother, at her grave."

Silence.

"Ohh," says Bernice finally. "You are? Well."

More silence. Then: "I am so grateful you are doing this. That you have found her. Hank would be so happy. Say hello to her from me, would you?"

We promise to.

THERE IS NO formal street address for Annie Carpenter Gauthier's burial site. It lies directly off the Queen Elizabeth Way. Turn south on Evans Avenue, and when you get to Horner Avenue, you'll see it on the northeast corner. There is not even a place to park.

Ed has a Tilley hat on and he is standing near the entrance to the cemetery, speaking to six people sitting on foldup lawn chairs. Some have wagons beside them, full of gardening tools and colourful plastic flowers. They are all volunteers. They come to tend to the graves, clear away the garbage, put new flowers down.

My mom, Natasha and I are a rarity here: actual family members who have come to visit. We are a bit nervous. Meeting a long-lost dead relative for the first time can do that to you. This meeting bridges distance, time and space. Being in such physical closeness to Annie is overwhelming. She was buried in 1937. I wonder, are we the only members of her family to have visited her here, alive or dead?

Ed leads us down the centre of the cemetery, where the old road used to be. He is consulting his map, looking for her plot, F-23. The ground is uneven beneath our feet, sloping and rising. We are conscious that we are walking on the dead. We half-heartedly joke that we are grateful for the plaques for World War One soldiers, put down as part of the Last Post Fund, a Canadian government initiative to give each veteran a dignified burial and gravestone. Without the program, there would be no plaques on the ground. The white military gravestones make it easier to find Annie.

Ed stops a little to the right of the plaque commemorating Daniel Colvin, a private in the 52nd Battalion, Canadian Expeditionary Force. He was born in 1893 and died in 1929. A little Canadian flag and an Ontario flag are stuck in the lawn near his headstone, which lies flat to the earth.

Edward Janiszewski points to the spot where Annie Gauthier (née Carpenter) is buried in the Lakeshore cemetery. (Photo by Jordan Huffman)

I take out my smudge kit. Ed stands respectfully off to the side, and I begin to burn the sage in the half shell. I use my eagle feather to generate a bit of oxygen and to get the spark burning. The sweet smell of sage soon surrounds us. My mother sits down on the grave, where we think her grandmother's head would be. She begins to cry. I begin to smudge the gravesite. I smudge my mother and my daughter. We speak to Annie. We tell her who we are and why we've come.

At this point, Ed is standing to the side, near the shade of a tree. Out of the corner of my eye, I can see he has taken out his map and he is studying it, looking perplexed. A few minutes later, he walks over to me. He wants a quiet word. I step aside from my mother and daughter and ask him what is going on. Sheepishly and apologetically, he tells me we are smudging over someone else—not Annie Gauthier.

After a few moments of awkward silence, we all begin to laugh, mixed with tears. It is so absurdly funny and typical that, at this precious moment, we've just smudged a white guy named Arthur Miller instead of Annie.

Then we move on. This is also the story of us—laughter has always been medicine.

Ed takes us farther up the row, about three-quarters of the way into the cemetery, and shows us to where Annie is. F-23. He says he is sure this time, and then he walks away.

My mother has brought fresh sage from her Scarborough home garden, along with a bouquet of pink and white silk flowers. Her long white hair is blowing in the breeze. She sits her small, nearly eighty-year-old self down gently on the uneven ground. Her still beautifully shaped strong hands work the stems of the flowers and sage through the grass and into the earth. Her hands have held the hands of her grandmother Liz, her mother Margaret, me, and then my daughter, Natasha. The circle continues, unbroken.

"I'm so happy we have found her," she says as she begins to cry.

My mom, Sheila Bowen, at the unmarked gravesite of her great-grandmother, Annie Gauthier (née Carpenter). Our family had been looking for Annie for eight decades. (Photo by Tanya Talaga)

EPILOGUE

I'M WALKING TOWARDS THE ROCKY CLAY BANKS OF ANDERSON POINT, STARING AT Kistachowan. It's early morning; the sun has just risen. Kistachowan is spread before me like a giant black mirror, still and peaceful. I flew in to Peetabeck with my film crew to attend the hundredth anniversary of the Old Post gathering. The Ininiw name for this celebration is Mamowihitowin, which means "remembering our ancestors." All of the Omushkego communities, from up and down the coasts of Weeneebayko and Kitchi Weeneebayko, have been invited to the Old Post. The gathering is held on Old Post Island, where the Hudson's Bay Company set up a trading post in 1659. We come here for three days of celebration, cookouts and a powwow.

The Old Post is more than a social or community get-together where we share a meal and exchange stories. While that alone would be worthwhile and fun, the reason we are here means so much more. We're here to remember our ancestors and to renew relations with each other, to try to put our proud and strong communities, which were almost destroyed by the crushing forces of colonization—almost, but not quite—back together again.

This book has illustrated the various ways the state and Crown have tried to assimilate us, to shake us down, to take away our belonging to each other and to the land. But, fundamentally, this book is about survival and the spirit that burns bright inside us. That, what unites us, is far stronger than what could ever divide us. We are our ancestors' wildest dreams.

Growing up in the suburbs of Toronto, not only worlds away from Omushkego traditional territories but unaware of my close family ties to these communities in Ontario's far north, I never felt Indian enough. People used to ask me if I was Greek, Italian, Israeli, Spanish, Iranian, Palestinian—anything but what I was. When I would tell people I was both Polish and Anishinaabe—particularly Ojibwe, because we did not know where Elizabeth was from—I'd usually be met with a bemused stare. No one knew what to say. Few had met a mixed First Nations and Polish person before. If I had a dollar for every time someone told me how "exotic" I was, I would be a millionaire.

In the 1970s and 1980s, beyond the Anishnawbe health centre on the eastern edge of downtown, to me Toronto had no visible Indigenous footprint. There were no murals painted on the sides of buildings, no giant Medicine Wheel—as we have now—at city hall, no landmarks to say the Anishinaabe were here. What *were* honoured, what *were* on public display—everywhere, it seemed—were people and names connected with the British Empire. As a First Nations person, you can't escape noticing the statues of Sir John A. Macdonald and Queen Elizabeth II at Queen's Park, the long-time name of Ryerson University (now Toronto Metropolitan University), and Dundas Street, which is named after Scottish-born Henry Dundas, who was involved in delaying the abolition of the slave trade in the late eighteenth century. Sure, there was a trace of Anishinaabe in the name of Spadina Road, which is the anglicized version of the Anishinaabe word ishpadinaa. But considering that First Nations people have lived here on the shores of what we call Niigaani-gichigami, or Lake Ontario, for thousands of years, the lack of any acknowledgement of traces of us added to my feelings of not being seen.

The only Anishinaabe I ever came across, other than members of my own family, were on television—and these were rare. Sometimes I'd catch Saugeen Ojibway First Nation reporter Duke Redbird on the news on Citytv. I thought he was so cool. There he was, somebody like me, telling stories on TV.

Despite this, as a girl I had no clue that my family was different from those of the other suburban Canadian kids around me. I thought, for example, that everybody had family members who had gone to residential school. Indian residential schools were never discussed at school—not once. I do remember scant lessons on the fur trade, but our crucial participation in this massively important part of early Canadian history, and its lasting effect on us as a people, was treated as a footnote—it was never discussed in any depth by the teachers. The message to me was that historians, teachers and, by extension, all Canadians did not think our history mattered. It wasn't *real* enough to be included in the classroom or in textbooks. Generations of Canadians would likely have grown up thinking the same thing.

EVERY FIRST NATIONS person who is a Status Indian—the Government of Canada's measure of who is Indian and who is not—has their name on the Indian Register, kept by Canada, and they are given a ten-digit registration number. Each Status Indian has a card that displays our birthdate, our date of issue and our date of expiration. No joke: there are a lot of "expired" Indians walking around out there, many of whom refuse to renew their cards or who just haven't gotten around to the indignities of applying for another one and learning whether they remain a valid Indian.

Luckily, our people have a good sense of humour.

My mother is a Status Indian under the Indian Act and so am I, thanks to Mary Two-Axe Earley and the women who for decades stood with her fighting, at great personal expense, to change the Indian Act so that we—women and our children—could be recognized.

Mary Two-Axe Earley was a Kahnawà:ke woman who grew up in her community of Kanien'kehá:ka on the South Shore of the St. Lawrence and who is credited with the 1985 changes to the Indian Act known as Bill C-31. This bill was created to reverse the inequity that had, for many decades, stripped official status from a First Nations woman if she married a non-Indian man. Before 1985, an Indian man who married a non-Indian woman could pass his status on to his wife and their children. But that was not the case for an Indian woman, who immediately lost status for marrying a non-Indian man. Their children also did not have Indian status. The way the Indian Act saw it, Indian women who married non-Indian men were "enfranchised," meaning they were now "civilized" enough to take care of themselves.[1] Thus, they dropped off the rolls.

But enfranchisement was no gift. It didn't make life better for these women. Look at Annie. After she'd lost her children, enfranchisement only added to her grief. Her status, her identity, was the last thing Canada could strip from her. And to make things irrevocably darker for Annie, she was confined, her freedom of movement stolen, until the day she died and her spirit was set free.

For a long time, I struggled with the concept of Indian status. I was reluctant to be put on a dehumanizing list and assigned my ten-digit number, much like what Nazi Germany did with prisoners taken to concentration camps.

I have publicly raged against the Indian Act in newspaper columns, on television sets, on radio waves and on stages across Canada. My anger came from my family's lived experience and that of my people, those forced to go to residential schools and live an "othered" life, under a separate set of rules. I knew full well that the whole point of the Indian Act was to not add more names to the rolls. Each name added meant not just more benefits the government would be forced to pay, but also a continued treaty relationship with the land that Canada would have to contend with. No, this was a system designed to engineer our extinction. The Government of Canada was in the business of getting rid of Indians.

And it must have thought, for a good long while, that it was doing a pretty good job. Since the act's inception in 1876, the damage done to families and individuals is incalculable—generations set adrift and set apart from their communities.

The specific reserves on which treaties and paylists placed us were often dictated by where our relations were at the moment in time when a treaty was signed. Hence Annie being a member of Mishkeegogamang, even though she was born in Peetabeck, or Fort Albany, six hundred kilometres away. Meanwhile, for generations, so many women and their children were, because of the Indian Act's bureaucratic rules, excised, almost surgically, from the communities and families they knew and loved. In many instances, this left the women the most vulnerable of the vulnerable. It has directly contributed to the epidemic of murdered and missing Indigenous women and girls, as well as to the overwhelming numbers of Indigenous children placed in foster care.

These exclusions and separations appear to be exactly what Canada wanted: communities dispersed, families split apart. And here's the kicker: status has long been used, not just by government authorities but also by our own people, to gauge who is Indian and who is not. Always, when questions of identity arise, one of the first questions asked is, "Do you have a status card?" The definitions within the act have pitted people against each other, contributing to lateral violence. In this way, the colonial system has promoted exclusion and division among us.

MY MOTHER, SHEILA, was not born an Indian registered with Canada. When Sheila was in her teens, she was adopted by John Dyck, a Canadian man of German Mennonite heritage who became the only father she ever knew. He formally adopted my mother after he married her mother, Margaret Bowen. Sheila Bowen became Sheila Dyck. It is remarkable how history repeats itself.

My mother never wanted to be under Canada's thumb, registered under the Indian Act. She never felt as though she belonged. She and her mother, who was born in 1925, lived significant portions of their lives before Indians in Canada were even given the right to vote in federal elections. (That didn't happen until 1960.) But my mother's enfranchisement left her with no grounding, no centre; she was legally separated from community. In the twentieth century, the Indian Act was a bizarre gold standard for identity before communities had the legal ability to write their own membership codes.

It wasn't until 1985 that Bill C-31 posthumously gave back to Annie her status—her identity. Eventually, more legal challenges and changes would return status to my mother—but the onus was on her to seek it out and apply for it.

Bill C-31 reinstated women who had been removed from band lists before 1951 or who had lost status if enfranchised after 1951. The legislation aimed to bring equality by bringing the act in line with the Canadian Charter of Rights and Freedoms. Bill C-31 also allowed First Nations to be in control of their own band membership codes, if they chose to. Section 10 of the Indian Act made it so that bands could create their own citizenship lists, meaning the band, rather than the government, could determine who belonged and who did not. However, this had to be opted into. If a band did not opt in, Section 11 of the act remained in force and it was Canada that decided membership.[2]

Legal victories do not mean the path to status or membership is clear-cut. Bill C-31 didn't solve everything. It was extremely difficult for women to actually execute the provisions in the act and regain their status. Indigenous Services Canada demands many supporting documents—from birth certificates to divorce and death records—and this book has shown how elusive, and often inaccurate, those documents can be. These demands contribute to lengthy wait periods.

Many changes have been introduced to root out the sexism still present in the law, and more are needed. Bill C-3, enacted in 2010, was supposed to fix the problems present in Bill C-31, but the reinstatement of status continues to be incomplete. Grandchildren born before 1951 who trace their heritage through maternal lines are still denied status, while those who can trace through their dads are not. The fight against the "second generation cut-off" continues.

It took the First Nations matriarchs who fought for the changes in Bill C-31 to make this fight possible, to begin to make things right again for all generations of children who'd been told they weren't Indian enough, whose spirits were nearly broken in the schools or the foster system. Indigenous women such as Mary Two-Axe Earley, Sandra Lovelace, Lynn Gehl, Jeannette Corbiere Lavell, Yvonne Bedard and Sharon McIvor stood up in the courts and demanded that the sexism prevalent in the Indian Act be reversed and our families be reinstated after enfranchisement. These women are heroes. When children's identities and languages were taken, it was First Nations women who valiantly fought for their families to exist. It still is. They threw their arms around us all, hugged us, told us we would persevere. And they do so to this day.

For this, and for so many reasons outlined in this book, we must stand up and be counted. Annie led us here. For my mother and I, our status cards represent all the pain our families have been through. But they do not dictate belonging. Only our people and our communities have that power.

I came to Kistachowan looking for answers. I needed to feel the river, see her power and flow, breathe in the saltwater air. I needed to do this so I could see Annie in my mind's eye, feel a connection to my ancestors, a connection that had been deliberately fractured, long before I was born, by the country I call home.

HERE IN PEETABECK, I felt it. I sensed it—how could I not? This feeling went beyond the remarkable discovery of finding Annie's younger sister Clara Carpenter's grave, her headstone weathered, covered in dry moss but still standing, here at the Old Post.

I felt it through the women in my family, and through the absences around me. Through the silences around my grandmother and her life story. Through Uncle Hank's lifelong quest for documents, evidence and answers. The sibi welcomed me home.

As I near the water's edge, the silence is broken by a loud exhale, the sound of air blowing up and out of the powerful lungs of a large mammal. I look to my right, and the curved back of a white beluga whale breaks through the surface of the water. It happens so quickly, so fast, I can capture only a glimpse of it—I live in the moment, grateful to witness this gift. Suddenly, another white beluga appears, swimming beside the first. Farther out, another slips in and out of sight.

Those standing where the freighter canoes are lined up at the landing of Anderson Point have stopped what they are doing to stare in wonder as the belugas swim along the edge of the sibi, on their way into the cold, salty waters of James his Baye, which leads to the Arctic Ocean. This is a rare sight, a pod of whales in the river. Our astonishment hangs in the air as they pass by. How many were there? Three, four, six? It's impossible to know for sure.

I am holding a small tobacco tie in my left hand. This medicine, this seema, is my offering, what I will give to Kistachowan, to pay my respects to the river that knew me before I knew her, before the whales revealed themselves.

I am entwined with my ancestors, I feel them dancing with joy around me as the circle spins. I kneel down and weave the tobacco into the light brown clay and shrubs. With both my palms, I touch the cold, damp earth, the aki, and I introduce myself by the name given to me in ceremony, Ka-musko pimojijet pinaysheesh. I thank Kistachowan for the gifts she has shown me during our return to each other.

Ininiw and Anishinaabe Glossary

ININIW

aski-gitchi bayou: traditional lands of the Omushkego
Ililiw: Cree from Moose Cree First Nation
Ininímowin: Swampy Cree language
Ininiw: Cree from Fort Albany First Nation
Kinosao-sipi: Norway House First Nation
Kitchi Weeneebayko: Hudson Bay
Nêhiyawêwin: Plains Cree language
Omushkego (Mushkegowuk): the people who live along Weeneebayko
Peetabeck: Fort Albany First Nation
Sipi: river
Washaybayow: the shoreline of the Weeneebayko coast
Weeneebayko: James Bay

ANISHINAABE

Aak-de-he-win: bravery
Aki: earth
Animkii Wajiw: Fort William First Nation
Anishinaabewi-gichigami: Lake Superior
Anishinabemowin: Ojibwe language
Dbaa-dem-diz-win: humilty
De-bwe-win: truth

425

Gwe-ya-kwaad-zi-win: honesty
Ininwewi-gichigami: Lake Michigan
Ma-na-ji-win: respect
Nbwaa-ka-win: wisdom
Zah-gi-di-win: love

Cast of Characters

ANNIE'S GRANDPARENTS

Dorcas Bunting, Annie's maternal grandmother
  (1821 FORT ALBANY–1899 FRENCHMAN'S HEAD, LAC SEUL FIRST NATION)
Tahkoonahkun (Jabez) Bunting, Annie's maternal grandfather
  (1821–DEATH UNKNOWN)
Madeline, Annie's paternal grandmother (1802–1882)
Metikonabe, Annie's paternal grandfather (DEATH UNKNOWN)

ANNIE'S PARENTS

Jane Carpenter (née Bunting), Annie's mother (1846–DEATH UNKNOWN)
Jean-Baptiste Carpenter, Annie's father (1841–1921)
Charles Carpenter, Annie's uncle, Jean-Baptiste's brother
  (1846 ATTAWAPISKAT–1930)

ANNIE'S SIBLINGS

Joseph Carpenter (1862–DEATH UNKNOWN)
Jane Carpenter (1864–1951 SIOUX LOOKOUT)
James (Jas) Carpenter (~1870 FORT ALBANY–DEATH UNKNOWN)
Charles (Chas) Carpenter (1877 KEEWATIN, ALBANY–DEATH UNKNOWN)
    Charlotte Carpenter, Charles's wife (1879–DEATH UNKNOWN)
    Tommy Carpenter, Charles and Charlotte's son (1905–2000)
        Doris Carpenter, Tommy Carpenter's daughter (1932–1937)
Sarah Carpenter (1874–DEATH UNKNOWN)
Clara Carpenter (1879 FORT ALBANY–1898)
David Carpenter (1883 FORT ALBANY–1883)

John Carpenter (1884 FORT ALBANY–1884)

Abraham Carpenter (1887 FORT ALBANY– DEATH UNKNOWN)

Henry Nevitt (1891 FORT ALBANY– DEATH UNKNOWN)

ANNIE'S FIRST HUSBAND

Samson Chapish Wemaystikosh, also Wemistekos (~1867 MOOSE FACTORY–1906/07)

ANNIE AND SAMSON'S CHILDREN

George Wamistikosh (Chapish) (1890 MOOSE FACTORY–1895)

John Wamistikosh (Chapish) (1892–1905)

James Wamistikosh (Chapish) (1894–DEATH UNKNOWN)

Sarah Wamistikosh (Chapish) (1895–DEATH UNKNOWN)

Christina Samson (EARLY 1900S–DEATH UNKNOWN)

Elizabeth (Lizzie) Samson (1904/05–1974)

ANNIE'S SECOND HUSBAND

Joseph Gauthier (1865–1935)

ANNIE AND JOSEPH'S CHILDREN

Louise Mary Gauthier, Annie and Joseph's daughter (1911–1963)

ANNIE'S GRANDCHILDREN AND GREAT-GRANDCHILDREN

Henry/Joseph Rodgers Bowen (Uncle Hank) (1924–2011)

Margaret Bowen, Annie's granddaughter (1925–2022)

Sheila Bowen, Annie's great-granddaughter (1944–)

Tanya Talaga, Sheila's daughter (1970–)

Natasha, Tanya's daughter (2003–)

William, Tanya's son (2001–)

Bernice Bowen, Annie's granddaughter (1932–DEATH UNKNOWN)

Sarah Bowen (1946–2007)

Christina Churchill (née Sampson) (1918 WINNIPEG–DEATH UNKNOWN)

Thomas Skelliter (1894–1912)

Samuel Skelliter (1898–1905)

Acknowledgements

THIS BOOK HAS BEEN WRITTEN FROM MY PERSPECTIVE, LOOKING BACK AT THE history of the women in my mother's family and the history of the country we now call Canada.

Any faults in research, any errors, omissions or misinterpretations, are my own. This will happen; records can't tell the whole story. This book was created with what we were able to access at this time.

The Knowing was written with the help of many hands. Elders, Knowledge Keepers, archivists, historians, editors, friends and family, all pitched in. Everyone has my deep gratitude and respect for your constant willingness to lend a hand. If I have forgotten to add your name, I apologize but know I'm grateful.

Thank you for the bravery of all our Survivors, past, present and future.

The backbone of *The Knowing* comes from Moose Cree Nation's Paula Rickard, who I met late one night on Facebook and am delighted to know we are relations. Paula's knowledge and love for the more than 10,000 Omushkego names connected along Kitchi Weeneebayko and Weeneebayko is unwavering. She is the keeper of us. Weenusk First Nation's Louis Bird, *The Knowing* would not have begun without your story and wisdom of where the spirit lies. You are the keeper of stories and Ininiw Knowledge. Luke Hunter, you have been so generous in sharing your deep understanding of all facets of Treaty 9, of the Ininiw and Ililiw families along the coasts and inland, and your notes on language. I'm honoured to also be your relation.

Elder Sam Achneepineskum, you've been there, every day, with your thoughts, your language lessons and your constant love for our communities, our People. Miigwetch for living the Seven Grandfather Teachings.

Scholar John Long is no longer with us but his book *Treaty No. 9: Making the Agreement to Share the Land in Far Northern Ontario in 1905* has been an incredible reference. I thank him and all that helped write his book.

My dear friends, brothers Mike and Edmund Metatawabin, you are both my teachers. From those early days on Kistachowan, more than a decade ago, to welcoming me to Peetabeck, you have always been there to answer my questions and to just listen. Joan Metatawabin, thank you for your invaluable gifts (and your cookies). Fort Albany Chief Elizabeth Kataquapit and Terry Metatawabin, Joyce Sutherland, Meeshan, thank you for welcoming my team.

Kanehsatake Mohawk Nation lawyer Kimberly Murray, Canada's Special Interlocutor for Missing Children and Unmarked Burials, your knowledge about Indian Residential Schools, the TRC, Indian Hospitals, sanitoria and most importantly, where to look and who needs to be held accountable, is unmatched. You are a warrior for our families, our children. Canada may not realize it yet, but you are the light this country needs.

Know History founder Ryan Shackleton and Leeanne Gaudet, you pushed me off on this journey and provided constant support along the way. I am in your debt.

Jenna Lemay of the Shingwauk Residential Schools Centre, your research and your endless knowledge about Shingwauk and Wawanosh has been a guide for me. My family and I are in your debt. You led us to Thomas and Sam. Miigwetch. To the Children of Shingwauk Alumni Association, your hard work, your relentless pushing, helped keep our truths safe. Miigwetch to the late Michael Cachagee.

Edward Sadowski, thank you for your research and dedication to record what happened at Shingwauk.

Garden River's Darrell Boissoneau, you are an encyclopedia of all things related to Chief Shingwaukonse and his mission. Your friendship, your willingness to help, is always appreciated.

David Chippewow Thompson, thank you for sharing your knowledge of John Ininway and the Kingfisher clan.

To Gary Williams, your daughter Collette and all the Williams clan, thank you for sharing yourselves with me and for bringing your canoe to Kamloops to take your children's spirits home. Miigwetch to Tk'emlúps te Secwépemc Kúkpi7 Rosanne Casimir; to Manny Jules for your strength and love for your community; to Ted Gottfriedson, thank you for all you do to protect the children's spirits, Le Estcwicwéy; to Racelle Kooy for contacting me and for all you do. You are a warrior.

To the *Globe and Mail*'s Natasha Hassan, Renata D'Aliesio, Adrian Lee, and David Walmsley for believing in our stories and truths and for your constant support. Thank you to the *Globe*'s library! Special thanks to Melissa Tait for your photos, your eye and spirit.

To University of Winnipeg's Dr. Anne Lindsay, thank you for all the work you've done; you have led the way regarding Indigenous forms of slavery in this country. And thank you to historian Jennifer Brown.

Miigwetch to you, Anna Baggio, for your friendship, for all the Wildlands League does, and for insisting I write about the caribou, the rivers.

A special thanks to Fogo Island Arts and Zita Cobb for making room for creatives to grow and explore—especially in the winter.

Thank you to Moose Cree First Nation's Lawrence Martin and Jason Martin, for listening to me and for always making the time. To MakeWay's Joanna Kerr, thank you for always creating space.

To Inuit Tapiriit Kanatami President Natan Obed, you are generous with your time and words. You are a true leader. Miigwetch Métis National Council President Cassidy Caron, thank you for your constant strength and leadership. To Dene National Chief Gerald Antoine, every time I sit with you, I learn. To Wilton Littlechild and Elder Fred Kelly, miigwetch for the sunrise ceremonies.

Dr. Kona Williams, you take care of our children, both here and those who are in the spirit world.

To Ellen Bond of Library and Archives Canada, miigwetch for stopping me at a conference and offering to lend a hand finding Annie.

Thank you to Nancy Hurn, former lead archivist to the Anglican Church of Canada, and to current lead archivist Laurel Parsons. Thanks to Kirsten Mercer for getting the fire going! Thank you to Laurentian University's archives assistant Marissa Walinga. Elders Lorne Bob and Paula Bob, you are inspirational. Keep teaching.

To the National Centre for Truth and Reconciliation Head of Archives Raymond Frogner, you carry so much and do so in a respectful, kind way. Keep going. To NCTR Executive Director Stephanie Scott and to all of the staff, miigwetch for safeguarding and protecting our stories and the memories of our children.

Miigwetch to Nishnawbe Aski Nation's Rachel Kakegamic and Ocean Moberly. Big hugs to Peter Sackaney, Stella Schimmens and my cousin Victor Chapais. I am honoured to know you and thankful for your strength. Miigwetch cousin Savannah Upton.

Miigwetch Jeremy Capay and Barabara Ruotsalainen of Bikiiwewinig Nindawaashishiiminaanak (Bringing Our Children Home) Initiative and to Chief Clifford Bull. As always, my dear friend Norma Kejick, executive director of the Northern Nishnawbe Education Council, your drive and spirit inspire me.

Edward Janiszewski discovered Annie's grave at the Lakeshore Psychiatric Hospital Cemetery. He organized psychiatric survivors and made sure the forgotten gravesite was cleared and protected. To you, to Dr. Geoffrey Reaume and to all the volunteers who care for the graves, I thank you.

Murray Sinclair has appeared in all three of my books, both behind the scenes and on the pages. The TRC's groundbreaking research, along with TRC Commissioners Wilton Littlechild and Marie Wilson, are the pillars of *The Knowing*. Murray, you have given of yourself to show us the way.

To my agent Michael Levine and to Executive Publisher of HarperCollins Iris Tupholme, you both believed in *The Knowing*'s vision, and Iris, your sharp eye and gentle guidance gave me the room to think and to write. Many thanks to Anita Lahey and Shaun Oakey—you are both masters of the copy edit. Anita, you gave all of your heart to this book. To Mikaela Roasa, thank you for always being there. I would also like to thank Craig Swinwood, Cory Beatty, Michael Guy-Haddock, Lauren Morocco, Neil Wadhwa, Canaan Chu and Alan Jones.

Kent Monkman, you are legendary. Miigwetch for your mind, your art.

To Jolene Banning, you were there from the beginning, and to Jordan Huffman, your persistence, your dedication and your unfailing effort is second to none. I'm thankful for your allyship, for all you do to bring our stories to light.

To Nishnawbe Aski Nation Grand Chief Alvin Fiddler and Tesa Fiddler, you are the strength our communities need. I am in awe of all you do and the love you show doing it. To Sol Mamakwa, I am honoured to walk with you on your journey. Every day, you fight our battles, you listen, you protect and you carry our stories with grace and love.

To the Coxe family, Erica and Anthony, you are kindness, cackles and love. Never lose your unwavering spirit. Stuart, you have held me up, even in the darkest hour.

My mother, Sheila Bowen, is my centre. Without her, this book would not be. Mom, you are my hero. Thank you, Alfred, for sharing her. Thank you to my brother Yuri, and to Maureen, Thomas and Joseph. Aunty Cheryl and Aunty Bernice, this is your story too. Thank you for your love.

To Natasha and William. Only you know what this means, what it has taken. You fill me with laughter and pride. You remind me what is possible. I wish nothing but the best for you both. Your ancestors walk with you.

The Knowing is one family's story, of many, who have lived through the mouth of genocide. I hope that other First Nations, Métis and Inuit families will see their own stories in this book and that it will motivate them to find their missing loved ones.

I also hope this will show our people how linked we truly all are—no Indian Act, government department or policy can tear apart the familial, generational lines of our families. We are more powerful when we are united.

By each of us telling our stories, we will rewrite the history of Canada.

Tkaronto, 2024

PROLOGUE: CHA-KA-PESH AND THE DIRTY SEA

1. My retelling is largely based on Louis Bird, "Cha-ka-pesh and the Sailors," in *Telling Our Stories: Omushkego Legends and Histories from Hudson Bay* (Toronto: University of Toronto Press, 2005), 153–57.

CHAPTER ONE: THE KNOWING

1. "The Toronto Purchase Treaty, No. 13 (1805)," Mississaugas of the Credit First Nation, November 3, 2020, https://mncfn.ca/the-toronto-purchase-treaty-no-13-1805/.
2. Bob Joseph, 21 *Things You May Not Know About the Indian Act* (Saanichton: Indigenous Relations Press, 2018), 8.
3. Tk̓emlúps te Secwépemc, "Kamloops Indian Residential School missing children findings but a fraction of investigation and work need to bring peace to families and communities," July 15, 2021, https://tkemlups.ca/wp-content/uploads/July15_Media-Release_Final.pdf.
4. Kim Murray, Indigenous History and Heritage Gather, June 6, Ottawa speech.
5. Ibid.
6. Truth and Reconciliation Commission, *Canada's Residential Schools: Missing Children and Unmarked Burials*, vol. 4, *The Final Report of the Truth and Reconciliation Commission of Canada* (Montreal: McGill-Queen's University Press, 2015), 1, https://publications.gc.ca/collections/collection_2015/trc/IR4-9-4-2015-eng.pdf.

CHAPTER TWO: THE END IS THE BEGINNING

1. Padraig Moran, "He saw Kamloops residential school as a monster. With poetry, he denied it 'the satisfaction' of killing him," CBC, June 4, 2021, https://www.cbc.ca/radio/thecurrent/the-current-for-june-4-2021-1.6053153/he-saw-kamloops-residential-school-as-a-monster-with-poetry-he-denied-it-the-satisfaction-of-killing-him-1.6053432.
2. "Canadian Pacific Railway (Plain-Language Summary)," *The Canadian Encyclopedia*, Historica Canada, published July 6, 2021, last edited July 6, 2021, https://www.thecanadianencyclopedia.ca/en/article/canadian-pacific-railway-plain-language-summary.
3. Manny Jules, interview by Tanya Talaga, Kamloops, B.C., May 2021.
4. "Missionary Oblates of Mary Immaculate," *Indian Residential School History and Dialogue Centre Collections*, University of British Columbia, https://collections.irshdc.ubc.ca/index.php/Detail/entities/1211.

5. When the discovery of potential graves at the Kamloops Indian Residential School was first reported, they were described by Tk'emlúps te Secwépemc as 215 confirmed remains of children (https://tkemlups.ca/kirs/). Tk'emlúps has since clarified this, saying there are 200 potential sites on the Tk'emlúps grounds with a possibility of more being found as they continue their search. Radio Canada International, "Tk'emlúps te Secwépemc release final report on unmarked graves at former Kamloops residential school," July 15, 2021, https://ici.radio-canada.ca/rci/en/news/1809374/tkemlups-te-secwepemc-release-final-report-on-unmarked-graves-at-former-kamloops-residential-school.

6. Truth and Reconciliation Commission of Canada, *Canada's Residential Schools: Missing Children and Unmarked Burials*, vol. 4, *Final Report of the Truth and Reconciliation Commission of Canada* (Montreal and Kingston: McGill-Queen's University Press, 2015), 4, https://publications.gc.ca/collections/collection_2015/trc/IR4-9-4-2015-eng.pdf.

7. Murray Sinclair, interview by Tanya Talaga, May 10, 2023.

8. Tanya Talaga, "Holding Back the River," *Toronto Star*, July 8, 2019, https://projects.thestar.com/climate-change-canada/ontario-eco-anxiety/.

9. Tanya Talaga, "24 more native men come forward in Boy Scout leader's sex abuse case," *Toronto Star*, November 8, 2011, https://www.thestar.com/news/canada/24-more-native-men-come-forward-in-boy-scout-leader-s-sex-abuse-case/article_412f-ca07-90bd-5ce9- b1d6-184cc105985b.html.

10. Sarah Law, "Settlement reached in class-action lawsuit against convicted ex-priest who abused First Nations youth," *CBC News*, August 9, 2023, last modified August 9, 2023, https://www.cbc.ca/news/canada/thunder-bay/class-action-lawsuit-ralph-rowe-1.6931362.

11. Tanya Talaga, "24 more native men come forward in Boy Scout leader's sex abuse case," *Toronto Star*, November 8, 2011, https://www.thestar.com/news/canada/24-more-native-men-come-forward-in-boy-scout-leader-s-sex-abuse-case/article_412fca07-90bd-5ce9-b1d6-184cc105985b.html.

12. Gloria Galloway and Bill Curry, "Residential schools amounted to 'cultural genocide,' report says," *Globe and Mail*, June 2, 2015, https://www.theglobeandmail.com/news/politics/residential-schools-amounted-to-cultural-genocide-says-report/article24740605/.

13. Ibid.

14. Tanya Talaga, *All Our Relations* (Toronto: House of Anansi, 2018), 40.

15. "A timeline of Residential Schools, the Truth and Reconciliation Commission," *CBC News*, May 16, 2008, last modified March 25, 2014, https://www.cbc.ca/news/canada/a-timeline-of-residential-schools-the-truth-and-reconciliation-commission-1.724434.

16. Tabitha de Bruin, "Indian Residential Schools Settlement Agreement," *The Canadian Encyclopedia*, Historica Canada, published July 11, 2013, last edited January 16, 2020, https://www.thecanadianencyclopedia.ca/en/article/indian-residential-schools-settlement-agreement.

17. Fay Brunning, email message to author, June 28, 2023.

18. Brett Forester, "Supreme Court refuses to hear St. Anne's residential school survivors' appeal," *CBC News*, October 20, 2022, https://www.cbc.ca/news/indigenous/supreme-court-st-annes-appeal-1.6621902.

19. TRC, vol. 4, 1.

20. Fort Albany Treaty Land Entitlement Claim: Historical Report, Fort Albany First Nation, 1.

21. "The James Bay Treaty (Treaty No. 9)," Ontario Ministry of Public and Business Service Delivery, accessed July 24, 2023, http://www.archives.gov.on.ca/en/explore/online/jamesbaytreaty/index.aspx.

22. Ibid.

23. John S. Long, *Treaty No. 9: Making the Agreement to Share the Land in Far Northern Ontario in 1905* (Montreal: McGill-Queen's University Press, 2010), 391.

24. Ibid.

25. Richard J. Preston, "Cree," *The Canadian Encyclopedia*, Historica Canada, published September 9, 2012; last edited May 18, 2021, https://www.thecanadianencyclopedia.ca/en/article/cree.

CHAPTER THREE: TK'EMLÚPS AND THE STICK WAVERS

1. Maureen Lux, "Indian Hospitals in Canada," *The Canadian Encyclopedia,* Historica Canada, published July 11, 2017, last edited January 31, 2018, https://www.thecanadianencyclopedia.ca/en/article/indian-hospitals-in-canada.

2. Lux, "Indian Hospitals."

3. Tanya Talaga, *All Our Relations: Finding the Path Forward* (Toronto: House of Anansi, 2018), 116.

4. Truth and Reconciliation Commission, *Final Report*, vol. 1, *Canada's Residential Schools: The History, Part 1: Origins to* 1939 (Montreal and Kingston: McGill-Queen's University Press, 2015), 423.

5. Thomas McMahon, "Indian Residential Schools Were a Crime and Canada's Criminal Justice System Could Not Have Cared Less: The IRS Criminal Court Cases," May 2017, http://dx.doi.org/10.2139/ssrn.2906518.

6. John S. Long, *Treaty No. 9: Making the Agreement to Share the Land in Far Northern Ontario in 1905* (Montreal: McGill-Queen's University Press, 2010), 393.

7. Long, *Treaty No. 9*, 393.

8. Andrew McIntosh and Shirlee Anne Smith, "Rupert's Land," *The Canadian Encyclopedia*, Historica Canada, published February 7, 2006, last edited August 18, 2022, https://www.thecanadianencyclopedia.ca/en/article/ruperts-land.

9. James Daschuk, *Clearing the Plains: Disease, Politics of Starvation, and the Loss of Indigenous Life* (Regina: University of Regina Press, 2013), 15.

10. Daschuk, *Clearing the Plains*, 15.

11. Ibid., 16.

12. TRC, vol. 1, 14.

13. Talaga, *Relations*, 46.

14. TRC, vol. 1, 15.

15. "Indigenous Title and The Doctrine of Discovery," Indigenous Corporate Training Inc., last modified March 30, 2023, https://www.ictinc.ca/blog/indigenous-title-and-the-doctrine-of-discovery.

16. TRC, vol. 1, 16.

17. Nicole Winfield, "Vatican formally rejects 'Doctrine of Discovery' after Indigenous calls," *PBS News Hour*, March 30, 2023, https://www.pbs.org/newshour/politics/vatican-formally-rejects-doctrine-of-discovery-after-indigenous-calls. For the full text of the repudiation, see https://press.vatican.va/content/salastampa/en/bollettino/pubblico/2023/03/30/230330b.html.

CHAPTER FOUR: PROFIT HUNTERS AND THE FALSE PROPHET

1. Ibid., 38.
2. Quoted in Jennifer S. H. Brown, "The Track to Heaven: The Hudson Bay Cree Religious Movement of 1842–1843," *Papers of the 13th Algonquian Conference*, ed. by William Cowan (Carleton University, 1982), 56.
3. Quoted in Brown, "The Track to Heaven," 57.
4. Brown, "The Track to Heaven," 57.
5. Egerton Ryerson Young, *The Apostle of the North Rev. James Evans* (Toronto, 1900), quoted in ibid., 58.
6. Jennifer S. H. Brown, "Abishabis," in *Dictionary of Canadian Biography*, vol. 7, University of Toronto/Université Laval, 2003–, accessed August 14, 2023, http://www.biographi.ca/en/bio/abishabis_7E.html.
7. Ibid.
8. Quoted in Jennifer S. H. Brown, "The Track to Heaven: The Hudson Bay Cree Religious Movement of 1842 to 1843," Northern Illinois University, vol. 13 (1982), 59, https://ojs.library.carleton.ca/index.php/ALGQP/article/view/808/698.
9. Quoted in ibid, 60.
10. "Abishabis."
11. Anne Lindsay, "'Especially in this Free Country': Webs of Empire, Slavery and the Fur Trade" (doctoral thesis, University of Manitoba, 2021), 32–33, https://mspace.lib.umanitoba.ca/server/api/core/bitstreams/139f739e-d939-4b8a-b60b-d64b8e38b50e/content.
12. Archives of Manitoba, North West Company, http://pam.minisis-inc.com/SCRIPTS/MWIMAIN.DLL/221635089/HEADING/North~20West~20Company?KEYSEARCH&DATABASE=AUTHORITY_WEB.
13. John Galbraith, *The Little Emperor: Governor Simpson of the Hudson Bay Company* (Toronto: MacMillan of Canada, 1976).
14. Thomas Saunders, *A Proud Heritage: A History of the St. Andrew's Society of Winnipeg, 1871-1982* (Winnipeg: Peguis Publishers, 1982).
15. John S. Galbraith, "Simpson, Sir George," in *Dictionary of Canadian Biography*, vol. 8, University of Toronto/Université Laval, 2003–, accessed August 14, 2023, http://www.biographi.ca/en/bio/simpson_george_8E.html.
16. Ibid.
17. Amelia Fay, "Shedding Light On the Darker History of Nonsuch," Manitoba Museum, December 5, 2022, https://manitobamuseum.ca/archives/53097.
18. Lindsay, "'Especially in this Free Country,'" 23.
19. "Sir William Baker Alderman of City of London," Legacies of British Slavery database, accessed August 28, 2023, https://www.ucl.ac.uk/lbs/person/view/2146650157.
20. Jacqueline L. Scott, "Hudson Bay Blanket and Black History," Black Outdoors, accessed August 14, 2023, https://blackoutdoors.wordpress.com/2022/02/25/hudson-bay-blanket-and-black-history/.
21. Sian Bumsted, "Manitoba History: Lady Selkirk and the Fur Trade," Manitoba Historical Society, accessed August 14, 2023, last modified October 13, 2012, http://www.mhs.mb.ca/docs/mb_history/38/ladyselkirk.shtml.
22. "John Wedderburn of Balindean", Legacies of British Slavery database, accessed August 14, 2023, https://www.ucl.ac.uk/lbs/person/view/2146634306.

23. Lindsay, "'Especially in this Free Country,'" 95.

24. Ibid., 100.

25. Lawrence J. Barkwell, "The Despicable Sir George Simpson," *Louis Riel Institute*, https://www.scribd.com/document/149140606/The-Despicable-Sir-George-Simpson#.

26. Melissa Gismondi, "The untold story of the Hudson's Bay Company," *Canadian Geographic*, May 2, 2020, updated May 17, 2022, https://canadiangeographic.ca/articles/the-untold-story-of-the-hudsons-bay-company/.

27. Barkwell, "The Despicable Sir George Simpson."

28. Quoted in Lindsay, "'Especially in this Free Country,'" 255.

29. Ibid., 83.

30. Quoted in ibid., 105–6.

31. Quoted in ibid., 110.

32. Quoted in ibid., 86.

33. Quoted in ibid., 80–1.

34. Quoted in ibid., 117.

35. "Our Origins Canada's Great Love Story: David & Charlotte," David Thompson Country, accessed August 14, 2023, https://davidthompsoncountry.ca/our-origins/.

36. Pambrun, *Sixty Years on the Frontier in the Pacific Northwest* (Fairfield, WA: 1978), quoted in Lindsay, "'Especially in this Free Country,'" 259.

37. TRC, 57.

38. Ibid.

39. Ibid., 66.

40. Ibid., 68.

41. Sir George Murray, quoted in ibid., 58.

42. See, for instance, Kenneth D. Nworah, "The Aborigines' Protection Society, 1889–1909: A Pressure-Group in Colonial Policy," *Canadian Journal of African Studies/Revue Canadienne Des Études Africaines* 5, no. 1 (1971): 79–91. https://doi.org/10.2307/484052.

43. John S. Long, "The Reverend George Barnley and the James Bay Cree," *The Canadian Journal of Native Studies* 6, no. 2 (1986): 314. https://cjns.brandonu.ca/wp-content/uploads/6-2-long.pdf.

44. Long, "The Reverend," 315.

45. Ibid., 316.

46. Ibid., 317.

47. Ibid., 315.

48. Ibid., 319.

49. Ibid, 320.

50. Ibid., 315.

51. "Canada Buys Rupert's Land," CBC, accessed August 14, 2023, https://www.cbc.ca/history/EPCONTENTSE1EP9CH1PA3LE.html.

52. "Canada Buys Rupert's Land."

53. Ibid.

54. "10 Quotes John A. Macdonald Made About First Nations," Indigenous Corporate Training Inc., June 28, 2016, https://www.ictinc.ca/blog/10-quotes-john-a.-macdonald-made-about-first-nations.

CHAPTER FIVE: THIS IS ANNIE

1. Karrmen Crey and Erin Hanson, "Indian Status," Indigenous Foundations, accessed August 16, 2023, https://indigenousfoundations.arts.ubc.ca/indian_status/.

2. For a photograph, see National Centre for Truth and Reconciliation Archives, https://archives.nctr.ca/uploads/r/National-Centre-for-Truth-and-Reconciliation-NCTR/5/b/d/5bd76c76e02fad49b5d30332c3c0d3826d517e02716df973b1501ce3361492c3/15c-c000317-d0001-001.pdf.

3. John S. Long, "Horden, John," in *Dictionary of Canadian Biography*, vol. 12, University of Toronto/Université Laval, 2003–, accessed August 16, 2023, http://www.biographi.ca/en/bio/horden_john_12E.html.

4. John S. Long, "Vincent, Thomas (1835–1907)," in *Dictionary of Canadian Biography*, vol. 13, University of Toronto/Université Laval, 2003–, accessed August 16, 2023, http://www.biographi.ca/en/bio/vincent_thomas_1835_1907_13E.html.

5. Ibid.

6. Ibid.

7. A. R. Buckland, "John Horden: Missionary Bishop; A Life on the Shores of Hudson's Bay," Anglican History, http://anglicanhistory.org/canada/horden/buckland/04.html.

8. Ibid.

9. Ibid.

10. "Coral Fund Children at Moose," *Coral Missionary Magazine*, November 1, 1874, page 167, https://books.google.ca/books?id=ES0EAAAAQAAJ&pg=RA1-PA167.

11. "Coral Fund, Children at Moose," *Coral Missionary Magazine*, September 1, 1875, page 141, https://books.google.ca/books?id=ES0EAAAAQAAJ&pg=RA2-PA141&dp-g=RA2-PA141.

12. "Children on the Coral Fund at Moose Factory and Albany," *Coral Missionary Magazine*, December 1877, page 184, https://books.google.ca/books?id=0z0EAAAAQAAJ&pg=RA1-PA184.

13. Donald J. Auger, *Indian Residential Schools in Ontario* (Ontario: Nishnawbe Aski Nation, 2005), 123.

14. Auger, *Indian Residential Schools*, 123.

15. Ibid.

16. Ibid., 131.

17. Letter from John G. Anderson, April 16, 1912, National Centre for Truth and Reconciliation Archives, https://archives.nctr.ca/uploads/r/National-Centre-for-Truth-and-Reconciliation-NCTR/a/b/5/ab50824cca090f84b25fb1c069ac2477d9ba523fcec1e40a3e209df0ff295e2b/c-7935-01798-01827.pdf.

18. Letter from D. C. Scott, October 25, 1910, in ibid.

19. Letter from Mary A. Johnson, St. Thomas Mission, to Frank Pedley, March 7, 1912, page 34, https://indiandayschools.org/files/RG10_467-1_PART_1.pdf.

20. Letter from John G. Anderson, March 25, 1912, pages 38–39, https://indiandayschools.org/files/RG10_467-1_PART_1.pdf.

21. Letter from John G. Anderson, May 30, 1914, National Centre for Truth and Reconciliation Archives, page 71, https://archives.nctr.ca/uploads/r/National-Centre-for-Truth-and-Reconciliation-NCTR/a/b/5/ab50824cca090f84b25fb1c069ac2477d9ba523fcec1e40a3e209df0ff295e2b/c-7935-01798-01827.pdf.

22. Telegram from Duncan C. Scott, June 2, 1914, in ibid.

23. Letter from Department of Indian Affairs, September 6, 1919, Algoma University Archives, page 9, http://archives.algomau.ca/main/sites/default/files/2010-006_001_001.pdf.

24. Letter from Department of Indian Affairs, September 6, 1919, Algoma University Archives, http://archives.algomau.ca/main/sites/default/files/2010-006_001_001.pdf.

25. Letter from William Rackham, October 13, 1919, page 59, https://indiandayschools.org/files/RG10_467-1_PART_1.pdf.

26. Letter from William Rackham, October 13, 1919, page 60, ibid.

27. Letter from H. N. Awrey to Royal Humane Association, September 22, 1921, Algoma University Archives, http://archives.algomau.ca/main/sites/default/files/2010-006_001_001.pdf.

28. "Lost Balloon Safe Near Hudson Bay," *New York Times*, January 3, 1921, https://timesmachine.nytimes.com/timesmachine/1921/01/03/103526616.html?pageNumber=1.

29. Ernie Bies, "Christmas Miracle at Moose Factory," *Ontario History*, October 28, 2014, https://www.ontariohistory.org/bies-miracle.pdf.

30. "Pathetic End of Anglican Rector," *Morning Citizen*, August 31, 1921, page 16, http://www.nrsss.ca/Resource_Centre/MooseFortIRS/MooseFortIRS_RG10_Volume6203_File467-1_Part1_Administration_1907-1947_wm.pdf.

31. Letter from H. N. Awrey, September 12, 1921, Algoma University Archives, http://archives.algomau.ca/main/sites/default/files/2010-006_001_001.pdf.

32. Truth and Reconciliation Commission, *Final Report*, vol. 1, *Canada's Residential Schools: The History, Part 1: Origins to 1939* (Montreal and Kingston: McGill-Queen's University Press, 2015), 66.

33. Auger, *Indian Residential Schools*, 153.

34. "Indian Schools Deal Out Death," *Daily Colonist*, November 16, 1907, quoted in "1906–1910 The Bryce Report," First Nations Education Steering Committee, "https://www.fnesc.ca/wp/wp-content/uploads/2015/07/IRSR11-12-DE-1906-1910.pdf.

35. "Bishop Horden Hall (Moose Factory)," National Centre for Truth and Reconciliation, accessed August 16, 2023, https://nctr.ca/residential-schools/ontario/bishop-horden-hall-moose-factory/.

36. Letter from H. N. Awrey, July 18, 1927, Algoma University Archives, http://archives.algomau.ca/main/sites/default/files/2010-006_001_001.pdf.

37. Letter from A. F. MacKenzie, July 26, 1927, Algoma University Archives, http://archives.algomau.ca/main/sites/default/files/2010-006_001_001.pdf.

38. Letter from T. B. R. Westgate, July 19, 1926, Algoma University Archives, http://archives.algomau.ca/main/sites/default/files/2010-006_001_001.pdf.

CHAPTER SIX: SEPARATION AND THE HUNT FOR RECORDS

1. "Man pleads guilty in grisly 1983 killings of 2 Toronto women," *CBC News*, October 5, 2023, last modified October 5, 2023, https://www.cbc.ca/news/canada/toronto/man-pleads-guilty-1983-toronto-women-killings-1.6988480.

2. Office of the Independent Special Interlocutor, *Moving from Our Heads to Our Hearts to Our Hands: Summary Report of the National Gathering on Unmarked Burials* (Edmonton: 2022), 42, https://osi-bis.ca/wp-content/uploads/2023/01/OSI-SummaryReport-Edmonton-Sept2022.pdf.

3. Ibid., 32.

4. "Charges laid against Bishop Hubert O'Connor," Indian Residential School History and Dialogue Centre, UBC, https://collections.irshdc.ubc.ca/index.php/Detail/occurrences/676; Tom Hawthorn, "Disgraced priest left legacy of pain," *Globe and Mail*, July 28, 2007, https://www.theglobeandmail.com/news/national/disgraced-priest-left-legacy-of-pain/article690143/.

5. Amanda Follett Hosgood, "A Nation's Journey into 'the Darkest Recesses of Human Behaviour'," *The Tyee*, January 25, 2022, https://thetyee.ca/News/2022/01/25/Williams-Lake-Findings/.

6. Ibid.

7. "St. Joseph's Mission Investigation," Williams Lake First Nation, accessed September 12, 2023, https://www.wlfn.ca/about-wlfn/sjm-investigation/

8. Office of the Independent Special Interlocutor, *Moving from Our Heads to Our Hearts*, 48.

9. Creeson Agecoutay and Anthony Vasquez-Peddie, "Cowessess First Nation working with Church to complete identification of 751 unmarked graves," CTV News, December 11, 2021, https://www.ctvnews.ca/canada/cowessess-first-nation-working-with-church-to-complete-identification-of-751-unmarked-graves-1.5704042.

10. "About," National Centre for Truth and Reconciliation, accessed September 12, 2023, https://nctr.ca/about/.

11. "About."

12. Office of the Independent Special Interlocutor, *Moving from Our Heads to Our Hearts*, 18.

13. "New England Company," City of London, updated May, 17, 2022, accessed September 12, 2023, https://www.cityoflondon.gov.uk/things-to-do/history-and-heritage/london-metropolitan-archives/collections/new-england-company.

14. Mark Hill, statement given at First National Gathering on Unmarked Burials, Edmonton, Alberta, September 12–14, 2022.

15. Dr. Kona Williams, interview by Tanya Talaga, 4th National Gathering on Unmarked Burials, Toronto, Ontario, March 28, 2023.

CHAPTER SEVEN: ANNIE AND THE SIGNING OF TREATY 9

1. "The Seven Teachings," Southern First Nations Network of Care, accessed September 12, 2023, https://www.southernnetwork.org/site/seven-teachings.

2. John S. Long, *Treaty No. 9: Making the Agreement to Share the Land in Far Northern Ontario in 1905* (Montreal: McGill-Queen's University Press, 2010), 110.

3. Ian Wereley, "Final Report: Research on the *Proceedings and Transactions of the Royal Society of Canada, 1898–1947*" (Ottawa: Royal Society of Canada: 2019), 5, https://rsc-src.ca/sites/default/files/Proceedings%20and%20Transactions%20-%20Final%20Report.pdf.

4. Wereley, "Research on the *Proceedings*," 8.

5. L. P. Weis, "D. C. Scott's View of History and the Indians," *Canadian Literature* 111 (Winter 1986): 30, https://canlit.ca/canlitmedia/canlit.ca/pdfs/articles/canlit111-Scott(Weis).pdf.

6. "'Until There Is Not a Single Indian in Canada,'" Facing History and Ourselves Canada, last modified July 28, 2020, https://www.facinghistory.org/en-ca/resource-library/until-there-not-single-indian-canada.

7. "'Until There Is Not a Single Indian in Canada.'"

8. "Duncan Campbell Scott," CanLit Guides, posted November 5, 2013, last modified August 19, 2016, https://canlitguides.ca/canlit-guides-editorial-team/poetry-and-racialization/duncan-campbell-scott/.

9. Weis, "D. C. Scott's View of History and the Indians," 28.
10. Long, *Treaty No. 9*, 119.
11. Ibid., 117–18.
12. Ibid., 136.
13. Ibid., 136.
14. "Indian Hospitals in Canada," Indian Residential School History and Dialogue Centre, University of British Columbia, accessed September 29, 2023, https://irshdc.ubc.ca/learn/indian-hospitals-in-canada/.
15. Long, *Treaty No. 9*, 147.
16. Ibid., 139.
17. Ibid., 140.
18. Ibid., 164.
19. Ibid.
20. "Making the Treaty," Ontario Ministry of Public and Business Service Delivery, accessed September 29, 2023, http://www.archives.gov.on.ca/en/explore/online/jamesbaytreaty/making_treaty.aspx.
21. Long, *Treaty No. 9*, 164.
22. James H. Marsh, "Obwandiyag (Pontiac)," *The Canadian Encyclopedia*, Historica Canada, published February 7, 2006, last modified March 25, 2021, https://www.thecanadianencyclopedia.ca/en/article/pontiac.
23. Marsh, "Obwandiyag (Pontiac)."
24. Long, *Treaty No. 9*, 288.
25. Ibid., 289.
26. Ibid., 292.
27. Ibid., 288.

CHAPTER EIGHT: STEALING CHILDREN

1. Tanya Talaga, "Episode 5: Honesty," November 25, 2020, in *Seven Truths*, produced by Antica Productions, podcast, https://www.audible.ca/pd/Episode-5-Honesty-Podcast/B08NY1LMJ8?ref=a_pd_Seven-_c4_1Asin_0_2&pf_rd_p=0c38abba-a42f-457d-a98a-dad4d340a9a5&pf_rd_r=0KYVRD35AM2RQCQXEGAC&pageLoadId=1uX3l-6w1vAs7cofO&creativeId=395f77c0-e1ec-4b1d-a47f-7395e710e18c.
2. Letter from J. D. McLean, June 4, 1908, page 2, http://www.nrsss.ca/Resource_Centre/CeciliaJeffreyIRS/CeciliaJeffreyIRS_RG10_Volume6187_File461-1_Part1_GeneralAdministration_1908-1925_wm.pdf.
3. Truth and Reconciliation Commission, Final Report, vol. 1, *Canada's Residential Schools: The History, Part 1: Origins to 1939* (Montreal and Kingston: McGill-Queen's University Press, 2015), 671.
4. Tanya Talaga, *Seven Fallen Feathers* (Toronto: House of Anansi, 2017), 81, electronic ed.
5. Talaga, *Seven Fallen Feathers*, 87, electronic ed.
6. Susan Gray, "Semmens, John," in *Dictionary of Canadian Biography*, vol. 15, University of Toronto/Université Laval, 2003–, accessed September 22, 2023, http://www.biographi.ca/en/bio/semmens_john_15E.html.
7. Gray, "Semmens, John."
8. Gray, "Semmens, John."
9. Ibid.

10. Natalie Cross, "Branching the Shingwauk Home: Residential School Networks and the Canadian Public 1885–1918," 5, and Shingwauk Letter Book of Rev. E. Wilson, 1887–1888, 48, https://archive.org/details/2013112004/mode/2up.

11. Cross, "Branching the Shingwauk Home," 5.

12. Richard Henry Pratt, *Battlefield and Classroom: Four Decades with the American Indian,* 1867–1904, ed. Robert M. Utley (Norman, OK: University of Oklahoma Press, 2004), 311.

13. Pratt, *Battlefield and Classroom,* 312.

14. Marcel-Eugène LeBeuf, on behalf of the RCMP. (2011). "The role of the Royal Canadian Mounted Police during the Indian Residential School system," 24. Government of Canada. https://publications.gc.ca/site/eng/9.692143/publication.html.

15. David Evans, "Francis Dickens," *The Canadian Encyclopedia,* Historica Canada, published January 22, 2008, last modified December 15, 2013, https://www.thecanadianencyclopedia.ca/en/article/francis-dickens.

16. LeBeuf, "The Role of the Royal Canadian Mounted Police," 25.

17. John Semmens, "Notes on Personal History" (1915), United Church Archives, University of Winnipeg, 93, http://uccarchiveswinnipeg.ca/wp-content/uploads/1915-John-Semmens-Notes-on-Personal-History-UCArchivesWpg-278-d1.pdf.

18. Semmens, "Notes on Personal History," 94.

19. Ibid.

20. Ibid., 95.

21. Ibid., 96.

22. Ibid.

23. Ibid., 99.

24. "The Davin Report, 1879," Nishnawbe Aski Nation, accessed September 28, 2023, http://rschools.nan.on.ca/article/the-davin-report-1879-1120.asp.

25. J. S. Milloy, "'Suffer the Little Children': The Aboriginal Residential School System, 1830–1992," submitted to the Royal Commission on Aboriginal Peoples, May 1996, page 82, https://publications.gc.ca/collections/collection_2017/bcp-pco/Z1-1991-1-41-155-eng.pdf.

26. Milloy, "'Suffer the Little Children,'" 77.

27. Ibid., 76.

28. Charles Stewart, quoted in ibid., 77.

29. Letter from Semmens to E. McColl, Inspector of Indian Agencies, February 19, 1895, quoted in "Brandon Residential School," The Children Remembered, United Church of Canada, accessed November 4, 2023, https://thechildrenremembered.ca/school-histories/brandon/.

30. Semmens, "Notes on Personal History," 96.

31. Ibid., 96–97.

32. Ibid., 97.

33. Ibid.

34. "Brandon Residential School," The Children Remembered, accessed September 28, 2023, https://thechildrenremembered.ca/school-histories/brandon/.

35. Ibid.

36. Ibid.

37. Ibid.

38. Semmens, "Notes on Personal History," 97–98.

39. "Brandon (MB)," Indian Residential School History and Dialogue Centre Collections, University of British Columbia, accessed September 28, 2023, https://collections.irshdc.ubc.ca/index.php/Detail/entities/74.

40. "Unmarked graves located near the former Brandon Residential School," Indian Residential School History and Dialogue Centre Collections, accessed September 28, 2023, https://collections.irshdc.ubc.ca/index.php/Detail/occurrences/437.

41. LeBeuf, "The Role of the Royal Canadian Mounted Police," 24.

42. "The Famous Five: The Women," Famous 5 Foundation, accessed September 28, 2023, https://www.famous5.ca/the-famous-five-women.

43. Sarah Carter, "Emily Murphy and Indigenous Peoples of Western Canada: 'On the Road to Extinction,'" Centre for Human Rights Research, University of Manitoba, August 16, 2021, https://chrr.info/blog/emily-murphy-and-indigenous-peoples-of-western-canada-on-the-road-to-extinction/.

44. Emily Murphy, *Janey Canuck in the West* (1910), *A Celebration of Women Writers* (blog), https://digital.library.upenn.edu/women/murphy/west/west.html#II.

45. Susan Jackel, "Emily Murphy," *The Canadian Encyclopedia*, Historica Canada, published April 1, 2008, last modified November 20, 2020, https://www.thecanadianencyclopedia.ca/en/article/emily-murphy.

46. "A Sumptuous Indian Palace," *Regina Standard*, November 26, 1896, Item 22, "Correspondence Regarding the Education of Indian Children," Library and Archives Canada, https://recherche-collection-search.bac-lac.gc.ca/eng/home/record?app=fonandcol&IdNumber=2058571.

47. Letter from R. S. McKenzie, October 26, 1915, page 26, http://www.nrsss.ca/Resource_Centre/CeciliaJeffreyIRS/CeciliaJeffreyIRS_RG10_Volume6187_File461-1_Part1_GeneralAdministration_1908-1925_wm.pdf.

48. Donald Auger, *Indian Residential Schools in Ontario* (Thunder Bay: Nishnawbe Aski Nation, 2005), 58.

49. Auger, *Indian Residential Schools*, 58.

50. Letter from Minokijikok (#83 Sabaskong), September 23, 1924, page 28, http://www.nrsss.ca/Resource_Centre/StMarysIRS/StMarysIRS_RG10_Volume6197_File465-1_Part1_SchoolEstablishment_1894-1927_wm.pdf.

51. Letter from Frank Edwards, October 4, 1922, page 16, ibid.

52. Jordan Omstead, "Search uncovers 171 'plausible burials' near Ontario residential school," *Globe and Mail*, January 17, 2023, https://www.theglobeandmail.com/canada/article-search-uncovers-171-plausible-burials-near-ontario-residential-school-2/.

53. Letter from R. S. McKenzie, March 15, 1917, page 42, http://www.nrsss.ca/Resource_Centre/CeciliaJeffreyIRS/CeciliaJeffreyIRS_RG10_Volume6187_File461-1_Part1_GeneralAdministration_1908-1925_wm.pdf.

54. Ibid.

55. Letter from Assistant Deputy and Secretary of Indian Affairs, August 4, 1917, page 46, http://www.nrsss.ca/Resource_Centre/CeciliaJeffreyIRS/CeciliaJeffreyIRS_RG10_Volume6187_File461-1_Part1_GeneralAdministration_1908-1925_wm.pdf.

56. Department of Indian Affairs report, March 29, 1917, Indian Office, Winnipeg, page 54, http://www.nrsss.ca/Resource_Centre/CeciliaJeffreyIRS/CeciliaJeffreyIRS_RG10_Volume6187_File461-1_Part1_GeneralAdministration_1908-1925_wm.pdf.

CHAPTER NINE: CHRISTINA AND THE GONE GIRLS

1. Luke Hunter, email to Paula Rickard, March 29, 2023.
2. Letter from R. S. McKenzie, April 27, 1912, https://heritage.canadiana.ca/view/oocihm. lac_reel_c7995/1236.
3. Telegram from R. S. McKenzie, June 2, 1912, https://heritage.canadiana.ca/view/ oocihm.lac_reel_c7995/1237.
4. Telegram from J. D. McLean, June 4, 1912, https://heritage.canadiana.ca/view/oocihm. lac_reel_c7995/1237.
5. Paylist for Fort Albany Band, paid at Lac Seul, July 9, 1915, https://heritage.canadiana. ca/view/oocihm.lac_reel_c7995/2354.
6. Ibid.
7. "Elkhorn Indian Residential School IAP School Narrative," National Centre for Truth and Reconciliation, last modified January 17, 2013, https://archives.nctr.ca/uploads/r/ National-Centre-for-Truth-and-Reconciliation-NCTR/f/6/a/f6a004f5f7d9ad9b d0eaa3b0cf0dcd629e6a751b0a0cdbc0ebd17092aac7b726/NAR-NCTR-037.pdf.
8. James Daschuk, *Clearing the Plains: Disease, Politics of Starvation, and the Loss of Aboriginal Life* (Regina: University of Regina Press, 2013), 164.
9. Daschuk, *Clearing the Plains*, xxii.
10. Kenneth Jackson, "Aboriginal children herded like cattle onto 'train of tears'," *APTN National News*, June 2, 2015, https://www.aptnnews.ca/national-news/aboriginal-children-herded-like-cattle-onto-train-tears/.
11. Jackson, "Aboriginal children."
12. Marcel-Eugène LeBeuf, on behalf of the RCMP. (2011). "The role of the Royal Canadian Mounted Police during the Indian Residential School system," 68. Government of Canada. https://publications.gc.ca/site/eng/9.692143/publication.html.
13. Ibid, 69.
14. Letter from Indian Agent R. S. McKenzie to the Secretary of the Department of Indian Affairs, Ottawa, June 14, 1915, https://heritage.canadiana.ca/view/oocihm.lac_reel_ c7995/2342.
15. Treaty annuity receipts from Indian Agent R. S. McKenzie and signed by Christina Samson and witnessed by John Semmens, August 20, 1915, https://heritage.canadiana. ca/view/oocihm.lac_reel_c7995/2353.
16. Letter from Indian Agent R. S. McKenzie to the Deputy and Secretary of Indian Affairs, Ottawa, August 13, 1918, https://heritage.canadiana.ca/view/oocihm.lac_reel_ c7995/2379.
17. Letter from Indian Agent R. S. McKenzie, Decemeber 28, 1918, to Asst., Deputy and Secretary of Indian Affairs, https://heritage.canadiana.ca/view/oocihm.lac_reel_ c7995/2383.
18. Darnell Dobson, "New agreement will assist the search for children who never returned home from residential schools," National Centre for Truth and Reconciliation, March 13, 2023, https://nctr.ca/new-agreement-will-assist-the-search-for-children-who-never-re-turned-home-from-residential-schools/.
19. Letter from Frank Edwards, August 19, 1925, Library and Archives Canada RG10, vol. 6888, file 486/28-3 part 3.
20. Letter from Indian Agent Frank Edwards, July 13, 1929, to Christina Sampson, https:// heritage.canadiana.ca/view/oocihm.lac_reel_c7996/1577.

21. Letter from Indian Agent Frank Edwards, October 16, 1931, to Christina Sampson, https://heritage.canadiana.ca/view/oocihm.lac_reel_c7996/2133.
22. Letter from Christina Sampson, February 28, 1933, to Dept. of Indian Affairs, https://heritage.canadiana.ca/view/oocihm.lac_reel_c7996/2353.
23. "J. Wolozub Charged with Armed Robbery," *Winnipeg Free Press*, July 24, 1944.
24. "W. Murray Is Held on Assault Charge," *Winnipeg Free Press*, September 29, 1944.
25. "Crowded Block Condemned for Fire and Health Hazards," *Winnipeg Tribune*, February 22, 1951, https://digitalcollections.lib.umanitoba.ca/islandora/object/uofm%3A2049890.
26. Letter from Margaret Matheson, Mary Jensen, Evelyn Fletcher, Archie Davidson, Marian Cole, Agnes Arnold, February 25, 1929, to Mrs. D. T. L. McKerroll, Cecilia Jeffrey School, https://central.bac-lac.gc.ca/.item/?op=img&app=microform&id=c-7922-02024.
27. Royal Canadian Mounted Police report by Constable E. Stanley, October 26, 1936, Library and Archives Canada, Indian Affairs, RG 10, Volume 6190, File 461-10, pt. 10, https://data2.archives.ca/microform/data2/dm09/d09/006003/c-7925/pdf/c-7925-00997.pdf.
28. Dedication of Cecilia Jeffrey Indian School, Nov. 9, 1929, *Kenora Miner & News*, Nov. 9, 1929, https://archives.nctr.ca/uploads/r/National-Centre-for-Truth-and-Reconciliation-NCTR/b/1/5/b1524ea583f51540d34fdede5a6a7cd23f08571d96628ee0609a73f-b245a75d1/c-7922-02081-02110.pdf.
29. Anonymous letter, undated, page 30, https://archives.nctr.ca/uploads/r/National-Centre-for-Truth-and-Reconciliation-NCTR/b/1/5/b1524ea583f51540d34fdede5a6a7cd23f08571d96628ee0609a73fb245a75d1/c-7922-02081-02110.pdf.
30. Application for Tuition Grant, page 45, https://indiandayschools.org/files/RG10_42129-3_PART_1.pdf.
31. Letter from T. P. Ross, August 8, 1949, page 51, https://indiandayschools.org/files/RG10_42129-3_PART_1.pdf.
32. Martha Troian, "Emerging from the Long Shadow of Canada's Indian Hospitals," *The Local*, June 15, 2021, https://thelocal.to/emerging-from-the-long-shadow-of-canadas-indian-hospitals/.
33. Department of Indian Affairs, "Memorandum of Inquiry into the cause and circumstances into the death of Doris Carpenter, Pupil No. 157 of the Sioux Lookout Indian Residential School," Indian Affairs RG10, vol. 6216, file 470-23, part 1.
34. Letter from Simon Wesley, February 14, 1937, Library and Archives Canada RB10, vol. 6216, file 470-23, part 1.
35. Letter from Philip Phelan, March 2, 1937, Library and Archives Canada RB10, vol. 6216, file 470-23, part 1.
36. Letter from Fred A. Mayo, March 11, 1937, Library and Archives Canada RB10, vol. 6216, file 470-23, part 1.
37. Pelican Falls website, National Centre for Truth and Reconciliation, https://nctr.ca/residential-schools/ontario/pelican-lake-pelican-falls/.
38. Fred A. Mayo, "A Statement of the Principal of the Residential School," pages 28–29, http://www.nrsss.ca/Resource_Centre/PelicanLakeIRS/PelicanLakeIRS_RG10_Volume6216_File470-23_Part1_DEATHS_1935-1949_wm.pdf.
39. Mayo, "A Statement," pages 24–25, in ibid.

40. Mayo, "A Statement," pages 33–34, in ibid.
41. Letter from Fred A. Mayo, October 19, 1937, Indian Affairs RG10, vol. 6216, file 470-23, part 1.
42. Letter from Fred A. Mayo, October 20, 1937, Indian Affairs RG10, vol. 6216, file 470-23, part 1.

CHAPTER TEN: IN THE MOUTH OF GENOCIDE

1. Robyn Doolittle and Tom Cardoso, "How Canada's FOI system broke under its own weight," *The Globe and Mail*, June 9, 2023, https://www.theglobeandmail.com/canada/article-canada-freedom-of-information-laws/.
2. "Edwards, Frank," Kenora Great War Project, accessed September 28, 2023, https://www.kenoragreatwarproject.ca/kings-own-royal-lancaster-regiment/edwards-frank/.
3. *Sessional Papers: First Session of Seventh Legislature of the Province of Ontario* (Toronto, 1891), 42-3, https://archive.org/details/n03ontariosession23onta/page/n69/mode/2up?view=theater.
4. Geoffrey Reaume, interview by Tanya Talaga, April 27, 2023.
5. Letter from Daniel Clark, May 8, 1890, Archives of Ontario, RG 63, Sub-series A-1, vol. 208, file 6317, "Burials and Burial Grounds" 1890–1906. Courtesy of Pleasance Crawford.
6. Agatha Barc, "The history of the Lakeshore Psychiatric Hospital in Toronto," *blogTO*, August 22, 2020, https://www.blogto.com/city/2011/04/a_brief_history_of_the_lakeshore_psychiatric_hospital/.
7. *Sessional Papers*, 50-51.
8. Ibid., 52-54.
9. Ibid., 55.
10. Geoffrey Reaume, *Remembrance of Patients Past: Life at the Toronto Hospital for the Insane, 1870-1940* (Toronto: University of Toronto Press, 2009), 32.
11. *Sessional Papers: Third Session, Ninth Legislature of the Province of Toronto* (Toronto, ON, 1900), 168-9, https://archive.org/details/n09ontariosession32ontauoft/page/n229/mode/2up?view=theater.
12. *Sessional Papers*, 169–70.
13. Reaume, *Remembrance of Patients Past*, 8.
14. Ibid., 16.
15. Carla Joinson, *Vanished in Hiawatha: The Story of the Canton Asylum for Insane Indians* (Winnipeg: Bison Books, 2016), digital ed., 15.
16. Joinson, 24.
17. Ibid., 26.
18. Ibid., 27.
19. Ibid., 33.
20. Pemina Yellow Bird, "Wild Indians: Native Perspectives on the Hiawatha Asylum for Insane Indians," 5, https://dsmc.info/pdf/canton.pdf.
21. Bird, "Wild Indians," 6.
22. Ibid., 7.
23. Wendy Mitchinson, *Mental Health and Candian Society: Historical Perspectives* (McGill-Queen's University Press, 2006), page 152, https://books-scholarsportal-info.myaccess.library.utoronto.ca/en/read?id=/ebooks/ebooks3/upress/2013-08-23/1/9780773576544#page=171.

24. *Toronto Star* photos by Bob Olsen, https://www.gettyimages.fi/search/more-like-this/515075249?family=editorial&assettype=image&phrase=lakeshore%20hospital.

25. Geoffrey Reaume, interview by Tanya Talaga, April 27, 2023.

26. Reaume, *Remembrance of Patients Past*, 19.

27. Ibid., 29.

28. Geoffrey Reaume, interview by Tanya Talaga, April 26, 2023.

CHAPTER ELEVEN: LOST, FOUND AND LOST AGAIN

1. Letter from R. S. McKenzie, April 5, 1918, Library and Archives Canada, https://heritage.canadiana.ca/view/oocihm.lac_reel_c7995/2371.

2. Murray Sinclair, interview by Tanya Talaga, May 10, 2023.

3. Kris Ketonen, "Over 170 'plausible burials' detected in search for unmarked graves at former Kenora residential school site," CBC, January 17, 2023, last modified January 18, 2023, https://www.cbc.ca/news/canada/thunder-bay/st-marys-residential-school-1.6716724.

4. David Thompson, interview by Tanya Talaga, October 15, 2022

5. Donald J. Auger, *Indian Residential Schools in Ontario* (Ontario: Nishnawbe Aski Nation, 2005), 149.

6. Robert J. Surtees, "Treaty Research Report: The Robinson Treaties (1850)," Treaties and Historical Research Centre Indian and Northern Affairs Canada, 1986, 4, file: ///D:/Users/MikaelaRoasa/Downloads/trerob_1100100028975_eng.pdf.

7. "The Robinson Treaties (1850)," Government of Canada, accessed October 12, 2023, https://www.rcaanc-cirnac.gc.ca/eng/1100100028974/1564412549270.

8. *Twenty-eighth Annual Report, Shingwauk and Wawanosh Homes*, Missionary Diocese of Algoma (Toronto, 1903), 29, http://archives.algomau.ca/main/sites/default/files/2014-020_001_004_1902.pdf.

9. Ibid., 18–26.

10. David A. Nock, "Wilson, Edward Francis," in *Dictionary of Canadian Biography*, vol. 14, University of Toronto/Université Laval, 2003–, accessed October 12, 2023, http://www.biographi.ca/en/bio/wilson_edward_francis_14E.html.

11. Rev. E. F. Wilson (ed.), Our Forest Children, And What We Want to Do with Them, vol. 3, no. 4 (July 1889), pages 17–21, https://www.canadiana.ca/view/oocihm.8_06666_28/2.

12. Wilson (ed.), "The Visit to Montreal" in *Our Forest Children*, vol. 3, no. 4 (July 1889), page 22, https://www.canadiana.ca/view/oocihm.8_06666_28/8.

13. "Battleford Hangings," *Saskatchewan Indian* 3, no. 7 (July 1972): 5, https://www2.uregina.ca/education/saskindianresidentialschools/wp-content/uploads/2020/09/Battleford-Hangings-1885-Riel-Rebellion.pdf.

14. Jenna Lemay, "Wilson and the North-West Rebellion," in *Shingwauk Narratives: Sharing Residential School History* (Ontario: Shingwauk Residential Schools Centre), https://ecampusontario.pressbooks.pub/shingwauknarratives/chapter/wilson-and-the-north-west-rebellion/.

15. Lemay, "Wilson and the North-West Rebellion."

16. Ibid.

17. Wilson (ed.), "Among the Blackfeet Indians" in *Our Forest Children*, vol. 2, no. 8, page 26, https://www.canadiana.ca/view/oocihm.8_06666_20/3.

18. National Centre for Truth and Reconciliation, National Student Memorial, Shingwauk (Wawanosh), https://nctr.ca/residential-schools/ontario/shingwauk-wawanosh/.

19. Wilson (ed.), "Among the Blackfeet Indians" in *Our Forest Children*, vol. 2, no. 8, page 26, https://www.canadiana.ca/view/oocihm.8_06666_20/3.

20. Bryan Newland, *Federal Indian Boarding School Initiative Investigative Report*, May 2022, 6, https://www.bia.gov/sites/default/files/dup/inline-files/bsi_investigative_report_may_2022_508.pdf.

21. Newland, *Federal Indian*, 6, 8.

22. Ibid., 7.

23. Wilson (ed.), "My Wife and I. A Little Journey Among the Indians" in *Our Forest Children*, vol. 3, no. 4, (July 1889), 26–27, https://www.canadiana.ca/view/oocihm.8_06666_28/12.

24. "Home," Carlisle Indian School Project, accessed October 12, 2023, https://carlisleindianschoolproject.com.

25. Auger, *Indian Residential Schools*, 101.

26. Ibid.

27. "Shingwauk (Wawanosh)," National Centre for Truth and Reconciliation, accessed October 12, 2023, https://nctr.ca/residential-schools/ontario/shingwauk-wawanosh/.

28. *Twenty-eighth Annual Report, Shingwauk and Wawanosh Homes*, Missionary Diocese of Algoma, Toronto: Warwick Bros & Rutter, 1903, page 6, http://archives.algomau.ca/main/sites/default/files/2014-020_001_004_1902.pdf.

29. Jorge Barrera, "Residential school group searches for identities of 2 boys who drowned while attending Shingwauk," *CBC News*, August 28, 2020, modified August 28, 2020, https://www.cbc.ca/news/indigenous/shingwauk-residential-school-pond-boys-drowned-1.5702306.

30. Letter from J. D. McLean, November 8, 1897, page 68, http://www.nrsss.ca/Resource_Centre/ShingwaukIRS/Shingwauk-WawanoshIRS_RG10_Volume6211_File469-1_Parts1-2_Administration_1872-1906_wm.pdf.

CHAPTER TWELVE: TRAIN SCHOOLS

1. "Canada's School Trains," *Ideas*, CBC Radio, January 9, 2023, https://www.cbc.ca/radio/ideas/school-trains-cn-cp-railway-remote-education-1.6704732.

2. Raymond Frogner, interview by Tanya Talaga, April 21, 2023.

3. *CBC News*, "Your questions answered about Canada's Indian Residential School System," June 24, 2021, https://www.cbc.ca/news/canada/canada-residential-schools-kamloops-faq-1.6051632.

4. Geoff Bartlett, *CBC News*, November 24, 2017, "A tearful Justin Trudeau apologizes to N.L. residential school survivors." https://www.cbc.ca/news/canada/newfoundland-labrador/justin-trudeau-labrador-residential-schools-apology-1.4417443.

5. Tom McMahon, SSRN, October 5, 2016, "The final abuse of Indian Residential School children: deleting their names, erasing their voices and destroying their records after they have died and without their consent." https://papers.ssrn.com/sol3/papers.cfm?abstract_id=2812298.

6. Ka'nhehsí:io Deer, *CBC News*, January 13, 2020, "What you need to know about filing an Indian Day School settlement claim," https://www.cbc.ca/news/indigenous/indian-day-schools-settlement-claims-1.5425226.

7. Letter from Chief Reg Niganobe, February 10, 2022.

8. Letter from Chief Joel Abrams, June 7, 2022.

9. Mickey Djuric, "'What about Timber Bay?' Survivor wants home recognized as residential school," CTV News, March 6, 2022, https://saskatoon.ctvnews.ca/what-about-timber-bay-survivor-wants-home-recognized-as-residential-school-1.5807915.

10. Mickey Djuric, Canadian Press, March 7, 2022, "Survivor wants Timber Bay Children's School recognized as residential school," https://globalnews.ca/news/8664089/survivor-timber-bay-childrens-school-residential-school/#:~:text=The%20Indian%20Residential%20Schools%20Resolution,%2D866%2D925%2D4419.

11. Federal Indian Day School Class Action website, Gowling WLG (Canada) LLP, indiandayschools.com, Schedule K—List of Federal Indian Day Schools, https://indiandayschools.com/en/wp-content/uploads/schedule-k.pdf

12. Cassidy Foxcroft, "Railway Car Schools," OISE Library News, January 11, 2018, https://wordpress.oise.utoronto.ca/librarynews/2018/01/11/railway-car-schools/.

13. *North Bay Nugget*, November 11, 1942, "Know your schools," newspapers.com, page 12, https://www.newspapers.com/article/north-bay-nugget/129672150/.

14. Mark Chochla, "The School Cars of Northern Ontario: The origin and accomplishments of an educational innovation" (Master's thesis, Lakehead University, 1987), http://knowledgecommons.lakeheadu.ca/handle/2453/954.

15. Chochla, "School Cars," 21.

16. Ibid., 43.

CHAPTER THIRTEEN: ROME AND AN APOLOGY

1. Tanya Talaga, "Swamped by teen suicides," *Toronto Star*, December 28, 2009, https://www.thestar.com/news/ontario/swamped-by-teen-suicides/article_be53be7e-c0f8-5297-a8e1-ad98de8f1ec2.html.

2. Tavia Grant, "Catholic Church ran most of Canada's residential schools, yet remains largely silent about their devastating legacy," *Globe and Mail*, June 5, 2021, last modified June 8, 2021, https://www.theglobeandmail.com/canada/article-catholic-church-ran-most-of-canadas-residential-schools-yet-remains/.

3. Jim Bell, "Fugitive Oblate priest Joannis Rivoire must be extradited, activists say," *Nunatsiaq News*, June 30, 2016, https://nunatsiaq.com/stories/article/65674fugitive_oblate_priest_joannis_rivoire_must_be_extradited_activists_sa/.

4. Jim Bell, "Nunavut court: Pedophile ex-priest Eric Dejaeger guilty on 24 counts," *Nunatsiaq News*, September 12, 2014, https://nunatsiaq.com/stories/article/65674nunavut_court_pedophile_ex-priest_eric_dejaeger_guilty_on_24_counts/.

5. R. v. DeJaeger, 2014, Nunavut Court of Justice 21, 46, https://nunatsiaq.com/stories/article/65674nunavut_court_pedophile_ex-priest_eric_dejaeger_guilty_on_24_counts/.

6. Ibid.

7. Ibid., 52.

8. Emily Blake, "'Get at the truth': Judge to study handling of sex allegations against former Nunavut priest," *CBC News*, June 12, 2023, last modified June 12, 2023, https://www.cbc.ca/news/canada/north/nunavut-oblates-abuse-1.6330449.

9. Jim Bell, "Runaway Nunavut priest left few good memories," *Nunatsiaq News*, September 23, 2010, https://nunatsiaq.com/stories/article/98789_runaway_nunavut_priest_left_few_good_memories/.

10. Bell, "Runaway Nunavut priest."

11. Kent Driscoll, "'They have a responsibility': Should the public have been warned about Eric Dejaeger's release?," *APTN News*, June 13, 2022, https://www.aptnnews.ca/national-news/eric-dejaeger-statutory-release-public-notice-nunavut-alberta/.

12. Blake, "'Get at the truth'."

13. David Lochead, "Canada-wide arrest warrant issued for priest accused of sexual assault," *Nunatsiaq News*, March 29, 2022, https://nunatsiaq.com/stories/article/canada-wide-arrest-warrant-issued-for-priest-accused-of-sexual-assault/.

14. Lisa Gregoire, "Marius Tungilik: Inuit leader, whistleblower and public servant, dead at 55," *Nunatsiaq News*, December 20, 2012, https://nunatsiaq.com/stories/article/65674marius_tungilik_inuit_leader_whistleblower_and_public_servant_dead_at_/.

15. Kelly Grant, Globe and Mail, July 20, 2022, "Nunavut residential school survivors hope for an apology, justice during the Pope's visit." https://www.theglobeandmail.com/canada/article-pope-visit-nunavut-residential-school-survivors/.

16. Kristy Kirkup and Patrick White, "Mounties charge priest living in France over sexual abuse allegations in Nunavut 47 years ago," *Globe and Mail*, March 29, 2022, last modified March 30, 2022, https://www.theglobeandmail.com/canada/article-mounties-charge-priest-living-in-france-over-sexual-abuse-allegations/.

17. David Murphy, "Nunavut RCMP seek another Oblate fugitive," *Nunatsiaq News*, November 28, 2013, https://nunatsiaq.com/stories/article/65674nunavut_rcmp_seek_another_oblate_fugitive/.

18. Murphy, "Nunavut RCMP seek."

19. Lochead, "Canada-wide arrest warrant."

20. Bell, "Fugitive Oblate priest."

21. Gregoire, "Marius Tungilik."

22. Kristy Kirkup, "Inuk woman says she came forward to RCMP several times before charge laid against Father Johannes Rivoire," *Globe and Mail*, April 8, 2022, https://www.theglobeandmail.com/politics/article-inuk-woman-says-she-came-forward-to-rcmp-several-times-before-charge/.

23. Sheila North, "Phil Fontaine's lifelong mission to get a papal apology delayed, but not over," *CBC News*, December 13, 2021, last modified December 13, 2021, https://www.cbc.ca/news/canada/manitoba/phil-fontaine-papal-apology-rome-trip-postponed-1.6282694.

24. Cassidy Caron, press conference, Rome, April 1, 2022.

25. Inuit delegation, press conference, Rome, March 28, 2022.

26. Ibid.

27. Tavia Grant and Tom Cardoso, "The Catholic Church in Canada is worth billions, a Globe investigation shows. Why are its reparations for residential schools so small?," *The Globe and Mail*, August 7, 2021, last modified October 25, 2021,https://www.theglobeandmail.com/canada/article-catholic-church-canadian-assets-investigation/.

28. Inuit delegation press conference, Rome, Hotel Universo, March 28, 2022, https://www.youtube.com/watch?v=Vcexij9oagQ.

29. Elder Fred Kelly, speech on bus heading to the Vatican Museum. Rome, March 29, 2022.

30. "Ethnological Museum *Anima Mundi*," Mvsei Vaticani, accessed October 12, 2023, https://m.museivaticani.va/content/museivaticani-mobile/en/collezioni/musei/museoetnologico/museo-etnologico.html.

31. Olivia Stefanovich, "Inuit leader says Vatican Museums open to repatriating Indigenous artifacts," *CBC News*, March 30, 2022, last modified March 30, 2022, https://www.cbc.ca/news/politics/vatican-museums-indigenous-repatriation-1.6402182#:~:text=Yakeleya%20says%20the%20artifacts%20should,them%20back%20to%20our%20people.%22.

32. Cassidy Caron, interview by Tanya Talaga, Rome, March 30, 2022.

33. Ibid.

34. Ibid.

35. Stefanovich, "Inuit leader says."

36. Tanya Talaga, "Reconciliation does not stop at the Vatican. It will not end until we bring all our children home," *The Globe and Mail*, April 1, 2022, https://www.theglobeandmail.com/canada/article-pope-francis-apology-residential-schools/.

37. "1983–1984, Inuvik, Grollier Hall Boarders," https://archives.nctr.ca/05b-c005511-d0001-001.

38. Crystal Fraser, "Inuit Experiences at Residential School," *The Canadian Encyclopedia*, Historica Canada, April 28, 2020, last modified April 28, 2020, https://www.thecanadianencyclopedia.ca/en/article/inuit-experiences-at-residential-school.

39. Truth and Reconciliation Commission, *Canada's Residential Schools: Missing Children and Unmarked Burials*, vol. 4, The Final Report of the Truth and Reconciliation Commission of Canada (Montreal: McGill-Queen's University Press, 2015), 102, https://publications.gc.ca/collections/collection_2015/trc/IR4-9-4-2015-eng.pdf.

40. Ibid., 103.

41. Ibid.

42. Talaga, "Reconciliation does not stop."

43. "Pope Francis: 'I ask for God's forgiveness,'" The Catholic Register, April 16, 2022, https://www.catholicregister.org/item/34237-pope-francis-i-ask-for-god-s-forgiveness.

CHAPTER FOURTEEN: THE PRIME MINISTER AND A POPE

1. Nick Boisvert, "Trudeau visits First Nation, apologizes for skipping invitation on National Day for Truth and Reconciliation," *CBC News*, October 18, 2021, last modified October 18, 2021, https://www.cbc.ca/news/politics/trudeau-kamloops-visit-1.6215084.

2. Open meeting, Tk'emlúps Powwow Arbour, Kamloops, B.C., May 23, 2022.

3. Tanya Talaga, "Canada has not truly released all residential-school records," *The Globe and Mail*, October 21, 2021, https://www.theglobeandmail.com/opinion/article-canada-has-not-truly-released-all-residential-school-records/.

4. Talaga, "Canada has not truly released."

5. Canada (Attorney General) v. Fontaine, 2017 SCC 47, [2017] 2 S.C.R. 205, https://scc-csc.lexum.com/scc-csc/scc-csc/en/item/16797/index.do.

6. NCTR, "Statement on the Prime Minister's comments on residential school records in Tk'emlúps te Secwépemc," October 19, 2021, https://nctr.ca/statement-on-the-prime-ministers-comments-on-residential-school-records-in-tkemlups-te-secwepemc/.

7. Tk'emlúps te Secwépemc, Kamloops, B.C., May 23, 2022, recording filmed by Makwa Creative.

8. Ibid.

9. Ibid.

10. Ted Gottfriedson, interview by Tanya Talaga, Kamloops, B.C., May 24, 2022.

11. Fakiha Baig, "Big crowds, road closures, and heavy security expected for Pope's visit to Alberta," *CTV News Edmonton*, July 14, 2022, last modified July 14, 2022, https://edmonton.ctvnews.ca/big-crowds-road-closures-and-heavy-security-expected-for-pope-s-visit-to-alberta-1.5987757.

12. "AFN National Chief Archibald and AFN Regional Chief Antoine Reflect on Papal Visit to Canada," *Assembly of First Nations*, August 2, 2022, https://afn.ca/all-news/news/afn-national-chief-archibald-and-afn-regional-chief-antoine-reflect-on-papal-visit-to-canada/.

13. "Pope apologizes to Irish sex abuse victims," *CBC News*, March 20, 2010, last modified March 2010, https://www.cbc.ca/news/world/pope-apologizes-to-irish-sex-abuse-victims-1.902607.

14. "Residential school survivors bear witness to apology by Pope Francis, CBC News Special," *CBC News*, July 25, 2022, http://www.cbc.ca/player/play/2055313475862.

15. Amy Tucker, "France won't extradite retired priest Johannes Rivoire, accused of sexually abusing Inuit children," *CBC News*, October 26, 2022, https://www.cbc.ca/news/canada/north/france-extradition-denied-johannes-rivoire-1.6630326.

16. "Oblates 'deeply saddened' to hear France won't extradite, prosecute Johannes Rivoire," *CBC News*, October 27, 2022, last modified October 27, 2022, https://www.cbc.ca/news/canada/north/oblates-johannes-rivoire-france-extradition-denied-1.6631835.

17. Jesuits of Canada, "Release of Names of Jesuits Credibly Accused of Sexual Abuse of Minors," accessed October 13, 2023, https://jesuits.ca/release-names-abuse/.

18. Letter by Erik Oland, "Release of names of Jesuits credibly accused of sexual abuse of minors," https://jesuits.ca/release-names-abuse/ (see disclosure list).

19. Ibid., 6.

20. "Residential school survivors bear witness to apology by Pope Francis," *CBC News*, July 25, 2022, http://www.cbc.ca/player/play/2055313475862.

21. Ibid.

22. "Full text of the Pope Francis' residential school apology: 'I am deeply sorry,'" *Global News*, July 25, 2022, last modified July 25, 2022, https://globalnews.ca/news/9013958/pope-francis-residential-school-apology-full-text/.

23. Danielle Paradis, "'It was not about religion': Littlechild defends gifting headdress to Pope Francis," *APTN National News*, August 5, 2022, https://www.aptnnews.ca/national-news/it-was-not-about-religion-littlechild-defends-gifting-headdress-to-pope-francis/.

24. Karen Pauls, "'I couldn't stay silent,' says Cree Singer who performed powerful message for Pope Francis," *CBC News*, July 29, 2022, last modified July 29, 2022, https://www.cbc.ca/news/canada/manitoba/cree-woman-singing-papal-visit-1.6535055.

25. Andrea Procter, "A Long Journey: Residential Schools in Labrador and Newfoundland," *Arctic Focus*, accessed October 13, 2023, https://www.arcticfocus.org/stories/long-journey-residential-schools-labrador-and-newfoundland/.

26. Natan Obed, interview by Tanya Talaga, July 27, 2022.

27. "'I am deeply sorry': full text of residential school apology from Pope Francis," *CBC News*, July 25, 2022, https://www.cbc.ca/news/canada/edmonton/pope-francis-maskwacis-apology-full-text-1.6531341.

28. Christopher White, "In Canada, Pope Francis apologizes for 'evil' of sex abuse, vows 'never again,'" *National Catholic Reporter*, July 28, 2022, https://www.ncronline.org/news/justice/canada-pope-francis-apologizes-evil-sex-abuse-vows-never-again.

29. Paul Tukker, "'I want to tell you how very sorry I am': Pope's Iqaluit speech hews close to earlier apology," *CBC News*, July 29, 2022, last modified July 29, 2022, https://www.cbc.ca/news/canada/north/pope-speech-iqaluit-visit-nunavut-1.6536444.

30. Gerald Antoine, interview by Tanya Talaga, July 29, 2022.

CHAPTER FIFTEEN: QUIET NO MORE

1. "Paylist of Osnaberg for Treaty Payment 1905," page 8, http://www.archives.gov.on.ca/images/jamesbaytreaty/making_the_treaty/Osnaburg_Fort Hope_Marten_Falls_Paylist_Booklet_1905.pdf.

2. Karl Hele, "Anishinaabe," *The Canadian Encyclopedia*, Historica Canada, published July 16, 2020, last modified October 19, 2022, https://www.thecanadianencyclopedia.ca/en/article/anishinaabe.

3. Truth and Reconciliation Commission, *Canada's Residential Schools: The History, Part 2 1939 to 2000* (Montreal: McGill-Queen's University Press, 2015), 395.

4. Ross Muir, "Poplar Hill closure remembered," *Canadian Mennonite*, Aug 26, 2010, https://canadianmennonite.org/stories/poplar-hills-closure-remembered.

5. Tanya Talaga, *All Our Relations* (Toronto: House of Anansi, 2018), 188.

6. TRC, *Canada's Residential Schools: The History, Part 2*, 395.

7. Sol Mamakwa, "National Day of Truth and Reconciliation," Ontario Legislature, posted September 28, 2023, YouTube, 8:43, https://www.youtube.com/watch?v=7vIIzjOkQdk.

CHAPTER SIXTEEN: ANNIE FOUND

1. Indian Act, Section 51, https://laws-lois.justice.gc.ca/eng/acts/i-5/page-5.html#h-332365.

2. "Bill C-38, An Act to amend the Indian Act (new registration entitlements)," Government of Canada, accessed October 13, 2023, https://www.sac-isc.gc.ca/eng/16621 42490384/1662142638971.

3. Native Women's Association of Canada, "Board engagement on Bill C-38: An act to amend the Indian Act (new registration entitlements)," August 2023, page 3, https://nwac.ca/assets-knowledge-centre/Board-Engagement-on-Bill-C-38-Final-Report.pdf.

4. NWAC, "Board engagement," 6 and 7.

EPILOGUE

1. "Remaining inequities related to registration and membership," Government of Canada, accessed November 28, 2023, https://www.rcaanc-cirnac.gc.ca/eng/1540403281222/15688 98803889#_Unknown_or_Unstated.

2. Robert Jago, "The Buffy Sainte Marie bombshell has been devastating. I fear some of this may be my fault," *Toronto Star*, November 5, 2023, https://www.thestar.com/opinion/the-buffy-sainte-marie-bombshell-has-been-devastating-i-fear-some-of-this-may-be/article_75dab525-9e5d-57e4-9ff3-d0137699b7f7.html.

INDEX

Note: IRS = Indian Residential School; Annie = Annie Carpenter. For the surname Chapish, *see* Wemaystikosh; for the surname Gauthier, *see also* Carpenter.